Science Plus Sentiment

César Daly's Formula for
Modern Architecture

Studies in the Fine Arts: Architecture, No. 7

Stephen C. Foster, Series Editor

Associate Professor of Art History
University of Iowa

Other Titles in This Series

Science Plus Sentiment

César Daly's Formula for Modern Architecture

by
Richard Becherer

UMI RESEARCH PRESS
Ann Arbor, Michigan

NA
645
.B4
1984

Produced and distributed by
UMI Research Press
an imprint of
University Microfilms International
A Xerox Information Resources Company
Ann Arbor, Michigan 48106

Library of Congress Cataloging in Publication Data

Becherer, Richard.
   Science plus sentiment.

   (Studies in the fine arts. Architecture ; no. 7)
   Revision of thesis (Ph.D.)–Cornell University, 1980.
   Bibliography: p.
   Includes index.
   1. Architecture, Modern–19th century–Philosophy.
2. Positivism. 3. Daly, Cesar, 1811-1893. I. Title. II. Series.

NA645.B4 1984   720'.1   84-2453
ISBN 0-8357-1566-3

To my sister Joan

Contents

List of Plates

Acknowledgments

Colin Rowe introduced me to the history and work of César Daly. Rowe's 1977 lectures on the French theoretician familiarized me with the general size and density of Daly *matérielle*. His commentary revealed the primary contours I had to recognize before attacking this mass of historical material, and from the earliest stages of my work, Rowe discerned those critical edges which would ultimately describe its shape.

Lee Hodgden gave me the visual techniques and tools with which to assess and address the substance of this book. His means of modelling allowed me to cut deep into the mass of Daly's built oeuvre, inscribing into it the *tracés régulateurs* upon which the form of my work might be composed.

Esther Dotson's contributions are evident in the study's most specific as well as its most geneal intentions. The breadth of her humanism has created a panoramic tableau of intellect against which to portray Daly. What's more, from her fine vision came the spotlight distinguishing this book's strengths from its weaknesses and emitting the energy to remedy its flaws. This clarification highlighted the necessary formal definitions which might otherwise have remained in shadow.

Charlene Castellano, my wife, offered a continuous incandescence for this work throughout its term of production. The intensity of her illuminations ranged from the level of brilliance, whereby the lines of the book's form fell into sharp relief, to that of sobriety, whereby the closer modelling of its surface took precedence. Most importantly, her insights provided the work with a quality of light which it might otherwise not have known. The many turns taken toward this light attest to the pleasure this book took in her intellectual spectrum.

Others have provided valuable criticism at various stages during the work's progress. Among these are James Boon, Peter Kahn, Dominick LaCapra, Ted Morris, and David Van Zanten. The contributions of graduate student colleagues, Sam Klingensmith, Mike Berns, and especially John Pratt, do not go unrecognized. Nor does the support of my family—mother, father, brother, sisters—whose support nourished my resolve.

Various libraries served as workshops within which much of this book's fundamental labors were undertaken. These include: in America, Columbia

University's Avery Library, Cornell University's Fine Arts and Olin Libraries, and the University of Virginia's Alderman and Fiske Kimball Libraries; in France, the Archives du Département du Tarn in Albi, the Bibliothèque Municipale of the City of Chartres, the Archives de Paris, the Archives de la Caisse Nationale des Documents Historiques et des Sites, the Archives Nationales, the Bibliothèque de la Ville de Paris, the Bibliothèque Fourney, and the Bibliothèque Nationale—all in Paris, and the Service Historique de l'Armée in Vincennes; in England, the Public Records Office in Kew, the Archives of the Royal Institute of British Architects, and the British Museum Library, both in London.

Chronology of the Career of César-Denis Daly

1811   César Denis Daly born 18 July in Verdun, France. Father, John Daley (Daly), is a purser in the British navy, prisoner-of-war during the Napoleonic Wars. Mother, Camille-Augustine Bernard de Calonne, is from an aristocratic family from Pas-de-Calais. The couple is unmarried.

1812   Marriage of John Daly and Camille-Augustine Bernard, 16 December in Paris.

1814   Father, mother, and son return to England, taking up residence in Greenwich.

1819   César Daly begins study of drawing.

1825   Death of John Daley.

1826   Camille-Augustine Daly and son return to France, living on family property near Douai.
        César Daly enters the Collège Royale de Douai, enrolling in a pre-law course.
        Studies rhetoric with Charles-Auguste Mallet and physical sciences and mathematics with Joseph Avignon.

1828   Wins first prize in drawing at the Collège Royale.
        Frustrated attempt to enter the army.
        Works with an architect in Douai.

1829-30 Enters Blouet's atelier in Paris, under the direction of Félix Duban. Enrolled in a preparatory course to prepare for entrance into the Ecole des Beaux-Arts. Daly fails to become a matriculating student

at the Ecole. Meets Henri Labrouste.
Extensive travel throughout France.

1830   Leaves Paris in July for Caen.
Attends Cours d'Archéologie given by Arcisse de Caumont.
Becomes involved with sketching Norman antiquities.
Introduced to circle of Prosper Merimée and Jules Barbey d'Aurevilly.

1831-32   Daly becomes involved with Fourierism.
Beginning of friendship with Victor Considérant.
Designs of child's phalanstery at Condé-sur-Vesgre, earning the admiration of Flora Tristan and provoking the criticism of Charles Fourier.

1836   Following fire at Chartres Cathedral in July, Daly proposes a project of restoration.
Prepares first articles, appearing in *Le Glâneur d'Eure et Loire.*

1837   Prepares first engravings—three views of Chartres Cathedral.
Contributes articles to Fourierist journal *La Phalange.*

1838   Travels to England.
Meets Robert Owen and Thomas Donaldson.
Named *architecte-adjoint* for restoration of Chartres, working under his former mentor, Félix Duban.

1839   Takes up permanent residence in Paris, living at 6 Rue Furstemburg. Begins publication of an architectural magazine, *La Revue Générale de l'Architecture et des Travaux Publics,* with the encouragement of Félix Duban and Henri Labrouste.

1840   Five month stay in England.

1841   Submits views of Albi Cathedral to the Salon of 1841.

1842   First major monographs, including: *Du Projet d'Achèvement de la Cathédrale de Cologne; Concours pour les Monuments Publics.*

1843   Travels to England and Spain.
Named honorary member to Royal Academy of Stockholm.

1844   Ministère des Cultes requests Daly to prepare restoration project for Albi Cathedral.
Named honorary member of Royal Institute of British Architects.
Barbey d'Aurevilly dedicates "Du Dandysme" to César Daly.

1845   Travels to England.
Submits restoration project for Albi Cathedral to Salon of 1845.

1846   Contributes articles to the Fourierist journal *La Démocratie Pacifique.*

1847   Prepares articles "De la Liberté dans l'Art", and "Solidarité entre l'Industrie et l'Art."
Appointed *Architecte-diocésain* at Albi.
Becomes member of the Société Centrale des Architectes.
Discourse at Congrès Archéologique held at Tours.

1848   Assists in establishing the "Société des Artistes Décorateurs et Industriels."
Runs as architects' candidate in the April elections for the *Constituent.*
Named secretary of the Société Centrale des Architectes.
Takes up residence at 6, Rue Sorbonne.

1849   Restoration begins on Albi Cathedral.
Named *rapporteur* to the Commission des Arts et Edifices Religieux, in the Ministère des Cultes.
Named honorary member of the Imperial Academy of Fine Arts in St. Petersburg.

1851   Suffers attack of pneumonia. Recuperates for three months.
Colleague in *Revue Générale,* Henri Sirodot, takes over Albi restoration.
Work stoppage at Albi Cathedral.

1852   Daly contemplates trip to Yucatan.
Address to the Société Centrale des Architectes.

1853   Continued problems at Albi. Entrepreneur files suit against Daly.

1854   Reorganization of Service Diocésain. Daly reappointed architect.
Travels to Germany, Austria, Saxony, Prussia, Bavaria. Bronchial ailment again leads to pneumonia.

1855   Daly embarks on journey to North America (February).
Sirodot takes over direction of Albi.
Visits Fourierist colony at La Réunion, Texas (May-June).
Named member of the Order of Saint-Stanislaus, Russia.

1856   Leaves New Orleans to visit Central America (March).
Discovery of pre-Columbian ruins.
Suffers from attack of yellow fever. Recuperates for two months in
Nicaragua.

1857   Returns to Paris (August).
Work resumes at Albi.

1858   Marriage to Marie-Josephine-Sydonie Aygaleng in Amélie-les-
Bains, Bas-Pyrénées.
Work stoppage at Albi. Entrepreneur files suit against Daly.

1859   Purchases former country house of Robespierre in Wissous.
Assists in founding Société d'Ethnographie Americaine et
Orientale.
Work resumes at Albi.

1860   Birth of first son, Marcel-Robert (15 October).
Major writing:
  L'Architecture Privée du Dix-Neuvième Siècle, volume I (Hôtels
  Privés).

1861   Named to Légion d'Honneur.
Major writings:
  *Du Concours Publics pour les Monuments Publics dans le Passé,
  le Présent, et l'Avenir;
  Blanchissage du Linge, Etude Comparative des Divers Systèmes.*

1862   Birth of twin sons, Victor-Camille and Raymond-Auguste (24
February).
Major writings:
  L'Architecture Privée, volume II (Maisons de Rapport);
  Vue Intérieure d'Un Tombeau Etrusque à Corneto.

1863   Daly receives awards at London Universal Exposition for *Revue
Générale* and *L'Architecture Privée.*
Named one of the presidents at the Congrès Archéologique, Albi.

Resides 30, Rue M. LePrince
Major writings:
  Motifs Historiques, 2 volumes;
  Un Puits de la Renaissance à Toulouse;
  Reponse à Deux Objections Adressées à La Revue d'Architecture;
  Chemins de Fer Bourbonnais, Gare de Vichy;
  Le Premier des Décorateurs, C'est l'Architecte.

1864   Trip to Rome.
        Major writings:
          L'Architecture Privée, volume III (Villas Suburbaines).
          Première Causerie d'Histoire et d'Esthétique: Ce Qui Peut Raconter une Grille de Fer.

1865   Named member of the Royal Academy of Belgium.

1866   Resides 6, Rue Sorbonne.

1867   A. Morel, Daly's publisher, wins awards for publications, *L'Architecture Privée* and *Motifs Historiques,* at Paris Exposition Universelle.
        Major writing:
          Deuxième Causerie d'Histoire et d'Esthétique à Propos d'Une Vase Amortissement

1868   Recuperates in Cannes from an attack of gastritis (January, February)
        Trip to Middle East; spends October through December in Egypt.
        Major writing:
          L'Architecture Privée (Deuxième Série).

1869   Visits Palestine with the English Palestine Exploration Fund, and visits the Aegean.
        Returns to France in April.
        Named member of the Order of Medjidié by the Sultan of Egypt.
        Named member of the Association of Portuguese Civil Architects.
        Major writings:
          Second edition of *Motifs Historiques,* with foreword, "Science Historique et Esthétique de l'Architecture."

1870   Leaves Paris in September for his house in Amélie-les-Bains.
House in Wissous sacked by Germans during Franco-Prussian
War.
Work stoppage on Albi Cathedral.
Major writing:
> *Des Droits et Devoirs de l'Architecte Envisagés Comme
> Constituant le Programme Nécessaire de Tout Journal
> d'Architecture.*

1871   Returns to Paris after Paris Commune.
Files suit against *architecte-adjoint* at Albi.
Major writings:
> *L'Architecture Funéraire Contemporaine;*
> *Funérailles de Félix Duban.*

1872   Named member of Académie des Beaux-Arts, France.
Named member of American Institute of Architects (Atheneum,
Boston).
Named member of Athens Archeological Society.
Major writing:
> *De la Société et de l'Architecture, A Propos de Notre
> Architecture Funéraire.*

1873   Address at Congrès des Architectes Français, entitled "Des
Rapports Qui Existent entre l'Archéologie Monumentale et
l'Architecture Contemporaine..." (June).

1874   Daly sponsors subscription to clean the Acropolis.
Speech at Congrès Archéologique, Stockholm, discussing Syrian
tombs.
Suffers attack of pneumonia.
Major writing:
> *Architecture Contemporaine: Les Théâtres de la Place du
> Châtelet.*

1875   Trip to the Western Sahara (January-May.)

1876   Founds new periodical, *La Semaine des Constructeurs,* coedited
with P. Planat and Daly's son, Marcel.

1877   Retires as *architecte-diocésain,* Albi.
Named *Président-honoraire* of Société des Architectes des Alpes-

Maritimes at Congrès National des Architectes, Cannes.
Major writings:
  L'Architecture Privée, Troisième Série;
  Ingénieurs et Architectes.

1878   Attends Congrès International des Architectes (August).

1879   Resides 51, Rue des Ecoles.
       Winters in Nice.
       Daly goes into partial retirement.

1881   Cares for Victor Considérant after death of Considérant's wife.
       Major writing:
         Motifs Divers de Serrurerie.

1884   Presides over Congrès des Architectes (Nice).
       Respiratory problems (February).
       Major writing:
         Des Hautes-Etudes d'Architecture et de l'Académie des Beaux Arts à Propos du Prix Duc.

1885   Named member of Accademia di San Lucca, Rome.
       Named honorary member of Royal Institute of British Architects, England and Ireland.
       Named member of Société Centrale des Architectes, Belgium.
       Addresses Congrès des Architectes Français, speaking on Hautes-Etudes (June).

1886   Final issue of the *Revue Générale.*

1887   Made *président d'honneur,* Congrès Provincial des Architectes Français, at Toulouse.

1888   Attends Congrès Scientifique, Section d'Ethnographie.
       Major writing:
         Des Hautes-Etudes d'Architecture; Un Appel à Nos Corps Constituée et aux Architects Indépendants.

1889   Addresses Société Nationale des Architectes in Paris, speaking on Hautes-Etudes (June).

1890   Daly named President of the Société d'Ethnographie (June).

1891   Trip to London to attend Salon of Hygiene.
Major writing:
"L'Architecture et l'Ethnographie."

1892   Receives the R.I.B.A. Gold Medal (May).
Major writing:
"De l'Evolution Historique de l'Architecture et la Place Qui y Occupe l'Architecture Americaine."

1893   Death of Victor Considérant (December).

1894   Death of César Daly, 12 January.
Secular funeral, body cremated at Cimetière Père-Lachaise.

1895   Final issue of *La Semaine des Constructeurs,* under the sole editorship of Marcel-Robert Daly.

Abbreviations of Works Frequently Cited

LDP: *La Démocratie Pacifique*

Le Glâneur: *Le Glâneur: Journal d'Eure et Loire, Politique, Commercial, Littéraire, d'Agriculture et d'Annonce*

La Phalange: *La Phalange: Journal de la Science Sociale Découverte et Constituée par Charles Fourier: Industrie, Politique, Sciences, Art, et Littérature.*

RGA: *La Revue Générale de l'Architecture et des Travaux Publics; Journal des Architectes, des Ingénieurs, des Archéologues, des Industriels et des Propriétaires sous la Direction de M. César Daly Architecte.*

LSC: *Le Semaine des Constructeurs: Journal Illustré des Travaux Publics et Privés.*

Introduction:
Remarks on History and Criticism

Nietzsche used an analogy to illustrate man's relationship to history. He described a bucolic scene, a herd of cows grazing tranquilly in a summery meadow, moving hardly at all, a peaceful vignette interrupted only by the momentary swish of a tail to ward off flies. To look at their composure, to see their faces, they appear contented. Their monotonous mastication evokes an image of almost mantric meditation. Have they in fact reached a transcendent state? Perhaps. At any rate, except for the pesky annoyance of insects, they seem unperturbed by the tensions of modern life. There is little concern, worry or effort in this scene, a suggestion of bovine satiety and gratification. A cow-world involves little about which to become upset. On an initial level, this may be a vision of happiness, yet, on another, one wonders.[1]

A central theme of nineteenth-century philosophy, both in Germany and elsewhere, was the development of the concept of history. It was during this century, "history's golden age," that history was legitimized and given substance, and that writers and philosophers alike felt the right to model its form consciously.[2] Seminal to the development of history as a literary genre, post-Enlightenment philosophy in Germany acknowledged the form-making significance of the Bible as precedent. Later, the Christian epic was especially informative in the period's researches into non-stylistic problems, especially with regard to historical structure. For example, Herder's view of historical progress, as outlined in his *Reflections on the Philosophy of the History of Mankind,* found important justification in Christian ideas concerning human perfectibility, yielding an optimistic temporality.[3] Hegel's dynamic of history, energized by the epistemological antagonism between mind and body, matter and spirit, found early resolution in the world-historical figure of Christ. Moreover, the evolution of spirit, the metaphysical premise of Hegel's *Philosophy of History,* could be traced meaningfully from its Old Testament origins among the Hebrews to its present advanced state among the German peoples.[4] Both varieties of historical determinism, either progressive or evolutionary, were based in a notion of the Bible as hopeful narrative, intent upon man's absorption into an existence of a different order in eternity. That chronicle might be summarized as follows.

The Old Testament produced a range of prophets who reveal to man the course of things to come. The New Testament puts the progressive, redemptive machine into motion, via the instrumentality of a Messiah. From that point, history cranks onward, as a train in its tracks, culminating in the final moments—the end of the line—the ecstatic, apocalyptic vision. At this point, human history ends, and divine history begins.

This scheme of history, interpreted perhaps too positivistically here, provided many in the nineteenth century with a holistic model of great persuasiveness. The unavoidable consequence of this scheme, however, was the devaluation of man in the face of humanity, action in the face of progress. For the mere human, failure to submit to the historical plot could only be regarded as error, as a potentially damnable offense. There was little to be done in the face of the divine forces governing prevision, for man had to submit to the will of God; that is, if he knew what was good for him. If day-to-day life became rubrical and preordained, at least man found a kind of satisfaction in the knowledge that his controlled, predictable life would one day bring him into contact with a transcendent existence. Trust in God and in his scheme would relieve man of worry, and he would ultimately find contentment.

From a personal point of view, I find a historical system that denies free choice unpleasant at best. Nineteenth-century historicism, like its distant ancestor, Mosaic law, is buttressed by clairvoyance and the vision of things to come. However, life deprived of clairvoyance becomes a series of alternatives, resolved not by a predetermined code of conduct, but by a kind of situational logic. Man, now lacking a sense of purpose within a larger scheme, is forced to discover what he is, without the presence of history to give his life meaning. In part, the search for self involves a denial of the precepts of life engendered by the old system, those being mass society, tradition, and standardized codes of conduct. The resulting alienation may well not be lawful, since legal structure is perhaps the best indicator of normalized social behavior. The search for self and its denial of law is seemingly absent from the Judeo-Christian scheme of history, for any lawlessness would be the cause of eternal expulsion from the Heavenly Jerusalem. Both these criticisms of divine order involve the internalized need for self-awareness, and a conscious questioning of the diminution of self in the face of higher consciousness.

However, it is not the skeptic or the egoist of whom Nietzsche speaks in his cow analogy. Rather, it is of those who follow law and tradition unconsciously. For these people, values and history have become vulgarized, cutting away the awesome responsibility of life on one's own terms. Life is no longer a labyrinth of alternatives, but a straight and narrow path ordered by God through his institutions. These people have neither a sense of history nor of self. It is of such people that Nietzsche speaks in his metaphor, satisfied, but cow-like in their existence.

If the nineteenth century has provided us with any notion concerning history, it is a sense of its being. The nineteenth century made history not only real, but something vital as well. It moved. It rose, it fell. It oscillated either erratically or rhythmically. It was a machine, a plant, and a river. It was everywhere and nowhere. It was God.

In the face of history, man was insignificant. Personal choice was not a life issue, for there were no alternatives to destiny. How could a single soul hope to alter the movement of the vast cosmic clock? How could a twig withstand a raging historical torrent? What could man do in the face of such temporal momentum? To attempt resistance was futile. All he could do was submit. Submit he did.

One wonders how Nietzsche saw himself, both as historian and individual within the historical frame of reference of the late nineteenth century. Did he imagine himself among the cows in the meadow, settled into the traditions of the time, comfortable in his day-to-day existence, unconsciously submitting to some higher order over which he had no conscious control? I think not. Nietzsche was certainly not an ordinary cow, for if his essay on history demonstrates anything, it is his sense of both historical and self-consciousness.

He was self-conscious, but at the same time historically controlled. In this regard, his life could be seen as imbued with a profound sense of tragedy, and he could be interpreted as a tragic persona. Although his life was forcedly rubrical, he was consciously aware of the historical forces that shaped him, and the schemes of which he was a powerless part. A sense of futility for Nietzsche as individual and historian must have coincided with his awareness of the monolithic world order.

Part of this alienation arose from his awareness of the inadequacy of increasingly vulgarized German philosophies of history. As noted above, for Herder, history revealed continuing progress. Hegel amplified Herder's optimism, asserting that human history was moving toward a prescribed goal: union with the Almighty. In the Hegelian school, Nietzsche perceived a parallel between the eschatological and idealistic views of history. A basic tenet of the latter school, the continuing 'realization of Idea' (Reason), implied a continuing revelation of divine essence as embodied in institutions. Simply stated, Hegel's dialectical development of progress terminated with the conception of contemporary Prussian society, epitomized by the Berlin situation circa 1820.[5] However, if the German state was the culmination of history, what then was the purpose of Nietzsche and his situation some sixty years after the paradigm's supposed achievement? Was Nietzsche merely an anachronism, waiting resolutely, as though in limbo, for the millenium (at that point, a lengthy wait), deprived of a future other than absorption into the world spirit—or was there something of an even more fundamental nature wrong with the prevailing view of history and man's place in it?

The differences between Nietzsche and Hegel can find illumination in an unexpected quarter. In this regard, I draw upon the third scene of Shakespeare's *Macbeth,* which is that point in the action when Macbeth and Banquo encounter the three witches. Hegel might be compared to a witch, able to see the future in his philosophical cauldron, and by his clairvoyance, able to control the destiny of humanity out of mere suggestion. Nietzsche, on the other hand, is more like Macbeth. Initially, the character has been made to feel superhuman by being made privy to information concerning the future. However, Macbeth not only aspires to the positive elements of the witches' vision, but furthermore, becomes instrumental in expediting its conclusion. After the climax of the prophecy, with its concomitant seizure of the throne, the historical drama grinds to a close. Although Macbeth puts the machine of destiny into motion, he is unable to stop it. At this point, he sees the futility of prevision, which, although momentarily improving his situation, ultimately impels him to create a situation that finally destroys him. He is now a victim of his own monster. Such is the case with many historians of Nietzsche's generation who embraced either idealistic or materialistic points of view. The tragic sense involves a paradox between the historian's awareness of a futile situation, one which he, in part, instituted and perpetuated, and his growing awareness that he himself became subject to forces of his own making.

If there was any resolution to the conflict that Nietzsche perceived as existing between the idealistic view of history ('historicism') and the historian, it was in the realm of "critical history." In contrast to "monumental" and "antiquarian" history, Nietzsche advocated "critical" history that concentrated upon repudiating rather than fetishizing the past. In part, this idea emphasized a component of personal aspiration which provided a critique of present-day life, now deprived of goal.

> Man must have the strength to break up the past, and apply it, too, in order to live. He must bring the past to the bar of judgment, interrogate it remorselessly, and, finally, condemn it.[6]

Critique on this order involved a conflict between unconscious historical inheritance, based in tradition, and a vision of the world as it should be. For Nietzsche, this view stems from a sense of awareness of a society not yet *arrivée,* and a continuing sense of idealism based in reason, which constituted part of the Hegelian legacy.

To digress for a moment, Hegel's dialectical process began with the idea of reason transforming itself from abstract thought into concrete reality in terms of institutions. However, this process of formalizing through imperfect interpretation by man is always incompatible or removed from the idea, a situation which Plato recognizes in his distinction between noumena and phenomena. Deviation from the ideal, as manifest in institutions, can be observed by social dissatisfaction or dissent (in Marxian terms, alienation), and the institution's incomplete rationality must call forth a critique or negation, resulting in the creation of new institutions. This process results in a cycle of continuing perfection until idea and institution, or content and form, are ultimately reconciled.

For Hegel, the philosopher of the Prussian state, a fetishized Germany as the perfect institution did not permit further critique. Surely, if the institution could be criticized, then the popular ideology could be considered erroneous. The present would consequently be denied as vindicator of the historical oscillations of the past. For Nietzsche, as for Hegel, the indicator of society's inherent imperfections was a sense of social alienation, an estrangement from the very institutions which were supposed to be ideal. In attacking institutions, Nietzsche mounted an offensive against historical inevitability, thereby demystifying the contemporary view of history. In his iconoclasm, he allowed the critical process to begin again.[7]

Nietzsche argues that consciousness can be used to criticize historical determinism in any of its scientistic permutations. Personal consciousness as critical mechanism provides the means to address the central problem of this essay—an analytical and evaluative biography of a historical figure, César-Denis Daly. By biography I mean that genre which attempts to illuminate the personal consciousness accounting for the singularity of a personality as it contrasts the backdrop of its age. Edmund Burke's writing is one source of this idea. His study of psychology in his *Philosophical Enquiry into the Origin of our Ideas on the Sublime and the Beautiful* stresses the value of self as the ultimate judge of aesthetic experience. Moreover, Burke was important from the point of view of critical history, for his *Reflections on the Revolution in France* elaborates upon the idea of individuality and personal valuation to combat the metaphysical abstractions—*liberté, egalité, fraternité*—underpinning the French Revolution. In like manner, latter-day critics of British utilitarianism and French positivism (Coleridge, Mill, Michelet, Saint-Beuve) exploited biography's psychological portraiture to underline the history-making qualities of certain polarizing figures.[8] More recently, David Watkin's study of *Thomas Hope and the Neoclassical Idea* focuses on the consciousness of an enlightened man with taste as seminal to a formulation of architecture totally separate from the utilitarianism of the day. Moreover, Watkin later uses notions developed in that work, when, in *Morality and Architecture,* he mounts a more comprehensive attack on nineteenth- and twentieth-century functionalism.[9]

César Daly stands apart from the historical backdrop of his age. Curiously enough, however, there is little to distinguish him as a historian from his contemporary schools of philosophical thought. Daly subscribed to the two major epistemologies most hostile to individuality. These systems were modelled on two metaphors: the machine and the plant. Mechanolatry and belief in the physical sciences implied an optimistic view of mechanistic progress, and led to a science-fascinated ideology. Organicity was an outgrowth not only of the natural sciences and the comparative method, but also involved an interpretation of history in terms of the cycle of growth, maturity and decay. Inherent in both systems of thought, however, lay a common philosophical bond—the notion of unfolding idealism. In mechanistic, historical systems, to submit the notion of progress to a causal analysis would involve a logical regression ultimately ascribing origins to a metaphysical source (reason), if not to the theological Prime Mover. If organicity could be described in terms of continual growth and integration, questions could be raised concerning the genealogy of the vital principle. Surely, if these questions were never effectively broached by the positivists, the phenomena of progress under both systems were elaborately described. And even if the idealistic sources were never really confronted for fear that a theological cause might be unearthed, an idealistic end was certainly foreseen. A paradisiacal existence, total harmony, gratification of all want, and oneness with the infinite awaited man upon completion of these scientific processes. However, this brief excursus into Daly's theoretical provenance gives little understanding as to why he was an individual.

An architect expresses himself in his built *oeuvre*. A historian does so in his writing. As a writer, Daly was involved with literature, and, as we shall see, occupied a middle ground between objective and expressive theories of literature. As a historian involved with a scientized point of view, it is not surprising that Daly utilized a spare, descriptive literary style. As an objective thinker, Daly was realistic. As an objective writer, he was factual. This stylistic feature is borne out in innumerable tracts of Daly's *Revue Générale de l'Architecture et des Travaux Publics*. Its articles are concerned with observation in an attentive, empirical way. Architecturally, they involve an extensive description of architecture's "constituent facts"—structural advances, mechanical services, new materials, new building programs. Socially, they deal with an enumeration of the effects of modern life— transportation, industry, communication. Historically, they conscientiously catalogue and compare the remains of past epochs. Supposedly, all is highly objective and non-judgmental. Daly's literary style espoused a kind of architectural *Beylisme* that attempted a dispassionate exactitude. Yet, much as with Stendhal's writing, that simple, Spartan quality of prose betrayed a kind of primitive passion.

The *Revue Générale* did more than summarize architectural knowledge in an encyclopedic sense. It was also a magazine. Moreover, it was among the first of the major architectural periodicals anywhere. From its inception in 1839, Daly maintained a pronounced commitment not only to inform, but also to reform. The *Revue Générale* was therefore more than an architectural catalogue; it provided a way of seeing, thinking and improving. In the early days, the journal provided its subscribers with the puzzle of the future, assembled incrementally on a monthly basis, much as the literary magazine's episodic format implied a program of gradual revelation on either a weekly, monthly or bi-monthly basis. The eager subscribers of such literary reviews the *Revue des Deux Mondes* or the *Mercure de France* waited for the next installment of Chateaubriand's *Le Génie de Christianisme,* Hugo's *Notre-Dame de Paris,* or Michelet's *Histoire de la France,* and thereby partook of a process leading to ultimate truth. It is my contention that the *Revue Générale* similarly provided an implicit ideology, using explicitly scientific forms as a means to express immanent philosophical content.

Furthermore, the problem of expression and ideology necessarily raises the problem of implicit idealism. Expressive literary theory must be seen as initially deriving from Platonic notions concerning rhetoric. In the *Phaedrus* Plato stipulates that the art of persuasion is to be used to convince the hearers of the Truth. Inherent in this view is the assumption that there is a soul within man that participates in the World-Soul. Divine truth is impressed on the soul in the form of ideas. The ideas can be presented to the public, albeit imperfectly, by encasing them within rational form. Appropriate form has certain limitations based upon the nature of the idea and the character of the audience, giving rise to certain formal patterns of speech. In classical literature, such form was described in terms of modal and genre theory. Although such classical notions disintegrate during the Romantic period, the notion lingers that the artist expresses truth; he is the mouthpiece of divine essence. This issue becomes especially important to literature where ideology is a central issue, particularly in the cases of propagandistic and *avant-garde* literary circles.[10]

In short, what I am proposing here is that Daly's writing style (and the style of any author with a point of view) cannot be superficially considered. Rather, form and content are intimately interwoven. Prose, no matter how dry or objective, should be regarded as metaphor for ideology; language implies meta-language.

I have moved far from the expressed purpose of this introductory essay. To return to the question posed earlier, why is Daly worthy of our study? Was he unique in terms of a point of view? With regard to the intellectual history of the early nineteenth-century in France, Daly was not alone. His ideas primarily stemmed from French positivism, hybridized by elements of English psychologism and German idealism. As an architectural theorist, however, he was singular as the first proponent of a doctrine developed to counter the classical humanism of the Ecole des Beaux-Arts.

However, Daly was also separate from the school of thought to which he vocally subscribed. Within the evolutionary system of positive reform, Daly's own human instrumentality would have to be considered a redundancy at best, and at worst, a contradiction. In terms of French positivism, vocal propaganda was a kind of ideological embarrassment, for it implied, first, a lack of total social integration, and second, a fear that progress would not occur without a certain amount of prodding. Furthermore, as explicit critic and propagandist, Daly was a symbol of the present as a "transitional" period, an epoch which all good positivists hoped would go away in as short a time as possible.[11]

Finally, Daly was alienated from the expressive, romantic movement by his half-evangelical, half-scientific literary style. Yet, at the same time, he was separate from pure objectivity by his implicit ideological motivation and his passion. César Daly stood out because he was both epitome and aberrant, faithful disciple and prodigal.

I am also historian, critic, and writer. As a historian, I am a receiver of the past. As a critic and writer, I am sceptical of it. To a considerable extent, historicism has provided a persuasive norm of scholarship in my own academic background, educated as I have been within the circumstantial, factualizing atmosphere of common sense, middle America and the value-free empiricism of liberal academe. This intellectual posture feared personal judgment and bias above all, epousing a kind of objective, "scientistic" method in imitation of the physical and natural sciences, in the attempt to relieve man of the awesome responsibility of evaluation. The resultant historicism stressed the factual and circumstantial over the abstract and ideational. Certainly, this "realistic" point of view was an integral component of the *détente* between idealists and positivists which has characterized our historical method since the mid-nineteenth century. Whereas in the nineteenth century, scientism was viewed as the superstructure to philosophical infrastructure, today the idealistic foundation has been devalued. What has resulted from this methodological counterrevolution has been a fetishization of process, which wholly overlooks the abstract principles that once governed. The process-fetish instituted a series of formal norms characterizing its sacred role, and expressing and idealizing process. For example, one effect of scientist academe was a preference for a terse, analytical literary style deemed most appropriate for modern exegetic writing. Abstract, "unclear" discourse having its basis in non-objective literary forms was rejected in favor of discursive techniques that were somehow concrete and positive. One never questioned the use of the third person in analytical writing for fear that use of the first person would introduce the accursed personal judgment into a feasible, scientific process. It is the sad lot of the self-denying historian to ignore his own instrumentality not only in the writing, but also in the shaping of history. In light of this realization, the question then arises, "Who (or what), then, does write history, if man does not?" Typical responses are "the facts," or worse still, "reason." Surely, the stock response, "reason," is no more acceptable today than it was in those early day's of history's existence, when historians gave up their interpretive position to "world view," "collective unconscious," "spirit of the age," or the reasonable ideal.

The task of the art historian is both analytical and evaluative. As an analyst, the art historian observes and dissects the object of his inquiry. Northrop Frye, in his *Anatomy of Criticism,* demands investigation based upon an empirical, comparative approach.[12] Roland Barthes, in *Le Plaisir du Texte,* describes discovery as a sadistic cutting away, a dismemberment even.[13] Barthes, however, emphasizes that this anatomizing is part of the passion that one has for the text as the object of one's affection, and this emotional intensity constitutes the artwork's vital principle. Passion gives rise to the desire to see what makes the organism tick. However, in the process of dismemberment, the sense of passion and artistic life is destroyed. The historian's task does not end here. Only when he brings the work back to life has he fully experienced the work of art. This is done in the evaluative process, and in the action of new, creative writing.

To evaluate implies a kind of artistic reconstruction. It involves the impact of the artwork on one's own situation, in terms of changing one's own set of aesthetic standards or norms. If Barthes' analytical disintegration moves from the abstract idea to a set of concrete components, the evaluator's involvement moves the artwork from the concrete to a new abstraction. Barthes illustrates this idea by his creation of a new prose poem, turning analysis into a higher language, itself subject to interpretation. This process is described by René Wellek's conception of "perspectivism," which recognizes an interpretive/ evaluative cycle in operation within the critic's mind. The first, analytical phase subjects the work to an investigation arising from a comparison with a preestablished set of norms or standards. All contiguities with and deviations from this norm are noted. Subsequently, a reverse process is enacted, in which the work of art instrumentally distorts and extends our own norms by affecting our frame of reference, both emotionally and intellectually. Hence, our norms of interpretation are directly affected by the work of art.[14]

To weigh the three components—history, criticism, and writing—one would be forced to say, like Nietzsche, that criticism is the central concern for those who deal with the past. Criticism necessarily involves history and writing style. First, out of initial assessment of the historical situation, it recognizes the norms imposed by historical tradition. Second, criticism embodies a conscious skepticism of these norms. Third, criticism recognizes its own instrumentality in effecting new norms, based in certain revised notions of history which are determined by personal ideology. Ultimately, this critique is embodied in writing style. Criticism presumes a mediating role between the work of art of the past and that of the future, between history and things to come, via the instrumentality of man himself. In short, criticality informs us of our role, not as the servants of the past, but as the potential determiners of the future.

1

Biography

César-Denis Daly's life history begins against the backdrop of the Napoleonic Wars. His father was John Daly (also spelled Daley), an Irishman serving as "Commissaire des Vivres" or purser on the English frigate, the *Yarico*. In 1807, the *Yarico* saw action with a French gunboat in the English Channel and was sunk. The unlucky officer was taken prisoner and interned in the town of Verdun, the site chosen by the French War Ministry for the incarceration of British aristocrats, officers and gentlemen during the duration of hostilities.

As a man of honor, Daly was placed on parole and allowed the freedom of the town. As a man of means, Daly quickly acquired a manservant, an apartment, and maintained a pleasant lifestyle, even in his imprisonment. Daly's financial resources must have been substantial, for on numerous occasions, we observe him lending large sums of money to fellow Irish soldiers of less comfortable circumstances.[1]

Having the freedom of the town permitted Daly a variety of pleasures. Before the Treaty of Amiens in 1802, Verdun was a sleepy town in the north of France, not far from the German border. The end of the Peace in 1803 initiated open hostilities between France and England, and the detention of any British subjects in France at the time. Verdun was the prison camp for the Britush upper class. Consequently, Verdun became a town of diversion catering to the moneyed Englishmen who were never cut off from their foreign money supply. Gaming houses, tearooms, horse tracks, and private clubs were quickly established, as well as distractions of a more illicit nature, better suited to the needs of men separated from their loved ones.[2] At this point, César Daly's mother enters the scene.

John Daly met Camille-Augustine Bernard in Verdun. Like many French women, she gravitated to the city to spend time with the British troops. Daly met this woman sometime between 1807 and 1809 and made a love-match. The fruit of their relationship was a son, named César-Denis Daly, born at four-thirty in the afternoon, 18 July 1811. On the child's birth certificate, the father is described as a purser of the British navy with Portsmouth as his home port. His age is thirty-two. The mother is termed a "démoiselle" or spinster, aged twenty-five, coming from the town of Calonne-Ricouart, Pas-de-Calais.[3] César Daly's legitimacy was established when father married mother on 16 December 1812 in Paris.[4]

Although little is known of the father's family, it is likely that John Daly came from the family of that name originating in county Galway, Ireland. The family is one of Ireland's oldest, with a lineage extending well back into the Middle Ages. At the moment of the Napoleonic Wars, the family was also one of Ireland's most influential. At that time, the most important family personality was Denis Daly, a conservative member of the English Parliament, violently opposed to the upsurgent Irish independence movement. He was furthermore famous for his private library, purportedly one of the largest collections in Ireland at the time.[5]

The mother's family is better documented. César Daly himself discusses his French ancestors:

> Ma mère était une de Calonne; son père avait été un des pages de la malheureuse Antoinette. La famille Sully s'est éteinte dans la nôtre, c'est un des ancêtres de ma mère qui prît le roi Jean prisonnier à Poitiers...[6]

> My mother was of the de Calonne family; her father was one of the pages for the unfortunate Antoinette. The Sully family was absorbed into ours; it was one of my mother's ancestors who took King John prisoner at Poitiers.

Like the Dalys, the Bernard family had a long history. Ennobled in the fifteenth century, it absorbed both the Bethune and Sully families, the latter's most notable member being Maximilien de Béthune-Sully, Surintendant des Finances under Henri IV. The Bernard family intermarried with the de Calonne family at the beginning of the eighteenth century. At that moment, the de Calonnes were very important politically, Louis-Joseph de Calonne being the first president of the Parliament of Flanders in the second decade of the century. His son, Charles-Alexandre de Calonne, served as Minister of Finances under Louis XVI following Necker. He was accused, perhaps unjustly, of embezzling millions of French francs from the feeble monarchy, an action which some say led to the financial crisis of 1788 and the Revolution. De Calonne fled to England in 1786, having the forethought to insure delivery of his art collection to his London address.[7]

The plight of the de Calonnes and the Bernard de Calonnes on both sides of the channel was unfortunate. In England, Charles-Alexandre was forced to sell his art for capital, largely spent on a futile attempt to organize a counterrevolutionary army. In France, his cousin, Marie-Louis Joseph Bernard de Calonne, César Daly's maternal grandfather, dropped the de Calonne portion of his surname because of general hostility to the family. Furthermore, dispossessed of their ancestral wealth and properties, the Bernard family found itself nearly penniless. Although Napoleon permitted the return of French emigrés after 1802, their properties remained nationalized.

This continued to be the situation of the former aristocracy until the Restoration. The penurious circumstances of the Bernard family may account for its dissolution during the Empire, and for the decision of an unmarried twenty-three-year-old woman to make her own way. Little is known of Camille-Augustine, but one aspect of her personality comes to the surface, especially from later accounts—her willfulness. For example, during the Franco-Prussian War, when bombs were falling around the Daly townhouse, she refused to flee the city as did her son and family, choosing rather to remain behind with a sick grandchild.[8] Together, the family's financial situation and the woman's fiery determination and independence may account for her attachment to an Irishman of means and position, and the resolution of her particular dilemma.

It is to be assumed that John Daly, his wife, and their son returned to London after the fall of Paris in 1814. They lived for a time in Greenwich, and it seems likely that John Daly remained in the service of the British navy.[9] For the next twelve years, the family lived in England, the young César completing primary education in the British system. Little is known of this period in his life. He learned to speak English, so well, in fact, that a trace of accent never left his otherwise perfect French. Daly himself recounts that at that time he cultivated a talent for drawing.

In 1824, César Daly's father died, and two years later, we find mother and son reestablished on de Calonne property near Calonne-Ricouart. Proximity to Douai, together with relatives in that city, were incentives for César Daly's enrollment in the prestigious Collège Royale de Douai for his secondary studies. He studied with two men, Joseph Avignon and Auguste Mallet. Avignon was a mathematician and physicist; Mallet, a mere five years older than Daly, taught rhetoric.[10] A course in rhetoric seems curiously out of place as preparation for an architect. The profession for which courses in both mathematics and rhetoric are required is law. Judging from family background on both sides, it would seem likely that Daly was being prepared, not for the Ecole des Beaux-Arts, but for the Faculté du Droit. After completing his courses at the Collège Royal de Douai in 1829, he made a futile attempt to join the army. However, when his candidacy was refused, he returned to Douai, and worked in an architectural firm. Late in 1829, he left for the capital. As the story goes, Daly walked with a backpack to Paris, where he sought to enter Abel Blouet's atelier at the Ecole des Beaux-Arts, at that time directed by Félix Duban.

That Daly walked to Paris is a significant feature of the story, for he certainly had no material reason to have done so. By that time, the family had recouped its Napoleonic losses, and surely could have afforded to send César to Paris in great style had it so desired. But Daly was probably going to Paris against his family's wishes. He had been prepared for law, not for the fine arts. Consequently, his family refused to sanction his entrée. Daly was never recommended for admission to the Ecole des Beaux-Arts; his name was never included on the various rosters of the ateliers.[11] Rather he worked independently in the Blouet atelier under Duban, perhaps in a preliminary course which would ultimately qualify him for admission to the Ecole at the *premier degré*. At any rate, his time at the Ecole was cut short by the July Revolution. Rather than build barricades like his contemporary, Viollet-le-Duc, Daly fled Paris for Caen.[12]

At this point certain observations are appropriate. First, Daly's flight from Douai, and his entry into the Duban circle under protest from his family, must be viewed as an act of defiance and willfulness. Rather than conforming to de Calonne intentions concerning his future, he had his own designs. César Daly was prepared to turn his back on his elders, even if it meant an impoverished existence.

Second, as his hasty departure from Paris at the advent of the July Revolution would indicate, Daly was not an unqualified republican. Daly states, "Je suis un républicain de raison, . . .", but also "Personellement, et sans l'effort de raison dont je parle plus haut, je serais monarchiste comme presque toute ma famille."[13] Rationally, he was libertarian, but temperamentally, he was aristocratic. Daly was both afraid of and ambivalent about the attack on Charles X. He was first and foremost an aristocrat, and could not be a party to the demise of that political system which had returned privilege and order to his family and society. Daly may have been a liberal, but at the same time, he was a monarchist, as were so many of his fellow romantics—Chateaubriand, Balzac, Gautier, Nodier, and Fourier. For Daly, and others of his generation, progressive social thought and aristocracy were not incompatible ideas: for example, they coexisted happily in the contemporary British representative monarchy.[14] Daly saw the monarchy as embodying certain positive attributes, most importantly, social continuity, a body of national values, and tradition, essential components for social order.[15] We come to two realizations about Daly, which together constitute a kind of paradox. On the one hand, we see a headstrong and individualistic Daly, desiring to shape his own destiny free of familial intervention. On the other, we see a cautious Daly, hesitant about political ideology when dealing with issues of social unity and the forces that constitute it.

The move to Caen was important for two reasons. First, Normandy, and particularly the city of Caen, was an important seat of French *légitimistes,* political conservatives in favor of the French monarchy. The city, at least initially, provided a retreat from the turmoil of Paris.[16] Second, Caen was the scene of the most advanced and comprehensive archaeological research yet seen in France. Two personalities were important to César Daly at the time, Barbey d'Aurevilly, critic, essayist, and major contributor to the short-lived *Revue de Caen,* and the archaeologist Arcisse de Caumont.

De Caumont was the focus of French archaeological activity in the early nineteenth century. Founder of the Société des Antiquaires de Normandie in 1823, he fostered the taste for orderly research of Norman antiquities, with Caen as the center of activity. He was appointed Professor of Archaeology at the Université de Caen in 1824, and published his lectures as the *Cours d'Archéologie* beginning in 1830. De Caumont impressed the young Daly, and although we have no firm evidence in this matter, surely the reverse was true as well. The archaeologist must have noticed his facility at drawing and his passionate interest in France's medieval heritage. Moreover, De Caumont must have observed the young man's elegance, his ease with the English language, and his unmistakable British bearing. Nikolaus Pevsner notes that at this moment, French antiquarian societies were modelling themselves on English models and methods.[17] Daly would have been useful as translator and intermediary between the two schools of archaeological thought. Although we have no evidence to support Daly's involvement in the graphic component of the *Cours,* it seems his work in the de Caumont circle served to familiarize him not only with documentary techniques but illustrative processes suitable to publication. Moreover, Daly's involvement with the de Caumont circle placed him in contact with many influential people, including Charles Nodier and Baron Taylor, authors of the enormously popular *Voyages Pittoresques dans l'Ancienne France,* Prosper Merimée and Eugene Viollet-le-Duc. The latter two would prove useful especially when the large French archaeological commissions and bureaux of the later thirties and forties were formed.

To digress for a moment, the Société des Antiquaires de Normandie was merely the first step in the bureaucratization of archaeological documentation, preservation, and historical research in France. De Caumont established in 1829 the Congrès Scientifiques de France, which were primarily concerned with historical problems. In 1834, de Caumont founded the Société Française d'Archéologie, which was held responsible for the Congrès Archéologiques and the *Bulletin Monumental,* France's first periodical specifically devoted to archaeology.

At this point, it becomes clear that de Caumont was a key figure to the French bureaucratic structure of archaeology in this seminal period. For as a member of the Institute's Académie des Belles-Lettres et des Inscriptions, he surely had a hand in forming the Commission Historique des Arts et des Monuments in the Académie des Beaux-Arts. It was this Commission which prompted the first major governmental agency, the Commission des Monuments Historiques in the Ministry of Public Instruction in 1837, presided over by Ludovic Vitet and Prosper Merimée, and whose membership included Félix Duban.[18]

Daly's involvement with restoration stemmed from the destruction of Chartres Cathedral by fire in 1836. He happened to be living nearby, at Condé-sur-Vesgre, and he volunteered his services to prepare a suite of three engravings of the church for purposes of subscribing money for repairs. The young architect's commitment to the project grew, particularly after the appointment of Félix Duban as architect of the restoration by the Conseil des Bâtiments Civiles. He assisted his former *patron* until 1839, the moment of the foundation of the *Revue Générale de l'Architecture*. This project was the necessary *entrée* to that system of archaeological patronage which would ultimately award him the restoration of the cathedral of Sainte-Cécile at Albi, as *architecte-diocésain,* in 1847.

His presence in Condé-sur-Vesgre was the result of another of his interests of the period, Fourierism. After he returned to Paris in the early 1830s, Daly, by virtue of his association with the Blouet/Duban atelier, found himself in a circle of progressive social thinkers. Duban, and to a greater extent his fellow romantics Henry Labrouste and Louis Duc, were involved with the French positivists, especially the *Saint-Simoniens.*

Doctrinaire *Saint-Simonisme* waned in the early 1830s, partially because of the deposition of Charles X and the Restoration monarchy, but more so because of the arrival of a new social avatar, Charles Fourier. Fourier attacked Saint-Simon's arguments primarily on metaphysical and economic grounds. Adherents to Fourierism became numerous during the two ensuing decades following the publication of *Le Nouveau Monde Industriel* (1829), his critiques of Saint-Simon and Owen (1830-31), and especially his periodicals, beginning in 1832, which spanned the length of the July Monarchy and the Second Republic. Following Fourier's death in 1836, his charismatic student, Victor Considérant, became the leader of this group.

Daly was intimately involved with this group in the 1830s. His visible presence among the Fourierists is best seen in these periodicals, *La Phalange, La Démocratie Pacifique,* and the regional journal, *Le Glâneur de l'Eure et Loire.* The earliest writings are dated 1836, yet it is apparent that Daly's participation with the Fourierists extends from an earlier date. In 1832 the Fourierists sought subscriptions for the new *phalanstère* at Condé-sur-Vesgre, and broke ground in 1833. At this time, Daly served as consultant to the group, and prepared schemes for some of the structures, most notably a phalanstery for four hundred children. Although nothing is known of the scheme, the phalanstery seems to have aroused admiration in socialist circles. Flora Tristan, upon viewing the project in the editorial offices of *La Phalange* in 1837, decided that it was Daly who should design the palace for her workers' union. She stated, "Je ne connais qu'un architect capable de faire le plan du Palais de l'Union Ouvrière, c'est M. César Daly."[19] Moreover, beyond supplying the group with necessary architectural plans, Daly provided the Fourierists with an even more precious commodity—money. He was a subscriber to both Fourier's and Tristan's journals, and loaned sums of money to the editorship of *La Phalange* and *La Démocratie Pacifique*. He later joined the staff on both journals.

It was early positivism—*Saint-Simonisme* and especially Fourierism—that provided Daly with his fundamental notions concerning philosophy, history, economics, and politics. Although these progressives were avowedly non-aggressive and preferred productive labor to social unrest and warfare, they did become activistic in the late 1840s, because of the government's continued lack of interest in phalanstery schemes, limitations to freedom of the press, opposition to universal suffrage, and indifference to the Polish independence question.[20] With the *coup d'état* of 1848, both Victor Considérant and César Daly became politically active. The two men ran as candidates for the Constituent Assembly in April 1848. Considérant was nominated by the Department of the Seine. Daly was selected by a "Comité Permanent des Architectes", created in March 1848 under Daly's encouragement for purposes of choosing an appropriate candidate for the election. Only Considérant obtained a seat in the Assembly.[21] As an offshoot of Daly's special interest group, however, the Société des Artistes Industriels, and its adjunct, the Ecole du Dessin came into existence, under the direction of Baron Taylor. These two organizations, the Société and the Ecole, ultimately developed into the Société des Artistes-Décorateurs and its adjunct, the Ecole Nationale des Arts-Décoratifs. Also in 1848, Daly assumed an active role as secretary in the fledgling Société Centrale des Architectes. In 1849 he joined the Commission des Arts et Edifices in the Ministère de l'Instruction Publique, by invitation of Prosper Merimée, Ludovic Vitet, and Hippolyte Fortoul.[22]

The early years of the *Revue Générale de l'Architecture et des Travaux Publics* must be judged against the backdrop of Daly's privileged Franco-English upbringing with its conservative tendencies, his romantic involvement in archaeology and architecture, and Fourieriest socialism. From the beginning, the journal had strong English ties, conditioned by the period of *anglomanie,* publishing the architectural work of Charles Barry (the Traveller's Club), reviews of A.W.N. Pugin's *True Principles of Pointed or Christian Architecture,* correspondence with Thomas Donaldson (editor of *The Builder*), and summaries of Britain's public works, particularly railway lines. The periodical was also heavily archaeological. It became the major mouthpiece of the newly formed Commission des Arts et Monuments, publishing articles by Prosper Merimée and Albert Lenoir. Fourierism was also present, not only in Daly's quasi-economic texts concerning the fortifications of Paris, but also in articles by F. Cantagrel and A. Perreymond, who discussed Parisian urbanism. Lastly, the *Revue* was family related and displayed *légitimiste* leanings by including articles by Daly's monarchist first cousin Alphonse de Calonne, especially those on the Hotel de Cluny and his attack on *Saint Simonien* Jules Bouchet's drawings of the Casino Pio IV.

A periodical spanning fifty years is subject to changes in editorial viewpoint, and in this, the *Revue Générale* was no exception. However, these changes were not merely arbitrary, but should rather be viewed against Daly's kaleidoscopic frame of reference. Editorial viewpoint must be seen in connection with Daly's numerous journeys, and his continual exposure to new architectural situations, his political involvements, which, in the case of the positivists had explicit artistic overtones, and his changing philosophy of art. Owing to family background, Daly's connections with Great Britain were strong. During the 1840s, Daly made frequent trips to England. For instance, in 1839-40, he spent five months in London; in 1841 he busied himself sounding the English Channel; he analyzed British proletarian housing in 1844. After the 1840s, his interests were less localized and more encyclopedic. In the fifties and sixties, Daly travelled to more exotic locales. In 1854 he spent time in Germany, visiting Saxony, Prussia, and Bavaria. In 1855 he was off again, this time for a two-year visit to the New World, visiting North and Central America. In 1868 he journeyed to the Middle East, spending three months in Egypt, and participating with the British Palestinian Exploration Fund in Jerusalem, Baalbek, and Damascus. On the return journey to France, he visited the Aegean and southern Italy. Daly travelled to North Africa in 1875, spending most of his time in Algeria.

Parenthetically, it should be noted that later in his life Daly's travels were intimately involved with his health. Daly was first and foremost a scientist, and was prepared to travel great distances to unearth or acquire new knowledge and insight. However, his passion for work drove his body to physical limits. Daly was prepared to chance his life in pursuit of knowledge. For example, Jean Laran recounts that Daly, intent upon sketching a detail on the uppermost platform of the Albi Cathedral tower, had himself dangled over the edge of the parapet on a rope, some three hundred feet above the ground.[23] That kind of behavior constitutes a risk that I think few of us would be prepared to take for either art or science. This driven existence taxed his health to a breaking point. Daly may have had a tendency toward respiratory problems, and in 1851 he suffered a three-month long bout with pneumonia.[24] His life thereafter was to be frequently interrupted by bronchial and coronary ailments. In 1854 he was again ill, and it is for this reason that Daly ostensibly wished to travel to America for a rest. He wrote to the Prefect of the Tarn in February 1855,

> Le mauvais état de ma santé m'oblige à délaisser pour quelques mois tout travail exigeant une application sérieuse, et de chercher dans un voyage le repos de l'esprit auquel la faculté me condamne momentanément."[25]

> The dreadful state of my health obliges me to foresake all exacting work and to seek in a voyage an escape from the exertions to which my faculties presently condemn me.

It is clear that rather than a panacea, the journey further complicated the fragile state of his physical condition, when during the spring of 1856 he suffered with yellow fever in Guatemala. Ironically, Daly returned to France in October of that year again seeking to regain his health. It is interesting to note that during his recovery period in 1857-58, Daly married Joséphine-Sydonie Aygaleng, his assistant on the *Revue Générale.*

Daly's problematical health became one of his most noteworthy characteristics. In *The Builder's* memorial of Daly, Edward Godwin is quoted as saying,

> If you call to see Daly, it is just a toss-up whether he is in bed with a cold, or whether he is away studying the aboriginal architecture of Kamschatka.[26]

To escape the winter cold, the cause of much of his discomfort, Daly bought houses in Cannes and in Amélie-les-Bains, in the Pyrénées Orientales. His journeys, particularly in the Middle East and North Africa, were undertaken with a vested interest in scientific documentation, but they also removed Daly from the winters in France, where even in the south, his health might be endangered.

The political stands of César Daly also had an impact on the *Revue Générale.* In 1839 Daly viewed a hybridized representative-monarchical and classical liberal system, exemplified by England at the time, as the best possible political alternative. Furthermore, as an admirer of Fourier and Owen, he simultaneously saw the importance of technology and organized labor as means to efficient production, the source of physical and social well-being. The inaction of the July Monarchy with regard to certain seminal Fourierist programs, and the king's press restrictions, turned Daly, like so many socialists, against the Duc d'Orléans, Louis-Philippe. Thus, Daly's view of history shifted from one where man was subject to the continual improvement via evolution to one where man took on a more instrumental role. Daly now became mediator and critic, a historical catalyst introducing the new age. The shift was apparent in the contrast between Daly's "Tableau of the Evolution of Styles" of 1846 and his letter to Ludovic Vitet of 1847, where he speaks of a new republicanism and the right to artistic self-determination.[27]

His short-lived satisfaction with the Second Republic ended with Louis-Napoleon's *coup d'état* in December 1851. The laws of the press of March 1852 culminated Napoleon's legal attempts to control journalism. One of the first victims of the emperor's displeasure was Victor Considérant, editor of *La Démocratie Pacifique,* whose journalistic attacks on the president forced his flight from France in June 1849. While in exile in Belgium, Considérant planned a great Fourierist expedition to North America for the establishment of a phalanstery in Texas. Considérant departed from Europe in 1855 to found La Réunion near the present-day site of Dallas. Daly followed soon thereafter.

César Daly's involvement with the community is problematical. He travelled from New Orleans to Dallas by boat and wagon during May 1855 in the company of M. and Mme. Considérant, Mme. Clarisse Vigoureux, and Mme. Cantagrel. He is listed as one of the members of the "Commission de l'Administration" of La Réunion in June.[28] We lose sight of Daly in the La Réunion archives after that date. One is forced to ask why it was that Daly left the colony so abruptly. One explanation may be that Daly never intended to stay permanently at La Réunion, but planned only a brief visit. However, if this was the case, why then did Daly accept a position in the phalanstery's board of directors? A more plausible interpretation might be that Daly had intended to remain for an unspecified time, but that the economic difficulties and general disorder of the community had become evident already, and insurmountable complications caused by discord hastened his departure.[29] Hence, this Fourierist experiment, like the one at Condé-sur-Vesgre, also failed. Daly moved on, exploring the tribes of the "Peaux Rouges" in North Texas, and painted mission structures around San Antonio. He then returned to New Orleans to plan for his voyage to Central America.[30]

Although Daly earlier likened the Indians of Texas to modern-day Greek heroes, it became apparent from his experience with the natives of Central America that the primitive man could also be cruel and vindictive. Unlike Rousseau, Daly perceived man in the primitive state to be morally deficient, and hence came to value modern civilization as an improvement upon Roussellian freedom and the concomitant lawlessness of life in nature.

Daly returned to France a changed man. He no longer disparaged Paris' bourgeois life style, but decided instead to participate in it. Single for the first forty-seven years of his life, he made the decision to marry, choosing his secretary Mademoiselle Aygaleng in 1858. Daly quickly became domesticated. He bought a villa in the Paris suburb of Wissous in 1859, where he was to raise a family. This was to be the only site of Daly's work as architect, although Albi's restoration also raised significant design issues. Children soon followed: Marcel-Robert in 1860, and a pair of twins, Raymond-Auguste and Victor-Camille, in 1862.

As Daly was partaking in the family institution, he also sought to join the architectural establishment surrounding Louis-Napoleon. He pointedly praised Napoleon III for his urban improvements in Paris in the dedication to the first series of *L'Architecture Privée du Dix-Neuvième Siècle* of 1863. It is worth noting, however, that he simultaneously criticized Baron Eugène Haussmann for the destruction of many of Paris' most important landmarks, particularly on the Ile de la Cité.

His jockeying for position had mixed results. For example, following his return from Mexico, he became one of the founders of the Société d'Ethnographie Americaine et Orientale in 1858. The group received imperial sanction after the French-assisted *coup d'état* in Mexico in 1863 as the

Commission Scientifique du Mexique of 1864. Daly and Viollet-le-Duc were founding members charged with the task of Pre-Columbian archaeology. After the overthrow of Maximilien and Carlotta in 1868, the group quietly disbanded.

Daly tried to gain other official appointments. Using Merimée as a means to gain the emperor's attention, he sought an appointment to the organizing committee for the French Exposition Industrielle of 1862. Daly, however, was not appointed. Other factors worked against him. Perhaps the most influential of these was Viollet-le-Duc, who never forgave Daly for remaining so quiet on the occasion of his lectures in architectural theory at the Ecole des Beaux-Arts in 1863-64. A rupture in attitude became even more apparent in the foundation of Viollet's *La Gazette des Architectes* which was viewed by both Daly and Viollet-le-Duc as a critique of the *Revue's* aesthetic posture.[31] Through the agency of Baron Nieuwerkerke, such antagonism could have been easily communicated to the emperor.

Ultimately, Daly built nothing official during the Second Empire. He was never given a major commission; he never became party to the enormous governmental system of public works. Daly's only architectural involvement during the period was as advisor to Gabriel Davioud's Théâtres du Chatelet—the Théâtre Impériale and the Théâtre Lyrique—lavishly illustrated and described in Daly's *Théâtres de la Place du Châtelet* of 1874.

Daly had mixed feelings about the Second Empire, both politically and artistically. On the one hand, he clearly admired the superficially stable social situation under Louis-Napoleon. He praised the emperor's emphasis upon technology and industry, and his progressive banking system making improvement possible. He also recognized and approved Napoleon III's achievements concerning the physical and psychological reorganization of the city of Paris. On the other hand, he disapproved of the implicit system of privilege practiced by this new monarchy, with its inherent prejudices against him as architect and intellectual. Daly's fundamental republicanism, with its joint emphases upon liberty and equality, compromised his positive feelings for the Empire, particularly since he felt himself discriminated against.

César Daly and his family left Paris in the fall of 1870 with the onslaught of the Franco-Prussian War and the Paris Commune. He despised them both. Part of his hatred must be ascribed to traditional bourgeois indignation at the loss of his private property. It should be noted that Daly invested much of his personal fortune in the apartment houses of the new Paris, many of which were damaged or destroyed by cannon fire. Daly laments his losses at the time.

The Prussians have occupied our country house near Paris since the third week of September. A battle took place in our grounds and the whole commune is devastated. The park and gardens which were improved at such great expense, and on which an endless amount of care was bestowed, are now a miry waste. All the shrubs, I am informed, were torn up for firewood by our amiable German visitors. My pictures were wantonly looted, as well as the library... The Bavarians ruthlessly cut down the fruit trees which we were at such great pains in collecting and planting, and smashed the melon and cucumber frames. The green houses are entirely things of the past, and there is not a door or window frame in the house. Whenever we get back, what shall we find of our house and grounds? A field and little more...[32]

With regard to the War and the Commune, it is important to note that Daly did not support conservative representatives of the newly proclaimed French republic, either *légitimiste* or imperialist, but rather the faction of Léon Gambetta, who was the major spokesman of the new radical republicanism. As minister of war for the interim government acting out of Tours, it was Gambetta who attempted a futile counterattack against German forces in France. Daly, however, soon tired of the revolution. By 1871, he saw the city's political struggle as "Jacobin," comparing it with Robespierre's Paris Commune. Hence, his political position wavered between conservatism and radicalism.

Moreover, his politics found close parallel in his aesthetics. Daly recommended neither liberal utilitarian art forms nor conservative *l'art pour l'art*. He illustrated his artistic, and specifically architectural, point of view using a political analogy:

En politique, il nous faudrait un gouvernement définitif généralement accepté, en architecture un style généralement acclamé. Mais nous sommes loin de là: car tandis que les politiques oscillent entre le jacobinisme et la légitimité, en passant par le doute timide et le scepticisme pratique, les architectes oscillent entre le rationalisme utilitaire et les renaissances historiques, en traversant l'eclectisme et la fantaisie.[33]

In politics, a generally accepted and definitive government is required; in architecture, a generally recognized style. But we are far from that; for while politicians oscillate between jacobinism and legitimacy, traversing regions of doubt and of practical skepticism, architects oscillate between rationalism and historical renaissance, passing through eclecticism and fantasy along the way.

Daly's political analogies expanded to consider art, like government, from a comparative and progressive point of view. France's social and political program from 1830 to 1851 seemed to parallel an artistic development that was similarly liberal, utilitarian and positive. However, Louis-Napoleon's ascendancy to president and then to emperor seemed to check that growth. In the course of one night, France's governmental structure was transformed from democracy to autocracy. This political upheaval reverberated in artistic circles.

Much as the Second Empire called the liberal-humanitarian social program into question, so did it foster doubts about romantic realism in art. Renouncing one world of artistic consideration, Louis-Napoleon sponsored interest in another. A vista was opened to an interpretation of art that was something other than purposeful or useful. Art was no longer to be considered as one with its socio-political context. This view of art was essentially that of Charles Baudelaire's *l'art pour l'art*. Daly always spoke contemptuously of Baudelaire's movement. Yet, like other members of the romantic realist movement, he could not escape the more subconscious play of Baudelaire's theories on his aesthetic conscience. The movement's impact on Daly's own artistic views is never direct. However, we can detect (in an indirect way) the effect of *l'art pour l'art* in his critical vantage, as evidenced in his review of Viollet-le-Duc's pedagogy at the Ecole des Beaux-Arts which he attacked as overly pragmatic and inartistic.

As support for the Second Empire waned, so did Daly's interest in any single artistic stand. The years between 1868 and 1894 found Daly returning to many of the themes of his early career. This shift is apparent in his introduction to the second edition of *Motifs Historiques* of 1869, an expansion of his "Tableau of the Evolution of Styles" dated 1847.

His change in theoretical position can be ascribed to a number of issues. First, he reestablished his involvement with various scientific societies, like the Congrès Scientifiques et Archéologiques, and the Société d'Ethnographie, of which Daly served as vice president in 1887 and president in 1891. Second, Daly renewed his friendship with Victor Considérant. Following the death of his wife in 1881, the penniless Considérant was forced to depend on the charity of friends. He lived for long periods of time with Daly during the last twelve years of his life.

The major themes of Daly's later writings concerned public competitions and *Hautes-Etudes* in architecture. His advocacy of open competitions stems from his hostility to the Second Empire and its practice of patronage. Daly's agitation for *Hautes-Etudes* originates in his rationalistic architectural posture, by which the fundamental questions of archaeology and architecture were to be assessed.

Although many of Daly's closest architectural colleagues—Merimée, Duban, Viollet-le-Duc, Labrouste, Duc, Garnier—were invited to join the Académie des Beaux-Arts of the Institut de France, César Daly himself was never to become a member. His single great achievement, the *Revue Générale,* went almost unrecognized in official circles. When Daly was nominated for the Légion d'Honneur, the archibshop of Albi mentioned one of the candidate's qualifications as "la publication d'un journal dont je suis persuadé que Votre Excellence apprécie l'utilité."[34] He was admitted to the Légion, however, by virtue not of his writing but of his restoration of Albi.

Daly's importance as writer and critic seemed always better appreciated abroad than at home. He was made a member of the Royal Academy of Stockholm in 1842, a correspondent of the Royal Institute of British Architects in 1844, named member of the Royal Academy of Fine Arts of St. Petersburg in 1849, of the Order of Saint Stanislaus in Russia in 1855, of the Royal Academy of Belgium in 1865, of the American Institute of Architects and the Academy of Fine Arts in Florence in 1872, member of the Academy of Saint Luke, and honorary member of the R.I.B.A. in 1885, and so on. Daly considered his greatest honor to be the gold medal awarded him by the Royal Institute of British Architects in 1892.[35]

In 1878 Daly went into partial retirement, having ceded his position as *architecte-diocésain* of Albi Cathedral to Ruprich Robert. He continued as editor and major contributor to his two periodicals, the *Revue Générale* and *La Semaine des Constructeurs,* founded two years before. For all practical purposes, the *Revue Générale* ceased publication in 1887. The *Semaine,* for which Daly was the titular editor, was managed first by Paul Planat, and after 1886 by Daly's eldest son Marcel. Its publication ended shortly after the father's death. César Daly remained active throughout his later years. He continued his customary circuit of lectures, enormous correspondence, theoretical writings on the *Hautes Etudes* and other topics, and even made plans for a dictionary of architecture. His last five years found him spending more time in bed, recovering from his frequent bouts with bronchitis. On 23 December 1893, Victor Considérant died. Two weeks later, on 12 January 1894, Céar Daly was also dead.

A biographical *précis* is to be perceived as a summary of factual information concerning some significant individual's history, a brief but pointed excursus discussing the background and provenance of a career. Names, dates, and places are laid out in single file or shoulder-to-shoulder order in an attempt to abstract and quantify a lifetime, a material matrix against which such important characteristics as inventiveness, traditionalism, or originality can be weighed or assayed. As earlier discussed in the Introduction, the scientific *précis* seeks to present historical data in a removed, objective way, at the risk of sacrificing personality, with its implicit values, idiosyncrasies, and contradictions, for a lifetime's data. Thus far, I fear that this *précis* has been no exception to the rule.

In the past Daly's architectural career has been subjected to some kind of intellectual distillation process, evaporating the extraneous historical fluid for some kind of material residue. The historiography of César Daly provides a useful means to convey the way in which his career has been dissected in search of meaningful issues. In the past he has been treated as a mere fragment in some great architectural edifice or a bit of debris on the surface of history's tidal movements. In the case of earlier writers, César Daly has been interpreted as part of a larger stream of historical consciousness. He is seen by Peter Collins in *Changing Ideals in Modern Architecture* as "proto-organicist," Sigfried Giedion in *Space, Time, and Architecture* as herald of functionalism, by

Donald Drew Egbert in *Social Radicalism and the Arts* as socialist/positivist.[36] My intention is not to criticize these three writers, for their set tasks were not specifically biographical. Collins attempted to deal with modern architecture as a composite intellectual history. Egbert chose to examine a "unit idea" of the modern movement, that is, its social purpose, and to examine its sources and implications. Giedion was involved with a subtle brand of propaganda by which he himself might have a hand in the birth of a new architecture, even if it meant delivery by Caesarean section. All three men, whether interpreting Daly as part of a social movement, ideology, or personal architectural stand, tended to distort or to disintegrate Daly as individual.

Giedion as historian can be attacked on a variety of levels. Giedion as critic, however, can provide us with certain interesting observations, which perhaps reveal more about the observer than about the phenomenon observed. Speaking about the relationship of architecture to engineering, he describes a situation in which the architect is alienated from the "spirit of the age," that is, historical consciousness which is immanently technological and progressive. Giedion sees this alienation evidenced in the architect's anxiety:

> With the quickening of the advance of industry in the middle of the nineteenth century, there becomes a feeling on the part of the architect that his privileged position is menaced and the traditions of his art outmoded. That anxiety grew in intensity with the progress of industrialization. But the contemporary statements of this feeling are of more interest than any deductions we might make concerning it.[37]

Giedion speaks from an early twentieth-century vantage. He views history as the gradual revealing of the technological and collective spirit in society. Past social upheavals can be explained by man's inability (or incompetence) in coming to grips with the spirit. Historically, man has been presented with a series of choices. At these points, pairs of alternatives or dualities, such as socialism or individuality, science or art, machine or spirit, presented themselves. They appeared as opposite but also equal. Although irresolution led either to historical stagnation (or "transition") or to revolution, a choice was inevitably made.

Giedion in the 1930s perceived himself in the best of all possible worlds. It is clear that in the past man had been confronted with a tortuous and forked path, but now, with destiny as both guardian angel and Saint Christopher, he had been placed on the straight and true path of progress. In Giedion's perverse "might equals right" argument, the present has vindicated the past.

Giedion may be correct in assessing the position of the architect in 1935. However, he fails to adequately assess the situation and status of the early nineteenth-century architects. Clearly, the twentieth-century architect, according to Giedion, believed himself able to resolve the apparent inconsistencies and inadequacies present in the nineteenth century. However, might not the architect of the nineteenth century also have regarded himself a commentator on the state of the craft a century before? And if so, what then was the achievement of the nineteenth-century architect?

In the seventeenth and early eighteenth century, architects were regarded as composite builders, producing anything from an interior to a bridge, a stage set to a fortification. Above all else, the French writer on architecture (with important exceptions) stressed technique over theory, intent especially on methods of construction.[38] There is an important connection between Le Muet's *Manière de Bien Bastir* of the early eighteenth century, Cordemoy's *Nouveau Traité de l'Architecture* of the mid-eighteenth century, and Rondelet's *L'Art de Bâtir* of the early nineteenth century.[39] All three treatises stressed a rationalistic posture, the first two maintaining a more conventionalized, common sense pragmatism, the third, a more scientific stand.[40] In all three, architecture was regarded more as a trade, craft, or technique rather than as an intellectual and artistic discipline. It had functional and empirical components that removed it from the pure sciences and the arts.

The *Encyclopédie* of Diderot and d'Alembert of 1751 had a major role in changing the conventional view of architecture. In its first volume the editors proposed a graphic "tree of knowledge" which divided architecture between three faculties—memory, reason, and imagination.[41] For our purposes, let it suffice to say that the architecture of memory and reason conforms to our present-day notions of public works and civil engineering. The third category, *architecture imaginative,* allied itself with the fine arts, particularly poetry, music, painting, and sculpture.

It is interesting to note that at a slightly earlier date, 1747, the Ecole des Ponts et Chaussées was founded to serve the needs of public works and engineering. Simultaneously, however, Madame de Pompadour and the Marquis de Marigny attempted to ally the Académie d'Architecture with the school of drawing in the Ecole du Louvre. Hence, it seems that at mid-century, there was considerable confusion concerning the nature of architecture. At any rate, an attempt was made to divide architecture between institutions committed to very different conceptions of architecture. Furthermore, it becomes clear that this categorical way of thinking about architecture existed in France before the arrival of the Encyclopedists, and that by mid-century, theorists and architects alike desired to separate themselves from the traditional craftsmanly conception, in favor of its imaginative persona. Architecture was now an art.

It is apparent that it was *architecture imaginative* that the latter eighteenth-century critics and artists, as well as those of the early nineteenth century, especially valued. Boullée's dedication to the *Essai sur l'Architecture* proudly states "Ed io anche pittore" or "I am also a painter," proclaiming the connectedness of architecture with the fine arts and imagination. Denis Diderot stressed the imaginative component of architecture, allying it with poetry, or figurative language, rather than the instrumental narrative of *Historia*. Upon the reestablishment of the Académie des Beaux-Arts, Quatremère de Quincy insisted upon having architecture grouped with the arts of painting and sculpture rather than with the sciences. The assessment of architecture as an art established it among the highest of man's faculties. It rose above the merely customary or contingent, partaking in divine rather than human life via inspiration. The architect as artist functioned on the highest plane of existence.

To return to the question posed above, the achievement of the early nineteenth-century architect was his attainment of a new status. The architect was now an artist with access to the highest levels of the mind. Although nineteenth-century architects of the romantic generation criticized Quatremère and the Academy, it is clear that there was no group more passionately interested in describing the philosophy of art, criticizing appropriate form, and discussing artistic metaphysics. Diderot and Quatremère, by separating technology and art, encouraged the architect to consider his situation, and to contemplate his discipline as an end in itself. As an artist, his main involvement was with the problem of form, which he might address by the expanded palette provided by new technologies.[42]

Technology, a heretofore undervalued consideration in the artistic process, was placed on an equal footing with other formal preoccupations. Equality was permitted out of the generosity of the liberal point of view. Liberalism's magnanimity was of the kind that William Gladstone displayed, as he prowled the streets of London's East End for young prostitutes whom he could proselytize. Gladstone set himself to his humanitarian task wholly convinced of his own sanctity. Or better still, one might consider officials of the British Foreign Office seeking to better the lot of the black African savages only after their own privileged station is assured.[43] Clearly one element in the legitimizing of technology during the early nineteenth century was the liberal point of view. The architects at that moment befriended poor, disenfranchised technology, because they had nothing to fear. For after its eighteenth-century defeat, how could it ever again rise to a position of merely functional, *retardataire* dominance? But as seen in numerous post-colonial situations, one-time colonies often turned their backs on the liberator who freed them from the dark ages of ignorance and gained the upper hand over their former oppressors. One wonders if the rationalists of the nineteenth century had any real idea of what their patronizing posture toward civil engineering would ultimately produce? For, as they would see a mere century later, Giedion declares the conclusive victory of science over imagination and idealism.

Daly himself embodies the paradoxical liberal position. As earlier discussed, Daly as a young *collégien* was being prepared for the study of law by courses in mathematics, physics, and rhetoric. The importance of mathematics and physics to the development of positivism has been noted by a number of authors.[44] In this positivist component, the functionalist critic Giedion might find the germ of Daly's progressive and materialistic stand. Yet Daly was also a student of rhetoric, significant for both functional and idealistic reasons. The study of rhetoric was regarded as essential to coherent argumentation. As such it was instrumental discourse. The functional form of rhetoric, however, was distinct from its objective. The purpose of rhetoric, in both the Platonic and Horatian senses of the word, was to convey the ideal. In short, rhetoric's object concerned inspiration which, as we have seen above, was also the end of the imaginative disciplines in the *Encyclopédie*'s tree of knowledge. As a scientist, Daly was a positivist; as an artist, he was idealistic; as a writer, he utilized positivistic argumentation for an idealistic end.

To return to my introductory comments concerning the scientific *précis,* I draw an analogy between drawing and biography. In this, I refer to the procedure of the academic *analytique* versus the *esquisse.* The *analytique* or measured hardline rendering of an archaeological facade or fragment described a particular architectural feature's structure and manipulation. Traditionally, the *analytique* told little about a building's character, for this was not at issue in scientific drawing. Rather, character was best communicated by the *esquisse.* In the shadows and tense lines, in the half-light of the chiaroscuro of the *esquisse,* character was convincingly depicted. Quick sketches and vignettes pertaining to plan and composition evoked visual associations, as much by what was implied and unresolved as by what was consciously depicted. The *esquisse* was neither holistic, scientific, or complete, but fragmentary and poetic. These drawing techniques might be likened to biographical methods. To contrast the preceding biographical discussion, one might further employ a literary technique akin to the *esquisse* or vignette, perhaps a colloquial, anecdotal method, to better portray Daly's character.

If we turn to a portrait of César Daly's family in the Considérant family album, we see the father, aged about fifty-five, seated with his wife and sons (plate 1). The twins, Raymond and Victor, sit with their father, listening intently while the father explains an illustrated book to them. The older boy, Marcel, stands beside his mother. Daly as the father is severe and imposing. His carefully cut, finely detailed black clothing suggests restraint, calculation and control. His posture is simultaneously meditative and didactic. His actions befit a good liberal—teaching the untutored for purposes of social improvement. Daly reminds us of education's central role in the ongoing drama of progress.

Implicit in this photograph, however, is a portrayal of Daly's psychology. We are presented with a depiction of Daly's intransigence. Although he was both democrat and socialist, Daly was profoundly distrustful of the state's educational institutions, and he insisted upon instructing his children himself. For their first fifteen years, the children remained at home under the tutelage of their dutiful and self-righteous father. With regard to Daly's attitude to child rearing, we see him flying in the face of bourgeois convention. This man with such a sedate, controlled, even middle-class exterior was a man of his own mind internally. He could be irreverant, iconoclastic, even passionate in life when his values were at stake. A man of conviction and action, Daly must have stood out dramatically from the bourgeois lifestyle of Second Empire Paris.

Our initial impressions about Daly from this photograph are confirmed by contemporary commentators. One writer describes Daly's "fiery temperament" which comes from the "blood of old Ireland" running through his veins. In this regard, an allusion is made to the Daly family's longstanding rhetorical heritage, stemming from the Celtic bardic tradition. [45]

What one commentator implies, another illustrates by describing Daly's fit of rage concerning administrative problems at Albi Cathedral in 1871. Ostensibly angry over an issue of free access to his office on the work site, he verbally attacked and humiliated one of his employees. The worker, Cyprian Magne, reported:

Mercredi 21 Mr et Mme Daly vinrent eux-memes au bureau. Mr Daly s'adressant à Mr Lacroux, lui demanda si tous les soirs il ne fermait pas les volets? Il répondit que si, mais, dit-il, ils étaient ouverts et vous n'étiez pas ici. Se tournant ensuite de mon côté, il me demanda si c'était moi qui y étais par la porte. Vous avez donc une seconde clef? Oui Monsier. Vous allez me la donner me dit-il. Mais lui dis-je Mme Bodin m'a donné cette clef et m'a recommandé de la garder moi-même je vais la lui remettre, et si elle veut vous la donner je vous la rapporterai tout de suite. A cette response il prît un air arrogant, se posta devant moi, me dit qu'il ne me connaissait ni à moi ni à Mme Bodin, me demanda si j'étais employé de Mr Le Ministre. Je lui repondis que non, alors continuant il me dit qu'il ne comprenait pas comment j'avais osé m'introduir dans son bureau, que j'ignorais pas que je parlais à Mr l'Architecte Diocésain, que Mr Bodin était son employé, que dans son bureau il y a des pièces importantes, qu'il n'était pas nécessaire que qui que ce fût y entrait, que ce bureau était pour Mr Bodin seul et pour les travaux de la cathédrale, que donc il me priait de lui donner cette clef, de sortir immédiatement, et qu'à l'avenir il ne voulait plus que j'y remis la clef qu'il donna à Mr Lacroux et je me disposai à sortir. Mr Daly changeant alors de ton, me dit de ne pas prendre cela en mal, qu'il ne s'adressait pas à moi personellement qu'il avait voulu donner une leçon à mon inexpérience. [46]

Wednesday the twenty-first Monsieur and Madame Daly came to the office. M. Daly addressed himself to M. Lacroux asking him if the window shutters were customarily left open in the evenings. Lacroux responded yes; they were left open when Monsieur Daly was not in town. Turning to me, he asked how I got in. By the door, I replied. "You have a second key?" "Yes, Monsieur." He told me to give him the key. I responded that Mme Bodin had given me the key and had instructed me to keep it myself, and that if she wished for Monsieur to have it then I would immediately turn it over. To this reply, he assumed an arrogant air, stood before me, and told me that he was as unacquainted with Mme Bodin as he was with me, and then asked me if I was employed by Monsieur le Ministre. I replied no. He continued saying that he failed to understand how I had the audacity to enter his office, that I was obviously unaware that I spoke to the Diocesan Architect, that M. Bodin was his employee, that in this office there were important and valuable materials, that this office was for the sole use of M. Bodin to use while working on the cathedral and no one else, and therefore, he demanded to have my key. He next told me to leave immediately and that in the future, I must leave the key he gave M. Lacroux in the office. I prepared to leave. M. Daly, changing his tone, told me to have no bad feelings, and that he was not addressing himself to me personally, but that he wished to give a lesson to my inexperience.

"Arrogance...giving a lesson to inexperience." In these lines, one can observe a perversion of the liberal responsibility to pedagogy. One wonders how a person of Daly's social position could possibly delight in the willful belittling of a simple draftsman. How could a socialist feel so little compassion for the plight of a worker? Lastly, why would Daly feel the need, not only to humiliate, but also to call upon traditional class distinctions in order to achieve his ends? It is apparent that the socially conscious Daly had considerable difficulty in dealing with those working under him at Albi. In the course of fifteen years, Daly went through three contractors, two of whom sued him for defamation of character at one point or other. Daly's most unpleasant labor dispute occurred with the site architect during the years 1869-71, an incident again ending in court. In the course of the proceedings, Daly was again accused of obstructionism and slander.

The core of Daly's problems at Albi probably lay in his inability to adequately orchestrate and supervise the restoration of the Cathedral. In 1859 M. Hamille in a candidacy letter for Daly to the Légion d'Honneur mentions that Daly is an architect *peu pratique,* an allusion to the numerous work stoppages and labor problems at Albi.[47] This resulted in the delegation of authority to various on-site people, and Daly's consequent loss of control. Control, however, was the one privilege that Daly was not prepared to concede. He subsequently maintained his position at Albi by effectively dismissing any opposition. His means of doing so, however, could be harsh and unfeeling.

This discussion of Daly's problematical political situation at Albi permits us to draw certain inferences about César Daly's personality. Although he was an outspoken socialist preoccupied with the problems of the working class, it is apparent that Daly had enormous difficulty in dealing with workers in real life situations. Furthermore, although a pronounced republican, Daly was easily threatened when faced with the reality of social equality and the obliteration of class barriers. Lastly, when feeling professionally or emotionally threatened, Daly had the means of lashing out against his opponent, using either his wit or his razor-like sarcasm, even if his antagonist had little defense. A strict liberal, an avid socialist? In theory, perhaps; in practice, no.

It is interesting to contrast our impressions of Daly from the family portrait earlier discussed—stolid, responsible, pedagogical—with the verbal description of Barbey d'Aurevilly of 1844. Barbey dedicates his essay "Du Dandysme" to César Daly.

A. M. César Daly
Directeur
de la Revue de l'Architecture

Pendant que vous voyagez, mon cher Daly, et que le souvenir de vos amis ne sait où vous prendre, voici quelque' chose (je n'ose pas dire un livre) qui vous attendra à votre seuil. C'est la statuette d'un homme qui ne merite guère que d'être représenté d'une statuette, curiosité de moeurs et d'histoire, bonne à mettre sur l'étagère de votre cabinet de travail...

Malheureusement je ne suis ni Montesquieu ni Beyle, ni aigle ni lynx, mais j'ai tâché pourtant de voir clair dans ce que beaucoup de gens, sans doute, n'eussant pas daigne expliquer. Ce que j'ai vu, je vous l'offre, mon cher Daly. Vous qui sentez la grâce comme une femme et comme un artiste, et qui, comme un penseur, vous rendez compte de son empire, j'aime à vous dédier cette étude sur un homme qui tira sa célibrité de son élégance. Je l'aurais faite sur un homme qui eût tiré la sienne de la forme de sa raison, que, grâce à la richesse des vos facultés, j'aurais eu bon de vous la dédier encore.[48]

To M. Cesar Daly
Director
of the Revue de l'Architecture

While you travel, my dear Daly, and while the memory of your friends scarcely knows where you will be next, here is something (I dare not say a book) that will accompany you to your doorstep. It is the statuette of a man who hardly merits being represented by a statuette, a moral and historical curiosity, good only to place in the shelf of your study.

Unfortunately, I am neither Montesquieu nor Beyle, neither eagle nor lynx, but I nonetheless try to see clearly into that which many men, undoubtedly, have not deigned to explain. What I have seen, I offer to you, my dear Daly...

You who emanate grace like a woman and like an artist, and who, as a thinker, comprehends his worldly empire, I lovingly dedicate to you this study of a man who draws his celebrity from his elegance. Had I modelled it upon a man who similarly drew upon his reason, I surely would have, because of the richness of your faculties, dedicated that to you as well.

Barbey was acquainted with César Daly and the Dandy "Beau" Brummel at the same time. They were in Caen simultaneously, Daly escaping from Paris, Brummel assuming the position of British Consul in the city. Although we have no reason to believe that Daly and Brummel ever met, we must assume that Barbey among others saw a kinship between the two. Each man spoke French with a genteel British accent, both affected an aristocratic air, each marked his own singularity in the company of others. Barbey's description of Brummel might just as easily have been of Daly:

Il avait les cheveux presque roux...et une chute de chavel, dans une charge, avait altéré la ligne grecque de son profil. Son air de tête était plus beau que son visage, et sa contenance—physiognomie du corps—l'emportait jusque sur la perfection de ses formes. Ecoutons Lister: "il n'était ni beau ni laid; mais il y avait toute sa personne une expression de finesse et d'ironie concentrée, et dans ses yeux une incroyable pénétration...Sa voix magnifique faisait une langue anglaise aussi belle à l'oreille qu'elle l'est à la pensée"...[49]

> He had almost red hair ... a fall from a horse, during a charge, altered the Greek line of his profile. The general impression of his head was even more beautiful than his face, and his countenance—his bodily physiognomy—carried him almost to the perfection of form itself. We hear Lister: "He was neither beautiful nor ugly; but his person embodied an expression of finesse and concentrated irony, and his eyes were unbelievably penetrating ... His magnificent voice made the English language as beautiful to the ear as to the mind...."

Fair, with reddish-blonde hair, handsome, refined, well-to-do and indisputably English, Daly was a physical recollection of Beau Brummel, at least to Barbey d'Aurevilly.

Moreover, it is clear that to Barbey, Daly was also a poetic figure. Daly was a man of reason. However, it was not so much his mind, but his "elegance" and his ability to "emanate grace like a woman" that must have inspired Barbey in his comparison between Daly and Brummell. Surely, Daly's influence on this ideal of the dandy was more than physical. For example, the dandy's personality exemplified defiance, independence, individuality, and egotism. As we have early seen, Daly could display all these tendencies on the appropriate occasion.

I call attention to the characteristic of *ironie concentrée* in Barbey's description of the dandy, for it is irony that aptly expresses the dualistic nature of Daly's personality. Charles Baudelaire amplifies the idea of dualism in his description of the dandy in *The Painter of Modern Life*. Baudelaire supplies a useful definition:

> (Dandyism is) ... an institution as strange and obscure as the duel ... Dandyism, an institution above the laws, has laws to which all its representatives ... are subject ... (the) dandy does not make love his special aim ... (he is) free from the need to follow any profession ... For the true dandy ... (personal appearance and material elegance) are ... symbols of the aristocratic personality. What then is this ruling passion ... ? It is above all, a burning need to acquire originality, within the apparent bounds of convention ... It is the delight in causing astonishment, and the proud satisfaction of never oneself being astonished ... The characteristic beauty of the dandy consists above all, in his air of reserve, which in turn arises from his remarkable resolve to not feel any emotion. It might be likened to a hidden fire whose presence can be guessed at; a fire which could blaze up, but does not wish to do so.[50]

Barbey's irony introduces the issue of paradox. Baudelaire's definition expands this idea. Duality alone can be used to explain the seeming contradictions in Daly's personality. Daly was blond, handsome, cool, Anglo-Saxon. His lifestyle consciously countered the temperamentality and individuality of such early romantic figures as Chateaubriand, Byron, and Gautier. He countered the romantic free spirit with his impeccable, aristocratic control. However, in this ostensibly individualistic period, it was restraint and control, above all else, which stood out. The controlled artificiality of his demeanor set him apart. Daly was not flamboyant, but cool, separate and cerebral.

César Daly's early social stand made him profoundly antibourgeois. He despised the artificial constraints placed on conventional manners by church, bureaucracy, and class structure. His own collective experience at Condé-sur-Vesgrê was clearly a commentary on the life-style of the bourgeoisie, "Etre comme tout le Monde."[51] In its own way, Daly's style was carefully conceived, his behavior as normalized, prescribed, and artificial as any under a church- or class-dominated system. The difference occurred in the realm of consciousness. Whereas other men's lives were controlled externally, Daly's was determined internally, by a self-imposed set of norms created by his own artistic, social and personal consciousness. This internality, however, must be contrasted with that of the Romantics, who felt that their genius must know no constraint of any description. Daly believed in genius, but he was convinced that genius must manifest itself in recognizable, self-imposed forms. Loss of control over the nature of these forms implied a loss of personal instrumentality in shaping one's own destiny.

The dandy was both a contingent and symbolic being. His life revolved around his needs and their gratification. In this regard, the dandy stressed the material components of his existence, in contrast to the metaphysics of religion which proposed the sublimation of earthly needs in the face of external higher purpose. In this regard, the dandy criticized religious ideology and symbolism which ultimately normalized and ritualized contemporary life. Yet the dandy, by virtue of his own distinct physicality, proposed an implicit ideology all his own. In this way, the dandy became a symbol representing a system of human values in much the same way as the Crucifix symbolized the Creed. In this way, Barbey described the iconic quality of Daly's emblematic persona first as a statuette. In so doing, Barbey inferred not only the monumental quality of Daly's persona, but more importantly, the affective role that this fetishized human portrait could play in shaping others' social norms.

The dandy embodied an implicit intellectual stand. Recognizing the ideological achievement of the dandy's personal form, Barbey stated, "On l'a considéré comme être purement physique, et il était au contraire intellectuel jusque dans le genre de beauté qu'il possédait."[52] Interestingly enough, nowhere in the nineteenth century did the equation of ideology, criticism, and form become so recognizable. On the one hand, the dandy recognized and repudiated existing norms and social forms. Yet, on the other, he posed a new, similarly formalistic system which replaced the former.[53] There was an inherent agonism in the dandy's stand. Ultimately, the irony of his system became apparent, for he came to realize that he himself was a norm, and that his critical vengeance must finally be unleased upon himself. He was forced to deny even himself in the end. In the case of Brummell, this alienation led to his insanity and confinement to an asylum in Caen. Daly, however, may never have plumbed the depths of his personal contradiction. In him, the two sides of the duality remain always in a tenuous balance.

Historical analysis is frequently taxonomic.[54] History, in one of its archeological variants, seeks to distinguish themes and issues within the historical situation in order to provide time with meaning and structure. Yet biography as historical genre should move the study of time beyond its scientific involvements. As historical portraiture it is not merely narrative but also pictorial. As such, biography should be addressed both analytically and formalistically. Formalism tied to the study of the significant historical personality calls to mind Barbey's and Baudelaire's discussions of the dandy. Both authors assert that the figure of the dandy visually articulates social and historical critiques. From his life style, the dandy's critical thinking can be adduced. Yet, his critical role is only a part of the dandy's personality. Whereas criticism, with its implicit ideological dismemberment and analysis, is one part of dandy's personality, it is balanced by a second, no less important attribute, his sense of artistic self-composition. Even after the social critique becomes clear to the world, the dandy never discards his guise. Were he to do so, he would extinguish that mark of self-consciousness, the formulative role of imagination, as contrasted to the taxonomic techniques of his social and historical critique. Likewise, the hermeneutic enterprise of this historical study of César Daly as dandy might surely unravel the threads of an intellectual design. In so doing, however, it must avoid destroying the tapestry of consciousness of which those strands are part.

Ellen Moers in *The Dandy: Brummell to Beerbohm* described the ornamental surface quality of the dandy's persona.[55] Moers regards fashion and manners as signs of the dandy's artificiality, creating a visualization of the dandy's consciousness, both critical and aesthetic. That artificiality, as any work of art, is marked by a distinctive composition. Like the painter's painting, the dandy's composed demeanor is his creation, the best evidence of his imagination. For within the form rest not only that stratum of epistemological concerns which most researchers seem compelled to unearth, but also a deeper one wherein those critical predispositions lay, creating a foundation for that edifice of mind termed an ideology.

For form also reveals a creative urge, the pre-historical motivation providing the focus for one's view of history of philosophy, as well as one's own self-formulation. Imagination, as the underpinning of self-consciousness, is best revealed in composition. Therefore, it is not so much in the particularities of analytical decomposition that we might detect the mind of César Daly, but in the realm of artistic composition, both in his writing and in his building. Perhaps the ultimate significance of this biography rests not so much with the purely informational as with the stylistic, the lasting index of the consciousness of César Daly.

2

The Ideology of Antagonism

There were widespread indications of impending social and political catastrophe when, in 1847, César Daly composed his first major architectural manifesto "De la Liberté dans l'Art."[1] Indignation and patriotism, sponsored by the social unrest apparent some six months before the February Revolution, moved Daly to take a political and artistic position and to discuss the future of both modern architecture and modern society. Fired by ideological discontent as well as by the optimism of French and German romantics, Daly sanctified his statement with epigrams from the inspired writings of popularly acclaimed men of genius—Vitet, Lamennais, Guizot, Michelet, Hugo, Goethe—and marked it with his personal rhetoric. Daly's manifesto alternates between antagonism and utopian vision.

In writing the manifesto, Daly deviates not only from the anti-critical stand set out in the early numbers of the *Revue Générale,* but from his indifference to explicitly political issues as well.[2] His rhetoric is no longer internalized, isolated or confined within the parameters of his own professional context. As he establishes connections with men of letters in other fields (politics, philosophy, history), his personal style becomes expansive, moving beyond architecture into a more generalized sphere. Processes of abstraction and coincident kinship are at play. The critique of architecture escapes its own orbit of influence, and Daly's polemic moves to an attack of society as a whole. Utopian urges know no classifications or boundaries. Daly's intellectual process is inherently cross-disciplinary and philosophically synthetic. Viewed against the background of Encylopedism, which treated knowledge as a collection of so many isolated and unrelated fields, Daly's approach is indicative of what is to come in the way of synthetic epistemology.

With regard to the statement itself, two factors are at play. The first is Daly's relationship to the increasingly powerful antiquarian movement and particularly to the figure of Didron l'Aîné, editor of *Annales Archéologiques.* "De la Liberté" followed closely on the heels of the Congrès Archéologique in Tours, at which Daly and Didron came to verbal blows over several issues: the nature of invention and stylistic imitation in architecture and restoration, the role of progress in shaping distinctly modern artistic phenomena, and the place of personal consciousness in the artwork.

Daly's own posture with regard to these issues is buttressed by a speech delivered at the assembly by the Minister of the Interior, Ludovic Vitet. Vitet's presentation, entitled "Des Etudes Archéologiques en France," initially focused on the more canonical concerns of archaeology—restoration, stylistic classification, and building technique.[3] Second and more importantly, however, he issued a warning to those architects who wished to normalize any single stylistic period. Especially provocative for Daly were Vitet's attacks on singleminded formal imitation, such as the following:

> Copiez le Parthenon, copiez la Cathédrale de Reims, vous subirez la même influence: les modèles restent sublimes, les contrefaçons feraient pitié.[4]

> Copy the Parthenon, copy the Cathetral of Reims [and] you submit to the same influence: the models remain sublime, the counterfeits produce only pity.

Moreover, Vitet proclaimed his admiration for the truly innovative modern architectural practice, free of typological thinking:

> Honneur donc à ceux qui, même aujourd'hui, ne désespèrent pas d'inventer une architecture nouvelle, c'est-à-dire une combinaison de lignes et un système d'ornementation qui n'appartiennent qu'à notre époque et qui en perpetuent le souvenir! Qu'ils ne s'inspirent ni des formes antiques ni des formes du moyen âge; qu'ils se pénètrent seulement de la pensée-mère qui les engendra, pensée d'artiste et non d'archéologue.[5]

> Honor to those who still do not despair of inventing a new architecture, that is to say, a combination of lines and a system of ornamentation which pertain only to our epoch and which perpetuate its memory! May they not be inspired by antique or Gothic forms; may they be imbued solely with the "mother-idea" which engendered them, the idea of the artist and not of the archaeologist.

Vitet's personal artistic stance was hostile to the past. Although not explicitly progressive, he was nonetheless fixated on the present, and regarded his epoch as different from others.

Vitet's discussion could be read as a biological analogy. He sees his own period in time as a kind of climate which necessarily affects the shape of the artwork. Yet the control exerted by that climate is counterpoised with the germinal urge contained deep within the work of art. As a plant grows in general conformity with instructions encoded in the seed, so does the work of art develop in conformity with an idea—in Vitet's terms, *une pensée-mère*—basic to the artistic intention. Vitet's judgments are thus conditioned not only by attention to historical circumstances, but also by the idea inherent in the artwork. In order to describe the "Good" in architecture, it would seem that

Vitet comes close to an academic predisposition whereby value in art can be not only ascribed to, but even prescribed by, the typological model.

Daly's editorial reply, "De la Liberté dans l'Art," also focuses upon artistic freedom in terms of art's general dissociation from institutional standards—particularly Gothic and Classic schools of thought. As a result, his treatment of artistic freedom resurrects the age-old academic problem of imitation versus invention. It also implicitly addresses the problem of artistic standards by which inventive artistic play might be confined.

Daly's essay elevated in significance the cognitive attributes of man's inventive faculty: free will and imagination. It is important to bear in mind, however, that for Daly, these notions possess metaphysical existences. Daly the moralist is suspicious of complete artistic freedom. Much as a theologian might argue that man's free will is held in check by an unconscious moral code, Daly also presumes a subconscious value system regulating the artistic impulse. He exemplifies this position by the artists of antiquity and the Middle Ages whose artistic impulses were controlled by similarly inspired artistic sensitivity:

> Jusqu'aujourd'hui l'artiste n'a connu qu'une seule loi, la loi de son sentiment. Il n'a obéi qu'à une seule influence, l'influence de son temps. Il en fût ainsi dans l'antiquité, et l'antiquité nous a laissé des merveilles. Il en fût ainsi au moyen âge et le moyen âge nous a legué des chefs d'oeuvre. Les uns et les autres sont les protestations contre la prétension de subsituer l'erudition au sentiment, la recette à l'inspiration, la tête seule à la tête inspirée par le coeur.[6]

> Until recently, the artist knew only a single law, the law of his sentiment. He obeyed only one influence, the influence of his time. He was thus in antiquity, and antiquity has left us marvels. He was also this way during the Middle Ages and that period, too, has bequeathed us masterpieces. These marvels and masterpieces stand as protestations against the pretension of substituting erudition for sentiment, recipes for inspiration, and head alone for the head that is inspired by the heart.

Daly's discussion also expands upon the notion of the artistic genius, who, like the artists of the past, instinctively grasps the divine nature of things.

Imagination, like free will, is controlled by a metaphysic. Imagination, for Daly, is first of all the faculty which allows for the creation of new artistic forms. In addition, Daly sees the process of imagination in a Platonic light, proposing that it draws upon a set of basic images impressed into man's memory—forms—wherein truth resides. Both attributes of the inventive faculty—free will and imagination—depend upon the *pensée-mère* in creating art at once good and true.

It appears, then, that invention for Daly and Vitet is valid only insofar as it is allied to a metaphysic. Daly thereby guards the integrity of the work of art, allowing human consciousness to tap into the divine. Daly states:

On proclame la liberté de la presse, c'est-à-dire de la parole écrite, et on nierait celle de l'art, c'est-à-dire de la parole chantée, sculptée, peinte ou bâtie! On n'aurait plus le droit d'obeir aux inspirations qui sollicitent l'âme de l'artiste, qui l'emportent dans les hauteurs où flottent les idées et les types que le génie incarne, à la gloire de Dieu, et pour le bonheur de tous![7]

We proclaim the liberty of the press, that is to say, of the written word, yet we would deny freedom of art, that is to say, of the sung, sculpted, painted or built word! We would no longer have the right to obey the inspirations that solicit the soul of the artist, that carry him into the heights where the ideas and the styles incarnated by genius float to the glory of God and the happiness of all!

Daly's and Vitet's discourses pose certain important questions. First, how is history viewed by Daly and his circle? Second, what is the role that man is to play in history's scenario? Third, what is the nature of man's activity? We might arrive at some tentative responses to these questions upon examining three illustrations from the period of the Second Republic. The first is a plate from the *Revue Générale,* designed as a visualization of Daly's stand in "De la Liberté dans l'Art" in 1849, conceived as an allegory of history, both architectural and social. The second is a tableau prepared by Daly in October 1847, likewise sketching an artistic progress, or "evolution" as the author states. The third is an anonymous newspaper illustration, an editorial cartoon, in which material confronts moral progress.

The first engraving, entitled "L'Architecture Contemporaine," was designed by Daly's collaborator, Ruprich Robert (plate 2). It illustrates Daly's attitude toward historical progress by a kind of sculptural frieze or stele in which an allegory of history, both architectural and social, unfolds. The composition is divided into two zones, one devoted to the arts and performers of the past, the Romans and the Goths (depicted as *Les Plus Vieux* and *Les Vieux*), the other ascribed to the present *(L'Art Nouveau).* Two readings coexist in this tableau. One comprises the recent history of architecture. The other, a more generalized interpretation, treats issues of historiography and historicism, or, the spatialization of history and the calligraphy of history's immanent forces.

In terms of recent history, Daly portrays a conflict between the two schools of retrospective architectural thought, both Gothic and Classic, and *l'Art Nouveau.* The rupture between the two is enormous. In spatial treatment, the distant past has been treated in terms of a compressed space, filled with the chaotic trappings of bygone formal systems and populated with an abject humanity trapped between the world of decomposing political and religious structures and the modern vantage point of the viewer. The peoples of the past traverse a pitifully narrow pictorial space, the slender edge of their artistic frame, teetering between that which they fear or do not want, and that which they cannot have. The personifications of modernity, however, are treated as fully-round figures portrayed against a limitless expanse of deep space. Daly, and his designer-engraver Ruprich Robert, attempts an analogy between the viewer's and modernity's visual frame, especially in the emphasis upon continuous space and the personally engaging perspective viewpoint.

An optimistic post-1848 vantage may be at the basis of Daly's interpretation in the contrast of peace and warfare. At that date, a battle between conservative and liberal factions in both artistic and political realms was resolved by the erection of a new order. In the case of politics this meant the presidency of Louis-Napoleon. In the case of architecture it involved an arbitration of the forces of disorder (termed elsewhere as free will) and harmony.

Moreover, I see a deeper meaning to Daly's tableau, resting in the historiographic dimension. This reading is introduced by the anagrammatic, almost hieroglyphic, inscriptions in the lower right hand corner of the plate. This sketch of the history of art, and civilization itself, focuses upon a conflict of antinomies—Persian versus Indian, Roman versus Athenian, Byzantine versus Latin, Roman versus Gothic. Only one period transcends this polarizing scheme—the Renaissance.

Daly perceives the antagonism between the most recent of these oppositions—Roman versus Gothic—as a tableau of antagonism and despair. A Roman legionary destroys a Gothic ogive; a Crusader demolishes a Roman arch. The two epochs are mutually hostile. Moreover, their destructive forces not only focus on the world external to their demarcation, but they are internally- or self-directed as well. The eras in both are peopled by blindfolded men physically separated from nature, and perhaps more importantly, psychologically isolated from each other. The tableau presents a study in alienation. Men are separated from the social and political architecture that envelops them; the social structure becomes a force that assaults mankind as well. For example, at the beginning of the Roman epoch, one man lies dead on the ground, while another falls prey to an exterminating baluster, his fate sealed. The institutional structure of these societies, rather than merely invoking a stifling presence, leads to alienation, or *anomie,* of a physical extreme. The very nature of these societies is destructive, the self reduced to rubble by an oppressive social and political superstructure. The characters of the tableau are not psychologically isolated to the extreme of suicide, the last great expression of self in defiance of fate. Yet, the figures are perhaps even more pathetic in being deprived of the last great act of personal will, performed in opposition to the futility of destiny.[8]

Despite the fact that the two periods—Gothic and Roman—are mutually exclusive or hostile, they are united in the process of the historical dialectic. Their reciprocal antagonisms fuse them. The automation of history as oscillation, rise and fall, growth and decline, is indicated by the undulating path that these peoples of the past tread. The mechanical chant underlying history— Venus, Mercury, Vignola, Venus, Mercury, Vignola, and Marcellus,

Pantheon . . . Reims, Chartres—speak of an almost mantric articulation and rearticulation of alternatives or opposites. The dialectical process becomes herein ritualized as the process underlying the motivations and actions of man and history.

The historical stage of *Art Nouveau,* however, presents a different scenario. The carnivalesque quality of the earlier scene of the tableau, personified by the dwarf, appropriate to the spirit of irreverence, reversal, and *mésalliance* implicit in the historical dialectic, is expunged from history's last chapter, modernity.[9] Whereas in the earlier phases of the tableau, dialectical history is ordered by a chronicle of antagonism, the future period is calm, cool, and ordered. As noted above, this final, unified phase of history commences with the Renaissance, the one period existing outside of the historical sketch presented on the lower right-hand edge of Daly's representation. Moreover, this last phase is idealized.

In history's final period, the personifications have a dual reading. On the one hand, the tableau is read as an allegory of architecture. The major seated figure, the genius of architecture, has standing beside her the Three Graces, here symbolizing line, form and color. All are superimposed upon the engine of progress—an indication that art still dominates contingency. On the other hand, the same group functions as visualization of the modern system of knowledge. The giant seated figure can be read as Athena, the goddess of wisdom, allied with the personifications of man's intelligent faculties—history, science, and imagination. The faculties are reinvoked in the classification of human knowledge etched on the wheels of the train of progress—Beau, Vrai, Utile. This triad marks a continuity between modern and ancient epistemologies, divided among art *(Beau),* science *(Vrai),* and morality *(Bien),* implicitly linked to the godly.

Whereas the first part of the tableau allegorizes alienation, the second symbolizes harmony and unity of system. The Three Graces are a traditional image of harmony; the unified treatment of knowledge is symbolized by a mechanistic image, the train. Stemming from traditional scholastic and rational epistemologies which visualized the unity of knowledge in terms of a machine, this image is similarly instrumental, self-contained, and complete, a symbol of filiation and unity among all varieties of knowledge. By way of analogy, Daly moves from philosophy to social science. As man's intellectual order is unified, so is his social situation in this period of modernity. The Three Graces, apart from symbolizing knowledge, also represent society. In contrast to the warring personifications presented in the early part of the tableau, this triad offers a unified grouping. Alienation and conflict are deleted from Daly's vision of *La Vie Nouvelle.* No longer are men blindfolded, separated from nature and from each other. Rather, the Three Graces' vision is seemingly unimpeded and their eyes are open. The deep space of Nature engulfs them, and expands limitlessly. Their eyes absorb it. Man and nature become continuous via perception. The world no longer crushes man as in earlier ages, but rather man supersedes nature. Daly discards the separation of man and nature in favor of a unity focusing upon human consciousness and will. Man replaces decrepit institutions which violate natural law with the predictions of his own invention built in conformity to the dictates of natural law, scientifically symbolized by the steam engine.

Unlike traditional representations of the Three Graces, where unity is formalized by a circular organization symbolizing their oneness, this grouping looks outward, toward an element external to their forms (plate 3). The inference is that social and artistic composition and harmony can be ascribed to a force outside of their persons. This element is represented by the sun and articulated by the final part of the motto crowning the tableau, "Faith in the Future." In Platonic terms, the sun, the source of illumination and life or inspiration, is coequal with the good, or Godhead. Faith in God is the final force facing art and society.

Much as society is unified by faith, so is knowledge. The *devise* of Daly's artistic program, "Respect pour le Passé, Liberté dans le Present, Foi dans l'Avenir," again invokes man's three intelligent faculties. The past, or memory, is the physical material of thought, the subject of empirical investigation; faith is related to logic, speculation, and metaphysics; liberty focuses upon the inventive and imaginative faculty. The three faculties are intimately interrelated. For Daly, liberty is most important for artistic invention, but creation is shaped by certain metaphysical conditions. Hence, faith is related to reason, to the highest faculty of mind, the one which attains the truth. Faith thus provides those predispositions by which valid artistic creation may proceed. Moreover, faith, sanctioned by morality, informs man's activities, and establishes criteria for right and wrong.

Daly's system of knowledge is dualistic. On the one hand, he associates scientific inquiry with the demystification of scholastic epistemology, continuing a process begun in the Renaissance. However, in the optimism surrounding an *episteme* founded upon faith and belief (Athena and the Three Graces contemplating the sun), Daly remystifies philosophy. The search for a unified epistemology which parallels the unity of society is predicated only on the assumption of a divine Supreme Artificer or Prime Mover. The engine of steady, historical movement, emblazoned with the epithet of progress, carries society and philosophy, with their unified triad of consciousness. It moves them toward the divine dawn that governs and orchestrates all, and transcends dialectical historical development.

The issue of faith and morality which is the basis of Daly's architectural theory is elaborated in a second illustration, Daly's "Tableau de l'Evolution des Styles," prepared in October 1847 (plate 4). For my purposes here, I will only discuss certain general features of the sketch. As in the tableau "L'Architecture Contemporaine," Daly's progress of architectural history modulates between alternative periods. But unlike the tableau discussed earlier, with its antagonistic system, this one presents a stadial development comparable to organic analogies of gradual revelation or growth. This sketch is structured in evolutionary or transitional periods, presumably marked by harmony or lack of harmony between art and society. Artistic periods in the tableau are correlated with stages in social doctrines. Ostensibly, the various architectural styles can serve as social statement, or as commentary upon the spirit of the age. Moreover, it is apparent that for Daly, the converse is also the case, that the state of society can equally inform architecture. It is especially significant that within Daly's historical sketch, social ideology is treated, not from material or scientific bases, but from moral, and specifically religious, ones. Drawing upon historical schemes of humanity's moral development, and particularly the *Saint-Simonien* historical system, Daly notes moments of transition as those characterized by conflicting religious views. For example, Roman antiquity juxtaposed polytheism, symbolized by rectilinear aesthetic systems, with monotheism, characterized by the circle and the arch. The implicit contradiction was the cause of Rome's social instability and consequent fall, and accounted for its transitional character.

In "L'Architecture Contemporaine," Daly interprets the Renaissance as a spatio-temporal continuum uninterrupted until the present day. In the tableau, however, he treats the Renaissance as a chaotic, transitional phase rather than as a peaceful, organic one. The intervening Revolution of 1848 may account for this difference in perspective between the two interpretations of recent history. In 1837 Paris was the scene of political turmoil, workers' strikes, and social disorder. Paris in 1849 was an enthusiastic city, optimistically proclaiming the revolutionary slogan "Order and Liberty" as an incantation against the evils of the past, and as a salute to the new social unity. [10]

Hence, for Daly the issue underlying a homogeneous, evolutionary historical period was the absence or presence of a cohesive social doctrine. This unity was especially marked by a moral order, resting particularly upon religion. For Daly, significant social characteristics were to be found less in the material (property, politics), than in metaphysical features. His idea of progress was involved less with personal wealth, production, or physical gratification in a utilitarian sense, than with the spiritual factors forming the basis of unity, particularly common belief and cohesive family structure. Both monotheism and monogamy led away from dissension and toward social harmony and organic unity.

Daly's personal valuation of the spiritual over the material components was paralleled by a comparable move in France's social life illustrated by a newspaper woodcut of 1849. This print, depicting the inauguration of a new train line between the Department of the Seine (Paris) and l'Aube, begs comparison with the engraving "L'Architecture Contemporaine" in which a machine likewise presents a visualization of human knowledge (plate 5). For the July Monarchy the steam engine was the consummate achievement of human intelligence, the proof of the interaction of science, reason, and imagination in man's daily life. The newspaper's steam engine partakes in the fetishization of engineering, while simultaneously presenting a critique of the cult of science, so fundamental to Louis-Philippe's positivism, like Daly's prints, this final illustration of human progress emphasizes that science must defer to religion, and not vice versa.

Garnier-Pages, in his *Histoire de la Révolution de 1848,* characterized this shift in attitude. He noted that it was the Bishop of Paris who set into motion the steam engine on the joyful day of inauguration, implying the preeminent position of religion in directing both science and society:

> L'évêque accompangné du clergé vînt bénir l'oeuvre des hommes. Il addressa à la foule, une allocution touchante, dans laquelle, rappelant que "toute idée vient de Dieu, les progrès industriels aussi bien que les progrès politiques," il signala son intervention toute-puissante dans ces grands évènements qui agitent aujourd'hui l'Europe et font disparaître les obstacles à la réalisation des promesses divines de bonheur, faites par le Christ il y a dix-huit siècles.[11]

> The bishop accompanied by his clergy came to bless the work of man. He addressed the crowd with a touching sermon in which, recalling that "every idea comes from God, industrial as well as political progress." He signalled the almighty's omnipotent intervention in the great events which energize all Europe and eliminate any obstacle to the realization of those divine promises of happiness which Christ made some eighteen hundred years ago.

Hence, the earth-bound poetics of the machine are supplanted by belief in a more abstract and less palpable *deus ex machina.*

The three plates constitute a series of intellectual oppositions. On the one hand, we acknowledge a stadial interpretation of history and knowledge which is implicitly open-ended and incomplete. On the other hand, we observe a vision of progress as a metaphor for the unity and stability of knowledge— philosophy as an ordered and self-complete entity. Progress as an idea is opposed to notions of stadial historical development rather than complementary. Furthermore, progress takes on an extra-historical dimension, relating more to utopian dreams of a golden age rather than gradual real-life physical and social improvement. Modernity, dominated by the attributes of progress, tends to be a culmination and end of history rather than a mere party to underlying motive force. Hence, progress is linked to a transcendent state of social unity and integration in opposition to the social factionalism and alienation of the past. The present is idealized by treating modernity as the end of a historical chain of being.

The apotheosis of the present is marked by characteristics of social unity and identity. No longer subject to the fragmentations that plagued past epochs, *l'art nouveau* and *la vie nouvelle* are based upon a set of idealistic assumptions. Life is to be structured and ordered in accordance with the precepts of a harmonious existence which has actually very little to do with the contingencies and material factors traditionally addressed by liberal proponents of progress. This vision of social integration and harmony supplants that of need for satisfaction and gratification. A new paradigm of modern life is revealed only via faith. Ultimately, the fundamental religiosity of the new age serves to shape and instruct man's physical control of nature and himself. Morality, revealed via the inspiration accompanying religious faith, must direct man's progressive efforts.

At this point, a momentary retreat would be in order to contemplate our present position. Our discussion thus far has raised the following issues concerning César Daly and his intellectual posture. First, we have observed a continuity between his view and the enlightenment tradition whereby human understanding *(Entendement)* comprises a union of the three faculties of knowledge. Like the *philosophes* of the eighteenth century, Daly speaks of their interrelationship in terms of a mechanical analogy—a train. For Daly, however, the source of this unity is due not so much to an internal condition, but to an unexplained external factor, a kind of *deus ex machina*. This posture places Daly more within the tradition of Cartesian rationalism, and concomitant idealism implicit within the theory of knowledge, than within that of empiricism. Second, Daly deals with the issue of history, particularly social history in terms of both physical progress and organic growth and development. Initially, his interpretation of social change is considered in light of material improvements, advances sponsored fundamentally by the growth of science and technology. Subsequently, however, he interprets the forces of history in terms of social order, marked by characteristics of cohesion, peace, and morality. Thus, Daly's view of history assumes not a materialistic but an idealistic basis. Third, it is in this idealism that we may gain an understanding of the nature of art and the role of the artist. No longer is it the artist who recommends or vindicates himself by the utility of his creations. Rather, his art is judged by its correspondence with those laws by which society is implicitly ordered, material or otherwise. It is an appreciation of artistic consciousness and personal genius which takes Daly to a realm beyond that of mere eighteenth-century sensationalism. Rather than in mere production, it is in the instinctive and spontaneous outburst of creative energies, which may be artistic, that the spirit of the age is grasped and formalized.

From Map to Tree of Knowledge

At this point it is useful to trace certain significant philosophical developments from which César Daly's own intellectual posture draws its provenance. As noted above, Daly maintained a systematized theory of knowledge, in which the different realms of intellectual inquiry were unified into a comprehensive epistemology. This epistemology partook in a tradition spanning the Classical and Modern eras, from Plato and Aristotle to Bacon and the Encyclopedists. It found its most articulate manifestation in the writings of Jean le Rond d'Alembert. His "Discours Préliminaire" of the *Encyclopédie* (1754) provided the best argued discussion of the division and systemization of the sciences. D'Alembert formalized his method of classification, by providing a "systematic chart" or "world map" of science, stating that such ordering rests not only in ascription of differences to the range of intellectual disciplines, but in filiations among them as well. D'Alembert claimed that he constructed his scheme by dividing all knowledge

> into natural and revealed knowledge, or useful and pleasing knowledge, or speculative and practical knowledge, or evident, certain, probable, and sensitive knowledge, or knowledge of things and knowledge of signs and so on into infinity.[12]

D'Alembert likened the surface of his system to a mapping, which, while pointing out visible natural features, more significantly sought the invisible, subterranean structure by which things are linked. Knowledge was like "a vast ocean, on the surface of which we perceive a few islands of various sizes, whose connections with the continent are hidden to us."[13] For d'Alembert the importance of his visualization lay in the connections of parts, and subsequent recognition of the shape of the whole.

The systematic chart, "Le Système Figuré des Connaissances Humaines," which d'Alembert provided for the edification of the *Encyclopédie's* subscribers, formalized this point of view (plate 6). He listed the faculties of knowledge in tabular form, grouping disciplines under the mental capacities of memory, reason, and imagination. These were filed in three separate columns. D'Alembert surely drew his sketch from similar tabulations used in both the natural sciences and economics. Among these were the contemporary synoptic tables of Carolus Linnaeus, and of successor Georges Cuvier, in the *Encyclopédie Methodique,* where various kingdoms, orders, classes, and families of plants and animals were distinguished (plate 7). The Abbé Turgot's comparative analysis of commodity values was also useful. Like these, d'Alembert's chart broke general fields of inquiry into disciplines and subdisciplines, noting external differences, gradations and shadings distinguished by a variety of empirical techniques. D'Alembert wrote,

> The most natural arrangement of my system would be the one in which the objects followed one another by imperceptible shadings which serve simultaneously to separate and to unite them.[14]

This statement indicates that d'Alembert's initial interest was in classification. Yet it might be said that his ultimate objective lay not so much in epistemological differentiation, as in detecting identity in and ascribing ontological unity to all areas of human inquiry. An analogy could again be made with the economics and natural sciences, for Turgot and Cuvier initially dealt with distinctions, and they too ultimately sought identities and ontology. Turgot's interest in comparative pricing sought a "real value" of commodities. Cuvier, in his researches into comparative anatomy, sought subsurface continuities between species, and in his analysis of functional physical systems (skeletal, muscular, digestive, nervous, respiratory and the like), sought unity between structures and organs.[15] Although d'Alembert derived critical perspective from parallel researches in both scientific and economic realms, he nonetheless fell short of his much sought-after objective. Despite its interest in disciplinary distinctions, d'Alembert's *Système Figuré* failed to portray the internal logic and unity accounting for and govering all categories of knowledge.

Methodologically, d'Alembert's system sought a static delineation and systematization which was self-contained and unconcerned with new discovery or innovation. This deficiency probably stemmed from the fact that d'Alembert described his system much as a blueprint might describe the construction of a building or machine.[16] Such a mechanistic system stressed completeness, efficiency, economy. Moreover, it assumed man's ability to understand fully the workings of the system. Like the parts of a machine, each discipline was individualized, serving a particular function within the workings of the mechanism, where it was carefully positioned to guarantee smooth operation. With the exception of architecture, each discipline was aligned with only one faculty. This arrangement suggested that the sciences derived no inspiration from the realm of imagination, and that therefore, the arts of memory and those of imagination had to remain forever separate. A machine was constructed; it worked only in accordance with a preconceived and prearranged scheme designed to produce a desired result. The parts of the system, like the system itself, were important not so much for what they were, as for what they did. By separating the faculties and their allied intellectual disciplines the machine analogy obviated the problem of ontology. D'Alembert's chart did little to create an ontological unity: it served more to designate and isolate the individual sciences than to link them. His scheme failed to deal effectively with an epistemological system unified in its search for truth. This was the inevitable difficulty inhering in an expressly materialistic methodology which expressed hostility to any metaphysic.

It seems, however, that d'Alembert foresaw and attempted to confront this difficulty. More than once in the "Discours Préliminaire", he termed his system an "encyclopedic tree" rather than a chart or map.[17] He also recognized the possibility of an organic analogy which might have served better than the mechanical one to portray the nature of his system's unity.

The frontispiece of a German edition of the *Encyclopédie* (1780) provided a new visualization of d'Alembert's theory of knowledge (plate 8). It replaced d'Alembert's earlier chartlike image with that of a tree.[18] The trunk of the tree was the seat of understanding *(Entendement)*. It quickly divided into three principal limbs, comprising memory, reason, and imagination. From these points, the range of disciplines proliferated while assuming the form of fruit upon this tree of knowledge. The bounty of this epistemological tree was presented as foliage, or leaves of paper, moving, folding, shimmering across its surface. These pages were partially overlapped and there was consequently an ambivalence in the readings. Although each discipline was fully described by a completed caption, the fragmentary readings of the leaflike visual portrayals— shaded, superimposed, partial—implied an understanding that was inherently open-ended or incomplete. Such incompleteness of form, *viz.* the relationship of sciences to plant life, made way for an interpretation of knowledge that sponsored rather than suppressed revelation and discovery. Furthermore, instead of describing epistemology in terms of a functional structure, the organic analogy treated knowledge in terms of a vital coefficient, growth.

Understanding was treated, not as source, but as an intermediate point in a continuum that moved from an invisible subterranean structure to a visible, external physical entity. It is from the earth via this substructure that the system above ground ultimately received its life. Moreover, in its shadowy, subsurface existence the source of epistemological life and unity evaded—or transcended—the rational inquiry generally considered to be the basis of d'Alembert's epistemology. Whereas d'Alembert's 1751 French system existed on a wholly analytical basis, and was ensured by empirical scientific method, the German treatment of the tree of knowledge involved an elusive substructure which unified the system and escaped logical inquiry. Hence, d'Alembert's metaphysical purge was countered in the German structure by the vital urge central to notions of organic idealism and vegetable genius.[19] Ontology was restored to epistemology, and a scientific position was established to account for new discovery, innovation, and invention.

Vitalism and Consciousness

D'Alembert's empirical stand explicitly opposed the presence of innate ideas in any phenomenon, man included. This opposition was directed against the conception of the soul in man, a belief central to religious and moral considerations. The empirical stand criticized the fundamentals of Descartes' rationalism (the mind-body dualism) and Leibniz' monadism, two philosophies involving the idea that a metaphysic operated in the world surrounding man. As a machine, man merely functioned; sensations were explained by actions and reactions within man's physiology.[20]

A particularly forceful exponent of the sensational point of view was Julien Offray de la Mettrie, who, in his *L'Homme Machine* (1748) maintained an essentially Baconian analysis of man and knowledge in terms of a mechanical analogy. In contradistinction to Descartes' rationalism, which stressed a dualism of mind and body, interior and exterior, spiritual and physical, de la Mettrie designated scientific inquiry as mechanical responses to sensory stimuli in the manner of Thomas Hobbes and John Locke. By the mid-eighteenth century, the limitations of the method were already recognized, e.g., Elie Luzac's attack on sensationalism and the mechanical analogy *L'Homme Plus Que Machine* of late 1748, and subsequently de la Mettrie's work entitled *L'Homme Plante,* first published in 1764. These contradictory interpretations of man paralleled interpretations of knowledge in terms of chart and tree. As noted above, d'Alembert's own philosophical system oscillated between empiricism and idealism.

It was d'Alembert's collaborator, Denis Diderot, who motivated the subtle shift from physic to metaphysic. Diderot, while officially maintaining the *Encyclopédie's* empirical stand, managed to communicate something quite different in his personal prose. The dichotomy inhering in his approach was best illustrated by Diderot's philosophical dialogues. By using the literary form of the dialogue, he effected a critique of both natural and conventional language. This was achieved by superposing critical faculty in the guise of personal consciousness, which acquired a quasi-corporeal identity under the designation *Le Moi.* In addition to the dialogue, such works as "Le Rêve d'Alembert" mystified self. According to Diderot, d'Alembert's dream was the flowering of inspired consciousness, itself interpreted in terms of an organic allusion and vitalism. Jean Varloot argues that Diderot saw d'Alembert's dream as "l'efflorescence d'une plante longtemps végétante."[21] It could be said that this vital principle was elevated to an idea in "La Mystification."

Diderot's appreciation of personal and artistic consciousness directly opposed generally accepted scientific method, especially as he stressed personal judgment in scientific inquiry, giving primacy to self. Previous philosophical systems failed to address this problem. Lockean sensationalism dealt fundamentally with empirical verification, reducing consciousness to the purely mechanical motions of the mind. Cartesianism, though recognizing the mind/body distinction, diffused the conception of individual mind, by allying mind's processes with logic, the intersubjective faculty. Differing from both scientific methods, Diderot viewed personal consciousness as a force to be reckoned with, as a mode of judgment and evaluation, as a human interpretive factor not necessarily congruent with logic.

Diderot's counterattack of consciousness upon both rational and empirical systems was elaborated by Jean-Jacques Rousseau. Rousseau attacked the empirical problem of classification and differentiation from the point of view of social organization. Rousseau's *Essay on the Origins of Inequality,* instigated by d'Alembert, stressed the implicit distinctions and differences existing within both nature and society. Yet, in *Du Contrat Social,* he focused more on philosophical and social unity than on differentiation. Rousseau engaged the factor of consciousness *(conscience)* to make his point.

Via consciousness, he addressed the problem of personal identity, and then generalized the idea in order to approach the problem of national or social identity and unity. Rousseau evoked Diderot's notion of *Le Moi,* or Self, associated with the idea of personal consciousness, and then attached it to its externalization, which he saw as volition *(volonté).* Subsequently, he moved from the idea of personal to group consciousness, *conscience* or *volonte collective,* which underlies the commonly held body of doctrine by which the social and moral order was to be assured. Moreover, Rousseau claimed that collective consciousness was to be finally formalized by society's institutions, thus physically marking precepts of common belief. He stated,

> Cependant pour que le corps du gouvernement ait une existence, une vie réele qui le distingue du corps de l'Etat, pour que tous ses membres puissent agir de concert et répandre à la fin pour laquelle il est institué, il lui faut un moi particulier, une sensibilité commune à ses membres, une forme, une volonté propre qui tende à sa conservation. Cette existence particulière suppose des assemblées, des conseils, un pouvoir de délibérer, de résoudre des droits, des titres, des privileges...[22]

> Yet in order that the governing body may have an existence, a real life that distinguishes it from the State, in order that all members may be able to act together and expand to the ends for which it has been instituted, it is necessary to have a particular identity [une moi particulier], a sensibility common to its members, a form, a will of its own that tends to the body's own preservation. This particular spirit presupposes in assemblies and councils, a power to deliberate, to decide upon rights, titles, and privileges.

For the *philosophes,* the independence of the scientific disciplines paralleled the freedom of man in nature. Yet society, like knowledge, comprised an order either below or above the level of the factual or the human singularity. For d'Alembert's and Diderot's epistemology, the sciences were finally unified in truth. In Rousseau's sociology, men were united by collective consciousness and sympathies, more easily described as a moral order.

Consciousness placed rationalism on the defensive. To be sure, the Rousellian identification of consciousness was central to the late eighteenth century's critique of ego-displacing scientific method. Its effects were most apparent in Kant's *Critique of Pure Reason.* Kant tied judgment to personal consciousness, and in so doing, questioned the existence of ontology, the final objective or rational scientific method, wherein personal consciousness was implicitly tied to reason. Diderot and Rousseau both questioned the existence of innate ideas, and the possibility of ontology, on the basis of personal subjectivity.

Yet, the goal of philosophy remained the ascription of ontology. This goal, however, was placed into question by consciousness. Response to this dilemma resulted in the notion of intersubjectivity, which allowed for the possibility of depersonalized or objective scientific evaluation, using such concepts as the group consciousness and the collective will. The Cartesian method, though initially criticized by psychology and sensationalism, was ironically reinvoked by the Rousellian notion of the supra-individual consciousness, although Rousseau replaced rational with moral order. For Diderot, this intersubjectivity was based in personal genius and inspiration uneasily tied to a divine unity underlying both his and d'Alembert's epistemology. For Rousseau, consciousness entailed a means to social unity, superseding or transcending the realm of individualized observation, or ego-motivated action. Rousseau's group spirit comprised a moral order, or secular religion, which recognized and sanctified the unifying social contact. Pierre Buguelin, one of Rousseau's commentators, notes the unity provided by the contract:

> La religion civile unifie les coeurs sans forcer les consciences, car elle n'impose rien qui ne soit raisonnable, y compris reconnaissance du caractère sacre du contrat.[23]

> Civil religion unifies hearts without coercing consciences, because it sponsors no unreasonable notions and recognizes the sacred character of the contract.

Philosophical and social systems stressing description, classification, differentiation, and individuality were hence replaced by systems fostering a new unity. With regard to philosophy, the empirical/sensationalist *détente,* focusing upon personal observation and emphasis upon external characteristics, gave way to an interest in internals. This moved scientific inquiry to a position again closer to that of innate ideas. Where man was the object of investigation, attention was now focused upon personal consciousness as the possible source of his essence. The relativistic scientific posture of Locke and d'Alembert, founded in sensationalism was replaced by an invariable idealization of personal consciousness, as introduced by Diderot and Rousseau. Thus, through the idealization of consciousness, analysis was moved out of the realm of personal to interpersonal judgment. It was generalized as *conscience collective,* the body of presuppositions or beliefs which linked man's minds and fused them into a single entity, a society, and encouraged social cooperation which was moral. The rehabilitation of metaphysics resulted in an emphasis upon systems of belief rather than of knowledge, supporting a moral rather than a merely scientific order.[24]

History, Consciousness, Genius

There was an implicit antagonism within the epistemology of the late eighteenth century between systematic history's domination of human affairs, and the free play of the man of genius. I see two possible explanations for this. First, there was a lingering rational bias stemming from Cartesianism by which personal consciousness was automatically equated with the intersubjectivity of reason. Hence, individuality of evaluation caused by subjectivity was diffused.

Second, a Christian prejudice asserted the implicit evil of the flesh, as well as those creative acts seeking to express the action of merely human will. Rousseau attacked this campaign of self-abnegation by his exaltation of the person and action of the noble savage, arguing that it was only through the institutions of man, the Church included, that man's basic morality was lost.

Be that as it may, the early schematization of knowledge and history was inhospitable to the notion of personal genius. This scheme, conceived in terms of a stadial development, was introduced to modern philosophical circles in the Abbé Turgot's Sorbonne lectures comprising *Le Tableau Philosophique des Progrès Successifs de l'Esprit Humain,* which were devoted to the progress of knowledge. As in other enlightenment *épistèmes*, knowledge was treated as an interaction of faculties and disciplines. Turgot, however, interpreted his tree of knowledge in terms of "four progressions," including science, industry, moral behavior, and art. Art was now conceived in a realm separate from either reason or morality.

His epistemology was synchronic. Like d'Alembert, Turgot initially spoke of knowledge from a single temporal vantage, seeking filiations which existed at one particular moment of inquiry. Yet Turgot desired to move beyond a scheme having relevance only to his own temporal situation. Hence, he introduced the idea of progress. Turgot approached the problem of progressive change from the realm of ethnography, and particularly the history of language. This research, best articulated in his *Reflexions sur les Langues* of 1751, presaged similar linguistic studies of a century later, most notably Saussure's. The outcomes of Turgot's researches have methodological traits in common with the work of his illustrious nineteenth-century inheritor as well.

As a historian of language, Turgot became interested in the transformations in language over time. He considered to be especially significant the rise of new morphemes, or neologisms, which he saw as linguistic forms accompanying a change of mental attitude or philosophical posture. As with Saussure, Turgot's interest in changes of linguistic forms moved analysis from a synchronic to a diachronic methodology. This program of morphological differentiation over time sought causal explanations. Turgot explained the causes of these differentiations in what became his law of progress. He emphasized that language was dominated by a move from metaphorical to philosophical or speculative form. He stated,

The study of language, if well done, would perhaps be the best of logics. In analyzing, in comparing the words of which they are fashioned, in tracing from the beginning the different meanings which they acquired, in following the thread of ideas, we will see through which stages, through which metamorphoses men passed...This kind of experimental metaphysics would be at one and the same time the history of the human mind and the history of the progress of its thoughts, always fitted to the needs which gave birth to them. Languages are once their expression and their measure.[25]

This formalization accompanied the progressive development of man's faculties from naturalism to abstraction.

To be sure, such a program of causal philosophical explanation was far removed from Saussure's position on synchronic and diachronic analyses. For Saussure, linguistic structures could only be ascertained within a controlled situation, i.e., the synchronic realm. Moreover, diachronically, particular parts of speech might be examined over time in order to evaluate and identify their transformations. Changes in usage of the morpheme might also be perceived, and a pattern of differentiation from moment to moment ascertained. As Jonathan Culler points out, a structure of transformation over time for all language is an impossibility, for differentiations do not lead to filiations.[26]

This was a difficulty which Turgot did not recognize. Turgot crossed the synchronic filiatory structure of his epistemology with the diachronic differentiations which he used in his linguistic researches. Rather than seeing the entire system as relative, Turgot made his linguistic method absolute. Moreover, he used analogies to link the progress of one discipline with another. By crossing the two-dimensional tree of knowledge with the time line by which morphological change could be described, Turgot created a three-dimensional matrix of mind, wherein all sciences were described and interrelated in all ages. Turgot assumed an inherent reciprocity between disciplines, through which the changes in one field might be used to inform or explain those of another. Like language, all arts and sciences were to be described in terms of a process of development away from the natural realm, and towards that of dematerialized speculation and pure reason.

Turgot analyzed historical languages and perceived in linguistics a path for the future. Although language began in a poetic/metaphoric realm wherein all nature was animated, language later moved to a realm of pure speculation, wherein the highest faculties of mind were represented. This notion was a natural extension of both Aristotelian and Cartesian linguistic systems which stressed the importance of a logical, philosohical language, subsequently reinvoked in Condillac's *Essai sur l'Origine des Connaissances Humaines* and *De la Grammaire*.[27] Thanks to Turgot's time-inclusive spatialization of knowledge, the move to reason and instrumentality was paralleled in all philosophical realms.

Turgot's progressive chord in the sciences reverberated throughout the following century. His student, the Marquis de Condorcet, wrote his *Esquisse* similarly mapping human history stadially, replacing the *Tableau's* three periods with ten.[28] Following both Turgot and Condorcet, Henri de Saint-Simon returned to a triadic view of progress, moving from polytheism to deism to physicism in his early writings, from polytheism, to monotheism, to positivism in subsequent writings, and finally from fetishism, to polytheism, to monotheism at the end of his career.[29] Especially in the later phases of his career, Saint-Simon used the history of religion as a schematic matrix suitable for generalization in much the same way as Turgot or Condillac had used language and ethnography, describing a progress from naturalism to abstraction. Appreciation of religion as a significant factor in man's mental life was an important deviation from the Voltairian philosophical disdain of clergy and organized religious life.

How did the progressive system move? Did it move of its own momentum, or, did it, as in both Cartesian and Newtonian scientific structures, act in accordance with the propulsion of the Prime Mover? On numerous occasions, Turgot's system was criticized as a theodicy. Surely the Abbé's fundamentally religious posture regarding human perfectibility was inspired by an apocalyptic vision. A moral order, speaking to man's continuing elevation from primitive depravity, surely underlay the progress of the material order. Nowhere, however, did Turgot specifically invoke the theological source of progress. Instead, he drew upon the man of genius as history's motive force.[30]

Turgot's appreciation of genius paralleled those treatments of fellow philosophers, particularly Diderot's. Of particular importance in this regard were the latter's philosophical dialogues, especially *Le Neveu de Rameau*. Particularly noteworthy was Diderot's appreciation of his hero's personal consciousness in creating new artistic paradigms, and in so doing, shaping the path of the future. For Turgot, the genius had the gift of prevision: "to know the truth in order to make the social order to conform to it, that is the source of public happiness . . ."[2] Furthermore, the special importance of the genius was of a moral order.

Turgot's posture regarding genius was, however, dualistic. Intellectually molded within a system of royal patronage, he was forced to ask if the man of genius was a true social singularity, or a person of talent allowed the complete development and expression of his faculties. A public functionary, Turgot avoided the revolutionary implications of the latter interpretation in favor of the former, which implicitly related genius to natalities. The proportion was constant. An increase of the number of geniuses must be related to an increase in population. Condorcet was of a different mind. A strict libertarian, he felt that all men were able, and should be allowed to rise to the level of genius, and that the antiquated, privilege-related social and educational system must be obliterated in order to allow man to develop to his fullest potential. Universal education was a natural outcome of this posture. For Condorcet's system, like Turgot's, rested on the hypothesis that the greater the frequency of geniuses in action within the human sphere of activities, the quicker would be the progress.

Although Turgot and Condorcet recognized in genius the ability to see the future, both missed one fundamental physical component necessary to the shaping of the future—the critical faculty. Both sought a proliferation of genius based in the unencumbered development of human abilities by way of education. Yet universal education would in itself establish an intellectual norm no less pervasive than the feudal or scholastic world-view that preceded the enlightenment. Genius, a faculty initially transcending social and intellectual norms, grew to be equated with talent, or with the ritual or cliché reiteration of social or intellectual conventions. This phenomenon has been discussed by F.R. Leavis. He notes the roots of the disdain felt by supporters of liberal education for the man of true ability:

> The academic authorities believing in such a system will tend to take as their first class man a type that may be described as the complete walking cliché - the man (it's often a woman) who unloads with such confident and accomplished ease in the examination-room because he has never really grappled with anything, and is uninhibited by any inkling of the difference between the retailing of his amassed externalities and the effort to think something out into a grasped and unified order that he has made his own. Those who like this type... will inevitably tend to dislike, and to undervalue as a student, the man who makes them uncomfortable by implicitly challenging their standards, their competence, or their self-esteem[32]

Leavis spotlighted an important opposition. To men of talent, dextrous manipulators of the widely accepted opinions, he opposed those who challenge academic conventions or norms. This is an opposition that Kurt Eissler has also used in contrasting talent with genius, defined as the ability to formulate new "paradigms," whereby old scientific systems are overturned to reveal a new epistemological norm.[33] Genius, unlike talent, ruptures with the status quo. By virtue of this resonant singularity, he comes to shape a new popular point of view.

For Turgot, singularity of this nature was not undesirable, at least initially, for as we have noted earlier, enlightenment epistemology revelled in distinctions—disciplinary or social. Yet as the implications of systemization and unity became more pervasive, genius became increasingly suspect. The critical faculty of genius was attacked as egoistic and self-serving in the face of social harmonies. In Saint-Simon's progressive system, there was an oscillation between critical and organic periods. Although in his dialectical history Saint-Simon viewed the critical phase as generating the organic, he subsequently rendered criticism obsolete by noting that his own moment marked the inauguration of the final organic phase of history.[34] In Saint-Simon's as in other positivist social systems, the outcome was the replacement of genius by talent, accessible to all via education. As genius was vulgarized by becoming universal, its function became lost. The gifted were immediately tied into the social structure, serving only to expand and strengthen it and the assumptions by which it functioned. The ideological norms by which the system was formalized were no longer to be questioned. Men of talent, men of facility, men of production, men of order replaced men of genius. The critical function of genius was now a thing of the past.

Fourier and Ironic History

An ambivalent attitude toward genius was apparent in the writings of Henri de Saint-Simon and Charles Fourier. Saint-Simon literally attacked the problem of genius in his early writings, replacing criticism with an emphasis on utility, in the interest of social unity. This posture was reinforced by his conception of meritocracy, which was central to his social program and which equated human potential with human production. At least in the early writings, vision was omitted from his world.

Charles Fourier proclaimed the advent of a harmonious society, and structured the economy of his social order on the bases of individual talent, labor and wealth. These faculties were to determine a person's share of the profits produced by Fourier's ideal commune, the *phalanstère*. In Fourier's view, personal value was equivalent to the physical results of a person's labor. This was made especially apparent by Fourier's retention of private property whereby class structure was tied to the material effects of life. Fourier thereby associated human value to what one did, made, and earned.

Curiously enough, however, whereas Turgot's, Condorcet's, or Saint-Simon's epistemological or social structures were designed in conformity with purportedly rational scientific method, it was Fourier who approached the problem from a different tack. Fourier began his construction, not by using instrumental discourse, but by a dialectical, critical attack upon the present-day social situation. Consequently, by a leap of faith, based in personal consciousness, Fourier devised a social science more psychologically personal than rationally interpersonal.

First, Fourier's approach originated from hostility to the existing social order. He hated modern civilization. Like other enlightenment figures, he conceived of history stadially. But, whereas the others viewed history as a continuing rise, Fourier saw it as a decline from an Edenic first phase to the depravity of the modern day. The periods of history culminating with the present-day were seen as a critique of the old order.

Second, Fourier's method was extremely suspect from the point of view of the pure rationalist. Although he cited Newton as the intellectual model by which his own social researches were undertaken, he invoked inspiration, and mathematics, as the germ of his idea. His initial social formulations began with a dream. Fourier recounted how Newton was awakened from his reverie by an apple dropping on his head. Reflections upon the incident resulted in the theory of universal gravitation. Like Newton, Fourier was inspired by an apple, serving as an example of commodity pricing. Whereas for Newton, the ruminations led to a theory of planetary mechanics, for Fourier, the episode resulted in a call for disposing modern finance and the searching for real values to underpin a modern economic order.

Fourier's historical scheme, begun within the Enlightenment's progressive sphere of influence, did not directly parallel it. He elaborated his system by references to both natural and biblical history. His historical scheme comprised four great phases of eight segments each, amounting to thirty-two distinct periods. The first phase began with the age of savagery, and was to end with a future age of harmonism, when Fourier's precepts became generally practiced. The midpoint of this phase, civilization, marked the nadir of the human condition. Although the *philosophes* celebrated civilization as bestowing a continual increase in the material lot of man, Fourier believed that the scientific process amounted to a continual dissolution of social structure and psychic well-being. With the sixth period, and world's first experiments with the *phalanstère* were to be attempted and with the eighth period, the reign of harmony would begin. The historical stages were to peak with the sixteenth period, and then society would again begin its gradual decline to savagery, the final of the thirty-two periods. It is noteworthy that Fourier likened his scheme to a growth cycle—infancy, adolescence, maturity, decrepitude. Yet there was a strong apocalyptic allusion, for, in Fourier's scheme, death introduced a regeneration and repetition of the process. The growth cycle began anew and harmonious society resurrected itself, phoenix-like from its own ashes.

It has already become apparent that Fourier fused mechanical with organic views of history. Moreover, Fourier juxtaposed methods from different scientific realms. The intermezzo between eighth and ninth periods, the "Birth of the Boreal Crown," Fourier likened to the anguish of birth, the coming of the new age. At this point, the earth would turn on its axis, the poles would be warmed, wild animals would be domesticated and new species would emerge, the souls of the dead would return, the universe would recenter itself upon the earth, and around it, the planets would copulate. Thematically, this second creation had a quasi-rational provenance. Fourier's planetary movements owed something to Newton's universal dynamics. The cataclysm accompanying the birth of the new age was related to dialectical historical schemes. In addition, Fourier invoked Cuvier's view of geological and natural history wherein some species disappear and others are introduced by global catastrophe. Furthermore, he used the emergence of new animal varieties to imply Lamarckian notions of genetic transformism. His recentering of the universe was a reversal of the Copernican universal view. Lastly, he exploited metempsychosis as an invocation of the Second Coming, a reference to the Apocalyptic narrative.[35]

Despite the patina of reason seeking to legitimize this scheme, it is, however, very difficult to take the great historical moment very seriously, at least from a rational point of view. By the juxtaposition and inversion of various scientific systems, Fourier's Harmonian birth distanced itself from any single rational, natural, scientific, moral, or religious system. It should be recognized that Fourier as critic of civilization separated himself as much from current intellectual as from current social systems. Surely, his critique of the sixth period was equally an attack upon philosophy as the mental norm of the age.[36] Nothing escaped his critical awareness or sense of irony. An ideological and social synthesis leading to a state of association was his own contribution to human progress. Fourier alone stood at the crucial juncture, bridging past and future, separating despair and happiness. As a prophet, he alone could fuse the intellectual oppositions of yesterday and sponsor the birth of tomorrow's unity.

Perhaps Fourier best embodied what a critical consciousness might achieve. Beginning with the rationalism of the cult of Newton, Fourier immediately went beyond reason by depicting the scientist as visionary or mystic. Likewise, he drew inspiration from the late eighteenth-century image of Newton as a seer. Critical of civilization, a period already associated with Enlightenment philosophy, Fourier proposed the rectification of history by a series of parodic reversals or ironic twists.[37] It was exactly this part of Fourier's character which appealed to nineteenth-century symbolists and twentieth-century surrealists, who valued above all else the personal expression of self.[38] For in that most fundamental of psychological realms, rational order was supplanted by the order of a pre-rational variety. Fourier drew upon alogical aspects of mind—the mythic, the millenial—in imagining a personal cosmos. Hence, the prophet of harmony left far behind the methods of the *philosophe,* and focused upon a world of his own making, legitimized only by ritual incantations to the god of Reason.

The uniqueness of Fourier's epistemology has often been tied to the singularity of his personality. Institutionalized at Charenton at the same time as the Marquis de Sade, the prophet of harmonism has been described as a case book of psychosis. His life was a model of social and psychological alienation and sexual frustration. Ultimately, his hostility to civilization was not merely outwardly but also inwardly directed, himself a most tragic proof of the failure of modern life. Sexuality was a *leitmotif* in all of Fourier's writings, and it was passional attraction which fueled his universal movement. Whereas d'Alembert, Condorcet, and Saint-Simon likened social organization to a machine or cooperative atelier, Fourier modelled a society on a cosmology based in passional attraction, in short, a kind of planetary copulation. This passional universal process generalized the idea of a psychological rather than a logical ordering system. As he described the universe, so did Fourier approach society and man himself.

For Fourier, society should be structured on the basis of the passions. The phalanstery, the germ of Fourier's harmonious social order, was to be populated by couples of 810 personality types, involving different passional permutations. Fourier described these personalities in terms of the interaction of twelve fundamental passions which were divided into three groups: sensual, affective, and distributive. The sensory faculties are self-explanatory; the affective passions were concerned with sexual liaison and social affinities. Distributive passions were directed toward superindividual social groupings, dealing with man's need for association, competition, and diversity. Ultimately, social structure and class distinctions were established on the basis of those personalities which combined larger passional groupings in the personality. The implicit superiority of those personalities which combined larger numbers of passions led to a psychological pyramid surmounted, of course, by Fourier himself.

The nature of Fourier's process of philosophical reversal presented an intellectual anomaly, particularly within the context of the lingering rationalism of the period. Whereas the *philosophes* and early positivists began their social experiments out of a generalized analogy with the logical mechanism of cosmology and epistemology, Fourier began on a different tack. He started not only with universal logic, but with illogic. Whereas the rationalists succeeded in mythologizing their *épistème* through a series of epistemological generalizations interrelating all areas of human inquiry, Fourier began with myth, with fantasy, with dream, and then rationalized them. Whereas the *philosophes* drew their scientific vantage into an inductive spiral taking their method far beyond the limits of speculation or empirical investigation, Fourier began with a flight of fancy and then brought it to earth, encasing it in logical structure, exploiting classification, taxonomy, historical stages, neologisms, and so forth, as vindication. Ultimately, Fourier, through his passional taxonomy of personality, moved self from the realm of mere subjectivity to a level of abstraction and absolute. Moreover, through his critical stand founded upon psychology and formalized by the creative act of his personal rhetoric, Fourier succeeded where the *philosophes* and early positivists failed, in an understanding of the value of self. Curiously enough, whereas Fourier's own cosmology focused upon a period of association which he introduced as the future's social prophet, his subsequent campaign of improvement would run the same risk as other programs. For in his campaign of universal education, in his world of total gratification, in his total psychological support structure, he sought a system where hereditary social distinctions disappeared and no want was left unsatisfied. In short, his was a world from which physical or psychological alienation, as cause of social discontent, was to be banished. However, once alienation ceased, so would criticism. The modus which had sponsored progress up to that point, especially in his own situation and construction, critical consciousness, would now become an outdated social characteristic. Like the *Saint-Simoniens,* Fourier also came to view a critical period as subversive once the organic period of harmony had been introduced. Ironically, Fourier's formulations envisioned a world in which such men as himself would cease to exist. Perhaps in the final regard, Fourier saw in himself a last vestige of civilization, a relic of a degraded moment in man's history, which must also, inevitably, be discarded.

Victor Cousin and Eclectic Spiritualism

Victor Cousin's philosophy of Eclectic Spiritualism, known more commonly at the time as eclecticism, was France's most important philosophical involvement during the second quarter of the nineteenth century. The sources for Cousin's eclecticism were three. First, in his early years, Cousin was a student of Lockean empirical or "sensationalist" philosophy, taught at the Ecole Normal by Pierre Laromiguière. Later, however, the young student fell under the sway of Paul Royer-Collard and Maine de Biron, figures central to the emergence of the spiritualist or early romantic phase of French philosophy, the second influence in Cousin's ideology. Third, in 1818, Cousin travelled to Germany, studying Kant and meeting the most important German philosophers of the age, the fathers of German idealism, Fichte and Hegel. During this seminal student phase of Cousin's life, three major philosophical systems were juxtaposed—English empiricism, French romantic spiritualism, and German idealism.

The first written formulation resulting from this ideological union appeared in 1826 with the publication of Cousin's *Fragments Philosophiques.* The title gives a clue as to its contents. In the *Fragments,* Cousin first defined and elaborated his philosophy of eclecticism, composed as a fusion of pieces taken from the three systems. This effort might be best described as a campaign of philosophical surgery, held together by a kind of rhetorical suture, an ideology composed of a collection of philosophical antinomies. First, Cousin exploited Locke's method of analysis and evaluation, expanding sensation to natural law, maintaining a method of logical induction, and lastly asserting that the scientific method can grasp absolute truth. Secondly, he used the emphasis upon personal consciousness central to Kant's *Critique of Judgment* and *Critique of Pure Reason,* and in so doing asserted the importance of self and personal judgment in scientific evaluation. Lastly, in his appreciation of French spiritualists and German idealists, he focused first upon modes of action involving free will and belief, asserting on the one hand the importance of liberty in action, and on the other hand, transcendant norms of moral, responsible behavior. The invocation of a moral order returned to French philosophy metaphysical considerations which had been absent since the polarization of science and religion by the *philosophes* in the mid-eighteenth century. Cousin treated his scientific method as an upward movement through a series of increasingly abstracted levels. It began in the empirical analyses of Locke and Kant, directed at both nature and at self, which he termed his method's psychology; then, by use of a sequence of judicious inductions, it arrived at the realm of absolute knowledge, or 'ontology'. Stated differently, the process comprised a move from substantiality to causality, with God as ultimate cause.[39]

The philosophy of eclecticism grew in intellectual importance during the Restoration, and subsequently became the state philosophy under Louis-Philippe.[40] Not adverse to exploiting those analogizing techniques so popular to the *philosophes,* Cousin sought to justify his philosophical scheme by a socio-political simile. It was in the second edition of the *Fragments,* published after the ascendancy of Louis-Philippe, that this analogy appeared, seeking to describe the form and hence the appropriateness of eclecticism to the present-day situation:

> Just as the human soul, in its natural development, includes several elements of which true philosophy is the harmonious expression, any civilized society has several wholly distinct elements, which the government should recognize and represent . . . The July revolution is no different from the English revolution of 1688, but in France, which has much less aristocracy and a little more democracy and monarchy . . . These three elements are necessary . . . The man who fought any exclusive principle in science has also to reject any exclusive principle in the state.[41]

He next addressed the problem of formulation. Initially, Cousin's philosophical method embarked upon a campaign of analysis, differentiation, and criticism. He stated,

> We must be able to separate the truths from the errors that surround them . . . and we can do this only if we know what is true and what is false in ourselves; and we can do this only if we have made an adequate study of philosophical problems, human nature, its faculties and their laws.[42]

Reconstruction can be attempted only after a stage of decomposition when the true has been separated from the false. Eclecticism sought to

> identify the true element in each of these systems and use them to construct a philosophy superior to all systems—one which governs all others by dominating them all.[43]

As noted earlier, the epistemology of the *Encyclopédie* began with man's faculties: thinking, feeling, activity. Various *philosophes* interpreted these psychological factors in different ways. For example, Jacques-François Blondel simply exploited a variant of the Platonic epistemology, raising the faculties to the level of ontology, *Le Vrai, Le Beau, L'Utile.*[44] It could be said that Blondel substituted *Le Bien* with *L'Utile,* in keeping with the liberal and utilitarian interest in divesting man's actions of any moral overtones. This change correlated with the general anti-religious feeling pervading the Encyclopedist school. Victor Cousin retained a triadic view of knowledge, had returned to the classical epistemology characterized by the true, the beautiful, and the good. In so doing, Cousin resurrected a metaphysic. Moreover, he discussed man's faculties as the modus and *matérielle* of philosophy, in contrast to the end of philosophy, ontology:

Philosophy in all times turns upon the fundamental idea of the true, the beautiful, and the good. The idea of the true is psychology, logic, and metaphysic; the idea of the good is private and public morals; the idea of the beautiful is that science which in German is called aesthetics, the details of which pertain to the criticism of literature, to the criticism of the arts, but whose general principles have always occupied a more or less considerable place in the researches, and even in the teaching of philosophers, from Plato and Aristotle to Hutcheson and Kant.[45]

The process of cognition began with what Cousin termed the psychological method, focusing upon the human faculties of reason, sentiment, and sensibility, described by Cousin as "head, heart, senses".[46] Sensibility was primarily the mechanical effect of external stimuli upon the senses, a process which Cousin likened to the working of Locke's sensationalism. Recognizing these influences would move the observer into another realm, for upon acknowledging perception, he would simultaneously admit to the action of personal consciousness. Moreover, with the realization of the play of personal consciousness in perception, Cousin further noted the existence of interpretive faculties, attention and reflection, both of which he tied to the impulses of volition or will. Hence, he related consciousness to what he considered to be the deepest level of being, ego or self, formalized in acts of will, on which any act of judgment depended.

At this point, it would seem that Cousin attached final significance to self, in terms of the epistemological problem of judgment central to the induction of ontology, the object of his or any other philosophical endeavor. The judgmental process, obviously based in self, Cousin described as either reflective or spontaneous. He defined reflective judgment, tied to conscious perception, as that wherein the mind's eye holds a phenomenon, either through simultaneous recognition or through memory, in order that it be regarded and analyzed. Although he saw the process as introduced by an act of will, the instrument controlling the act was seen to be reason. Reason allowed one to come to a conclusion and act accordingly. Moreover, reason, being part of consciousness, yet greater than consciousness, was a factor escaping human subjectivity. Reason as an instrument was activated by the will, but escaped its control. The faculty moved beyond the sway of the individual personality, to a mediate position between man and truth, permitting the grasping of ontology in human consciousness.

Man's faculties, however, seemed to Cousin not coequally, but hierarchically arranged, with reason ascending to a transcendant position above both sensibility and action in the triad of consciousness. Yet at the same time, reason escaped individual consciousness by virtue of intersubjectivity, and hence, was inflated in significance as a superindividual faculty.

Cousin countered the implications of his own argument in his treatment of the spontaneous action of will. He saw spontaneity of judgment as coming from a realm wholly separate from reason. Perceptions sponsored by consciousness were superseded by that realm's apperception. In this view perception became the instinctive acknowledgement of a reaction to phenomena unlike that gained by reflection. Spontaneous actions were hence differentiated from those which had been carefully considered. Curiously enough, however, the realm of spontaneous judgment, like actions sponsored by reflection, stood apart from the individual personality at work informing judgment. For Cousin, apperception was governed by a moral factor, formalized in a system of social belief, and thus as ideal as the instrumentality of reason transcending self in reflective action.

As already noted, this concept was presaged in philosophy by Rousseau's notion of *conscient* or *volonté collective.* This idea engaged a range of social factors which attempted to regularize or ritualize man's activity. For Rousseau, collective will was akin to a "natural philosophy" of man, the intellectual realm in operation in cases of instinctive reaction. Belief, common sense, tradition, habit, these comprised the subsurface undertow by which the natural man, that is the man unencumbered by the superstructure of culture, might arrive at decisions. In *Le Vrai, Le Beau, Le Bien,* and the 1853 expanded edition of the *Fragments,* Cousin described the consideration of 'collective consciousness' in terms of the first of man's institutions, language:

> Individual consciousness, concerned and transferred to the entire species, is called communication. It is common sense that has made, that sustains, that develops language's natural and permanent beliefs, society and its fundamental institutions. Grammarians have not invented languages, nor legislators societies, nor philosophers general beliefs. All these things have not been personally done, but by the whole world—by the genius of humanity.
>
> Common sense is deposited in its works. All languages and all human institutions contain the sentiments that we have just called to mind and described, and especially the distinctions between good and evil, between justice and injustice, between free will and desire, between duty and interest, between virtue and happiness, with the profoundly rooted belief that happiness is a recompense due to virtue, and that crime in itself deserves to be permitted, and calls for the reparation of just suffering.[47]

Ultimately, the consensus of a civilization and the implantation of a belief system within the minds of men became, for Cousin, the impulse of the subconscious and instinctive judgment. It is important to note that in acts of spontaneous judgment, he believed reason to have no part. Within man's faculties, the realm of sentiment owed nothing to reason. Logic was displaced from the passional sphere. In his recommendation of spontaneous action, Cousin called for the exercise of an area of activity and judgment bypassing logical truth and the rational faculty necessary to the attainment of ontology. Hence, he created an antagonism between the philosophical factors of reason and tradition, whereby habit, history, and myth became as important to action as instrumental rational consideration. Needless to say, this realization held important implications for the artistic world. Cousin's recognition of spontaneous judgment and action provided a necessary alternative to the systems of logical thought and concomitant cognitive literary and artistic languages which had fettered free artistic experimentation since the neoclassical ascendancy of the God of Reason. In this regard, the alogic and historicity of the early romantics found significant support.

Although the realm of spontaneity countered rational action, Cousin did not perceive in it an ideology of total freedom or libertarianism. Rather, in those cases of judgment and action where reflection did not enter, norms of responsible and dutiful behavior would come into play. Ultimately motivations in these cases would be restrained by moral and ethical systems. It is curious to note that Cousin, the spokesman of belief and tradition, supporter of the Restoration and July Monarchies, was simultaneously anti-Catholic. Although religious in a pantheistic sense, Cousin, like Voltaire, was steeped in the eighteenth-century Enlightenment tradition of anti-clericalism.

The implications that the eclectic system held for art were likewise ambivalent. On the one hand, artistic spontaneity connoted an instinctive act, free of aesthetic norms and reflection. Yet, it was in artistic creation that Cousin most criticized the process of spontaneity. For example, he criticized Diderot's poetic language, citing excerpts from *Jacques le Fataliste,* as overly personal, impressionistic, and inattentive to those formal and syntactical norms by which effective communication occurs. As noted above with regard to Diderot's philosophical dialogues, the author came under Cousin's fire because he championed personal genius. Critical consciousness was to be replaced by a language more instrumental and traditional in its intentions.

With regard to the arts of imitation, Cousin drew upon Plotinus and on Burke's discussions of the sublime and the beautiful. Although Cousin recognized transcendent poetic genius at play in the sublime work of art, for him, the appropriate artistic model was the work of beauty governed by rules of taste. Cousin drew upon Quatremère de Quincy in arguing against freely poetic art forms ('ut pictura poesis') to those stressing rationalized natural formulations. Opposing the doctrine of the sublime according to which fundamental interest in natural forms or episodes ungoverned by law or decorum may be portrayed ('je ne sais quoi'), Cousin, like Quatremère, argued for a pictorial language transcending the natural, aspiring to the artificial, rationally composed.[48] For both Quatremère and Cousin, this was the realm of Zeuxian method, by which natural models are improved or constructed from a range of examples in accordance with taste and decorum. Both theorists required these models to underpin the beautiful work of art.[49]

The imitative arts were transferred from the realm of imagination to that of memory, from spontaneous to reflective act. In memory, purified, idealized artistic norms or 'types' were seen to be stored, ready to be called upon in order to inform judgments. Hence, the making of art invoked an inductive method.

Cousin wished to move away from the personal into interpersonal standards of excellence or achievement. As in Quatremère's campaign of cognitive art, the individual artistic consciousness was to be gradually superseded. For in his frame of reference, the individual, personal work of art had meaning only in so far as it related to a larger whole. Moreover, in the shift, art was to move from a subjective, to an intersubjective realm. This was a process which we have already observed in the absolutized criticality of the early socialist Fourier, and in the group who also attempted to raise personal psychology to the level of an abstraction via taxonomy, and in the group spirit of Rousseau. Cousin's psychology sought to delete subjectivity from the artistic process by allying cognition with either the conscious, rational workings of mind or with the subconscious, Roussellian *conscient collectif*. In so doing, the artistic product, as mark of cognition, would approach nature of an ideal order.

If we ask to which faculty Cousin gave precedence in the artistic enterprise, we must conclude that it was reason. In Cousin's epistemology, ontology was attainable only via reason. Cousin thus defused much of his own psychological method. In considering spontaneity as the great expression of self, he initially elevates personal consciousness in much the same way as either Rousseau or Kant. Yet his artistic disclaimer of spontaneous action, particularly free artistic activity, depersonalized judgment and, consequently, invalidated personal consciousness as a retreat from the absolute Cartesian and Lockean cognitive modes. The course of Cousin's own program of phenomenological abstraction retraced the course of the early Enlightenment. Personal consciousness was irretrievably left behind.

Cousin's artistic admixture was inherently unstable. On the one hand, artistic camps of the period were polarized between spontaneous and reflective action. In architecture, for example, alternative camps of romantics and rationalists articulated this dilemma during the July Monarchy. Yet polarities were difficult to demarcate strictly even when the *groupements* were so easily described. Although the canonical classical unities may have been questioned by one camp or the other, romantic movements in literature, painting, and architecture devoted enormous amounts of time and effort to the construction of distinctive forms. Furthermore, the rationalists embodied covert elements of personal criticism within their metaphoric language, communicable only to the initiated, and even then, with considerable difficulty.[50] Rationalists, like the romantics, also had their personal language. Surely criticism, internal form or deep structure, and self-expression were as important to those involved only with supposedly self-denying, functional, and 'real' aesthetic structures as to those who freely supported individuality and spontaneity.

Curiously enough, the logical, cognitive structure which Cousin sought in his philosophy eluded the would-be creator. The various systems at play in Cousin's own Eclectic philosophy could only at best be called a syncretism reached through the power of his own rhetoric. Moreover, it was primarily by means of his own prose style, steeped within the rhetorical tradition of French nineteenth-century academe, that any synthesis, albeit ephemeral, was achieved at all.[51] Cousin reconciled ideological oppositions primarily because the philosopher deemed that they cease to exist. By virtue of his own provocative personal prose, Cousin succeeded in spotlighting major themes around which ideological issues could be grouped while obscuring his philosophy's perimeter where alternative systems could inconspicuously do battle with one another. Total congruence of philosophical systems was a consideration outside of Cousin's own personal psychological method. As with Fourier, it is interesting that Cousin should stress the importance of self, especially in opposition to rational epistemologies, as an outgrowth of post-Kantian philosophies, only to deny it again in the face of a metaphysical order. Ultimately, a metaphysic dominating human intention or volition under the guise of reason, morality, or beauty, sponsored the recognition of truth. As with human consciousness, Cousin's personal statement, fashioned as a heroic expression of personal criticism and self, was likewise to be devalued by a rational deconstruction of a necessarily superindividual order. Finally, rather than being self-sustaining, Cousin's was an agonistic philosophy, for, as the inevitable outcome of Cousin's implicitly liberal point of view, deconstruction called for the destruction of his personal formalization and self.

Daly's Punchinello

By way of summarizing the preceding discussion, I will return to Daly's tableau "L'Architecture Contemporaine" and develop a reading that finds in the central figure, the jester, a convenient reference for the themes by which I have characterized Daly's intellectual background.

Classical philosophy bequeathed to the eighteenth century the opposition between man and nature. The classics also deposited in Enlightenment minds the possibility of bridging the gulf between the two using perception as a means. Via perception, man could confront, contemplate, and draw conclusions from nature. In the process of cognition, man could reach the fundamental truths which underlay the world about him.

Neoclassical philosophy and aesthetics developed these themes. A particularly significant demonstration of lingering classical epistemology appeared in the form of Claude-Nicolas Ledoux' *L'Architecture Considérée sous les Rapports de l'Art, des Moeurs, et de la Législation* (1804). Two plates from the work are particularly suggestive. The first "L'Abri du Pauvre" establishes the dualism between man and nature (plate 9). An Arcadian shepherd sits beneath a tree, beside the ocean, contemplating the world. Customarily, the ocean signifies the sublime experience, which convinces man of his finitude in the face of infinity. But the shepherd's meditation has caused him to look not at the ocean, but at the sky, where he envisions a tableau of

Parnassus. His vision has revealed a natural order transcending the world's incomprehensibility. The divine light in which he is bathed confirms that he has seen the truth underpinning the universe and its history.

Ledoux elaborates that "L'Abri du Pauvre" is not merely that space where primitive man resides. Rather, it is that domain where man might casually encounter the panoply of classical gods. Ledoux' *Abri* is an ideal realm. The architect posits that the spirit of this space might inform contemporary architecture. Ledoux describes "L'Abri du Pauvre" as an enclosure, supported by landscape features, trees acting as columns, and covered by the heavenly soffit, "la voûte azurée pour dôme."[52] Although Ledoux recognizes the difficulty of transferring these features to a distinctly architectural situation, he nonetheless reasserts that architectural, like natural space, must be ideal.

Ledoux visualizes his ideal interests concerning built form in a second plate "Vue du Théâtre de Besançon" (plate 10). He deals with two principal themes in this tableau. The first concerns a method of composing architectural form consonant with nature's ideality. The second deals with man's perception and cognition of this ideality. Ledoux' view reflects his ambivalence between a desire to illustrate his building and to represent the process of one's seeing the architecture that the architect has created. In the plate, Ledoux represents a human eye with a depiction of his theater inserted into its pupil. This arrangement suggests that he deals not merely with a reflection of the external world in the eye, but addresses the problem of perception in nature, and the interpretation of nature in ideal terms. The circularity and geometrical purity of the eye is transferred from the organ to that which it perceives. Ledoux hence implies the ideal, typological quality of the building by virtue of its explicit mathematical order. Yet it is unclear whether we are looking from external nature toward the eye or from the inner eye toward nature. In this second interpretation the reflection signifies the viewer's recognition of the architectural idea. A ray of light moving back and forth between the interior of the building and the interior of the eye substantiates the connectedness between external nature and the mind. Here, Ledoux summarizes the Platonic dialectic: cognition occurs when nature, illuminated by the light of God, fuses with the inner light of the mind. Via the processes of sensory perception, nature and mind are one.[53]

The relationships among nature, mind, and perception are of central concern to classical art, and particularly, Greek tragedy. Sophocles, for instance, explores the themes as he studies human alienation in *Oedipus Rex*. When Oedipus commits the crime of patricide, he alienates himself, albeit unconsciously, from the divine forces governing nature. He is thus at odds with destiny. However, he rectifies the situation by putting out his eyes. Although blinded, he regains his harmony with the will of the gods.

It is important to note that when Oedipus alienates himself from mankind, he loses sight of the truth as well. Furthermore, when he literally loses sight, his access to the truth is reopened. Moreover, as he approaches knowledge, he also attains self-knowledge. Because Sophocles confers truth, knowledge, and self-knowledge upon a blinded, and especially a voluntarily blinded man, his play can be understood as a critique of Platonic epistemology. Cognition and the unity of man and nature do not necessarily depend upon sensory perception.

César Daly's tableau "L'Architecture Contemporaine" draws explicitly upon Platonic imagery (plate 2). The sun on the right side of the tableau, discussed earlier in this chapter as symbolizing the progressive ideal, is illustrative. In Platonic terms, the sun is the image of the divine light that illuminates nature. In the tableau the reflection of the divine light from nature enters the mind, as signified by the open eyes of Athena and the Three Graces. Hence, Daly represents the moment of inspiration so important to Platonic perception and cognition.

Similarly, Daly's tableau makes use of the principles organizing classical tragedy. Earlier, I described how historical progress becomes the plot of Daly's historical narrative. Hayden White has noted the congruence between progressive historical schemes and the classical understanding of destiny.[54] In both cases man is guided by a force outside himself, as he moves toward a predetermined and arbitrary goal.

Whereas the figures on the right side of the tableau see God, those on the left are deprived of vision. In the first period of the tableau, blindfolds cover the eyes of the performers in Daly's historical narrative. In the second Daly obscures the characters' eyes with closing or by means of pictorial devices that preclude our awareness of their eyes. As we will see, the jester is the exception to both situations.

The contrast between right and left sides of the tableau suggests a contrast between modes of consciousness and inverts the Oedipal scheme. While the blinded Oedipus signifies mankind conscious of self and harmonious with the forces of nature, Daly's blindfolded characters are unconscious. They stumble and fall along the rocky way of dialectical improvement, and their difficulty in making their way suggests that they are unaware of the historical course they are following. This view of unseeing man's relationship to history parallels Sophocles' understanding of reconciliation with destiny, achieved when cognitive means provided by vision are eradicated. On the right side of the tableau man's eyes are open and his course smooths out: he has achieved conscious understanding of the order of things. In the final period of the tableau we can see that man's recognition of historical structure allows him to ride, not walk, to paradise. In this, man achieves a godly realm, where personal and divine consciousnesses intermingle.

But Daly is not attempting to resurrect a purely Platonic epistemology or tragic narrative structure in this tableau. Rather, he is placing that epistemology into a new perspective. For a blindfolded mankind is a social entity quite different from a blind mankind. There is an important existential permanence in Sophocles' narrative that is absent from Daly's. Unlike Oedipus, Daly's characters can regain their powers of perception simply by discarding their blindfolds. Daly thus describes a state of false blindness, and treats it as a masquerade.

As such, Daly's narrative pokes fun at the Oedipal tragedy as genre, and implicitly, at tragedy's narrative structure, an optimistic history regulated Platonically by divine law. This comic reading is reinforced by the figure of the jester, who subverts historical *gravitas* and epitomizes the composition's satirical quality. The jester symbolizes the tableau's spirit of irony, and his significance permeates all levels of the tableau. Superficially, his dress and attributes assist us in establishing the jester's precise identity. In contrast to the frock coat of those figures to the right of the jester, his costume—tights, jerkin, floppy hat—is theatrical rather than conventional dress. His grotesque appearance, including such bodily deformities as a distended stomach, humped back, and beaked nose, and his attributes, stick and bird, provide us with a key to his identity.

For us, the stick relates the jester to a figure from our childhood experience, the marionette figure, Punch. Moreover, both club and bird refer to Punch's ancestor, the *commedia dell'arte* character, Pulcinella. The bird especially relates to Pulcinella's most familiar theatrical antics, including chirping like a bird, clucking like a chicken, and strutting about like a barnyard fowl. It suggests the Latin root of his name, *Pullus Galliniensis,* which associated Pulcinella with the birds he imitated.[55] In other words, the attributes specify Daly's jester as none other than the *commedia's* Pulcinella, Polichinelle in the French, and Punchinello in the English tradition.

For Daly it appears likely that Punchinello was significant for two reasons, one historical and the other cognitive. First, he was among the oldest characters performing in the mid-nineteenth-century presentations of the *commedia dell'arte.* Thus, his every appearance was invested with history. Second, within the frame of the *commedia* itself, he personified the course of human events from antiquity through the present day. A biographer of Punchinello, Maurice Sand, in his *Masques et Buffons* (1860) points out his significance when he recounts the character's life story. Punchinello rebukes his youthful audience and its taunts, as naive:

> J'en aperçois d'ici certains gens qui ne partagent pas à mon opinion: libre à eux. Ils sont encore jeunes.[56]

> I see here certain people who do not agree with my opinion. So much for them. They are still young.

He contrasts this naiveté with his pessimism stemming from a personal experience of history:

S'ils avaient...vu des cités entières disparaître sous les cendres volcaniques, s'ils avaient eu leurs chaussures brulés par les laves du Vesuve; s'ils avaient vu se ruer les peuples sanguinaires du Midi sur les peuples farouches du Nord, et réciproquement...je vous assure que je m'en souviens, mes enfants...[57]

[For they would think differently] if they had seen entire cities disappear under volcanic ash, if they had had their shoes burned off by Vesuvius' lava; if they had seen [as I] the yellow people of the East attack the fierce Northern tribes, and vice versa...I assure you that I remember these things, my children.

The history that Punchinello describes is a violent one. The history depicted in Daly's tableau is similarly violent. The history into which Daly has placed his jester is thus the one that Punchinello himself remembers and recounts. In narrative, then, discourse and memory coincide, and since Daly's narrative is pictorial, the coincidence extends to include the space enclosing the speaker, Punchinello. This shallow pictorial space can thus be read as the formalization of the dwarf's mind. A reciprocity exists between Punchinello's personal and historical consciousness.

The means by which Daly accomplishes this historical reading suggests a device from the tropic theory of figurative language. I speak particularly of the trope of metonymy, a literary structure which ascribes significance to an object by reference to one of its attributes.[58] That structure moves meaning outward, from the attribute to that object to which the attribute is contiguous. You recall that I finally identified Punchinello by referring to one of his attributes, a bird. The bird is a visual pun on the name of Punchinello, hence a symbolic element providing meaning for that figure to which it is attached, the dwarf.

Lastly, in the third of a series of metonymic expansions of meaning, the significance of the Gothic period attaches itself to those time slots which precede and follow, "Les Plus Vieux" and "L'Art Nouveau." As a historical attribute, it moreover identifies not merely adjacent time frames, but also all time itself. History is hence signified and formalized, substantiated by a series of interactive figural relationships between the tableau's major formal features. History has two functions. First, history is the repository of significant historical personages and episodes. Second, history as a literary form with more than a merely narrative function is an entity which transcends those events which it contains. Rather, it has a metahistorical significance, a structure of a mythical character, which orchestrates those events.

Up to this point, I have argued that Daly metonymically signifies a series of implicit readings radiating outward from the central image of his tableau, Punchinello. In so doing, Daly implies that the dwarf is not merely the signifier of the idea of history, but its form as well, hence making concrete what heretofore had remained wholly in the realm of ideas. Daly's historical narrative is composed not only of perceptible events, but of real purpose and structure as well.

Metonymy suggests a periodified and optimistic historical reading that seems compatible with Daly's general theory of history.[59] Both mechanistic and organic views of historical progress are present in his tableau. Moreover, Daly implies man's relationship to and acceptance of these historical views, either consciously or unconsciously, by the poses of his characters representing humanity. Mankind is oriented in the direction of the sun, the symbol here of history's immanent divine order. The implication is that sooner or later, all will unite with God.

However, Punchinello turns away from the sun, and by implication, the progressive, optimistic world view. Unlike the others whose poses comply with the direction of history, Punchinello resists. Unlike the poses of the others, which together form a rhythmic composition reinforcing the spatial frame itself, Punchinello's stance violates the explicit pictorial and implicit historical order. Rather than posing frontally, Punchinello spirals outward from the course of time. His head turns from the divine light that awaits him at history's end. He rotates toward his audience.

I have suggested that Daly depicts the dwarf's personal account of human existence in the space surrounding Punchinello. Hence, it is the dwarf who provides the documentation for Daly's history. The dwarf is history's narrator. In addition, Daly's Punchinello also looked toward us, his audience. Hence, his linguistic stance is rhetorical, not merely discursive. His concern is with communication and by implication with the processes of human perception and cognition.

Much as Daly's tableau formalizes the first of Punchinello's preoccupations, that is, history, it also spatializes the second, the human processes of cognition. Punchinello violates the pictorial structure of the tableau. By extension, he also disrupts the tableau's historical and narrative structure. Violation of narrative frame suggests a connection with romantic irony as a literary form, where the narrator turns away from his own carefully developed seriousness, in order to undermine that seriousness. Punchinello's turning from his context violates the temporal frame that he has assisted in constructing. In addition, Punchinello's lack of interest in his historical frame marks the first step in establishing a consciousness distinct from history. This distinction allows for a criticism of history, and concomitantly, a discovery of self.

Like historical consciousness, personal consciousness has a distinct spatial frame in Daly's tableau. However, the construction of this space is implicit rather than explicit, phenomenal rather than literal.[60] We can see what is meant by the phenomenal quality of the spatial frame by looking at Antoine Watteau's portrait "Gilles" dating from the early-eighteenth century (plate 11). The portrait is particularly pertinent to this discussion because it, like Daly's tableau, represents characters from the *commedia dell'arte,* Gilles and other members of the company. Gilles faces the viewer; he stands in a foreground zone which is a dais framed by a small hill. A second spatial slot is established by the same hill and by the foliage placed deeper into the pictorial space, where we observe other partially obscured figures from the *commedia*.

The composition is further elaborated by other pictorial devices that playfully explore and engage the various spaces of the painting. Processes of vision and perception are addressed in order to fuse discrete spatial zones. The *gaze* accomplishes this fusion by establishing visual connections among viewers both inside and outside the canvas. For example, the figures on the right side of the composition look at Gilles, thereby joining the deeper and shallower spatial zones by their sight lines. In a similar way, a link is established between the fictional space of Watteau's canvas and the real space of the observer. The dais on which Gilles stands has no foreground demarcation, implying that pictorial space might extend beyond the picture plane into the real world. The pictorial means of gaze reinforces this reading, for Gilles creates a visual connection with his audience in much the same way as background figures meet Gilles. Moreover, the background characters of man and donkey establish eye contact with the real space of the viewer. This sight line slices across three zones—background, foreground, real—joining them by a compositional means which violates explicit pictorial structure. These oblique lines do not merely skewer the three spaces implied by the tableau. Rather, their relationship establishes a second matrix of lines unlike the basic compositional geometries of the canvas. They portray a perceptual field. This spatial frame constitutes a second structure apart from the pictorial which serves to formalize the process of seeing: the visual and cognitive realm from which nature, both pictorial and real, is interpreted and understood.

Punchinello operates pictorially in much the same way as Gilles. The dwarf addresses the viewer and implicates the audience's perceptual and cognitive realms. Therefore, we can say that Daly's Punchinello signifies personal consciousness, becoming a metaphor of self.

To summarize, we can say that Punchinello is dually significant for Daly and yields two readings in the tableau. The first reading is metonymic, giving Daly's narrative its historical structure. The second is metaphorical, shaping personal consciousness in Daly's literary and artistic creation. Punchinello is part of both frames of reference, history and mind. Yet Punchinello fits uncomfortably into either realm, and therefore can be regarded as a figure yearning to be independent from both.

Historical and personal consciousness are formalized pictorially in Daly's tableau. Daly's formal means are essentially academic: he uses line rather than color to compose his spatial zones. The geometries of the two spatial frames, however, are not congruent. For Punchinello's rotation dictates that the line between his figure and the viewer reads perpendicularly to that of historical progress. The two spatial frames have only one feature in common—their intersection in the figure of Punchinello himself.

The intersection between the two spatial frames warrants comparison to the intersecting axes of language described by linguistic theory. Roman Jakobson, for example, calls these axes the metonymic and the metaphoric, and finds that they distinguish narrative from poetic literary modes.[61] The metonymic and the metaphorical readings of Daly's tableau yield a similar distinction, and imply a parallel in mental activity, the mnemonic and historical versus the speculative and the ideational. These, in turn, correspond to two epistemological categories, history and reason, as indicated by Punchinello's dual significance.

Yet, as I maintained earlier, Punchinello's discomfort in both historical and cognitive realms suggests that a third space is about to emerge. This suggestion again finds linguistic support, now in Roland Barthes' structuralism. As a development of Jakobson's formal categories, Barthes posits a third, *écriture,* a literary form occupying the space between axes of narrative and poetic literature.[62] By implication, we might say that the existence of a third literary form also implies a third category of mind. Three literary modes in turn suggest the traditional tripartite epistemologies of both classical and Enlightenment theories of knowledge.

Both philosophical systems consider the faculties of memory, reason, and imagination. Were Barthes to pair mental faculty with its representative literary form, he would possibly associate the narrative with memory, poetry with reason, and *écriture* with imagination. Were Daly to similarly pair mental faculty with formal means, he would probably associate his explicit narrative frame with memory, his implicit perceptual frame with reason, and Punchinello, as a form separate from the others, with imagination.

Barthes' categories correspond to eighteenth-century epistemological faculties. The significance of Barthes' reading as it pertains to eighteenth-century epistemology is in imbuing the "space" of *écriture* with a quality by which imagination can be recognized. However, absence is more than a quality for the nineteenth century: it is the *modus* by which imaginative activity is accomplished, much as metaphor is the means of poetry or metonymy the means of narrative.

Barthes' argument is instructive by contrast. The space of *écriture* reinforces the distinction between the two other models while maintaining itself as a distinct entity. This view of literature as well as epistemology is inherently taxonomic, intent upon establishing meaningful distinctions. We have seen, however, how the third spatial zone in Daly's tableau, formalized by Punchinello, seeks not to establish distinctions but to merge them. Hence, we might conclude that the tableau's "space" serves to fuse literary modes as well as epistemological categories. As such, Punchinello symbolizes a critique of both classical and Enlightenment epistemologies.

Nineteenth-century writers also address the concept of absence, discussed variously as "rent," "pause," or "Verfremdung."[63] Although not epistemologically directed in intention, these discussions also collapse the Enlightenment's three categories of knowledge. Most noteworthy among these is Hegel's, which implicates "pause" as the central moment of imaginative activity. In *The Phenomenology of Mind,* Hegel divides that moment into three parts. The first part is perception, the grasping of a physical event in the mind's eye. The second part is history, when the event is compared with historical paradigms held within the memory. The third part is formalization, when the physical event is integrated into the historical paradigm carried in memory, hence establishing a new form for knowledge. [64] It is important for our investigation of Daly to note that this view was essentially that of France's Hegelian, Victor Cousin, discussed in his *Fragments Philosophiques.*

Punchinello symbolizes the collapse of epistemological categories. Yet, his figure does not merely mark the rubble of philosophy. For Punchinello, as the sole survivor of philosophy's end, establishes a supervening significance. He becomes the symbol of humanity's one constancy, as depicted in the passage of time—man's basic antagonistic impulse.

We can return to Daly's tableau in order to evaluate Punchinello's new significance. As noted earlier, Punchinello marks the split between antiquity and the Middle Ages. In addition, the division within the left-hand side of the tableau has a second historical reading, which distinguishes the eighteenth from the nineteenth century. This reading originates in the Gothic arch framing Punchinello's head and bearing the caption "Du Style Gothique au XIXe Siècle." The arch specifies the nineteenth century as that which Punchinello initiates: the metonymic reading elaborated earlier implies that the period he closes is the eighteenth century. Punchinello is located on a line dividing the two, and that line balances the *coulisse* at the right end of the tableau. The *coulisse* probably signifies the Revolution of 1848, the event marking the rupture between Daly's present and his future of "L'Art Nouveau," since the tableau was created in that year. Similarly, the line on the left of the tableau might signify the 1789 revolution. Since the tableau's lines of historical demarcation could be seen as coinciding with revolutions, Punchinello, standing next to the first, might likewise be imbued with revolutionary spirit.

We might imagine the effects of Punchinello's revolutionary spirit by looking at the narrative portrayed in the tableau from his point of view. As he rotates his head, casting his eye across history, historical periods become fused. Temporal distinctions are lost in the same way that colors in a centrifuge are neutralized.

In the tableau, the differing costumes serve to reinforce periodic identities. However, the wearers of these costumes perform actions that are indistinguishable from period to period. Mankind's actions thus articulate a metahistorical theme which transcends historical epochs. This consistent activity is, moreover, destructive. To interpret Daly's tableau in the light of Marxian philosophical distinction: the supersturcture of historical moments may change; the deeper structure of history, i.e., the actions of man, remain constant.

Punchinello himself describes the terrifying invariance of man's violence and inhumanity. Maurice Sand's *Masques et Buffons* recounts Punchinello's words:

> ...les nations les plus orgueilleuse de la terre n'étaient que de peuplades de toutes de sauvages.[65]

> ...the proudest nations of the earth are nothing more than herds of savages.

There is an Rousseau-like quality to Punchinello's assertion. Like his eighteenth-century counterpart, Punchinello recognizes the degenerate quality of modern life, and the corruption of modern man. Unlike Rousseau, who would advocate a return to man's primitive existence by the eradication of institutions, Punchinello would argue that no social structure, old or new, would ever yield a better existence or a better man. Nothing could change man's basic evil. Punchinello is pessimistic about man's spiritual composition. However, his pessimism does not alter the fact that his view of man's history is as fatalistically conceived as is that of his more optimistic *Encyclopédist* counterparts, Rousseau and Diderot.

Punchinello's attitude introduces into Daly's tableau a question as to the validity of progress, whether material, social, or ideological. As a result of the static quality of man's basic impulses, all temporal, social and epistemological structures are to be seen as identical. Names, characters and fashions may vary from moment to moment as part of the historical superstructure, but these trivial historical features are immaterial to the essential fact: the destructiveness of humanity. Punchinello embodies history's destructive character as he stands on the ruins of Enlightenment epistemology, modern man's most cherished institution.

The collapse of the faculties is especially well portrayed in a depiction of Punchinello from 1820 (plate 12). Gone are the tights, jerkin, and cap of Daly's tableau. In their place, Punchinello wears what would seem to be the theatrical costume of a Spanish captain. Its provenance, however, is problematical. Punchinello's hose, ribbons, lace, and velvet intimate the costume of the mid-eighteenth-century gentleman. However, his tricorn implies a Napoleonic historical frame. Punchinello's facial features and pose imply a second historical duality. His face, bespeckled by moles, appears an offshoot of eighteenth-century bourgeois realism. His pose, however, is marked by the self-consciousness of the nineteenth-century *poseur,* the predecessor of Barbey's and Baudelaire's cerebral dandy. Punchinello's dress can be seen as informed by both eighteenth- and nineteenth-century sartorial convention.

As history is fused in this Punchinello, so too is ideology. Eighteenth-century bourgeois realism can be seen as a starting place for the empirical method governing the physical inquiries of *Encyclopedism*. Furthermore, self-consciousness, the mark of eighteenth-century cerebrality, can imply an idealistic ideology of a metaphysical order. Hence, it might be said that while Punchinello depicts both bourgeois and Napoleonic fashions, he also presents empirical and idealistic epistemologies.

This peculiar combination of ideologies can be interpreted in light of the 1820 portrait of Punchinello described above. The portrait suggests that Punchinello is traditionally a farcical character, whose humor largely derives from the incompatibility of his physical and ideological features. Mikhail Bakhtin points out that this incompatibility tends to profane its component parts.[66]

Karl Marx discusses criticism as a kind of profanation that "demystifies" its object. By demystification, he means a dethroning of modern social and epistemological conventions that have acquired a more than real value. Like Marx, Punchinello's profanation also criticizes historical and epistemological conventions. It is thus a demystification, but one which takes the form of parody. Using the ironic mode, Punchinello's form visualizes his parody of social and epistemological conventions. As we can see from his 1820 portrait, Punchinello's periodic form resurrects and recomposes the forms of the past. This form uses history as a means of creating the contrasts necessary to its own profanatory intent. Hence, in order to profane ideological paradigms, Punchinello must construct another, albeit a satirical one, on the model of its predecessor. Likewise, in order to profane history, Punchinello must construct an alternative recognizable as history, although in a perverse way. In its playful antagonism, parody resurrects its antecedent, hence forcing a repetition of history.[67] There is an almost apocalyptic undertow in parody for it must necessarily reconstruct the historical object of its derision, hence giving form to its own critical significance. Therefore, parody necessarily resurrects history and its formal paradigms in the course of its own formalizations. Parody's relationship to its temporal antecedents recall the opening lines of Marx's "Eighteenth Brumaire of Louis Bonaparte":

> Hegel remarks somewhere that all great, world-historical facts and personages occur, as it were, twice. He has forgotten to add: the first time as tragedy, the second as farce.[68]

Hence, two features of parody become important to our consideration of Punchinello. The first, stemming from Marx, is the critical commentary which is the purpose of parody. The second is the paradigmatic reconstruction and profanation which is parody's means. The first recognizes the importance of personal consciousness, the second the importance of history in shaping parody's formalizations.

I have discussed how Daly's tableau recognizes both mechanistic and evolutionary views in its form. Moreover, in the introduction to this study I have argued how both paradigms stem from the Bible as their ultimate source. Nineteenth-century thinkers owe a debt to this source, particularly as it pertains to notions of periodic history and of the perfectability of man.

Likewise, César Daly's tableau intimates a Biblical provenance in its historical frame. The Bible is a narrative, divided between two parts, human and divine history, and among three major periods, Old Testament, New Testament, and Revelation. Daly's historical portrayal is similar, divided between human and divine history, and among three periods "Les Plus Vieux," "Les Vieux," and "L'Art Nouveau."

The major Biblical periods are separated by two cataclysmic moments, the birth of Christ and Christ's second coming. Similarly, as I argued earlier, Daly's periods are distinguished by revolutions, much as cataclysm is marked by the appearance of Christ in the Bible, revolution is formalized by Punchinello in the tableau.

In *Ecce Homo,* Nietzsche saw Christ's coming as a great revolution, thereby suggesting that the distinction between revolution and apocalypse was tenuous.[69] By extension, Punchinello's revolutionary significance could be seen as apocalyptic. I have noted above that Punchinello seeks to fuse all temporal periods: his present metonymic reading implicates past and future. Hence, although positioned at the beginning of the nineteenth century, his significance is not limited to it. As past and present telescope into Punchinello's present, we realize that Daly's narrative becomes an apocalyptic vision.

St. John established the literary pardigm for the narrative of the Apocalypse. The artists of the Middle Ages established the visual paradigms. César Daly discovered these paradigms in their unembellished states, and in their original locations, in the tympana of Gothic cathedrals. When Daly was entrusted with the task of documenting and restoring Chartres Cathedral, the moment arose to explore these formal paradigms. Their impact shaped the form of his tableau's pictorial narrative. For the purposes of exploring their meaning for the tableau, I find the Chartres "Last Judgment" portal particularly useful (plate 13).

Its tympanum displays two major zones, the lower populated by the souls of mankind, the upper of Christ and intercessors. The lower panel depicts the resurrection of humanity, and humanity's history. Mankind is divided into good and evil, the good on the left being led to Paradise, the bad on the right to hell. Above them, Christ the judge determines who is to go where.

The figures on the lower level, as well as the intercessors on the upper, establish a space congruent with the picture plane of the tympanum. The Christ figure, however, reads differently. His frontal orientation establishes a line reading perpendicular to the picture plane. Symbolic and formal similarities with Daly's tableau become immediately apparent. The rhythmic movement of humanity in the lower level relates closely to that in the tableau. By extension, the history of the tympanum finds a close correlation to that surrounding

Punchinello in the tableau. The central position of the jester in the tableau, moreover, parallels that of Christ in the Last Judgment.

However, important differences also exist. These distinctions occur primarily in the realm of consciousness. Emile Mâle notes the didactic character of these panels' narratives. [70] As such, the episodes depicted on the tympana of churches seek to establish a sensory contact with its audience as part of its rhetorical function. Yet Chartres' Last Judgment fails to accomplish this.

It is useful to contrast Watteau's "Gilles," as a theatrical depiction which succeeds in reaching its audience, with the tympanum. I noted above that Watteau accomplishes his didactic intention by establishing eye contact between various characters in his tableau and his audience. This contrast moves the canvas from being a mere portrayal of the *commedia* troupe to a depiction of a number of real personalities not unlike ourselves. The Last Judgment orders all characters within the same abstracted spatial frame, with the sole exception of Christ. Christ could be seen as occupying a position in his space similar to Gilles. Yet unlike Gilles, Christ fails to establish the eye contact necessary to specify him as a character apart from the spatial and historical context into which he is placed. Christ remains a hieratic figure, removed from the realm of sense and perception. Although seemingly unaware of his historical frame, Christ is ironically centered within that narrative which was his own divising. Although the two layers of the composition seek to distinguish humanity's past from Christ's present, the two remain essentially interwoven. Christ remains internal to the historical narrative. He is moreover unaware of a cognitive frame that could establish his as a consciousness apart from history, and that could serve to separate him from the narrative he has devised.

Daly's Punchinello portrays a reversal of this reading. Located on the upper level of the tympanum, Christ is physically separated from history, whereas Punchinello is embroiled in it. Yet whereas Christ fails to perceive his audience, Punchinello forges a vital link with us. Unlike Christ, we recognize in Punchinello a consciousness separate from history.

Daly's tableau heightens the conflict between history and individual consciousness by a number of ironic means. Whereas Christ is overscaled in the tympanum, the dwarf is underscaled. Whereas Christ is beautiful, the dwarf is grotesque. Whereas Christ is sightless, the dwarf sees. Christ is physically separate from and spiritually a part of his narrative frame. The dwarf is physically a part of but spiritually separate from his context. As a result of this parodic structure, Daly's tableau not only recognizes the importance of critical consciousness, but understands critical consciousness as a source of Apocalypse, a causal factor that the creators of Chartres' iconographic paradigms do not acknowledge.

Punchinello's significance for the tableau grows from this comparison to Christ. Yet, Punchinello, by virtue of his profanatory role in the tableau, must be seen as an anti-Christ. This feature is crucial to our understanding of Punchinello's relationship to ideology. For Hegel, Christ is ideology's formalization. He is the initial substantiation of the ideology underlaying man's spiritual evolution. The ideology articulated is the Word.

Unlike Christ, Punchinello's major utterances are not linguistic. Rather Punchinello's intellectual posture is marked by laughter. In Sand's *Masques et Buffons,* Punchinello emphasizes that laughter is his primary means of self-expression: "Je suis le rire en personne, le rire triomphant, le rire du mal."[71] Whereas ideology is marked by instrumental discourse, Punchinello's anti-ideology is characterized by a vocal means that frustrates any linguistic instrumentality. Punchinello not only parodies Christ as ideological spokesman, but by his laughter, satirizes ideology, Punchinello is a critic of ideology in any form.

Ironically, Punchinello apotheosizes the role of the critic. He opposes all ideologies and historical schemes that ignore man as he is, impulsive and irrational. He knows the futility of historical and epistemological schemes as means to order man's life, for he speaks from the experience of history. By reason of his privileged knowledge, his role is to thwart holistic schemes of thought of any kind. However, in a perverse way, Punchinello becomes the final word itself.

As I noted earlier, Punchinello opposes the optimism of Enlightenment historical and philosophical schemes. However, he does not question a basic tenet which underlay those schemes, that there is a basic force which predetermines the actions of mankind. Unlike that of his opponents, Punchinello's attitude toward life is pessimistic. Like his antagonists, however, Punchinello's world view is essentially fatalistic.

As fatalist, Punchinello understands the way in which the world works. He conveys that understanding by overturning the false constructions of man's mind, his philosophical and historical schemes. Although his authority is carried in the form of actions rather than words, his power is as great as the philosophers. By dethroning philosophy, Punchinello's criticism takes its place. Punchinello becomes king of the farce that he perceives about him.

In the historical scheme, Christ the redeemer is supplanted by Punchinello the rogue. In taking Christ's place, Punchinello attaches special importance to Christ's privileged consciousness, imbuing his own performance in his comic history with a sense of prophecy.[72] Punchinello's prophetic significance was noted by many in the nineteenth century, including George Sand, Champfleury, and Charles Baudelaire.[73] Yet few of these commentators saw him as the prophet in a farce, a context placing the character's own prophetic *persona* into question. As prophet, he could be seen as a member of the *avant-*

garde, his superior vantage directing man to the future. Yet, as a false prophet, Punchinello's utterances are parodies of rhetoric; *en avant* becomes a mere jingle.[74] The dwarf might just as well direct mankind down the primrose path as along the yellow brick road.

Punchinello's pronouncements resemble more a monologue from a *commedia* presentation than a statement of ideology. His monologues are false ideologies, profaning philosophical paradigms in much the same way as historical. It is not insignificant that César Daly's essay "De la Liberté dans l'Art," which Punchinello's tableau was designed to illustrate, appears in three different periodicals. Each of these journals, the *Revue Générale, La Démocratique Pacifique,* and the *Revue du Monde Catholique,* espouses a different political and ideological stand: respectively, liberal, and radical, and conservative. This disparity is the final testimony of the havoc that Punchinello wreaks upon ideology. His written form juxtaposes systems of thought in much the same way as his person contrasts historical periods. By dismissing all, Punchinello fabricates a comprehensive profanation of popular social programs, and in so doing, constructs an almost universal critique of ideology itself.

The nineteenth century establishes Punchinello as the icon of criticism. He directs his critical weapons at all that seems solid and sure. Punchinello's club disintegrates the monolithic form of history. Its blows demolish the monumental structure of ideology. Punchinello's criticism emerges from the fray victorious. It is not surprising that the apotheosis of Punchinello parallels the apotheosis of criticism which becomes the mid-nineteenth century's reigning literary form. Punchinello's parodic sensibility transfigures criticism into a literary mode having equal stature with *Historia* and poetry.

It should be noted, however, that parody as figurative mode must acknowledge, like the others, a distinct ideology. Hayden White links parody with anarchism, hence imbuing it with ideological significance.[75] Once this is recognized, parody must be seen to turn upon itself as receptacle of ideology. This metatropological parody would leave intact neither ideology, nor any narrative structure conveying ideology. As parody turns upon itself, it begins the disintegration of narrative literature. As such, history falls out of sight as a legitimate realm for linguistic inquiry and formalization. Slowly but surely parody turning upon itself increasingly removes man from history. Man's alienation from history parallels his discovery of self. Surely, Nietzsche's conceptions of "monumental" history, Bergson's *élan vital,* and Freud's study of psyche bear the marks of man's increasing involvement with self-discovery. Linguistically, the result is the discovery of private languages and symbolic literary forms that have more to do with the workings of the mind than with the scheme of history and man's place in it. Rather, they seek the scheme of man and history's place within him.

This alienation sponsors a proto-existential posture which neither Punchinello nor Daly can really understand, much less approve. Both view the existence of mankind as the evidence of the antagonism between history and self. For both, criticism as a potential narrative form suitable for man's existence marks a balance between the two. We saw earlier that Daly as dandy fails to turn his anti-conventional conceits upon himself as new convention. Similarly, Daly as Punchinello fails to parody his own methods.

Daly's Punchinello must be seen as a character who cannot live external to the history he parodies, who cannot spiritually survive a final rent with his temporal situation. Hence, Daly's Punchinello remains essentially a romantic rather than a modern personality. Total self-consciousness separated from time remains ironically external to his own vision. The seeds of literary as well as architectural modernity lie planted within Daly's corpus, especially the *Revue Générale*. But they will have to wait another half century for their ultimate germination.

3

César Daly's Architectural Theory: Motifs and Their Composition

We now turn to the problem of interpreting César Daly within the context of the modern intellectual history outlined in the preceding chapter. Briefly stated, the intellectual developments of his time could be seen as involving a transition from a liberal to a socialist political position, from an empirical to an inductive scientific method, from sensational to metaphysical epistemology and from an instrumental to a poetic aesthetic language. Central to all shifts was a continuing reassessment of the classification of the human faculties, perception, and the place of criticism and personal genius within the overall historical scheme.

Daly spoke to these issues, and in so doing, marked continuity with the concerns and predispositions of his immediate intellectual forebears. Frank Manuel interprets the post-revolutionary "prophets" as crisis philosophers.[1] He sees these men, including Saint-Simon, Fourier, and Comte, as ideologues reacting to the confusion sponsored by revolutionary libertarianism. Manuel exploits a generalized psychobiographical technique to explain the early positivists' interest in order and systematization. Daly, like his spiritual fathers, might likewise be seen as the product of such a revolutionary *crise de conscience*. Daly's childhood bore important resemblances to those of Manuel's prophets. As noted earlier, Daly was the illegitimate offspring of a war-time affair between an Irish prisoner of war and a disinherited French aristocrat. As such, Daly's origins were impoverished and sordid. Stability did not arrive in his life until the return to his mother's ancestral properties in 1826. Perhaps the chaos of these formative influences accounted for Daly's early need to discover a social and epistemological order.

Unlike his intellectual forebears, however, Daly was an implicitly religious man. A sense of morality and a love of tradition pervaded Daly's writings in contrast to those of the pre-revolutionary thinkers, especially the *Encyclopédistes*. This predisposition made him uncomfortable within the circle of the stricter positivists. It was only after the Restoration made France aware again of religious and historical issues, that Daly toyed with utilitarian and liberal social themes. At this point the late writings of Saint-Simon and Fourier became important. In the 1820s Saint-Simon, as noted earlier, altered his mechanical social physiology, invoking the history of religion as a means of deciphering the epistemological and social order. Fourier's method remained a slightly insane syncretism of rationalism and positivism, as well as a collage of Christian themes and images of an apocalyptic nature. Like Saint-Simon, and perhaps Fourier, Daly saw in tradition a system of moral norms and an ordering method basic to much of his philosophical and aesthetic stand. The implications of this shift can be examined in a series of directed discussions.

The Socio-Political Departure

To turn to the political views under which César Daly operated, we first encounter an antagonism between liberal and socialist schools of thought. On the one hand, Daly tied social order to basic utilitarian notions of need satisfaction or social programmatics, an outgrowth of the philosophy of gratification which linked the eighteenth century—Bentham, d'Alembert, Rousseau—to the nineteenth century and Fourier. Daly emphasized, "L'ordre social conforme aux besoins de la nature de l'homme."[2] Daly implied a social order conforming to certain physical considerations. Generalized, this could further mean a system of free economy, based in man's right to work. This system further proposed that all men are entitled to wealth, provided they are productive. In an ideal sense this wealth would be commensurate with talent and labor.

Yet, clearly, Daly did not advocate a *laissez-faire* social or economic system. It is interesting to note that the liberal Rousseau stressed the innate goodness of primitive man. Man, in his primitive state, embodied a moral impulse. In contrast, there was no moral factor for utilitarians Bentham, Priestley, or Mill.[3] For these men, need satisfaction would eliminate any cause of aggression, hence enable men to evolve into a peaceful, harmonious society without any metaphysical imposition. As the French Revolution subsequently demonstrated, however, liberal and libertarian notions yielded little other than mutual hostilities, distrust and social fragmentation. Liberalism's critics ultimately reconstituted a moral order to foster a spirit of national unity.

Daly reflected these interests in the *Revue Générale*. Early numbers of the magazine were filled with technological innovation. In 1840 Daly illustrated the latest advances in bridge construction—the Town truss (plate 14). In 1842 he proudly displayed a mechanical street-sweeper, proclaiming its utility for public sanitation. Later, however, Daly turned from the technological to the institutional nature of society. In 1849 for instance, he lavished great attention on a children's *crèche,* an early display of the new social order following the 1848 Revolution (plate 15). Daly came to stress society's institutionalization, through which a standardized, high quality of life would be assured. However, the notion that men are entitled to certain cultural amenities provided by its institutions flew in the face of the liberal assertion that education, like so many of man's social attributes, was an acquired privilege and not a right. Moreover, in Daly's theory, government moved from its role as mere middleman, effectively orchestrating economy and industry, to a public task master, a defender of the public right and moral order in opposition to any special interest. Government took on a regulatory role as defender of the public weal.

Daly's vacillation between free and controlled economies was tied to both Fourierist and Owenite social systems. As noted above, Charles Fourier maintained class distinctions based upon wealth. Class distinction, however, implied a stratification in the social structure Fourier outlined. To combat potential social fragmentation, Fourier exploited a theory of passional attraction which focused upon man's activities, rather than his possessions. Especially important was harmonious labor, or "travail productif attrayant."[4] Passional attraction turned disruptive human motivations against themselves, channelling such vices as envy, greed, and competitiveness into productive activity. Moreover, passional attraction, the emotional link unifying mankind, became the basis of Fourier's social unity.

Daly, like Fourier, dabbled with economic ideas concerning division of labor and attractive or passional work. In his articles appearing in *La Phalange,* he spoke of the breakdown of labor into fields of specialization, in Fourierist terms "groupes" and "séries." Daly describes them much as Linnaeus classified plants by distinguishing genus and species:

> Chaque espèce d'industrie donne lieu à autant de groupes qu'elle offre de variétés, et chaque groupe se divise en autant de sousgroupes que la division de son industrie de fonctions.[5]

> Each kind of industry gives rise to as many groups as it has divisions, and each group divides itself into as many subgroups as there are functions of that industry.

Yet close on the heels of this statement, Daly effected a critique of liberal division of labor, as evidenced by his study of Robert Owen's socialism. Daly first criticized the libertarian tyranny of the passions, the utilitarian component implicit in Fourier's *épistème,* by commending Owen's ascetic socialism.

> Partant de là, il s'efforçait, de démontrer l'absurdité de la colère, de la haine et de la malveillance.[6]

> Departing from there, he [Owen] was forced to demonstrate the absurdity of anger, hatred and ill-will.

He recognized the value of Owen's paternalism and the equality of all residents in New Lanark. He particularly commended Owen's system of education, no longer the property of the privileged few, but the right of all.

Daly's critique extended to free enterprise. Although fascinated with technological advance, the flowering of the intellect fertilized by industry, Daly did not unreservedly accept scientific innovation as the mark of social progress.

> Les sciences physiques et cliniques, qui devaient servir à faciliter la fabrication des produits et à leur donner une plus grande perfection, ont été consultée depuis lors dans le but d'embellir l'apparence de la marchandise, souvent aux depens de sa bonté réelle...[7]

> The physical and experimental sciences, which should facilitate the fabrication of products and serve ever to perfect them, have been consulted for some time with the goal of improving the appearance of merchandise, often at the expense of its real goodness...

Disillusioned with production, he went on to attack industry's major sponsor, free economy.

> Les anciens économistes adoptèrent donc dans toute sa latitude le principe du "laissez-faire, laisser-passer"... [par conséquent]... La science s'est mise au service du mal et l'act de la falsification est aujourd'hui plus avancé sous beaucoup de rapports que l'act de la bonne fabrication.[8]

> The ancient economists adopted in all its latitude the principle of "laisser-faire, laisser-passer." [As a result]... science placed itself in the service of evil, so that today the act of falsification prevails over the act of good fabrication.

He criticized the disorder of modern society, primarily caused by its engagement in and involvement with such an economic system. Attacking the social anarchy caused by free enterprise and competition, Daly made his first major call for order:

> ...qu'en *morale*, en *science*, en *art*, et en *industrie*, toujours le désordre *appelle le désordre*, comme aussi *l'ordre engendre* l'ordre.[9]

> ...in morals, in science, in art and in industry, disorder always calls for disorder, as does order engender order.

Curiously enough, Daly's assault on *laissez-faire* economy did not force him to abolish personal property from his social theory. Property as the hereditary source of power (hence, historical order) was a realm unaffected by the supposed equalization effected by socialized economics. As a result, Daly leaned closer to both Saint-Simonien and Fourierist views—wealth being a necessary compensation for labor—than to the paternalism of the Owenite social order, with its system of common ownership of property, or to the early communism of the Icariens.

> Nous aurions à relever encore, ce qui est l'essence même de tous vos sermons, l'étrange confusion que vous faites entre la communauté et l'association; mais c'est une thèse générale

que nous reprendrons en temps d'opportune et nous aurons à défendre contre les mépris le droit de propriété.[10]

We will have to bring up again that which is itself the essence of all your [Owenite] sermons, the strange confusion that you make between community and association; but there is a general thesis that we will reassert at any opportune moment, and we will have to defend against all your adversity: the right to property.

As one of that class disenfranchised by the French Revolution and the Napoleonic Wars, Daly vigorously asserted the right to personal property. As a democrat Daly believed in equality in terms of human rights and personal wealth. Daly further believed in inheritance, a factor which called his egalitarianism into question. Ultimately, in his vision of society, total equality via equitable distribution of wealth was not taken for granted. Hence, we see that Daly's social system was increasingly fraught with social distinctions and discontinuities. Whereas an older social system might make distinctions on the basis of birthright, Daly's class structure, like that of other positivists, was based in merit. This meritocracy, like the pre-revolutionary class structure, would ultimately yield a social pyramid, each level having its own set of privileges. However, unlike class structure determined by natality, position in this pyramid resulted from talent. Modern society was thus stratified by positive means, yielding a class structure no less rigid than the pre-revolutionary.

The idea of the *phalanstère* as symbol or social order lingered in Daly's memory. Fourier introduced this architectural form as a means to resolve the problem of personal property, manifest in the parcelling of arable terrain, as against social unity. Within this structure, each household would have its own apartment, the size and comfort of which would depend upon the importance and wealth of the individual relative to the whole. Unlike the housing of the Owenites and *Saint-Simoniens,* which resembled nothing so much as an army barracks, Daly's and Fourier's phalanstery came closer to the modern-day cooperative apartment building, whose units vary in price relative to their sizes and locations. The Fourierist group dwelling likewise included a number of dwelling types, coordinated with the productive character types of the commune, the Harmonian social organization.

We are only too familiar with Fourier's sketch of such a *phalanstère,* designed on the model of Versailles. Daly recommended other buildings as models as well, his favorites being the Palais Royal, and a new building type, the residential club. For Fourier, the Palais Royal was the embodiment of the richness, luxury, and brilliance that life should offer all men. Biographers of Fourier, such as Charles Pellarin, noted the importance of this building for the socialist's own architectural forms.[11] The structure was likewise provocative for César Daly. For example, in 1840, he stated,

Le Palais Royal est un magnifique exemple de ce que peut le réunion d'un grand nombre de personnes pour donner de l'essor à l'architecture domestique.[12]

The Palais Royal is a magnificent example of what a large assembly of people can do to take domestic architecture to new heights.

Later, in 1863, he provided a series of details from the Palais Royal in his *Motifs Historiques* (plate 16). He first emphasized character in the facade of the individual dwelling unit, and second implied unity in the multiplicative quality of the type, ultimately yielding the structure's carefully orchestrated total form.

The second prototype informing Daly's social architectonic was the residential club, effectively portrayed in Charles Barry's Travellers' and Reform Clubs in London, discussed in the 1840 and 1857 numbers of the *Revue*. In the 1857 article, he discussed the social unity of such organizations as founded in the common ideology of the membership:

Un club anglais, on le sait, se compose d'un nombre limité de membres qui paient chaque année une somme fixe pour les frais généraux de l'établissement. Les hommes seuls y sont reçus. Les membres sont naturellement des gens que rapproche une affinité de goût ou d'occupation.[13]

An English club, we know, is composed of a limited number of members who pay fixed annual dues to offset the general expenses of the establishment. Only men are received there. The members are naturally those who share an affinity of taste or of occupation.

The Reform Club as planned constituted a curious duality. On the one hand, there was a series of public rooms and a floor of residential quarters devoted to the membership. The bedrooms were seen as identical, implying the equality of all involved (plate 17). Yet Daly also noted servant quarters, both in the basement and in the attic. Likewise identical in kind, these rooms also indicated a social class different from that of the membership, yet similarly homogeneously treated. Daly stated,

D'après ses règlements, le Club de Réforme peut avoir 4,600 membres. On en comptait 1,500 au moment où je me suis occupé à en faire l'étude. Il s'y trouvait aussi environ 60 personnes, tant employés que domestiques des deux sexes, aux gages du Club, sans compter les domestiques de passage qui servaient leurs maîtres momentanément logés dans l'établissement.[14]

According to its own rules, the Reform Club membership can number as many as 4,600. At the moment of my study, it is comprised of 1500. There are also about 60 persons, as many service employees as domestics of both sexes on the club payroll, not including those transient domestics which serve their master temporarily lodged in the establishment.

Ultimately Daly superimposed one class upon another. Although ideology was the unifying factor for one group, it is clear that the organizing factor for the other was merely its service function. Daly failed to address satisfactorily the problem resulting from the juxtaposition of class structures, ideological versus utilitarian. The club was treated merely as a syncretism, unified in form only by its homogenized envelope. Whereas the program of the Reform Club implicitly delineated class distinctions and the decomposition of a total social order, the elevations displayed for Daly composition and unification (plate 18). With regard to the exterior of the Travellers' Club, Daly stressed a formal unity based in its linearity and its window placement.

> ...Nous ne confondrons pas la monotonie avec l'unité, et nous félicitons... M. Ch. Barry d'avoir si convenablement combiné la disposition des pièces qu'elles éclairent; disons mieux, vue de l'intérieur, vue de l'extérieur, cette disposition semble avoir été conçue en vue de jeter quelque mouvement dans les lignes du monument...[15]

> We do not confuse monotony with unity, and we congratulate Mr. Charles Barry in having so suitably arranged the rooms of the interior so that they may take fullest advantage of the windows; better said, seen from the interior, and seen from the exterior, the inside and outside organizations of the building seem to have been considered with a view toward activating the primary lines of the monument. . .

Daly's treatment of the Travellers' and Reform Clubs as a social order in microcosm leads to certain realizations. First, for Daly, the building's form served as a middle ground between the idiosyncracies of program on the one hand and unity of composition on the other, subsuming functional and decorative consideration within a higher means of systematization. Hence, the buildings embodied a meeting place for variety and order, contingency and principle, not unlike the synthesis encountered in Cousin's philosophy. Formally, as Daly stated, the order of buildings, both in plan and elevation, rested in lines of composition, "les lignes du monument."[16]

The second realization stemming from Daly's treatment of the Clubs derives from his suggestion that club ideology be considered a means of social unity at least among club members, if not among the club's resident classes. By this suggestion Daly inferred that men were united not so much by their function in society as by shared belief. As noted earlier, this was Saint-Simon's later sociological stand, arising from a rupture with the liberal and social ideas held earlier with regard to material progress. The resurrection of a belief system, with its implicit basis in tradition, involved an inversion of the Encyclopedic *épistème*. For Saint-Simon reason, the supervening human faculty for the eighteenth century, was replaced by memory. History replaced material progress.

For Daly the role of ideology in the creation of social unity became apparent with the burning of Chartres Cathedral in 1836. He recounted how he became immediately aware of this building in terms of France's national architectural heritage, and of religion, i.e., Catholicism, in fusing the French people. Daly imagined the forces of religious unity in his steel-plate etching of the cathedral, dated 1837. He articulated his feelings some ten years later. In his *Introduction Traitant du Symbolisme dans l'Architecture* (1847), he described the realization:

> Seul enfin avec mes pensées, mon esprit obéit aux sollicitations du chef d'oeuvre que j'étudiais, et mon imagination peupla bientôt le vide que s'était fait autour de moi. Je voyais sortir par la porte centrale une procession d'hommes voués à Dieu et de petits enfants, dont le chant, d'un style large et simple, semblait faire tressaillir jusqu'aux immobiles figures assises dans les voûtes.[17]

> Alone at last with my thoughts, my spirit obeyed the solicitations of the masterpiece that I have been studying, and my imagination quickly peopled the void about me. I saw a procession of clerics and children emerge from the central portal, whose broad and simple song seemed to thrill even those stony figures seated in the tympana.

The exact provenance of the religious theme in Daly's writing is difficult to trace. It is certainly affected by the romantic spiritualist philosophies of both France and England, sponsored largely by France's conservatives, Chateaubriand and Royer-Collard, and England's Edmund Burke. Generally speaking, its sources can be found in the climate of thought simultaneous with the Restoration of the Bourbon Monarchy and the rise of French nationalism.[18] Surely an important source lay in contemporary German idealism. This factor became especially evident with Daly's involvement with the Cologne *Domverein* in Paris in 1842.

Cologne Cathedral became the *cause célèbre* of early nineteenth-century German romanticism and idealism. Encouraged in Germany by both Goethe and Hegel, the movement also received support from non-German intellectual circles. Most important of these was the group established by Heinrich Heine in the early 1840s in Paris to support the completion of Cologne Cathedral. Heavily populated by *Saint-Simoniens* and romantic spiritualists, this group agitated for financial support of the cathedral's restoration and completion.[19] Daly was a member of this group and in 1842 made a written contribution to the church campaign, *Du Projet de l'Achèvement de la Cathédrale de Cologne.* He noted especially the social program sponsored by the church. This he treated in his description of the throngs celebrating the church's rededication:

> ... Dès le matin, une foule immense remplissait le majestueuse vaisseau de la Cathédrale: l'espoir et le bonheur rayonnait sur tous les visages; enfin chacun se recueillit avec une solonnelle grandeur; on fût vraiment pieux ce jour-là.

Vers la fin du service, la foi inondait toutes les âmes, l'enthousiasme allait toujours grandissant, et au moment de quitter l'enceinte sacrée on se forma en procession...

Précédés par des trompettes et des drapeaux nationaux, deux conducteurs des travaux ouvraient la marche, portant sur des coussins les anciens plans de l'Eglise, puis venaient les ouvriers de la Cathédrale: les vitriers, et les peintres, chacun revêtu de tablier et tenant les instruments de sa profession, gaiement ornés de rubans et de fleurs. A leur suite, entouré de quarante drapeaux aux couleurs nationales de l'Allemagne et des pays voisins, était porté un immense étendard dont le champ était occupé par une image de la Cathédrale complètement terminée, et dont l'encadrement était formé par les armoiries des pays qui se sont déjà côtisés pour achever le monument. Les membres de la nouvelle société, des rameaux à la main, des palmes au chapeau, fermaient la procession, qui se composait de plus de cinq mille personnes.[20]

As the day began, an immense crowd filled the majestic nave of the Cathedral; hope and joy beamed from every face; each collected his thoughts and the religious ceremony was accomplished with solemn grandeur. We were truly pious on that day.

Toward the end of the service, joy innundated the souls of all present and enthusiasm increased in magnitude, and as soon as we departed the ancient precinct, we found ourselves in a procession...

Preceded by trumpets and national flags, the two labor supervisors began the march, carrying on cushions the ancient plans of church, then came the Cathedral's workers: the glassmakers, and the painters, each dressed in an apron, and holding the instruments of his profession, gaily ornamented with ribbons and flowers. Behind them, surrounded by 40 flags in the national colors of Germany and neighboring countries, was an immense standard of the completed Cathedral. Its honor guard was composed of the armoried regiments of countries who contributed to the monument's completion... The members of the new society, with branches in their hands and palms in their hats, closed the procession, which numbered more than 5000 persons in all.

Daly called this great social unity a society: "Une société s'est constituée... le 16 février dernier."[21] [A society was created... last February sixteenth.] The social link was the Catholic religion. Daly noted that at Cologne, it was important

... de réaliser dans toute son intégrité cette belle expression de l'unité catholique telle qu'elle fût formulée sur le vélin par son auteur.[22]

... to realize in all its integrity this beautiful expression of catholic unity, in the same way that it was formulated on [ancient] parchment by its medieval author.

Ultimately, Daly considered the moral order rather than the physical nature of progress as source of social unity. He thus was moving implicitly from the liberal or utilitarian social system, which denied metaphysics and morality, to ideology.

Furthermore, whereas the phenomenon of Cologne began with a nationalistic implication, Daly, like Heine and other *Saint-Simoniens,* recognized a social unity within the international sphere. Like other early positivists—religious and secular—Daly envisioned a total, worldwide social harmony. Like Saint-Simon and Comte, Daly foresaw a religion of humanity, a moral order by which all peoples might be joined. The common ideology would be conveyed by art.

> Oublions donc un moment des discordes nationales, ou plutôt souvenons-nous nous que l'art est une partie commune à tous ceux qui se consacrent au culte du beau; que les artistes aussi forment une grande nation dans l'humanité; rappelons-nous que sur les bords du Rhin on se dispose à terminer un monument qui sera la gloire de l'architecture ogivale; prouvons notre sympathie pour cette belle entreprise; qu'un pilier, un arc-boutant, ou un vitrail, portant le nom de *France* dise aux âges futurs que nous fûmes là, et que dans le temple chrétien, on reconnaisse un jour avec bonheur ce germe de l'Union des nations éclos sous le souffle de l'art.[23]

> Let us forget national discord for a moment, or more so let us remember that art is a common part of all who consecrate themselves to the cult of beauty; [let us forget that] artists also form a great nation within humanity; let us recall that on the banks of the Rhine, a people readies itself to complete a monument that will be the glory of ogival architecture; let us express our sympathy for this beautiful enterprise; may a pillar, a flying buttress, or a stained glass window carrying the name of France say to future ages that we were there, and that in the Christian temple, we may one day recognize with happiness this germ of a national Union budding under the breath of art.

Returning to Chartres, Daly similarly noted a reciprocity between ideology and the forms which convey it. Formal unity could be achieved in the process of architectural composition via regulating lines. Architectural composition, therefore, with its implied geometrical system, had a relation comparable to that of ideology to society. Moreover, in as much as built architecture could be compared to a structure of theory, architectural composition could be considered the externalization of the subliminal forces of unity, belief or religion. Daly termed geometry, "l'esprit générateur de la composition."[24] The generative act, linked with spirit, was, he believed, formalized by composition, "les grandes lignes de la forme plastique dans lesquelles cet art s'est incarné."[25]

To briefly recapitulate, Daly's social views alternated between liberalism and socialism. Daly was in favor of material progress like his forbears, the Encyclopedists. Thus, Daly acknowledged the importance of scientific advance for the lot of mankind. Initially, his economic position, closely related to his approval of technical progress, was likewise liberal, focusing upon the effective deployment of "dépenses productives" for technological advance. Yet Daly became increasingly disaffected with technology. Like so many of his contemporaries, Daly noted a lack of parallelism between man's physical and psychic health. He saw the potential deleterious influence of free economy on man's social development and unity. Hence, he came to attack *laissez-faire* and concomitant libertarian/utilitarian social forms.

With the emergence of a governmentally controlled economy, Daly came to advocate governmental paternalism, through which man's natural rights are protected. These rights and responsibilities comprised a moral order transcending contingency or need. Daly's investigations of this order, like those of the *Saint-Simoniens,* focused upon ideology, the repository of moral norms. Rather than philosophy, which he initially criticized as party to the liberal system, Daly focused upon systems of belief like the late writings of Saint-Simon. Such belief structures were most obviously articulated in terms of religion. Daly saw men as socially united in the moral order. It was in terms of an analysis of the history of religion that Daly attempted to develop a sociology. His social interpretation of man thereby moved from material to metaphysical considerations.

Lastly, Daly drew an analogy between social and architectural progress. His analogizing system found its source within the encyclopedic *épistème,* where all knowledge was unified synchronically in a tree-like order. Moreover, Daly used Turgot's morphological matrix of time-transcending filiations to construct a diachronic system of architectural progress which he equated with social progress. He thus used researches into art as a basis for interdisciplinary researches.

The *Encyclopédie* stressed differentiations in knowledge. Mental faculties vied with one another for primacy. Yet as subsequent interpreters noted, all facets of human existence were unified by an undefined yet nonetheless present germinal urge. Daly's social ideology, like the *Encyclopédie,* was more than a program of differentiation. Rather, it constituted a battle plan between philosophical oppositions. It sought to orchestrate antagonisms. *Laissez-faire* countered social responsibility; individuality opposed unity; detail countered composition; contingency vied with principle. Philosophically, these confrontations implied a general confrontation between idealism and sensationalism. However, try as it might, neither antagonist was victorious. In this battle between science and sentiment, neither system came to the fore. Rather, what emerged from the fray was the glorified process of opposition, a generalized dialectic, formalized in the artistic act.

Scientific Method and the Faculties of Mind

Like Victor Cousin, Daly used a social analogy to describe his epistemology and scientific method. Daly compared society to an organism, making a direct link between the study of man, together with his institutions, and the natural sciences. In a discussion inspired by Saint-Simon concerning "social physiology," Daly likewise provided an organic definition of a society:

> Une société étant un organisme, et les lois de la constitution et du développement des organismes étant la matière de la science physiologique, la science sociale c'est simplement la physiologie sociale...[26]

As a society is an organism, and the laws governing the constitution and development of organisms are the subject matter of the science of physiology; social science is simply social physiology. . .

Continuing the biological analogy, Daly further emphasized that society could be analyzed and evaluated like objects of natural science. Like Comte, he placed sociology at the pinnacle of man's tree of knowledge, as the most sophisticated and intricate field of human inquiry.

La science sociale est plus haute, la plus noble et la plus utile science qui soît et qui puisse être; c'est la science des interêts généraux de toute société humaine, ni plus ni moins, et c'est parce que la santé public est un intérêt général, c'est-à-dire social, de premier ordre, que l'Association nationale constituée en faveur des progrès de la science sociale, c'est-à-dire de l'étude des lois qui gouvernent les intérêts de l'homme en société, et qui ont pour but le développement de l'ordre et du bien-être général ainsi que celui de notre état moral et intellectuel.[27]

Social science is the highest, the most noble and useful science that may and could ever be; it is no more and no less than the science of the general interests of all human society, and that is because the public well-being is a general interest, that is to say a social interest of the first order, which the national Association created through the progress of social science, that is to say the study of the laws which govern the interests of man in society and which aim to develop order and general well-being in both our moral and intellectual states.

Daly seems here to associate social sciences with both pure and natural sciences, a view reinforced by his involvement with early positivism. Moreover, on first view, Daly's attack in these areas, paralleled positive method. Daly recommended the scientific approach of the positivists, described as the last in a succession of methodological advances originating in the empiricism of Bacon and Locke.

What was the positive method? Auguste Comte treated method in his discussion of *l'état positif* in the *Cours de Philosophie Positive*. He explained:

Dans l'état positif, l'esprit humain, reconnaissant l'impossibilité d'obtenir des notions absolues, renonce à chercher l'origine ou la destination de l'univers et à connaître les causes intimes des phenomènes, nous s'attacher uniquement à decouvrir, par l'usage bien combiné du raisonnement et de l'observation, leurs lois effectives, c'est-à-dire leurs rélations invariables de succession et de similitude.[28]

In the ... positive state, the mind has given over the vain search after absolute notions, the origin and destination of the universe and the causes of phenomena, and applies itself to the study of their laws—that is, their invariable relations of succession and resemblance. Reasoning and observation duly combined are the means of this knowledge. What is now understood when we speak of an explanation of facts is simply the establishment of a connection between single phenomena and some general facts, the number of which continually diminishes with the progress of science.

Moreover, John Stuart Mill further elaborated the positive method in his *Auguste Comte and Positivism,* and in so doing, linked English and French empirical schools. He stated,

> We have no knowledge of anything but Phaenomena; and our knowledge of phaenomena is relative, not absolute. We know not the essence, nor the real mode of production, of any fact, but only its relations to other facts in the way of succession or of similitude. These relations are constants, that is, always the same in the same circumstances. The constant resemblances which link phaenomena together, and the constant sequences which unite them as antecedent and consequent, are termed their laws. Their essential nature, and their ultimate causes either efficient or formal are unknown and inscrutable to us.[29]

Both authors asserted that the positive method should focus upon the observable externalities of phenomena. In their empirical approach, phenomena and their interrelationships remained the basic material of knowledge. Positive method sought *a posteriori* filiations between facts. This was an extrapolation of the old Encyclopedic epistemology implicit in the tree of knowledge, in which all disciplines, and inferentially all phenomena of nature, were seen as interconnected. The final problem implicit in the move from the world of facts to the world of relationships involved a quantum leap of evaluation and judgment. What might be reasonably asserted in the pure sciences, by virtue of its predictability, became much more problematical in the social sciences.[30]

Comte himself was aware of the difficulties of such induction from the social fact. To achieve the desired result—the ascription to law of man's acts in history—he felt a need for some kind of predisposing means of interpretation. He stated,

> Si d'un côté, toute théorie positive doit nécessairement être fondée sur des observations, il est également sensible, d'un autre côté que pour se livrer à l'observation, notre esprit a besoin d'une théorie quelconque.[31]

> If on the one hand, any positive theory must necessarily be founded on observations, then, on the other, it is equally apparent that our mind needs a theory of some kind in order to give itself over to observation.

In this shift, the empirical *a posteriori* method as the positive basis of knowledge came into question. The problem arose when the uncontrollable mass of social facts was orchestrated by the superposition of a theory, or by an interpretive structure. This theory became an assumption through which social observations were sifted and ultimately assessed. The result of such hypothetical induction was a vicious circle—the assumptions shaping scientific inquiry being identical to the conclusions reached. Such tautological thinking shaped the sociology of the positivists.

Like Comte, Daly recommended positive method to begin with *a posteriori* empiricism—the registration of the observable facts of phenomena.

> [La methode]... consistaient simplement à observer les faits et enregistrer les observations, laissant au temps le soin de faire naître de ce travail... la révélation des lois générales.[32]

> [The method]... has consisted simply in observing the facts and registering observations, leaving it to time to bring forth from this work the revelation of general laws.

To illustrate the program of scientific investigation as it pertained to archaeology and architecture, Daly noted especially the classifications of the naturalists, Linnaeus and Cuvier. Such comparativistic thinking is one of the major propositions of the *Revue Générale*. For example, in an article of 1852, Viollet-le-Duc argued in favor of an architectural history, perceived as a kind of "comparative anatomy,"

> Quand donc notre pauvre école verra-t-elle surgir son Cuvier pour nous enseigner cette anatomie comparée des monuments antiques et modernes, et pour nous apprendre à ne pas mêttre des pattes de lapin à un corps de singe...[33]

> When will our poor school see the rise of its own Cuvier to instruct us in the comparative anatomy of ancient and modern monuments and to teach us that we must not put the feet of a rabbit on the body of a monkey?

For Viollet, and Daly too, the campaign of architectural anatomizing should result in a filiatory structure by which styles could be distilled, abstracted, idealized. Similarly, for Daly, the positive historical program should seek to establish a historical line of progress, by which styles could be unified in a scheme of increasing architectural complexity and perfection:

> ... Une définition du Style en architecture, et une classification des styles (... comme les premières classifications des naturalistes...) marquait un notion précise de la loi du progrès social et architectural, des rélations diverses de l'Architecture et de la Société, ainsi que des liens qui rattachent entre eux les styles d'architecture...[34]

> ... A definition of Style in architecture, like a classification (... like the first classifications of the naturalists), marks a precise notion of the law of social and architectural progress and of the diverse relations between Architecture and Society, as well as of the ties binding architectural styles with both architecture and society.

The tautological nature of the method is apparent. Daly assumed the existence of a law of progress. He then went about illustrating the action of the law by appropriately classifying fragments in accordance with that law. He finally used the physical evidence to verify the law. Daly hypothesized the law of progress so that he could ultimately induce its existence.

We have just observed an example of the kind of vicious circle that permeated Daly's argumentation. The problem stemmed from a superposition of scientific methods—empirical upon speculative. As we can see, the propositional nature of logical argumentation fits uncomfortably into the positive frame of reference, too easily allying itself with unacceptable *a priori* assumptions. Daly directly confronted this systemic contradiction when he asserted the need for a predisposing theory to organize facts. He cited the importance of an *a priori* approach in contrast to the *a posteriori* method which characterized both utilitarian and positive schools of thought. For example, in an 1842 discussion of the politics of public works, specifically, roadways:

> Une verité ne saurait contredire unedautre verité...; donc, la bonté, l'utilité et l'économie doivent être autant de conditions de la beauté; ou, en d'autres termes, la bonté, l'utilité, l'economié, doivent être proportionelles à la beauté, de telle sorte que le système qui réalise la viabilité la plus belle doit réaliser en même temps les routes les plus utiles et les plus économiques, tandis que le système qui réalise la viabilité la plus laide doit réaliser nécessairement aussi les routes les plus mauvaises et les plus dispendieuses. La beauté est donc la boussole qui doit servir de guide dans la recherche de meilleur système d'entretien des routes.... [Il] reste à soumettre cet *a priori* à l'épreuve de l'expérience, et il ne restera plus qu'à conclure. [35]

> A truth would not think of contradicting another truth...; so, goodness, utility, and economy must necessarily be proportional to beauty, such that the system that realizes the most beautiful viability must also recognize the most useful and economical routes, while the system that realizes the least attractive viability must also realize the worst and costliest routes. Beauty is thus the compass that must serve as guide in the research of the best system to maintain roadways... we have yet to subject this *a priori* to the proof of experience; there exists nothing more than to prove.

This quotation is illuminating. First, we observe Daly's difficulties in argumentation. Daly initially proposed that beauty is affected by goodness, utility, economy, or that a subset of beauty's shaping forces are the three social considerations. Alternatively, however, he asserted that these three components may be used to assess beauty. Clearly, the first proposition does not imply the second. There may be many factors that mold beauty, including utility, economy, goodness. But this is not to say that these three considerations are the sole ones. In this case, Daly fell into the logical fallacy of taking the converse of his proposition as true.

Second, the superposition of inductive upon deductive systems, or *a posteriori* upon *a priori,* allowed Daly to attach a syllogistic, propositional logic to empirical interpretation. As a result, the proposition served as a predisposition or prejudice shaping interpretation, which in turn, reinforced the validity of the initial proposition. Moreover, in imposing logic upon experimental argumentation, Daly confused philosophy, and finally, metaphysics, with empiricism.

Daly cited the importance of philosophy for ordering and interpreting mere historical facts.

L'introduction de l'élément philosophique dans les travaux historiques modernes a fait apporter un esprit moins étroit, moins exclusif dans l'étude de l'historie de l'art, et par suite dans le *pratique* de l'art lui-même.[36]

The introduction of philosophical elements into historical research imparts to history a less restrictive spirit, less exclusive in the study of art history, and consequently, in the *making* of art itself.

The implication here was that cognizance of ontology could precede observation. This assertion was tantamount to a reinvocation of innate ideas as ultimate causes in the natural order, an epistemology that empiricism sought to circumvent.

In describing Kepler's moment of faith, Daly spoke of the interrelationship between metaphysical and positive epistemologies, of the consonance between religion and science:

It was in a moment of ecstacy, before the revelations of nature, that Kepler exclaimed the first time, "Mathematics are co-existent with God." And this grand man, at once so profoundly religious and so knowing, rather than pretend to formulate limits for the powers of the Omnipotent One, wished to emphasize the absolute perfection of the Divine being... His (God's) perfection refused him the power to act outside the conditions of order and harmony.[37]

The commingling of science and religion, which Daly described, would imply the need for a scientized religion or a deified science. The implication here was that the metaphysical should coincide with the scientific order. Daly's interpretation of valid scientific method finally moved from a conception in which speculation was separated from empiricism, to one in which these systems fused.

We have encountered a similar methodological consolidation earlier, in the psychological method of Victor Cousin's Eclecticism. Here, the facts of sensation—man's sensory empirical data—were idealized by the action of reason, the philosophical faculty. The precedence of the transcendental over the physical order of things was always implicit in Cousin's philosophy. Metaphysics provided a means for ordering the facts of life. Daly likewise questioned the separation of the metaphysical and positive realms of human knowledge and consciousness. In contrast to the present "transitional" period of history, which he characterized by "une separation de l'Eglise de l'Etat, de la Théologie de la Science, du Sentiment de la Raison," he sought an era of reconciliation between disciplines and systems of thought.[38] During such an organic era, he hoped to see "un accord plus ou moins parfait entre les efforts de l'esprit et les inspirations du sentiment; car la société est alors en voie de déduire les conséquences logiques du système d'idées qui la constitue."[39] In his "L'Architecture de l'Avenir" of 1869, César Daly came to criticize strict positivism expressly as "une lutte au jour le jour," seeking a method transcending empiricism.[40] In this method, the order of facts and essences would be reversed, with religion taking precedence over science. Daly asserted, quoting Vincent de Beauvais, "La Foi préside aux efforts de la Science."[41]

Daly's method clearly had moved far from the purely empirical method which he, like other positivists, initially encouraged. From a scientific posture wholly focused on the external facts of phenomena, he shifted first to a method of hypothetical induction, and finally to a metaphysic by which facts are organized and explained. In so doing, Daly paralleled current eclectic philosophy, seeking to fuse mind and body in much the same way as German and French spiritualist schools.

You will recall that the psychological method of Victor Cousin combined faculties of reason, sentiment, and sensation, or head, heart, and senses. These elements constituted human consciousness. Moreover, he saw the object of philosophy to be the elevation of the facts of consciousness to an ideal level, *le vrai, le beau, le bien.* César Daly clearly drew upon Cousin's method and classification of faculties in his own epistemology. For instance, in 1845 he stated,

> L'âme humaine [le conscient] presque tout entière trouve à y développer son activité; le vrai, le beau, et l'utile sont les divers aspects de cet art sublime, aspects correlatifs à l'intelligence, au coeur, et aux sens.[42]

> The human soul [consciousness] concentrates above all upon developing its activity; the true, the beautiful, and the useful are the diverse aspects of this sublime action, aspects which correlate with the intelligence, the heart, and the senses.

Slightly later, however, Daly asserted

> L'univers est un. L'industrie, l'art et la science ne sont que les trois grands aspects de l'unité universelle. Ils correspondent à l'utile, au beau et au vrai; qui sont aussi trois aspects de l'unité universelle; comme les sens, les affections et l'intelligence sont les trois grands aspects de l'âme humaine, ce miroir de l'univers.[43]

> The universe is one. Industry, art, and science are but three aspects of a universal unity. They correspond to the useful, the beautiful and the true. These are also three aspects of universal unity, just as the senses, the affections, the intelligence are the three aspects of the human soul, that mirror of the universe.

These quotations are interesting in two ways. First, Cousin's and Daly's psychological model provided a means for examining the inner being of man as well as the ontology of the world. This middle ground provided a resting place between the outer, or *l'univers,* and the inner, or *l'âme,* or as Daly later termed, the *non-moi* and the *moi*.[44] Moreover, consciousness implicitly assumed its own congruence with the metaphysical forces governing the universe, because of the reciprocity between self and other, mind and body, whereby the visible facts of nature could be used to inform nature's true being.

Second, the Cousin-Daly model posed certain interesting questions concerning man's actions, and their relationship to the faculties of consciousness. Despite the deism implied by "Le Bien" in both Daly's and Cousin's systems, Daly made a concerted attempt to purge action, described as "utile" and allied with industry, of any moral overtones. This fact stemmed primarily from Daly's continuing involvement with liberal and progressive epistemologies, most importantly, Encyclopedism. As noted earlier, Bacon's and D'Alembert's Tree of Knowledge proposed a classification devoid of reference to a moral order. Man's process of inquiry, the motivation behind scientific method, was likewise amoral.

For D'Alembert, art rested in man's imaginative faculties, treated as free, creative, shaping activity, unimpeded by historical or formal norms. For Encyclopedists like Diderot, art's alienation from history in the scheme of knowledge was the cause of its amorality. This was not the case with César Daly. There were few nineteenth-century architects more history-fixated than Daly. Although on numerous occasions Daly, like Diderot, cited the importance of spontaneity, or intuitive acts of artistic creation, he simultaneously stressed the importance of history to the process of formalization. In so doing, he made artistic creation less a spontaneous than a reflective act, tempered and informed by the norms of the past.

On the one hand, Daly commended the spontaneity of genius:

> Il faut donner à la tradition son contrepoids, et ce contrepoids, c'est le génie créateur de l'architecte...Ce génie devient d'autant plus grand, il s'élève d'autant plus haut, qu'il sait mieux observer les besoins de son temps, se pénétrer de ses sentiments, et se servir des puissantes ressources scientifiques et industrielles que la société moderne met à sa disposition.[45]

> It is necessary to give to tradition its counterweight, and this counterweight is the creative genius of the architect... This genius becomes ever-greater, and rises ever-higher, so that the architect may better observe the needs of his time, penetrate its sentiments, and make use of the powerful scientific and industrial resources that modern society places at his disposal.

Yet the artistic act governed by genius and characterized by complete liberty was not to be an end in itself. The bold creative act, like any externalization of will, was to be governed by an intervening conscience, directed by behavioral and artistic norms. Whereas technique lay in the realm of science, artistic norms were the property of history.

Daly also addressed the faculty of imagination. He maintained its importance as the legitimate basis of artistic endeavor. Yet he opposed unrestrained artistic creativity, or fantasy, by a counterattack of historical norms and scientific practice,

Dire que la science est *l'ennemie de l'imagination,* c'est dire encore que l'art ne relève que de la fantaisie et du caprice. De cette doctrine, à nier que l'architecture elle-même ait droit de prendre rang parmi les beaux-arts, il n'y a qu'un pas, et ce pas, quelques-uns l'ont fait...

Toutefois c'est commettre à la fois une injustice et une sottise; j'allais dire une impiété; et n'en est-ce pas une, en verité, que de nier l'alliance intime, profonde, indestructible de la science et de l'imagination dans les grandes oeuvres d'art? N'en est-ce pas que d'affirmer que le beau existe en l'absence de tout ordre? qu'il existe, et que l'ordre, qui est l'essence *mathématique* n'en est pas la base, et pour ainsi dire aussi *l'essence?* Le Beau, disait Aristote, en prenant cette expression dans un sens incomplète, mais élevé, le *beau,* c'est *l'ordre dans la grandeur;* et qu'est-ce s'il vous plaît que *l'ordre dans la grandeur* si n'est pas la regularisation par la science des grands essors de l'imagination?[46]

To say that science is *the enemy of imagination* is to say that art arises only from fantasy and caprice. From this position we deny that architecture itself has the right to take its place among the beaux-arts...Nevertheless [such a doctrine]...is at once injustice and foolishness; I was also going to call it an impiety. For doesn't this separation also deny a profound, intimate, and indestructible (spiritual) alliance that also exists between science and imagination in all great works of art? Isn't it yet to be confirmed that the beautiful cannot exist in the absence of order? That if (beauty) exists, is not order, which is essentially *mathematical* in its basis, and even its *essence*? The *Beautiful,* said Aristotle, while understanding this notion in an incomplete yet elevated sense, the *Beautiful* is the *order in grandeur;* and what is, if you please, *order in grandeur* if not the regularization through science of the great flights of imagination?

In Daly's formulation, artistic process intermingled imagination, order, and art. Art, as the recipient of beauty, combined sublimity (grandeur) and beauty (order). Morever, Daly emphasized that imagination must be restrained by historical norms to be revealed in archaeology. This must be a central concern of any artistic enterprise. He stated:

Tout homme d'imagination qui se complaît dans l'idéal, qui s'ennuie de la vie monotone de chaque jour, et se réfugie dans ses rêveries, pour y rencontrer l'émotion, la couleur, la vie heureuse qui manque à son existence habituelle; tout architecte,... enfin aimerait à coup sur les études archéologiques, surtout les études d'archéologie monumentale et s'en occuperait peut-être, s'il en avait une notion élémentaire quelque peu précise...O la beauté de la tradition! par vous le présent se lie au passé; par vous l'humanité reconnaît son unité à travers les variations infinies des races, des pays, des temps![47]

Any man of imagination who delights in the ideal, who is bored by the monotony of daily life, and who takes refuge in his reveries in order to chance upon the emotion, the color, and the happy life that his habitual life misses, any architect, any poet should at least love archaeological studies, especially those concerning the archaeological facts of monuments. The architect...should perhaps engage in these studies if he wishes to have a more precise, fundamental notion...O the beauty of tradition! through you, the present connects to the past; through you, humanity recognizes its unity across the infinite variations of race, country, and time.

History, in its association with religion, was seen as coexistent with the traditions and the concomitant moral order by which society is ordered. Likewise science, as the analysis of history and its laws, involved a prolonged search for truth. Science also was tied to a moral order. In making this assertion, Daly quoted Kepler, "les mathématiques sont coexistantes avec Dieu."[48] He subsequently elaborated his stand:

> Et si donc l'Etre suprême, si le Dieu de l'univers ne créa les merveilleuses beautés de la nature qu'en se conformant aux lois de la science, pourquoi, artistes, qui vous êtes admirateurs de la nature, prenez-vous ces lois en suspicion?[49]

> And if then the Supreme Being, if the God of the universe created the marvelous beauties of nature only while conforming to the laws of science, why, artists, if you are admirers of nature, do you hold these laws suspect?

Daly turned the Aristotelian dictum of natural imitation back upon the artist. True depiction of nature, he maintained, must deal not merely with the range of external situations which the world offers, but also with an underlying order— *la belle nature*—by which these events are orchestrated.[50] This basic order might be portrayed by means of typological representation, implicit within the rarified realm of man's memory, within history, as well as in properly induced scientific law. Art hence might move from a depiction of reality to unreality, from the merely natural to the supernatural, from the realm of the characteristic to that of the truly beautiful.

Daly's artistic position left far behind the liberal views of Diderot and d'Alembert. His artistic campaign proceeded along a route closely paralleling that of his major artistic opponent, Quatremère de Quincy, particularly in his assertion of artistic types revealed in history, and scientific methods of composition. Moreover, in drawing his aesthetic stance into line with a complete epistemology, Daly generalized his discipline, taking it into the realms of philosophy and ethics, concomitantly drawing it into a metaphysical *épistème* not unlike Victor Cousin's philosophical theodicy. He had moved far from the simple positive method.

To summarize briefly, the empiricism of the Encyclopedists and the positivists was crossed with metaphysics in César Daly's hybrid ideology. This was achieved fundamentally by the fusion of D'Alembert's faculties of mind— history, science, imagination—with Cousin's—intellect, sensibility, sensation. D'Alembert sought to demystify the artistic process by dissociating it from history. Cousin opposed this interpretation, especially in the artistic realm, where artistic creation was governed consciously by rational process or subconsciously by types stored in the memory. Daly replaced d'Alembert's libertarian notions of free artistic activity, with the orderly, and the residually academic doctrine that valid artistic creation must take place through reflective action.

On one level, Daly succeeded in deemphasizing personal genius as a creative impulse separated from history or science. On another, he elevated genius to new existential heights, by virtue of the creator's participation in a quasi-divine world. Competent works of art became apotheosized through their respect for and continuity with both tradition and reason. Daly placed the artistic enterprise between mind and heart, science and sentiment, mediating between them, and more importantly, supervening them in ontological significance.

Daly's early identification of art as a middle ground between fantasy and order, idiosyncracy and composition, was superseded by a system which saw an order in all. For example, Daly initially perceived a dialectical relationship between detail and composition. In 1854, for example, he stressed the importance of *motifs* to architecture, especially in their ability to contrast with and give variety to composition.[51] Daly formulated this interest in the publications of his *Motifs Historiques* of the 1860s, which concentrated especially upon ornament, and *L'Architecture Privée* of the late 1850s and 60s, which was concerned primarily with planning and compositional issues. Yet as his thought evolved, ornament was drawn into Daly's systematizing campaign, leaving little to the dialectical process. No longer interpreted as mere contingency, detail was also elevated to the level of order. Daly's aesthetic program succeeded in elevating all, in banishing distinctions between architectonic and decorative elements, rational and fantastic components.

Much the same was true of Daly's critical campaign. He frequently referred to his critical writings as *fragments* or *motifs,* implying that the formalizations of his consciousness were something apart from this conventionalized scheme of things. Criticism was an expression of his individuality, or sense of self, much as an architectural detail might be a foil to the architectural composition. He first noted the separateness or detachment of his own critical fragment from history and tradition.

La vraie critique n'est qu'un fragment détaché de l'historie des peuples.[52]

True criticism is only a fragment detached from the history of peoples.

Daly subsequently moved from acknowledging criticism's negative function to asserting criticism's positive role in shaping a modern ideology.

Une négation, c'est une pas fait vers une nouvelle affirmation.[53]

A negation is only a step made toward a new affirmation.

It would seem that the dialogical means of criticism was replaced by a discursive form, i.e., a rational aesthetic. As Daly stated in 1867, "There are no limits upon the liberty of the critic than those of science."[54] It would appear that

Daly transformed his role as critic, as commentator upon the *status quo,* into one of spokesman of scientific truth.

Yet, in a review of 1845, "Bibliographie—'Revue de l'Architecture et des Travaux Publics'," Daly is quoted as making a distinction between "la verité", or scientific fact, and "le Vrai", or absolute truth. It appears, then, that Daly saw himself less as reporter of scientific advance than as evangelist or prophet. He reinforces this interpretation in a metaphor wherein he sees his journal as a trail which he blazed, steeled by "Le Bien", through the "forêt de Nemesis", filled with "errors and false cries." The path—the *Revue Générale*—passed through the forest and led inexorably to the land of the True *(le Vrai)* and the Beautiful *(le Beau).*[55]

In this regard Daly swayed between the romantic notion of genius, to one in which his personal significance was mitigated by his utility, a social function. A genius for Daly was neither a romantic island, whose very alienation criticized social convention, nor was he the enlightenment figure whose value ultimately derived from his reading of the future. Rather, Daly saw the genius as an arbitrator, pulling order out of conflict or chaos, mediating between extremes. Not necessarily inspired, but indisputably dextrous, this was a man whose own sense of ideological composition served to obscure philosophical antagonisms by a form so persuasive as to leave his audience wholly convinced. His externalizations were shaped but not dominated by either history or reason. Yet his formalization could not be explained by imagination. Rather, in its ritualized incantation concerning man's scientific past and present form sought a vindication at once positive, metaphysical, personal and impersonal. Form was hence elevated to cult, transcendental, intersubjective and superhistorical.

Daly's notion of personal genius began at an epistemological gap formed by the relevant philosophical shortcomings. This was an ideational crevasse traversed only by way of his own personal form and style—his criticism. For Daly form could do all things. It could expand outward into the realm of nature; it could contract inward to the psychic realm of the self. Moreover, it could move laterally into science, society, life, or alternatively, into the most individuated realms of art. Daly's rhetoric, an inherently unstable admixture, sought to fuse, generalize, analogize all, under the cabalistic wrapping of its own form. Itself vital, it synthesized its environment, then reached out for more. Mortal as well, Daly's rhetoric lost its vitality once dissection of its form began.

From Detail to Composition

Daly's treatment of the individual architectonic element developed from specific and antiquarian to a generalized and compositional understanding. He began by thinking of the detail in isolation, as an end in itself. Later, however, he considered the detail in an expanded way, within the context of a larger formal system. We can discover the meaning of this generalizing process by comparing it with contemporary advances in the natural sciences. As we have already seen, Linnaeus' taxonomies of biological parts (plate 19) similarly gave way to Cuvier's treatments of anatomy in terms of unified bodily systems (plate 20).[56]

Daly's interest in archaeological classification began under the influence of Arcisse de Caumont. De Caumont's task, as set out in the *Cours d'Antiquités Monumentales* (1830-41), was the description of France's architectural patrimony. He first divided history into broad time spans: antique, Celtic, Gallo-Roman, Romanesque, Gothic; he then proceeded to dismantle various chronologically significant artifacts into their component parts. A single plate serves to illustrate the antiquarian's archaeological point of view (plate 21). De Caumont's "Tableau des Fragments d'Architecture Romane" juxtaposed Romanesque details of different locales sufficing to describe their characters as "zigzag, checkered, spiral," and so on. De Caumont introduced the descriptive, differentiating technique of the comparative anatomists into archaeological studies in France. The continued use of this technique by the nineteenth- and twentieth-century antiquarians has reinforced its importance. For the connoisseur these acute statements of difference served to educate the eye in its striving to understand stylistic and formal distinctions. Yet valuable as this approach may have been in the past, concentration upon detail tended to obscure other important formal issues. Most importantly, it underemphasized the interrelationships between parts. The understanding of compositional means transcending individual features, and the creation of artistic totalities, were important considerations within the artistic and architectural formalizing campaign.

For Daly an important shift in this regard came from the architectural contributions of Louis Batissier and the team of Albert Lenoir, Prosper Merimée, and Charles Lenormant. Each in his own way concentrated on the interrelationships between details, attempting to induce principles of composition. In 1845 Louis Batissier published his *Histoire de l'Art Monumental dans l'Antiquité et au Moyen Age.*[57] Immediately following its appearance, Daly printed excerpts from the work in the *Revue Générale,* supplementing Batissier's illustrations with some of his own devising. If de Caumont could be likened to an architectural Linnaeus, then Batissier might be compared to Cuvier. Whereas de Caumont stressed taxonometric differentiation and detail, Batissier stressed identity and composition. This was accomplished in two ways. First, Batissier provided classifications, not only of distinct architectonic features, but of different combinations of features as well. He gave a comparative analysis of composition, as illustrated in his plate of four different Gothic nave bays, or *Travées* (plate 22). Second, Batissier established filiations by analogy with the organic processes of life. In this regard the titles of Daly's illustrations of Batissier's theory, the "Tableaux Synoptiques," are suggestive. Cuvier's discussions of filiatory structures for natural classifications were also called synoptic tables (plate 7). Cuvier's tables imply interconnections of parts in terms of an anatomical subsurface, internal biological systems which ultimately established true identities. For Cuvier, it was not in the separateness of parts but in their interrelationship through organic composition that ontology, in the biological sense, could be ascertained.

Batissier's parallel illustrations dealt with comparable issues. On the one hand, the "Tableau Synoptiques" served in much the same way as de Caumont's "Classifications Chronologiques," by attempting to give a broad range and description of individual architectonic features assembled over time. One such "Tableau Synoptique des Divers Eléments du Moyen Age" focused upon individual details—archivolts, cornices, column profiles—and ordered the series in terms of date (plate 23). Clearly, Batissier chose these elements (for surely there must have been an infinite variety of choices for any given period), so that the juxtaposition of details illustrated a meaningful movement or flux, from simplicity to complication of forms. The judiciousness of his choices was best illustrated by the careful progression of column sections, moving from Romanesque through Tertiary Ogival periods. Evolution of form was persuasively portrayed, from simple square and round piers to clustered columns whose horizontal sections presented a complex interplay of circles and ellipses. Square, circle, square and circle, multiple squares, multiple circles, and all permutations in between, constituted a continual movement from basic Romanesque to flamboyant Gothic form.

The sequence from simple to complex implied an important biological concept. Not only was Cuvier's system of comparative anatomy suggested by Batissier's first tableau, the *Travées*, but a second notion was implicit as well—evolution. Daly discussed the *Tableaux* from the point of view *transformation*, stating,

l'observateur saisit d'un seul coup d'oeil les tranformations subies par chacun de ces éléments depuis le XIe jusqu'au XVIe siècle.[58]

In a single glance, observation seizes the transformation that each of these elements underwent from the eleventh until the sixteenth century.

He implied a connection with an important pre-Darwinian evolutionary theory, Lamarck's Transformism.

Jean-Baptiste de Lamarck first discussed transformism in 1815 in his *Histoire Naturelle des Animaux sans Vertèbres*. Four major assumptions shaped his theory of evolution:

1. Life by its proper forces tends continually to increase the volume of every body possessing it, and to enlarge its parts, up to a limit which it brings about.

2. The production of new organs in an animal body results from the superposition of a new want continuing to make itself felt, and a new movement which this want gives birth to and encourages.

3. The development of organs and their force of action are continually in ratio to the employment of these organs.

4. All that has been acquired, laid down, or changed in the organization of individuals in the course of their lives is considered by generations and transmitted to the new individuals that proceed from those which have undergone these changes.[59]

In the light of Lamarckian evolutionary theory, Batissier's development scheme had certain important implications. First, Lamarck proposed a cell, or *germule,* as the basis of all forms. For Batissier, this could be likened to the initial primitive circular column or square pier. Second, Batissier proposed a scheme of development, in which the germ, provoked by architectural or social climate, could take on fully new characteristics. Hence, the architectural, like biological, transformism invoked a scheme of material process and physical improvement, wherein forms continually strived for and achieved new levels of sophistication. Third, Batissier's scheme postulated a sequence of changes, which ultimately incorporated their ancestors. This was a scheme of history in which characteristics were never lost, but acquired and overlaid. Throughout history, architectural or biological form was seminally unchanging and constant, though it acquired an increasingly complicated external envelope. The exterior of any class of vital or architectural elements necessarily moved from a primitive simple state to a later complex one.

Daly first articulated his connection with Lamarckian transformist notions in 1847 in the earlier-discussed "Tableau l'Evolution des Styles," especially in his use of the terms "evolution" and "germes" (plate 4). Moveover, Daly depicted all of architectural history in much the same way as Batissier viewed the Middle Ages, as a movement from the simple to the complex. Daly discussed architectural progress some ten years later in explicitly Lamarckian terms.

> L'architecture de nos jours est donc forcément plus complex que celle des siècles passés; serait-ce un signe de décadence? Nullement. Sa complexité croissante, on le comprend aisément, correspond à un progrès de la société, à des raffinements autrefois inconnus, à une plus grande culture de l'homme et des rélations sociales. Cette marche progressive du *simple* au *complexe,* dans le développement regulier d'une création, est une loi dont la nature nous offre à chaque instant des belles applications.[60]

The architecture of our time is forcedly more complex than that of past centuries; could this be a sign of decadence? Not at all. Its increasingly complexity which we easily see, corresponds to the progress of our society, to refinements hitherto unknown, to an ever-greater culture of man and of social relationships. This progressive march from the simple to this complex is, in the regular development of creation, a law whose nature offers to us, at every moment, beautiful applications.

Like Batissier's "Tableau Synoptique," Daly's evolutionary sketch focused first upon the geometric simplicity and abstraction of the primitive germ, and then on a succession of permutations whose form depended upon both old inherited and new acquired characteristics over time.

Daly expanded Batissier's notions of increasing complexity of geometrical means. Whereas both Daly's and Batissier's synoptic tables stressed an increasing articulation and complication of detail and profile, Daly further described his evolution mathematically. The germ types for Batissier—square pier and circular columns—were treated by Daly in terms of primitive dwellings—hut, cabin, tent—and characterized by elementary geometries—rectilinear, circular, triangular. History melded these three types and complicated them via new formal concerns.

What was the source of this geometrical treatment for Daly? It was not Batissier, for he never spoke of geometry in his articles. Rather, it was the *Comité Historique des Arts et Monuments,* comprising Lenoir, Merimée, and Lenormant, whose "Instructions" stressed geometrical composition. Merimée's presentation, devoted to the Romanesque and Gothic periods, followed an implicitly progressive scenario. Generally speaking, he noted a development from abstract to naturalistic form during the period in question. For example, Merimée's description of archivolts stresses the initial geometric simplicity at the outset of the Romanesque period, the increasing complexity and articulation through succeeding generations, and finally the moment of "imitation plus ou moins pure," or naturalism, at the outset of the sixteenth century.

Concomitant with the historical scheme moving from abstraction to naturalism, Merimée proposed a diagrammatic means for evaluating the historical process (plate 24). This technique was depicted in two representative pages from the report, where earliest moments of the Romanesque style were characterized by a single circle, and where the full development of international Gothic was marked by a double circle, or by inference, an ellipse. This process might be described as a process of architectural mitosis, in which after a certain length of time, the architectural germ experiences a kind of convulsion, breaks apart, and ultimately duplicates itself. The resulting form implicitly contains the original cell, yet simultaneously presents a new, more complex biological art form.

The transformism of Lamarck and Batissier and the mathematical description of progress were fused in Daly's 1847 Tableau. Daly moved his

Lamarckian evolution through six major phases. The first introduced the primary formal "germs," comprising circular, rectilinear, and triangular typologies. The generative process began with the second "evolutionary" phase, in which the rectilinear system dominated. The third "transitional" phase merely juxtaposed orthogonal and circular systems. The fourth "evolutive" period synthesized the two. The fifth period contrasted all elementary forms and the final period, which included Daly's own time, should have fused all. This was to be the period of architectural form characterized by the ellipse.

Needless to say, the scheme had its difficulties. For instance, all three types existed as germs in some primitive phase of architecture's existence. Yet, what happened to the curvilinear and triangular systems while the rectilinear was evolving? How could some forms be shaped by time and others not? Did some forms deny or transcend history, rather than being shaped by it? These were difficulties that Daly hoped to rectify in his 1869 "Tableau de la Génération Géométrique et Successive des Styles-Types d'Architecture" (plate 25). In this table, Daly addressed the problem of the suspended animation of certain forms by assigning to each period its own distinctive form—primitive with rectilinear, secondary with curvilinear, tertiary with elliptical. In so doing, however, Daly lost the beauty of his Lamarckian scheme by eliminating "primitive germs", thus placing into question the essentially typological system.

Daly nonetheless maintained that architectural progress should be characterized by a scheme of synthesis, in which individual architectural components were to be drawn into new formal wholes. Perhaps even more importantly, Daly's publication of the 1869 tableau as a foreword to the second edition of *Motifs Historiques* officially marked Daly's move from considering isolated details to total composition, in which details were linked and orchestrated in a coordinated artistic campaign. Like Cuvier's notion of biological unity, that of artistic unity was accompanied by unified systems—structural, functional, or formal.

The architectural unity of Daly's system involved a program of conscious geometrical overlay. Batissier's *Travées* tableau implied geometrical relationships between parts in a synchronic frame of reference, at certain ideal moments in time. Yet filiation over time, the major preoccupation of Batissier's evolutionary studies, was a diachronic problem. Although linguists have disputed the possibility of establishing filiations in a diachronic fashion, Batissier and Daly in their "Tableaux Synoptiques," argued otherwise. For Daly, evolution was a historical law, regulating human events and shaping the future. Moreover historical, like physical laws, were mathematical. History, like any science, was orderly and logical. Once man was aware of this order, history could be manipulated and composed like a figurative architectural facade. For Daly, diachrony was as geometrical as synchrony.

Hence, for César Daly it was geometry that provided the unifying system in all temporal frames of reference. Viollet-le-Duc spoke to these issues in his articles in the *Revue Générale* of the early 1850s. He noted that archaeological taxonomy was not enough, but rather that order and identity were to be objectives of any scientific inquiry, archaeology included. Moreover, he asserted that this order rested in the logical order that man's rational faculty superimposed upon the facts of history. Viollet stated,

L'amour de la classification l'emporte aussi sur l'observation des faits; on pose des règles absolues afin de n'avoir pas la peine de constater et d'étudier les exceptions.[62]

The love of classification also prevails upon the observation of facts; [upon them] we impose absolute rules in order to avoid being troubled with ascertaining and studying exceptions.

He further noted that the formalization of this mental or psychic order lay in geometry. The implication was that the order of history converged with the order of the mind. Architecture, like the study of history, had its own sense of composition. Viollet noted that this compositional order resided in geometry:

L'architecture du XIIIᵉ siècle est plus encore peut-être une science qu'un art, et un science aussi positive que la géométrie, dont les règles sont basés sur les raisonnements d'une exactitude absolue.[63]

The architecture of the thirteenth century is perhaps even more a science than an art, a science as positive as geometry, whose rules are the basis of reasonings of an absolutely exact order.

Likewise for Daly, the impact of history on art, like the Lamarckian systemization of animal evolution was portrayed in basic compositional techniques. Much as Batissier and Merimée discerned, Daly traced in architecture a contour similar to that of the sciences, moving from simplicity to complexity along the outline of evolution. In "L'Architecture de l'Avenir" (1869) where he set out his theory of historical order, Daly stressed the importance of filiatory structure in both the synchronic and diachronic developments of architecture. He stated a need to study history in order to discover its laws, to find, "La loi des filiations géométriques et du progrés des styles types depuis les temps historiques les plus reculés."[64]

In the synchronic filiatory structure, the force unifying architectural elements was use and convention. In the diachronic filiatory structure, the force of unity was history itself. Yet it was history of a specific kind. It was a history built of laws, forces, and movements. It was a history hierarchically constructed of layers. It was a history striated by periods, characterized by their congruence with abstraction and nature, pantheism and monotheism, polygamy and monogamy. It was a history which was itself spatialized and turned into an architectonic. It was finally a history composed and geometrized.

The sources of his idea are not difficult to trace. Daly often spoke of men's lives, or personal histories, in a geometrical way, as for example, in his characterization of Napoleon:

> Météore brilliant, sa vie décrît une immense et harmonieuse parabole dont les extremités s'éteignent dans les ténèbres.[65]

> Brilliant meteor, his life described an immense and harmonious parabola whose extremities were extinguished in the shadows.

A similar idea served as the point of departure for Constant-Defeux in his linear, *Néo-Grec* monument of Dumont d'Urville (plate 26). Here, Daly's historical analogy of life took form. The monument's parabolic contour served to allegorize not only the stateman's death, but also his life and also his afterlife. Constant-Dufeux stated,

> Nous avons adopté pour le contour du monolithe la parabole; cette courbe si belle, qui décrît le projectile lancée dans les airs, et qui nous a paru être celle que l'oeil suit avec le plus de plaisir... Ici le but que nous nous sommes proposés étant un peu du domaine de l'imagination, on est obligé de se créer des données à soi-même pour préciser et justifier la forme qu'on adopte... [créée avec]... un motif vrai et positif de la glorification.[66]

> We have adopted the shape of the parabola for the contour of the monolith. This curve, so beautiful, is described by the projectile thrown into the air, and appeared to us to be that which the eye follows with the greatest pleasure... Here, the end that we have proposed, being somewhat of the imaginative realm, obliges one to create givens for himself in order to specify and justify the form that one adopts... [created with]... a true and positive motif of glorification.

The parabolic outline of the monument represented the trajectory of life, involving not only events, past, present and future, of the statesman's existence, but also by inference, our own imaginative life. Interestingly enough, the end of Dumont d'Urville's life history lay in an image of union with God in the hereafter. These themes were developed in the work itself. A frieze depicting Dumont's archaeological exploits encased the base of the argument. His voyages, and especially, his discovery of the Venus de Milo, were portrayed on it. At mid-point of the tomb, the observer confronted a bust of Dumont, treated as a herm, a classical acknowledgement of his death. Above, d'Urville, wife and daughter were apotheosized. Personal history was embodied in the form of this monument, introduced by general contours, then more completely described by composition and detail.

From personal history Daly turned to social history. He gained support from more generalized historical schematizations in the writings of Saint-

Simon and Auguste Comte. Especially significant here was Comte's Positivist Calendar, composed in 1849, in which all history was graphed in accordance with significant men and moments.[67] Moreover, much as d'Urville's history involved a religious component, so did humanity's. As noted earlier, both Saint-Simon and Auguste Comte assessed social history in essentially theological/religious terms. In so doing, they moved their focus from the history of material progress to ideological development. The shift in the historical scheme reinvoked a metaphysic, and attached valuation to the system itself. We are led to believe that a transcendent or vital urge underlay historical evolution, rather than any single physical law. The final emphasis on ideology marked a shift in mental attitude away from a material to a moral progress, implying the ultimate perfection of spirit rather than body. The emphasis was on the divinity of the workings of nature and society, and on the prophecy of a glorified future.

The diachronic systematization of all history in either *Saint-Simonien* or Comtian terms was an especially felicitous advance for predictive (or prophetic) progress. History's stages were now seen as a graph, and progress was that mathematical function that played across it in algebraic fashion. August Comte's famous dictum—"savoir pour prévoir, prévoir pour pouvoir"—focused upon the function of foretelling as the central concern to both historical and sociological study. Moreover, he compared the law of social progress to astronomical projection, an allusion which called to mind Daly's metaphor of Napoleon's life. Like astronomy, with its techniques for predicting future planetary positions, Comte noted that sociology could use comparable techniques of extrapolation, similarly leading to meaningful prediction. Daly made the same scientific connections as Comte. First, he emphasized the need for science, especially sociology, to address the problem of *prévoyance* (prevision). He asserted in 1845,

A la bonne heure! Nous acceptons complètement cette doctrine qui est aussi le nôtre; elle établit nettement la relation entre le passé, le présent, et l'avenir, entre l'archéologie et l'architecture. L'archéologie est donc un instrument destiné à accroître la science de l'homme, à lui faciliter les moyens de prévoir, et par conséquent de mieux faire que dans le passé.[68]

It's high time. We are accepting completely this doctrine as our own; it neatly establishes the relationship between the past, present, and future, between archaeology and architecture. Archaeology is thus an instrument destined to enlarge the science of man, to help him promote certain means of foreseeing, and consequently to do better in the future than in the past.

Later, he reiterated the Comtian, "Savoir, c'est prévoir."[69]

Like Comte, Daly's method of prediction involved a mathematical model for social history based on an astronomical analogy. In 1848 he advocated positivist predictive technique:

Lorsqu'un astronome veut déterminer la marche d'une étoile il cherche... à quelle courbe les points successifs appartiennent, et ce problème resolvé, il est en mesure d'indiquer la marche future de l'astre; un travail analogue est à faire pour l'architecture... La prédiction de sa position prochaine, est-elle connue?[70]

When an astronomer wishes to determine the movement of a star... he seeks the curve to which its successive points belong, and once this problem is resolved, he is in a position to indicate the future movement of the star; an analogous labor remains to be done for architecture.... The prediction of its future position, is it known?

Later in his career, he asserted that the technique is known. Expanding the astronomical analogy, he stated,

Vous me permettrez... de rappeler ici le procédé des astronomes qui, pour déterminer la trajectoire ou courbe parcourue par le centre de gravité d'un corps céleste, observent trois points qu'il occupe successivement dans l'espace et déterminent ensuite, au moyen de ces trois points, la courbe entière du parcours.... Notre prétention, pour n'être pas si grande que celle des astronomes, a quelque analogie cependant avec elle; car après avoir determiné l'expression géométrique du progrès humain depuis l'origine des grands civilisations jusqu'au future et à plus forte raison marquer exactement le point éloigné où passera cette courbe du progrès après une longue période de temps nous pourrons indiquer la direction générale de sa marche prochaine.[71]

Permit me... to recall here the process by which astronomers, to determine the trajectory or curve travelled by the center of gravity of a celestial body, observe three points that the body successively occupies in space; they then determine, by means of these three points, the entire curve of the trip.... Our claim, less grand than that of the astronomers, nonetheless has some similarity with theirs; because after having determined the geometric expression of human progress since the origin of the great civilization until today without pretending to trace the course of the future and with greater reason to mark exactly the distant point where this curve of progress passes after a long period of time, we will be able to indicate the general direction of its future march.

Ultimately, the progressive scheme, in contrast to mere history, generated a means to order the past, already situated by periodization. Progress penetrated the levels of history, giving it unity. As a kind of algebraic play across the imaginary graph of history, it proposed a superhistorical mathematical order, by which events, already meaningfully temporalized, were to be given value by an unfolding scheme of universal improvement. Moreover, like a differential equation which had no limits, this order could be infinitely expanded. The future was within its ken.

To recapitulate briefly, it might be said that a shift occurred in César Daly's historical point of view. Generally speaking, this shift involved a move from taxonometric considerations focusing upon isolated historical moments or episodes. It concerned an increasingly comprehensive understanding of moments conceived as parts of a whole, whose unity transcended the contingencies of any single temporal situation. Evolution, which gave individual historical moments an organic unity, was important for Daly because it was a progressive means of improvement embracing rather than denying the past. Evolution also implied a historical vitalism, giving Daly's epistemology its life. As a scientific law, the order to evolution was an essentially mathematical one, whether interpreted in terms of certain architectural germs built upon geometrical systems, or in terms of the algebraic equation of progress. In both views history was vital, but also mathematically ordered. The animistic factor of history was thus mathematized. History was organized by periods and united by evolutionary progress so that the confusion of historical (and archaeological) incidents was given both synchronic and diachronic order.

For César Daly and other ostensibly empirical historians, the past was assessed in terms of its social artifacts. Yet Daly moved beyond the realm of mere documentation or antiquarianism.[72] The past contained an ideology which served as the unifying force governing society for Daly, objectified in the forms that a society created. Modern society as history-shaped and history-involved necessarily reflected the historical subconscious, in which lay the intrinsic order of all time. The forms of architecture created by societies over time became for Daly the spatial embodiment of history. As a component of modern life, architecture needed to be synchronically involved in society's other involvements, whose time frame it shared. Lastly, architecture was to represent that vital urge which shaped man's life, but did not cease with man's passing. For Daly architecture was also to induce history's trajectory into the future, and ultimately, the social perfection of tomorrow. Architecture became a statement of past, present, and future. In so doing, the architectural program resulted in a glorification of the present, which simultaneously concentrated into itself the whole of history past, present and future. Finally it, apotheosized self, as formalizer of the life of history.

For Daly the life of history was in composition. But what was this life? Progress? Evolution? In the 1847 Tableau Daly discussed historical movement in terms of a religious shift from fetishism to monotheism, or from natural pantheism to an abstract, otherworldly deism. Alternatively, at the same time, he saw architectural history as moving from abstraction to naturalism, especially in Lamarckian terms. It was clear, however, that one historical scheme was incompatible with the other: Daly's artistic order contradicted the social. Neither the historical drive to abstraction nor to naturalism could serve as animistic principles.

Perhaps it was Daly's program of synthesis and resultant unity in social and artistic realms that served as the basis for his historical scheme. Yet if historical order was dominated by a movement toward unity as either Fourier and Cousin asserted, how then could polygamy, the ultimate form of material and familiar fragmentation, exist within Daly's historical system? These situations, pulled somewhat randomly from Daly's scheme of total evolution, indicate a basic confusion with regard to modes of unity between historical manifestation, and also illustrate some of the logical difficulties of any eclectic (Cousin) or synthetic (Spencer) philosophical position. [73]

It might be concluded that Daly's historical understanding was shaped by a series of fragmentary perspectives, each contributing to the architectonic, yet none individually dominating the scheme. His ideology could be viewed as a series of *Motifs Historiques,* wherein the historical events of France were somehow formalized. Yet, just as the architectural *Motifs* were countered by the compositional principles of *L'Architecture Privée,* so was Daly's eclectic historical system also ultimately ordered. This was not accomplished in terms of any single method of philosophical attack, rather the synthesis came from an absent, but nonetheless implicit formalizing consideration: Daly's own mind. Daly's genius did not merely document, but dominated history in his own acts of rhetorical form. Form, the externalization of all, provided a middle ground between self and other, past and future mediated by present. Form in itself became microcosmic.

Finally, in his rhetorical actions, César Daly consciously sought to deemphasize individuality and singularity. It might also be said that Daly tended to continually defuse or redirect any potentially dominating point of view. Rather, Daly sought an epistemological unity which might provide a means to attain ontology. Yet ontology itself was likewise questioned in his system. History was turned into a fiction. Daly was left with the artwork and himself. As noted earlier, Daly's formalizations were implicitly microcosmic. Ironically, they were also the only residents of his rhetorical world. In the vicious circle underlying Daly's ideology, in his campaign of total antagonism, only Daly's personal consciousness was left intact.

Literary Forms

Having discussed César Daly's attitudes toward architectural composition, I now turn my attention to style in his writing. Daly exploited three basic writing techniques, which could be termed the realistic, the dialogic and the poetic modes. The first technique, the realistic, characterized the greatest part of Daly's written *oeuvre.* It was both expository and practical. Generally speaking, his realistic writing paralleled his engagement with positive scientific method, stressing pragmatic description and facts in contrast to criticism. Daly explained his anti-critical campaign in the second volume of the *Revue Générale:*

Beaucoup de nos lecteurs se sont étonnés de rencontrer dans la Revue si peu de travaux de critique, et nous avons souvent reçu des observations à ce sujet ... Ensuite on aurait pu se méprendre sur notre but, et confondre la Revue avec les publications qui n'ont pas pour object principal la diffusion des connaissances utiles. [74]

> Many of our readers are shocked to discover in *La Revue* so few articles of criticism, and we have received many comments in this regard ... [It appears] then, that they have misunderstood our goal, and confused *La Revue* with publications which have not had as their primary objective this diffusion of useful knowledge.

The *Revue Générale* provided prolific examples of this utilitarian style. In the same volume in which he stressed factual discourse, Daly formalized his point of view in two distinct ways. The first was the list or catalogue, which succinctly enumerated statistics that convey information in a simple, comparative way. Particularly interesting in this regard is Daly's enumeration of American railway advances, mileages of track laid, and locations (plate 27). The chart, a favorite diagrammatic device of the Encyclopedists, provided the means of elaboration. Second, especially in the early numbers of the *Revue Générale,* Daly displayed a predilection for scientific formulae, which he described as modern hieroglypics.[75] The titleplate of the theory section bore the formula $Tm - Tr = 1/2(mv^2 - mv^{12})$, an allusion to physical, and I suspect historical dynamics. Such uses of scientific language heavily populated the theory, history, and practice sections of the journal. The scientific language was especially appropriate to Daly's positivist leanings. Indeed, such symbolic linguistic forms might be compared to that of the logical positivists a half century later. Scientific language, unlike critical language, was useful, value-free, cognitive, and perhaps the most impersonal of all Daly's literary styles.

However, Daly moved away from such instrumental writing techniques. This shift was motivated by his increasing disillusionment with the positive method, and by his critical position which sought a reevaluation of language itself. A second literary technique, the dialogue, was the most ready manifestation of this critical posture.

With the third number of the *Revue Générale,* Daly initiated a critique of strict utilitarianism, instigated by the Versailles train crash that killed Dumont d'Urville and one hundred others. With the disaster, technology's favorite son, the train, became suspect. At the same time, in 1842, Daly also composed a series of articles critical of free economy and *laissez-faire* capitalism, issues central to the liberal social view. His critical posture implied a dialogue between himself and the status quo, a confrontation of a new personal viewpoint and the current social and political convention, utilitarianism.

More than any other literary form, the dialogue posed the issue of mental reciprocity and critique. Although Daly exploited this technique infrequently in the *Revue,* limiting it primarily to the *Correspondence* section, he did use it in one important theoretical essay, his *Ce Que Peut Raconter Une Grille de Fer* (1864). The dialogue focused upon two interlocutors, *L'Architecte* and *Le Poète,* engaged in a discussion of esthetics. The poet was spokesman for spirituality or the metaphysical forces underlying the artistic enterprise of symbolization. The architect was the voice of function and pragmatism and his function was to demystify. Their discussion focused on an illustration of a piece of rococo ironwork. The first respondent, the poet, provides a romantic interpretation, communicated in Daly's prose style:

> D'ailleurs, je m'aperçois que ce dessin gagne à être examiné attentivement: j'y trouve par endroits, un peu à mon étonnement je l'avoue, quelque chose de moelleux; le cadre de la composition est rigide, il est vrai, on y sent la bâtisse, mais les accessoires ont certainement de l'ondoyant; ces branches fleuris, par exemple, se courbent gracieusement autour des médaillons à monogramme placés au centre des panneaux. Mais quels sont les noms qu'on rappelle par les lettres entrelaces S.G., S.V.... cette grille, en effet doit appartenir, à une église, et ce sont la des monogrammes des *saintes* assurément... Sainte Geneviève ou Sainte Gertrude, Sainte Victoire ou Sainte Véronique... ne le pensez-vous pas Messieurs et Mesdames?[76]

> ... Besides, I see that this drawing merits being attentively examined; here and there it is, I find, a little to my astonishment I admit, something soft; the frame of the composition is rigid, it's true; one senses something solid in this part, but the accessories have something undulating; these flowered branches, for example, curve graciously about the monogrammed medallions placed into the center of the panels. But what are the names that are recalled by the interlaced latters S.G. and S.V.? A light dawns, Madame: this grill, in effect, must belong to a church, and these are the monograms of female saints surely, not male: Saint Genevieve or Saint Gertrude, Saint Victoria or Saint Veronica; don't you think so, ladies and gentlemen?

The architect does not agree. He replies with a characteristic, hard, factual, commonsense interpretation. He criticizes the poet's attempt to personalize the historical situation, for in so doing the poet distorted the original, historical meaning. The architect asserted,

> ... Par vos interprétations, je pense que vous venez de fournir une preuve nouvelle de la réserve et de la mesure qu'il faut apporter dans l'appréciation des oeuvres d'art historique; et, je le dis en passant, vous avez également fait comprendre, sans le vouloir toutefois, combien il est impossible de reproduire dans les compositions modernes les anciennes formes de l'art, sans risquer d'en dénaturer le sens.[77]

> Your interpretations lead me to think that you have just furnished a new proof of the measured reserve that must be carried into the appreciation of historical works of art; and, I say, in passing, that you have also made me understand, inadvertently, how impossible it is to reproduce in modern composition the ancient forms of art without the risk of distorting the [original] sense.

He then proceeds to associate the style of the grill with an eighteenth-century *jubé* program at Saint-Germain l'Auxerrois, and in so doing, identifies the monograms:

> Les monogrammes S.G. et S.V. ne se rapportent aucunement à des vierges saintes; ce ne sont les initiales ni de vierges ni de saintes, mais bien celle de Saint-Germain d'Auxerre et du diacre Saint Vincent, les patrons de l'ancienne paroisse de Saint Germain l'Auxerrois.[78]

The monograms S.G. and S.V. do not at all relate to the holy virgins [of St. Ursula]; they are neither the initials of virgins nor of saints, but those of St. Germain d'Auxerre and of the deacon St. Vincent, the patrons of the ancient parish of St. Germain l'Auxerrois.

From his historical vantage, the architect destroys his opponent's poetic, as well as denies any kind of personal, value, interpretive or otherwise, in the understanding of the historical artifact. The architect is a documentarian, the historical empiricist.

These two points of view are subsequently mediated by a third party, Mme. X, the hostess of the salon at which the dialogue takes place. Her position establishes a middle ground between the poetic and historical frames of reference. On the one hand, she criticizes the romantic idealism of the poet, stating:

> L'antiquité...se gouvernait...par les lois esthetiques différentes de celles qui paraissent ressortir logiquement des croyances chrétiennes.

> Antiquity...is governed...by aesthetic laws different from those which would appear to logically derive from Christian beliefs.[79]

She maintains that art forms are affected by historical circumstances, and consequently, that art cannot be wholly based upon necessary and time-transcending principles.

On the other hand, she also attacks the pragmatism of the architect, who believes that art must result from natural and historical circumstance:

> Il me paraît incontestable... que l'art émanant d'une réligion comme la nôtre, qui exige la foi en présence d'insondable mystères, et affirme la possibilité d'une intervention miraculeuse à tout moment dans les affaires de ce monde, neutralisant l'action des forces de la nature par un pouvoir divin confié parfois à un simple mortel, il me semble manifeste qu'un art sorti d'un pareille source ne peut avoir pour les luis de la matière et de la vie psychologique le respect absolu que vous paraissez demander.

> It appears...that art, emanating from a religion like ours, which demands faith in the presence of unplummable mysteries and which affirms the possibility of a miraculous intervention at any moment in the affairs of this work, thus neutralizing the action of the forces of nature by a divine power conferred sometimes to a simple mortal—it seems to me to be obvious that an art deriving from such a source cannot have the respect for the laws of matter and of life that you demand of it.[80]

Thus it appears that Madame X's position entails a romanticism stressing the possibility of an "unfolding" idea, a body of ideology which is nonetheless conditioned by contextual circumstances. This context forces the poet to acknowledge the time frame into which his pronouncements were placed; it also forces him to take into account the linguistic discipline necessary to make both idea and circumstance communicable.

Both poet and architect come to agree upon her moderate point of view. The architect, for example, asserts the need for a poetic. But he qualifies his stand, saying that poetry too is a linguistic form, and as such, has a responsibility to communicate ideas. To accomplish this, it needs to conform to a set of syntactical rules, restraining and ordering the mere artistic caprice. Using eighteenth-century art as a point of departure, he maintains:

> Le XVIIIe siècle n'avait pas la foi profonde et la piété fervente du moyen age. Sceptique au contraire, peu réligieux dans l'art, peu préoccupé même de la Nature, mais amoureux passionné de la Fantaisie, il la laissait marquer d'une empreinte arbitraire ses moeurs, ses habitudes, ses parures. Il y a quelquefois une raison simple et toute particulière qui explique suffisamment certaines altérations des formes naturelles dans une oeuvre d'art comme celle qui nous occupe: c'est la nécessité pour l'artiste de réaliser une parfaite harmonie dans les formes matérielles de son oeuvre... Quelquefois il méconnaît ainsi les droits légitimes de l'expression symbolique; il sacrifie de l'idée à celle de la vue, le sentiment à la sensation, la poésie à la volupté. C'est regrettable.

> The eighteenth century did not have the profound faith and fervent piety of the Middle Ages. On the contrary, it was sceptical, and hardly religious in matters of art, little preoccupied even with Nature, but passionately in love with Fantasy; it permitted Fantasy to arbitrarily imprint its morals, habits, and adornments on art. There is sometimes a simple and particular reason to sufficiently explain certain alterations of natural forms in a work like the one with which we are presently occupied: it is the necessity for an artist to realize a perfect harmony among the material forms of his work.... At the same time, however, sometimes he is mistaken as to his legitimate right concerning symbolic expression; he sacrifices idea to physical appearance, sentiment to sensation, poetry to seduction. That is regrettable.

The architect consolidates two literary forms—poetry and logical discourse. He thereby invests literature with both structure and ideology. The verbal process by which the consolidation is accomplished is the dialogue. Ironically, the dialogical process, in rising above either alternative literary position, attained a super-literary status as language's arbitrator and judge.

Daly's third literary form, the poetic, did not deal with alternative ideologies in a critical way. Instead, via poetry, he fused antagonisms in a creative act. To illustrate Daly's poetic, I note especially his review of Constant-Dufeux' tomb of Dumont d'Urville, treated as a letter to the architect. This letter revealed the authors threefold intention for the review. First, Daly stated that the artist saw and interpreted the tragic moment of the train crash killing Dumont and his family in 1842. Second, Daly described the way in which the historical event informed Constant-Dufeux' artwork. Lastly, Daly portrayed the rhetorical means that Constant used in creating forms suitable to evoke emotions in an artistic audience comparable to his own as spectator of history.

In speaking to the artist, Daly focused upon Constant-Dufeux' consciousness, which was both audience of and participant in history. Daly spoke of the participating artist as one equipped to accurately and objectively chronicle the historical event, creating a journalistic narrative. Yet, when Daly addressed Constant-Dufeux as audience, he spoke of a consciousness which was super-historical, external to the action of history. As artist, Constant was a journalist. As audience, he was the receptor of the chronicle, the ultimate judge and interpreter of the verbal and pictorial narrative depicting the historical event. Moreover, each reference to Constant-Dufuex as audience referred to a larger audience, which includes ourselves.

Daly describes the scene to both Constant and the *Revue's* readership:

> Témoin et acteur dans cet horrible drame du 8 mai 1842, qui a donné une si funeste illustration du chemin de fer de Versailles (rive gauche), vous avez dû éprouver, en traçant les contours de ce tombeau, des émotions que seul vous pouvait exprimer. Placé au sommet d'une voiture du convoi, vous avez senté les premiers oscillations accentuées qui revelaient le danger; immobile au sein de ce mouvement impetueux, vous avez vu la locomotive dérailler, se pencher, creuser le sol et se précipiter avec une violence contre les talus de la route,—puis successivement entraînées par le fatal mouvement, les diligences se heurter, se broyer, rouler les unes au-dessus des autres, au milieu des charbons rouges et des nuages blancs de la vapeur brulante... cri déchirant, épouvantable, de cent victimes humaines torturées jusqu'à la mort,—ce cri, vous l'avez entendu retentir par-dessus le sifflement de la vapeur et les craquements des voitures incendiées. Et pendant que cet horrible tableau se créait sous vos yeux, vous vous êtes senti entraîné, précipité par une force invincible cette affreuse torture et cette morte—et vous vivez.[82]

> Witness to and actor in this horrible drama of 8 May 1842, which gave such an awful illustration to the Versailles railroad [Left Bank], you must have put to the test, in sketching the contours of this tomb, the emotions which only you can express. Placed above a carriage, you sense the first sharp oscillations that revealed the danger; immobile in the midst of this impetuous movement, you saw the locomotive derail, turn and cut into the ground, and then violently rush headlong against the train tracks themselves—then in turn dragged by the fatal movement, the coaches collided, overturned and rolled one upon the other, in the midst of blazing coals and white clouds of burning steam... [you heard] the heart-rending cries, unbelievable, of one hundred human victims tortured to death—this cry, you heard it resound above the shrieks of steam and the crackle of the burning carriages. And while this horrible tableau unfolded beneath your eyes, you felt yourself swept away, thrust toward this horrible torture and this death—and you live.

The quotation was provocative, particularly for its comments upon perception and ontology. What was Constant's and the audience's cognitive and perceptual mechanism? How did the audience see? It saw with its eyes, and also without its eyes. What did it see? On a conscious level, it saw a piece of architecture—Dumont's tomb. On an unconscious level, it saw a fragment of history. Vision moved between the real and the unreal, the physical and the imaginary. Yet this was not a fantasy. The audience's vision was an imagined moment of things and times past. The imagination that reconstitutes was not free, but restrained by history and memory. The experience of viewing Dumont d'Urville's tomb moved from mere empirical description, to something much more. The process of initial observation, dispassionate and analytical, was put in question as the viewer was transported into an imaginary realm. Yet this realm was not merely sentimental and subjective. Rather the world the viewer saw was a domain of memory, the resting place of historical types, an unreal and perhaps ideal terrain. Total knowledge of the monument involved perception and apperception revealing both immediate and transcendent significations.

By virture of complete knowledge of the monument, coming from transcendental experience fusing with the past, the audience was confronted with essential meanings (types), which, as Platonic philosophy asserts, were stored in the memory. Consequently, the limited, situational nature of the monument's empirical and critical interests became generalized and apotheosized, moving personal perception to impersonal truth. With regard to this move, Daly stated.

> J'ai le désir sincère, et je l'ai tourjours eu d'élever la critique, dont cette *Revue* est l'organe, à la dignité de l'histoire contemporaine. Votre discours, comme le monument de Dumont d'Urville appartient à l'histoire contemporaine de l'architecture française. Il doit être consacré dans les annales qui j'ai eu le bonheur de fonder.[83]

> I have the sincere desire, and I have always had it, to elevate criticism, of which this *Revue* is the mouthpiece, to the dignity of contemporary history. Your discussion, like the monument of Dumont d'Urville, belongs to the contemporary history of French architecture. It must be considered as such within the annals which I have had the happiness to found.

Daly's criticism of the monument was designed to have the same effect as the tomb. Daly's prose shifted from a negative to a positive style, allowing his audience, the reader, to expand upon mere discovery of circumstance or detail by participating in history with its full range of laws and symbolic types.

Thus, this poetic effort was seen to be something more than mere romantic evocation or personal fancy. The arbitrariness of personal judgment and romantic language was deleted from the sketch in Daly's depersonalized poetic enterprise. Clearly, many compositional techniques marked Daly's style, drawing it into context with both conventional and instrumental language. Daly's prose style was clearly crafted and structured in order to communciate the desired effects to the reader as if he were the viewer. For example, Daly believed the carefully modulated assonances stressing u and i sounds signal lugubrious and strident atmospheres simultaneously. Consciously onomatopoetic signifiers, such as *sifflements* and *craquements,* attempted to portray both sound and action. These and other effects characterized Daly's careful attention to detail and craftsmanship in shaping his art form. In such acts of fastidious composition, Daly was being self-consciously artistic. However, the assertion of self formalized in acts of will questioned ontology. To counter this factor, Daly raised personal consciousness to transcendental heights when he states, ". . . vous vous êtes senti entraîné, précipité par une force invincible vers cette affreuse torture et cette morte—et vous vivez." He elevated self, initially conceived as a passenger on the train and party to the tragic consequences of the accident, to the level of an entity apart from the incident. Daly asserted that the observer (which is Constant, himself, and ourselves) was first a reporter, then a victim, then an omniscient presence immune to the worldly forces that affect mere mortals. Ultimately, the observer and Daly, were seen as dispassionate, separate, and godlike in their visions. Perception circled from scientific observation to empathy, empathy to transcendence, transcendence to ontology, and lastly, back again to external observation and objectivity. At this point, the psychic process was to begin again.

Daly's poetic alternated between poles of subjectivity and objectivity, personality and impersonality. This he accomplished by treating his poetic first as a part of the realistic prose described above—analytical, factual, scientific. He subsequently moved beyond scientific restriction to an assertion of self in terms of critical consciousness. Much as the dialogue form attempted to stress personal understanding over any kind of conventionalized artistic or intellectual system, Daly's poetic emphasized the value of personal experience implicit within the perceptual process. Yet Daly countered the inherent relativity of the critical stance by idealization of self. At first he accomplished this by his careful craftsmanship and awareness of the means appropriate to effective and consistent communciation; then, by the connectedness of his personal poetic with a diachronic syntax extending backwards into his and humanity's memory. The resulting experience—dare I say synesthetic—confronted one not only with a real physical situation perceptible through the senses, but also with the norms stored in history, and history's laws, which when grasped, could lead one to the future. Hence, the written text like the architectural one became a time machine, by which mind could not move back and forth in time at will.

Submitting such work to positivist method is telling in two ways. First, as noted earlier, the inductive method involved a process of increasing generalization, by which perceptions were raised to the status of scientific law. Submitting Daly's poetic to the inductive method of evaluation moved the reader outward into the realm of ontology. Second, the process also moved the reader inward into self, which concomitantly became idealized. Self and other finally merge, forming an ontological continuum, focusing upon the work of art at the center of the inductive process.

I alluded earlier to Daly's poetic efforts as "synesthetic"; they serve not merely as stimulus for a set of impressions or sensations, but as an embodiment of those impressions. Experience of such texts placed the viewer into no hermeneutic dilemmas, but rather, confronted him with both psychological and physical truths. Daly suggested that his criticism could be taken as a *fetish,* in short, a physical art form which was simultaneously one with the idea represented.[84] In so doing, he intimated that form sufficed to achieve ontology. Such an aesthetic posture found close parallel in Baudelaire's theory of types as discussed in *The Painter of Modern Life*. Baudelaire's types mutually criticized conventionalized ideology and subsequently became the embodiment of another. The product of man's artistic efforts moved from the realm of personalized, individual dialogue involved with its environment, to an intersubjective, instrumental and ultimately cognitive art form. Daly's artistic stand may have begun within positivist scientific method and aesthetics, but it soon moved far beyond. Like Baudelaire, Daly occupied an aesthetic middle ground between the useful and the artistic, the factual and conceited, the critical and the ideological, the real and the imaginary.

Theory of Language

In the preceding section I established the ideal nature of Daly's developed literary form. I described it as poetic because of certain resonantly symbolic features prevailing in portions of his *corpus*. My inquiry now turns from issues of form to more general questions concerning Daly's theory of language.

Language, whether written or architectural, was one of Daly's major preoccupations during his entire writing career. A series of articles devoted to Louis Duc's July Monument of 1840 and 1841, published in the *Revue Générale* and *La Phalange* early testified to this interest (plate 28). He began his discussion with a formal analysis; then he posed questions of a more general nature. Daly described the monument centered in the Place de la Bastille as an "emblem" which signified both the French and July Revolutions. He saw the design as a kind of rostral column akin to Napoleon's Colonne Vendôme, erected in 1805. Yet Daly pointed to important differences between the two. He said the composite July Monument differed from the Doric severity of the Colonne Vendôme, in that it used a wider range of natural decorative devices and formal means (plate 29).

Daly's argument centered on the didactic qualities of both monuments. He noted that the two columns developed the theme of the *volumen,* i.e., the antique scroll, as a major decorative motif, but each in its own way. On Napoleon's column, the scroll winds slowly upward around the perimeter, completely enclosing it within its figurative discourse. For Daly the linguistic component implied by this metaphorical text achieved the monument's didactic purpose. Daly found the same to be the case with the July Monument in that it also implied a text. The difference was that the July Monument embodied symbolic rather than natural lexicography, not pictures of action, but written alphabetical lists of the victims of the Revolution. Daly commended Duc's progressive instrumental language as an improvement over the representational picture writing of its predecessor. In this respect, Daly's critical method was like Turgot's: both critics deployed modern written form as support for an abstract rather than a natural lexicography.

Furthermore, whereas the Napoleonic project tended to obscure the tectonic nature of the monument by its use of figurative means and by treating its surface as a pictorial *volumen,* Duc's monument clearly articulated distinctions between structure and decoration. Daly noted that the lists of the Revolution's victims filled the spaces between the bosses of false rustication. Vacant zones were left beneath the capital and above the base, and in these, the column's fluting appeared. Similar distinctions, decoration versus structure, were likewise carried into the July monument's capital. Unlike the column's shaft where decoration obscured structure, in the capital, natural forms explicated the order's supportive function. Figures of Hercules carrying garlands symbolized the structural nature of the column. The mere curvilinear patterning of other leaf decorations, the legacy of the composite order was subordinated to Herculean figures.

Daly's discussion of Duc's column contrasts the formal and didactic function with the Colonne Vendôme. Moreover, it seems that Daly finds in Duc's treatment of the texts an abstract language which displaced an earlier, natural one. In both architectural and literary form, then, functional and instrumental language took precedence over the veristic or natural.

Some forty years before Daly's discussion, Quatremère de Quincy likewise made a distinction between functional and decorative language. Natural decoration, which Quatremère termed "hieroglyphics," was an important component of primitive architecture, through which functional and didactic intentions of these societies fused.[85] In primitive architecture, all was allegory. Quatremère spoke of two types of allegory—natural and artificial—described as representational and non-objective. In preference to natural allegory, the critic preferred the artificial and the abstracted. It was in this world of abstracted language, fictional, artistic, cognitive, that truth lay. Quatremère elaborated,

> ...strange systems, which scarcely merit refutation, arise from the ignorant and false ideas which are entertained concerning Allegory, of which there are two distinct kinds. The first of these sprang up in the early ages of society, from the figurative mode of speaking and writing in those times, and which only appears mysterious at the present day, because the mode of speaking and writing have changed. The other kind appertains to the taste men have for fiction, and in this respect, differs essentially from the first; which although now the least intelligible is nevertheless the truest, being only a lively and simple representation of objects, affections and sensations, expressed in a striking manner...[86]

Quatremère noted elsewhere in the discussion that architecture's primary language could not have arisen from poetic, i.e., figurative sources, but only from constructed, artificial origins. He reasserted the essential rationalism of the original architectural language as demonstrated in "la cabane primitive." He asserted that functional necessity and utility preceded poetry and imagination, that "...the idea of making a shelter must have preceded that of making a symbol."[87] In so doing, he reemphasized that primary meaning in the structural composition of a building was like the construction of language and thus recapitulated his basic rationalistic stand.

For Quatrèmere the column was the basic element of architecture's classical language. It was first a structural element defying any natural or poetic signification. Second, it was an elemental form embodying an idea. Quatremère believed that articulation of idea was to be accomplished with the barest possible instrumental means. On this basis it could be assumed that the Colonne Vendôme defied Quatremère in its use of naturalizing detail, as well as in its indistinct rendering of its own structural form. The July Monument, in turn, could be interpreted as a critique of the Colonne Vendôme, because it conformed to instrumental aesthetic and linguistic positions.

Daly drew upon Quatremère's distinctions between natural and artificial form. He cited his debt to Quatremère's academic theory in a footnote to his discussion of the July Column:

> Il y aurait a ce sujet un travail très curieux et très interéssant à faire qui consisteraient à établir une classification regulier des symboles variés qu' offre à chaque instant la nature et des symboles dans les oeuvres de l'homme. Cette classification embrasserait ainsi deux catégories, l'une des *symboles naturelles,* l'autre des *symboles artificiels.*[88]

> There should be performed upon this very curious and very interesting subject a study which would consist in establishing a regular classification of various symbols which nature offers at every moment, and of those drawn from the works of men. This classification would thus comprise two categories, one of natural symbols, the other of artificial symbols.

In addition, Daly asserted the necessity of scientific symbolization and cognitive signification; as an example, he recommended scientific language, typified by the formula for momentum, $F = MV$. Daly hence likened instrumental language to the physical sciences, an association that Quatremère also made in his association of idealism with structural rationalism.[89]

In the light of this assertion, we see that Daly's and Quatremère's theories of language have much in common. How then do we explain Daly's earlier recommendation for the construction of Alavoine's elephant on the Bastille site (plate 30)? Daly's recommendation seemed to fly in the face of his own instrumental linguistic predilections: he called for a natural symbol over an artificial. This apparent contradiction might be understood as deriving from Daly's technique of situational argumentation. Daly argued that the Place de la Bastille, unlike the architectonic Place Vendôme, was a space defined by trees. The grandeur of the Colonne Vendôme was perceived only in relation to the smaller scale architecture surrounding it. In contrast, the grandeur of Alavoine's natural symbol could be sensed only within the context of nature itself. In this case, the urbanistic situation demanded naturalistic, poetic form.

On the incentive of Quatremère, Louis-Philippe's administration effectively suppressed the Elephant in favor of an artificial symbol: a column. Moreover, Louis-Philippe demanded that Duc's column improve upon Gondoin's Colonne Vendôme. As a result, distinctions in formal language were made more explicit. Daly noted these merits in Duc's final design, and he described them in terms not unlike Quatremère's. Daly states:

> Le Monument de Juillet... c'est une parole éloquente qui doit raconter en beau langage le fait qu'il consacre; en le regardant, chacun doit le comprendre sans interprète...
>
> Mais il y a une telle association entre certaines formes et certaines idées, que les unes, étant devenues les symboles des autres font trop souvent oublier que l'art doit satisfaire a d'autres conditions qu'à celle de rappeler un souvenir ou d'éveiller une idée par une correlative forme.[90]

> The July Monument... is an eloquent word that must recount in beautiful language the fact it consecrates; in looking at it, each [of us] must understand it without interpreter...
>
> ... There is such an association between certain forms and certain ideas that the former, having become the symbols of the latter, too often make us forget that art must satisfy conditions other than those by which forms recall a memory or evoke the idea of a correlative form.

Moreover, although Daly maintained a need for variety of details in architecture, his own formal preferences remained profoundly anti-imitative. He asserted, "Cette imitation intelligente tue l'art."[91]

The notion that architectural language is tied to ideation was central to Daly's linguistic theory. His was basically a Cartesian position, a point of view continued into the eighteenth century by Condillac and Turgot, and in the nineteenth century by Quatremère and Cousin. Instrumental language associated ideas through logical syntax, formalized in a rational grammar. Grammarians, beginning with the Port-Royal Cartesians, sought to formalize this conception, creating a language which was immediate, value-free, interpersonal, and logical. There was no period in French literature more given to conceits and consciously artistic than seventeenth- and eighteenth-century classicism. Moreover, it was as scientific as it was artistic in its search for connections between systems of thought and their externalizations.

Daly reinvoked the ideational nature of thought, and the necessary cognitive means of expression. Late in his life, Daly comments upon the Platonic conception that ideas are inscribed upon the memory:

> Tout édifice est une pensée... matérialisée. La première esquisse se trace sur le cerveau. La pensée inspiré par le sentiment conçoit l'idée générale du monument avant que le crayon n'en élève les murs.[92]

> Every building is a thought... materialized. Its first sketch is traced upon the brain. Thought inspired by feeling conceives the general idea of the monument before the pencil begins to design walls.

As we have seen, Daly developed the ideational nature of architectural thought in terms of typologies. He drew upon Jean-Nicolas-Louis Durand's *Recueil et Parallèle des Edifices* (1799) as a means to induce types (plate 31). Citing Durand, Daly also invoked Quatremère. Daly's interests in typology stemmed from his examinations of architecture utilizing a comparative method. In the resulting formal differentiations, Daly sought architectural germs or essences. The comparative method first articulated in his *Concours pour les Grands Prix* of 1842 was first visualized in the anatomizing of plans of his *L'Architecture Privée* of 1863 (plate 32). In this treatise, residences of similar programs and destinations are compared and evaluated. Ironically, typological ascriptions escaped his ken, and essences remained limited to their definition in terms of architectural programs.

Ultimately, Daly's linguistic interests moved from formal concern with a single idea, to the creation of an instrumental, artistic language. He realized that this shift entailed the problem of connecting ideas, and more importantly, it involved the issues of commuunciating complex thoughts between individuals. Communication presupposed that the mechanism by which speakers formalized their thoughts was compatible with the mechanism by which listeners interpreted auditory stimuli. This mechanism was logic. Hence, Daly sought to formulate a grammar of architecture congruent with cognition.

Although on numerous occasions Daly strived for poetic form, he realized the inadequacies of poetics for language's social function. For example, in his discussion of Owen Jones' *Alhambra,* he noted the present-day proliferation of personal languages.

> Les races humaines ne sont-elles pas aussi differenciés de couleur, de formes, de caractère, de langage et de goût? N'habitent-elles pas des climats différents nécessitant des costumes et des règnes différents? Comment se pourrait-il donc que ces races si dissemblables au physique et au moral, ne le fussent pas dans leurs manières de sentir et de concevoir le beau? Evidemment chacune d'elles a son sentiment spécial d'art, son beau particulier, sa poètique...[93]

> Aren't human races differentiated by color, form, character, languages and taste? Don't they live in different climates which necessitate different clothing and fashions? How then would it be possible that these races, so dissimilar physically and morally, would not be dissimilar also in their ways of feeling and conceiving the beautiful? Evidently, each of them has its own special sentiment of art, its particular beauty, its poetic...

Later, Daly came to oppose this formal variability recommending to restrain stylistic proliferation using taxonomic means. He likened his rarified classifications of the styles of architecture to definition supported by orderly architectural nomenclature:

> [Aujourd'hui] il manquait une définition du style en architecture et une classification des styles fondée sur cette définition; il manquait ... la nomenclature des styles, les sens des renaissances et des écoles.[94]

[Today] there is no definition of style in architecture nor classification of styles founded upon such definition; there is no nomenclature of styles, understandings of renaissances and of "stylistic" schools.

In citing Boileau's famous dictum, "Que toujours la raison s'accorde avec la rime," Daly noted that rational linguistic structure goes hand in hand with beauty; he thereby reasserted the classical academic posture toward linguistic instrumentality, artistic composition, and truth.

Daly's advocacy of an instrumental architectural language characterized his entire career. For example, in 1883, *La Semaine des Constructeurs* again asserted his connection with Quatremère's idealist school, when it reassessed Charles Landon's *Le Symbolisme dans l'Art* of 1802. Landon and Quatremère collaborated on the 1803 *Description de Paris;* this work will be discussed at greater length later in this study. Especially noteworthy in this regard was the journal's emphasis on Landon's recommendation of a philosophical language. In this reading, Landon's linguistic preoccupations were with the interplay of form and idea and with grammar's status as the formalization of a theory of cognition. In architecture, said Landon, ideas and thought processes were to be articulated in comparably similarly logical language. In general, Landon, like Quatremère, interpreted this linguistic structure in terms of the abstracted, classical language of architecture. *La Semaine* acknowledged Landon's typological preoccupations:

On croit fermement ... [says Landon] ... que l'antiquité ne s'est amusée qu'à des chimères, à la vénération des animaux, à des simulacres représentant les héros; que les anciens n'ont élevé des monuments que pour le gloire de surcharger la surface de la terre ... Erreur! Les types mystérieux, les emblèmes parlant de la divinité, les rapports qui la fécondent ... (existent toujours) ... [95]

There are those, he [Landon] says, who firmly believe ... that antiquity was preoccupied only with spirits, with the generation of animals, with effigies representing heroes, that the ancients only erected monuments for the glory of overloading the surface of the earth ... Error! Mysterious types, emblems speaking of divinity, the attributes of divine power imprinted on all their monuments, earth, the nourisher of human life, ceaselessly represented under ingenious forms, expressing all the relationships that she fosters; all these different objects have escaped modern researches, all of which have considered them to be arbitrary ornaments.

In addition, it seems that Daly asserted the need for appropriate manipulation of these types and ideas, with regard to the logic of the mind. He saw thought processes as translated into the terms of architecture's classical language. *La Semaine* continues:

Du symbolisme aux âges fabuleux nous parlerons peu cette fois, laissant tout à l'heure à feu Landon lui-même le soin d'arrêter d'un ferme burin, les traits éternals, et d'en fixer la véritable signification, dégagée de toute vaine utopie; d'en rappeler en même temps l'importance supérieure, avec une élévation de pensée que nous ne saurons atteindre.

Dans le mysticisme des premiers âges chrétiens, le symbolisme fut en extrême développement, héritant du symbolisme antique qu'il adopta a ses propres besoins et qui'il étendit à tout; il est alors bien près de remplacer l'art tout entier, et de substituer a l'architecture ordinaire, qui vit de piliers, de supports, de pleins et de vides, l'architecture *psychique* qui laisse les pleines de coté et se nourrit des vides.[56]

We will speak little this time of the symbolism of the fabulous ages, leaving it to the dead Landon himself to fix the eternal lines with a firm burin, and to ascertain the true meaning, detached from all vain utopia, and to recall at the same time a superior importance, with an elevation of thought which we will know how to attain.

In the mysticism of the first Christian ages, symbolism attained an extreme development, inheritor of antique symbolism that it adapted to its own needs and that it extended to everything; [Landon] is close indeed to replacing art entirely and to substituting for ordinary architecture, which grows from columns, supports, solids and voids, a *psychic architecture* that leaves solids aside and nourishes the voids.

Daly emphasized the importance that the notion of an apotheosized emptiness has for his theory of architectural language. The implications of this emphasis could be seen in the illustration of Charles Vaudoyer's "Maison d'un Cosmopolite" engraved by Landon, accompanying the essay "Le Symbolisme" by Daly and Paul Planat (plate 33). The house was characterized by an abstracted geometrical form. It was supported by a simple ring of Doric columns which carry a straight entablature. The indefinable spaces of the heavens were allegorized in the signs of the zodiac occupying the defined circular entablature. The two saw space, or the cosmos, as being signified by Vaudoyer's project, resulting in the substantiation of what was by definition insubstantial. This idea was not unfamiliar to Daly. For as we have seen earlier, Madame X came to personify the invisible dialogical process which structured the aesthetic argument of Daly's *Ce Que Concerne une Grille de Fer.* Daly saw Vaudoyer and Landon as giving significant absences shape. In so doing, they modelled insubstantial fictions—ideas—and substantiated ideology.

To conclude, César Daly's linguistic attitude drew close to the philosophical language standardized by the academic system. Daly's stand was rooted in the idealist/rationalist *détente* sponsored by Quatremère and his circle, which included Landon and Durand. It is interesting to note that idealism gave rise to rationalistic as well as formalistic stands in architectural circles after 1830.

Daly was not alone in his recommendation of instrumental language. The romantic, Viollet-le-Duc and the *Saint-Simonien,* Léonce Reynaud, whose *Traité de l'Architecture* closely paralleled the *Revue Générale,* both stressed the desirability of an instrumental architectural language.[97] The American, Henry Van Brunt, seemed also to advocate a cognitive language, as illustrated by a passage from *Greek Lines:*

> Like the gesture of a pantomine, which constitues an instinctive and universal language, these abstract lines, coming out of humanity and rendered elegant by the idealization of study, are, it is hoped, restoring to architecture its highest capacity of conveying thought in a monumental manner.[98]

On the one hand, Van Brunt advocated an ideal language made universal by its conformity to rational laws. He also claimed, however, that such language is instinctive. Thus, Van Brunt confused spontaneous linguistic acts with reflective, studied language. In so doing, he bypassed the problems of craftsmanship, technique, and willful composition in linguistic acts. For Daly instinctive utterances were important only in so far as they commented upon a larger cognitive system. This hierarchy allayed the confusion present in Van Brunt's discussion; however, Daly's method had its own problems. His system was inductive, thereby creating a tension of its own between spontaneous and conscious utterance. More than a rigor of method, it was Daly's own artistic consciousness and self that underlie any one of his literary enterprises. His refusal to acknowledge the involvement of self in science accounted for one of the spaces in his theory. As in Landon's architecture, perhaps that space too might be invested with significant form.

Religion, Ritual, Rhetoric

As noted in the preceding section, Daly's linguistic theory was legitimized by ideological and cognitive structures. His attack upon poetic language was constant. In 1852, for instance, Daly's sometime collaborator, Ruprich Robert, attacked personal language in favor of linguistic purity:

> ... pour faire partager ses impressions, il faut parler juste; la poésie est incomplète sans la pureté de language.[99]

> ... in order to share one's impressions, one must talk correctly; poetry is incomplete without the purity of language.

As we have just seen, this purity lay in a grammar, the outcome of considerations of cognitive structures. Such instrumentality was to be the basis of intersubjectivity, the assumption upon which all social language was predicated. Daly stated,

> La raison est la même pour tout le monde: on ne peut pas avoir raison contre raison.[100]

> Reason is the same for everyone; one cannot have reason against reason.

Consequently, it appeared that Daly valued rational language over any kind of self-consciously artistic, personal poetic.

Yet Daly's logical formal stance was put into question by the inclusion of certain explicitly poetic projects in the *Revue Générale*. Daly used the occasion of the Paris Opera competition to discuss the nature of the monumental building which was devoted to art and poetry. He accomplished his analysis by establishing an analogy between architecture and opera as *Gesamtkunstwerk*. Daly saw an inherent reciprocity existing between theatrical and architectural forms. The poetic mission of this building was not seen as utilitarian but inspirational:

> [La] mission [de l'Opéra] est d'élever sans cesse les âmes par le sentiment du beau, et de donner un corps palpable à l'idée: [l'Opéra est]...une aile ouverte sur l'infini.[101]

> The mission [of the Opéra] is ceaselessly to elevate souls by the feeling of beauty, and to give palpable substance to this idea; [the Opéra is]...a wing open to infinity.

Moreover, he commended Joseph Nicolle's stable at Marly as a work of utmost poetry involving individuality and private language (plate 34):

> Je loue sans réserve cette jolie composition; elle est pénétré d'un sentiment à la fois profond et naif, il y a une communication intime de l'artiste avec son sujet...Les artistes archéologiques, n'y reconnaissant aucun style historique, seront aussi tentés de passer outre; mais vous jeunes gens, vous poètes, qui sentez des battements sous la mamelle gauche, arrêtez-vous quelques instants, vous avez sous les yeux un oeuvre d'art véritable.[102]

> I praise without reserve this pretty composition, it is penetrated with a sentiment simultaneously profound and naive; there is an intimate communication of the artist with his subject...Archeological artists, not recognizing any historical style in it, would be tempted to pass it over, but you young people, you poets, who feel a beating under your left breast, stop for a few moments: you have under your eyes a true work of art.

Here, Daly alludes to an artistic rationale that transcended logic or use, recognizing art forms that were personal, natural, and finally, non-historical. The implication was that the careful structure of ideology, and its concomitant rational theory of cognition was condemned by a theory which divorced itself from rational typologies and philosophical thought processes of any kind. Rather than stressing reason in consciousness, it emphasized sentiment in terms of "les battements sous la mamelle gauche." Daly came to address this duality.

He spoke to the problem of consciousness in his later writings. Moving away from a belief in ideology that superseded self, Daly took a mediate position between ideology and sensation. No longer was art to be merely equated with philosophy or religion. Art came to dominate both. This was accomplished by a dissection of ideology, discussed in terms of religion, into components of dogma, morality, and liturgy.

Daly associated dogma with the intellectual faculty. As such, it became the director of reflective action. Morality and sentiment informed man's instinct. Art had to be associated with liturgy, moving between reason and feeling. It focused upon neither intellectual nor social norms. Ideology and morality were both absent from art. Rather, liturgy dealt with human will, volition, the ultimate cause behind any action, artistic or otherwise. With respect to dogma and morality Daly stated,

> Les réligions, en effect, se sont adressés à l'intelligence humaine par leurs dogmes et les dogmes ont été invariablement d'accord avec la science contemporaine au moment de leur adoption... ; les réligions s'adressent au sentiment contemporaine par leur morale...[103]

> In effect, religions are addressed to human intelligence by their dogmas, and dogmas have invariably been in agreement with contemporary science at the moment of their adoption... ; religions address themselves to contemporary sentiment by their morals.

With regard to cult, or the formalization of the artistic impulse, Daly stated that

> ... les réligions, par leurs, *rites et ceremonies* s'adressent *à nos sens esthetiques*...[104]

> ... religions, by their *rites and ceremonies* address themselves to our esthetic senses ...

Moreover,

> Le culte, ou l'ensemble des cérémonies exterieures de la réligion, emprunte ses ressources au sentiment de la poésie et l'esthétique.[105]

> Worship, or the collection of the external ceremonies of religion, borrows its means from the feeling of poetry and aesthetics.

Daly's tripartite division of religion parallels similar schemes in the philosophies of Victor Cousin and Encyclopedists. For example, the categories of mind, sensation and sensibility were popularized by Victor Cousin's Eclecticism. In contrast to Cousin, however, Daly links ritual to more than one of these categories. He discusses *culte* in terms of mind, or "esthetic," and sensation, thereby making links where Cousin had carefully marked distinctions. Similarly, Daly blurs distinctions between Cousin's idealistic epistemology and the empirical method. He interrelates aesthetic, deriving from man's rational faculties, with sensation, presumed by the Baconian and Lockean method of Encyclopedists to be the mechanics of consciousness. As Daly uses ritual to concentrate various faculties of mind into one form, so does Daly see in ritual a middle ground between two opposing schools of thought.

It seems that Daly accomplishes this conjoining via a number of very legitimate scientific principles of the day. The first is the comprehensive matrix of mind proposed by the Encyclopedists. The *détente* between Turgot's diachronic transformations of language and d'Alembert's synchronic classification of mind suggests that all aspects of man's intelligent faculties are necessarily interrelated over time, and that any of man's faculties necessarily connects to others. Second, the tranformism of Lamarckian evolution and Comte's positivistic "progress" both suggest that each attribute of mind has gone through a developmental process wherein it has built upon, and absorbed, others. Comte, of course, placed "sociology" at the summit of this ladder of progress. Daly, on the other hand, placed art in this location.

As an analogue for art, ritual, in Daly's view, is the most complex, the most synthetic of religion's various manifestations. It is consequently the most elevated in significance. Ritual is not controlled by either ideology or morality, and is not subservient to the ideas it incorporates. It constitutes not an icon of belief, but rather, a fetish. The art-fetish does not allude to a body of ideas so much as it embodies those ideas. The result in Daly's view is the fusion of art and the idea, by which a quasi-divine entity is created.

We might observe a parallel between Daly's eclectic philosophical program and the conflicted cosmology of Fourier, as discussed in chapter 2. The comparison is useful because art occupies a place in Daly's scheme similar to that which Fourier occupies in his own cosmology. Earlier, I argued that Fourier's cosmology was less a rational than an imaginative act. Here, as we have seen, Daly connects *culte* with poetry, imagination's most distinctive form in the view of the Encyclopedists. In consequence, it can be concluded that imagination is the underpinning of what is for Daly a hieratic human act.[106]

Much as we might say that the shape of Fourier's cosmology reflected the arcane workings of his mind, so might we say that Daly's view of art was similarly indebted to the imaginative faculty. Art, for Daly, was the focus of epistemology, and thus moved from the periphery of various epistemological circles to the center. Consequently, art became an epistemological circle whose empty center came to be occupied by César Daly's own creative consciousness.

It is not immaterial that the editorship of *La Semaine des Constructeurs,* i.e., Daly and Planat, came to regard emptiness in architecture in a substantive way. For example, Daly and Planat viewed the intercolumniations of Vaudoyer's "House of a Cosmopolite" not so much as simple voids as "l'espace psychique," i.e., as space pregnant with the presence of human consciousness. Such space was occupied, the two suggest, by Vaudoyer's creativity. Various Romantic theoreticians had discussed similar spaces in comparable terms: 'rent', 'pause', 'Verfremdung'.[107] These terms all visualize a gap between perception and cognition inhabited by the real life of the mind, imagination.

It might be said that the workings of imagination are less indebted to ratiocination than to unknown processes whose manifestations exploit forms contained within both nature and memory. At once perceptual and cognitive, imagination supersedes both. For it is in the act of imagining that man creates, becoming most godlike. Does it then seem so surprising that Daly replaces a religion subservient to ideology with one that sees art as the active workings of God in man?

If one wishes to discover the ultimate religion of César Daly, one must look beyond his pronouncements, examining those imaginative processes from which they derive. Daly's writing must be seen as creative rather than functional, and must be evaluated in formalistic as well as in philosophical terms. This approach explicitly deemphasizes signification and meaning, and implicitly places into question that linguistic instrumentality to which we historians are so indebted. I propose that we look at Daly's written legacy as ultimately personal and poetic—as so many imaginative acts pulling order from the chaos of differences. In this regard, a citation from the poetry of W.H. Auden is provocative:

> For poetry makes nothing happen it survives
> In the valleys of its saying where executives
> Would never want to tamper; it flows south
> From ranches of isolation and the busy griefs,
> Raw towns that we believe and die in; it survives
> a way of happening, a mouth. [108]

This mouth metonymizes a way of happening, a creative process. It is in searching for the immanent, creative process, somewhere between science and sentiment, that we will be able to discovery the essence of César Daly's positive theory of architecture.

4

History and the Cathedral

For César Daly there were two varieties of text. From our experience in earlier chapters, we have become familiar and comfortable with the first type—the written. Up to this point, however, the second type of text—the architectural—has been more elusive. Whereas César Daly left an enormous legacy of written texts, the number of his built works was small indeed. As we have already seen, the Daly corpus can be subjected to a number of literary distillations, of hermeneutic examinations, to assess the author's system of thought, intellectual provenance, and value system, by which his analysis and evaluation took place. Much as with prose, the work of architecture, or the architectural text, might be submitted to similar examinations for purposes of determining meaning.

Victor Hugo writes on the idea of building as book in his *Notre-Dame de Paris.* The chapter, entitled "This Will Destroy That" deals primarily with the problem of ideology and its formal expression, especially in human institutions. He states,

> ... during the first six thousand years of the world—from the most immemorial temple of Hindoustan—architecture has been the great manuscript of the human race. This is true to such a degree, that not only every religious symbol, but every human thought, has its page and its memorial in that vast book.[1]

He cites examples of significant buildings of the past as the manifestations of a body of ideas. For example, Solomon's temple is the great manuscript of the Word of God.

> The parent idea, the Word, was not contained in the foundation of these edifices, but in their structure. Solomon's Temple, for example, was not simply the cover of the sacred book, it was the sacred book itself. On each of its concentric enclosures the priest might read the Word translated and made manifest to the eye, might follow its tranformations from sanctuary to sanctuary, till at last he could lay hold upon it in its final tabernacle, under its most concrete form, which yet was architecture—the Ark. Thus the Word was enclosed in the edifice, but its image was visible on the outcovering like the human figure depicted on the coffin in a mummy.[2]

Much as Hugo saw an important connection between architecture and religious ideology, he saw a relationship with political ideology.

Hugo was an ardent republican. He viewed past history as the domination of monarchy, privilege, and class structure over society. The physical evidence of this domination was the institution: architecturally speaking, the monument. Hugo asserted that the first major attack upon the aristocracy came from the middle class. The form that this critique was to take was not plastic, but printed. The book was the great evidence of the bourgeoisie as political force in the eighteenth century. This critique resulted in the French Revolution, an uprising which eradicated old institutions, hence the architectural text, and presaged the ultimate victory of the written. The printed text heralded the birth of republicanism.

Hugo was a writer, and espoused an interpretation of history and politics that would give substance and meaning to his role as social critic. Needless to say, moved as architects were by the iconographic implications of Hugo's essay, they could not wholly accept the political component. For whereas Hugo was the builder of the monuments of the middle class, i.e., the written text, the architect's task was first and foremost to clothe institutions. Surely, architects were justified in their scepticism of Hugo, as was any man interested in social order underpinned by strong government. In every strong, centralized political system which presented an alternative to monarchy (liberalism, socialism, even communism), governmental structure necessarily gave rise to institutions. The only political alternative which precluded the need for institutions was anarchism, a point of view which few middle class intellectuals (perhaps not even Hugo) were prepared to accept. Rather, architects opted for a moderate interpretation of Hugo. They embraced, not a revolutionary posture which would have been professionally nihilistic, but a tentative, relativistic, evolutionary one. They believed in the institutional nature of government and society, although they maintained that these structures should and must change on the basis of a fluctuating socio-political climate. Architects asserted the need for local modifications within institutional form, without questioning the static character of those institutions, and the paternalistic posture that their very existence implied.

Hugo was a radical critic. Like Hegel, he stressed that discrete historical periods made themselves apparent by the obliteration of old institutions and the growth of new. For Hugo the new institution was the printed text. This assertion had a markedly revolutionary tone, and was questioned by history itself. The antiquarians of the early nineteenth century argued that certain institutions, which maintained an existence transcending historical periods (for example, the church), inhabited distinctive functional architectural types. Perhaps the most recognizable of these was the temple, which Hugo himself discussed in various permutations.[3] J-N-L. Durand, for instance, in the *Recueil et Parallele des Edifices* explicitly articulated the continuity of political, social and religious programs over time in terms of traceable building types (plate 31). It was apparent, especially to the nineteenth century, that markets, schools, and fora had existed from the time of the Greeks, courts and legislatures from the time of the Romans. The assertion that periods of history were parallel to an institutional history of architecture, as exemplified by building types, was disputable. It seemed more likely that instead of obliterating existing political and institutional structures, new political regimes merely modified them. In so doing, new regimes invoked a conscious critique of the old political system. Yet, this action implied a subconscious continuity, for the purpose of preserving social values and order. Hugo, Marx, or Proudhon may have desired the "annulment of the state" and its bureaucratic structures, but the institution builders, the moderate architects, preferred a less catastrophic course.[14] The evolutionary posture of the Romantic architect stressed a continuity with the formal types of the institutionalized government (house, church, school), overlaid with progressive values asserting necessary change overtime, reflective of a modern social "climate." Characteristic of the architecture of this generation was an interplay between formal continuities and discontinuities, between types and culture, between static and dynamic components of modern life.

For many in the early nineteenth century, the institution was housed in the building type. The type was the vehicle of the ideal. The institution was a metaphysical notion relating not to a natural but a supernatural existence. This conception was conveyed by Quatremère de Quincy in his famous definition of "Type" from the *Dictionnaire*. The type was first of all Idea.

> The word 'type' presents less the image of a thing to copy or imitate completely than the idea of an element which ought itself to serve as a rule for the model... the type... is an object after which each (artist) can conceive works of art...[5]

Second, the type is the fundamental theme to which any number of variations can be attributed:

> ... all things, in spite of subsequent changes, have conserved, always visibly, always in a way that is evident to feeling and reason, this elementary principle, which is like the sort of nucleus about which are collected, and to which are coordinated in time, the developments and variations of forms to which the object is susceptible. Thus we have achieved a thousand things in each genre, and one of the principal occupations of science and philosophy is to discover their origin and primitive cause in order to understand the reasons for them. This is what must be called 'type' in architecture, as in every other universal field of invention and human institution.[6]

Anthony Vidler mentions the Neoplatonism of this definition and suggests that Quatremère is preoccupied with the issue of ideality.[7] Furthermore, Quatremère incorporates these concerns into the primer of artistic education, *Essai sur l'Imitation dans des Beaux-Arts* (1823), emphasizing that it is the goal of representation (imitation) to invoke the ideal. He proposes a method interposing artistic "means" and "execution." Although he makes the distinction between type and model, it is clear that in his discussion of means, he considers a formal norm by which the type might be most fittingly represented.[8] Most important among his "means" of representation is the generalized form. Generalized forms are derived from the traditional Zeuxian method, i.e., the assembly of the most perfect characteristics from a number of models into a visible norm.[9] In addition the method of execution is handed down to the academy from Nicolas Poussin, which is an emphasis upon "dessin" or line drawing over colorism.[10] Line drawing implies geometry, hence a mathematical compositional basis which might underlay meaningful form.

Quatremère opposes "generalized" with "particularlized" forms. He furthermore contrasts type with character. If the linear and the generalized indicate the typological, then the rugged and idiosyncratic must represent the characteristic. Furthermore, if the typological epitomizes the ideal, then the characteristic must describe the real.

This polarity is important for the early nineteenth century. We can find an application of this duality in an early print illustrating Chartres Cathedral, prepared by César Daly in 1837 (plate 35). Daly provides an oblique view of the north portal, complete with ogival and rose windows, tribunes, sculpture, and so forth. He furthermore adds an element of local color to the scene by the procession trailing out of the central doorway of the portal. He lastly overlays the ensemble with a play of light and shadow, heightening the volumetric play of the composition, as well as providing atmospheric variety across the building's surface.

This kind of view is an extension of the characteristic representations in the antiquarian publications of the day. In France, the Duc de Caumont's *Cours d'Archéologie* and *Bulletin Monumental* make great use of this kind of picturesque composition. Its provenance is indisputably English.[11]

In his *Cours d'Archéologie* (reprinted in the second volume of the *Bulletin Monumental*), De Caumont cites his literary and historical sources, both French and English. This applies to his graphic sources as well. An ultimate origin of this picturesque illustrative technique can be found in William Gilpin and his writings on the picturesque.[12] Gilpin first coined the terms "picturesque" and "characteristic" with regard to the representation of the natural and architectural landscape. He contrasted "picturesque beauty" with Burkian notions of "Beauty" and "Sublimity," the first of which he likened to typological beauty of an abstract cerebral kind, the second, to cathartic, emotional experience. Picturesque beauty emphasized temporality, stressing the momentary, the transitory, the atmospheric, and the contingent qualities of pictorial representation. He likened the character in landscape to a Hogathian genre scene, filled with action, idiosyncracy, movement, and contrast (plate

36).[13] Action, idiosyncracy, and movement are the key to Gilpin's assessment of Burkian sublimity. A major implication to the aesthetic is its opposition to complete, stable, and methodically composed kinds of formal representations. Gilpin, like Burke, suggests the inadequacy of academic typology as a means of affecting significant artistic experience. He describes the distinction between ideal and characteristic formalizing systems in terms of a Palladian analogy:

> A piece of Palladian architecture may be elegant to the last degree. The proportion of its parts—the propriety of its ornaments—and the symmetry of the whole, may be highly pleasing. But if we introduce it in a picture, it immediately becomes a formal object, and ceases to please. Should we wish to give it picturesque beauty, we must use the mallet, instead of the chisel: we must beat down one half of it, deface the other, and throw the mutilated members into heaps. In short, from a smooth building we must turn it into a *rough* ruin. No painter, who had the choice of the two objects, would hesitate a moment.[14]

Palladio transcended time and space; he provided us with formal types that ignored situation. The ruin was the norm distorted and affected by time. Palladio's villa was the "beau idéal." Similarly, Gilpin's ruin could only be defined as the "beau réel."

In time, the picturesque graphic form became the standard means of providing architectural views for early Gothic antiquarianism. This technique was practiced both in England and France for representations other than the documentary. As mentioned above, the Duc de Caumont used this technique in his own work. Similarly, another great antiquarian of the day, the Comte Alexandre de Laborde, used this descriptive method in *Les Monuments de la France.* This was an extremely important work to that generation of young architects now interested in France's architectural heritage. Its intention paralleled the work of statistical inventory undertaken by De Caumont in his *Bulletin Monumental.* The plates were provocative.

An illustration from the second volume, published in 1836, depicting the north porch of Chartres, provided a representative example of this graphic work (plate 37). It furthermore begs comparison with the earlier described Daly print. Like the Daly print described above, de Laborde's plate exploits oblique perspective, a play of light and shadows, and genre figures. The two plates, however, display as many dissimilarities as likenesses. The differences begin with the techniques of execution. de Laborde's is a *gravure à l'eau forte,* a steel plate etching. Here, the etching technique is important, for it is a means especially appropriate to the artistic intention of creating character via roughness of line, dramatic juxtaposition of light and shadow, energetic contrasts of surface, and variety of other formal and spatial effects. That the etching was difficult to control in areas of detail was less important than considerations of provocative pictorial quality.[15]

Daly's print is a *gravure à burin,* an etching on steel plate reworked by engraver's burin for greater subtlety, control, and line quality. Gilpin, in his

Essay on Prints, describes this technique as a means of restraining the freedom of the etching, and of retrieving clarity of line. It was line that ultimately dominated composition, not light and shadow. Unlike the de Laborde print, the Daly etching is surprisingly restrained. Whereas for de Laborde the surfaces of Chartres, including upper stories, piers, and buttresses, become one in a sea of shadow, in Daly's work careful use of line, silhouette, and back lighting, ensures that edges and surfaces are never equivocated or confused. Lighting effects, which seem to mold and fuse forms in the de Laborde print are exploited to separate and to analyze the same forms for Daly. Whereas de Laborde tends to obscure detail, particularly of sculptural elements, Daly seems to revel in fastidious description. de Laborde's cathedral seems made of a single monolithic material. César Daly portrays Chartres' masonry in all its jointure. Enormous attention is paid to the way in which the building is assembled.

Perhaps more importantly, in both works the building takes on a kind of personality by virtue of the human activity unfolding before it. In an empathic way, the building is not only setting for, but also party to human life. But what a difference of scene! de Laborde presents a series of vignettes, which although consciously humorous, are equally mundane in character. On the steps of the portal a young rake woos a fair damsel (dressed in *Néo-Grec* fashion); beside the main door a woman begs for alms under the surveillance of a sinister figure (depicted in silhouette) presumably waiting for an appropriate moment to divest her of a day's gleanings. In the foreground, mother and child walk to Mass, but the child seems to be taking greater interest in the event under the portal than in the church itself. Family life, romance, penury, robbery—the effects of modern life are caricatured. No less clearly is the church parodied. Masonry collapsing, *ad hoc* additions, graffiti on walls (provided by the plate's engraver Fortier), detail disintegrating: this may well have been a close representation of the church's appearance in 1835. The church takes on a comedic character, perhaps as a kind of jester or fool, and the total episode provides the viewer with a pleasant diversion. Yet this depiction also leaves an unpleasant aftertaste, for if the church necessarily parallels life, then both seem tawdry and pathetic.

The picture of Chartres that Daly presents embodies a very different view of life. The seamier elements of day-to-day existence seem to disappear. Rather than acting as a backdrop for life's comedy, the church is instead represented as a kind of tragic scene, a setting for public ritual and civic virtue. A religious procession is in progress. The participants are not engaging in life's more mundane activities, but are witness to and actors in an important religious ceremony. This is a portrait of man's loftiest aspirations as embodied in religion, as well as the social unity fostered by common values. In place of its sordid appearance in the earlier print, Daly's Chartres appears young, strong, and heroic, untouched by time. Furthermore, the building is not merely backdrop to, but intimately involved with, the unfolding drama. The procession from the church's portal gives an impression of the building's instrumentality, perhaps causality, in the moral lives of its people.

To summarize, the Daly engraving clearly comes from the same pictorial tradition as the de Laborde print. Unlike the earlier depiction, however, Daly's is a rarefied, hieratic, even idealized depiction. Hard, muscular, direct, heroic, his image of Chartres Cathedral is one which orchestrates life and dominates time. Daly's Chartres is emphatically *not* real. De Laborde presents a view of religion and society on the brink of disintegration. Daly's implies a view of social reconstruction, utilizing the church as *modus*. This print presents a positive, optimistic statement, interested not so much in a veristic depiction of life as it is, but in a view of life as it should be, unified in religion, with the church as orchestrator and focus of society.[16]

My tentative assertion at this point is that Daly was interested less in realistic depictions of the architectural situation than in an idealistic interpretation. This is communicated in two ways by the Chartres engraving. First, rather than stressing the transitory, circumstantial and idiosyncratic in his print (like de Laborde), he preferred an analytical, logical and rational depiction. Daly's depiction of the church emphasized reason, order and control. Second, the church dominated human life. Rather than atmosphere molding the church, Chartres manipulated light and context. It achieved its objective by an implicit ideology, communicated to the people by means of form. In the subliminal communication of this knowledge, it orchestrated society. The conception of the building as instrument of inspiration, as vehicle of ideology, as symbol, forces us to reconsider a basic stand of Quatremère, that is, the relationship between form and idea, and a synthesis of these concerns in the architectural type.

These ideas, stemming from pictorial evidences, are reinforced by Daly's writings of the same period. His earliest articles appeared in a regional newspaper *Le Glâneur: Journal d'Eure et Loire,* and they discussed among other topics the annual *envois* from the Ecole Française de Rome. His architectural associates of the period—Felix Duban, Henri Labrouste, Louis Duc—were young Romantics, all ostensibly opposed to the leadership of the Ecole de Rome.[17] Their criticism was directed primarily at one figure, Quatremère de Quincy, theorist of the Académie, questioning his doctrines particularly with regard to typology. Was Daly equally critical? Like the Romantics, Daly was hesitant to accept the Romans as standards of excellence. He stated,

Les Romains n'ont été généralement que de médiocres artistes par eux-mêmes, ils étonnent par le grandeur de leurs monuments et l'immensité de leurs entreprises, mais les détails montrent généralement peu de goût. Dans l'art de profiler, par exemple, les Grecs et les artistes gothiques des temps ogivaux et du commencement de la renaissance leur ont été très supérieurs.[18]

> The Romans were generally only mediocre artists themselves; they astonish by the grandeur
> of their monuments and the immensity of their enterprises, but the details generally display
> little taste. In the art of profiling, for example, the Greek and the Gothic artists of both ogival
> and early renaissance periods were very superior to them.

He is hostile to the Romans, and prefers to have Greek, Gothic, and Quattrocento models used as examples. His criticisms, however, are directed primarily at details. With regard to larger scale planning, he returns to ideas of the functional building type, stressing certain architectural forms which transcend historical situation. For example, in this same article he proclaims a great admiration for the Forum of Trajan, interpreting it as a great model worthy of imitation and application in present-day situations.[19]

> Le forum romain correspond à ce que les Grecs appellaient *agora* et à ce que nous désignons
> marché. L'agora grec était carré, mais le forum romain était oblong. Ces marchés chez les
> anciens, étaient entourés de portiques et ornés de statues des dieux et des grands hommes;
> Rome en renfermait dix-sept, mais aucun n'était comparables au forum de Trajan pour la
> liberté et la richesse des sculptures.[20]

> The Roman forum corresponds to what the Greeks call *agora* and to what we designate a
> marketplace. The Greek agora was square, but the Roman forum was oblong. These ancient
> markets were enclosed by porticos and ornamented with statues of gods and great men;
> Rome had seventeen of them; but none of them was comparable to the forum of Trajan for
> the liberty and richness of sculpture.

Was Daly anti-typological? Tentatively, we must say no. Although critical of the Romans, he attacked them not on the basis of the appropriateness of their solutions to modern needs, but on the basis of detail. Just as the market was a persuasive formal paradigm, one must imagine that the basilica, or the bath, would have its place within Daly's architectural frame of reference. Although Daly criticized Roman detail as inappropriate or clumsy, he found certain Roman design solutions wholly applicable to similar modern problems. Surely, from all the major periods of the history of architecture, paradigms could be gleaned. Greece gave Daly the temple, Egypt the tomb, Gothic France the cathedral. Details might vary, but the type as organizational device was important.

This proposition can be examined in the light of Daly's work on Chartres Cathedral. A fire of 1836 destroyed the church's roof, leaving exposed to the weather the building's irreplaceable stained glass and sculpture. Nave, transept, and choir had to be covered as quickly as possible. During the next three years, Daly and his teacher Félix Duban worked to recover the church. Their solution, understandably enough, conformed to the original configuration of the roof. However, rather than using a wood structure, which would be susceptible to another fire, they substituted a non-inflammable material, cast iron. Retrospective or progressive, how should this reconstruction be viewed?

If a doctrinaire modernist like Sigfried Giedion were preparing the evaluation, he would have been certain to emphasize the use of cast iron as "constituent fact," a mark of the spirit of modernity. However, if we return to Quatremère's distinction between means and execution, the interpretation becomes something different. Quatremère was primarily concerned with rational execution, especially embodied in line drawing and rules of composition. Technique was to be logical. The means, however, were to be controlled by typological notions of form. Logical technique was moot to the consideration of type. In the case of César Daly, who immediately interpreted Chartres in an idealistic, typological way, violation of primary form would be unthinkable. Technique and detail were variables, but only in so far as they maintained the basic rationality inherent in the type. Any strict materialist would have been uneasy with the preoccupation of structure conforming to predetermined envelope. For Daly, this hesitancy was absent. The utilitarian was to be the underpinning for the ideal. The attention of the public was never to be diverted from Chartres' timeless form, for, at least in this case, progressive elements could be kept "under wraps." The roof configuration did not bend to new needs, circumstances, or epochal considerations. Old profiles and volumes were maintained. In the case of Chartres, if progress or the present was to be articulated, it was in the details. The type, however, transcended detail. It was impervious to time, situation, or the spirit of the age.

Albi Cathedral in History—*Proem*

Although Theseus made his labyrinthine way by use of Ariadne's thread, I can only think that he would have much preferred a roadmap. Upon rereading the forthcoming section, with its various windings and *cul-de-sacs*, I have decided to facilitate the reader's task by clarifying the central themes of the discussion. This *proem* has been devised as a kind of roadmap of things to come.

There are two central issues at play. First, this discussion confronts materialistic readings of history with idealistic. Second, it deals with Daly's attack on the problem of architectural meaning: whether ideology can transcend time, or whether it must be interactive with its historical climate. In short, is César Daly's attitude toward ideology absolute or relativistic?

First, as stated above, César Daly viewed Chartres Cathedral typologically. He assessed other northern Gothic churches using Chartres as a norm. However, César Daly was unable, at least initially, to use Chartres Cathedral as a meaningful precedent to inform his estimation of Albi. He could not interpret Albi as a church modelled on the example of Chartres. Instead, he chose to interpret Albi Cathedral as related to fortification.

This interpretation of Albi Cathedral gave it a second meaning within the historical climate of thirteenth-century Languedoc, instead of the meaning within the context of the church as institution and building type. Architectural types transcend history. By virtue of formal consistencies over time, they lead to an interpretation of building form that exists outside of the action of history. However, if Albi Cathedral cannot be assessed typologically, is it then to be seen as an example of history and its forces in action upon a building's fabric, transforming it into something unfamiliar and singular? If so, then does it lose meaning with regard to its ontology as institution and church? Perhaps. Daly's early interpretation of Albi Cathedral as fortification indicates a view of history of a materialistic causal variety. Architecture no longer ignores history, but seems fundamentally affected and shaped by it.

Third, although Daly's early historical and architectural understandings of Albi were materialistic, as the decade moved on, his historical vantage changed. Although he initially saw the cataclysmic events of the thirteenth century and the Albigensian controversy as affecting building form, a second issue later came into play—the spirit of the age. This idea that individual incidents were the phenomena of the action of higher consciousness invoked the issue of the historical metaphysic. If Albi was shaped by explicit historical events, was it not also imbued with implicit historical purpose?

Last, how was such higher purpose conveyed? How was such a historical force recognized? Historically, there was the vindication of posterity, and the then-current presence of national unity and social order. The modern day sought the thread of its present social fabric in the events of the past. Tectonically, there was the issue of architectural unity or composition—the geometrical and proportional rules of order. The presence of such rules indicated the involvement of a higher consciousness in action upon the course of both history and architecture. This same concern reinvoked factors of social and architectural unity stemming from ideological continuities, seeming to echo certain pre-materialistic concerns.

Did such overriding historical will to order exist immanently, subconsciously orchestrating the events of history to some eventual outcome? Possibly. A variant of this idea also existed, however. There was the idea that spirit or historical purpose was best conveyed by certain special vehicles or individuals. This seemed an adjunct to the idea that Chartres Cathedral could be conceived as an emphatic instrument. Likewise, a person could shape destinies. Daly's view of history exceeded an idealistic belief in the *Zeitgeist*. Rather, he believed that he himself could be the manipulator or medium of higher consciousness. He, therefore, had an instrumental role in the shaping of history.

Daly's reassessment of history from a purely materialistic to an increasingly metaphysical view affected his perceptions of architecture. Although he early interpreted Albi as fortification, he came to recognize that such a view failed to account for the building's primary role as church, and ignored its true institutional meaning of intention. Ultimately, he sought necessary spiritual meaning in the consciously artistic components of its architecture rather than the functional. It was in the consciously artistic elements of architecture that ideology and spirit were best conveyed. This posture was the only idealistic alternative to considering Albi as a type in and of itself. Moreover, later Daly was to consider not only the artistic parts of Albi as especially representative, but the church itself as empathic instrument, and vehicle of inspiration as well—as a symbol and as a type.

Chartres versus Albi

The restoration of Albi Cathedral, the church of Sainte-Cécile, was the major architectural project of Daly's career. His official involvement with the building began in 1844, when the Ministère de la Justice et des Cultes, on the recommendation of the Commission des Monuments Historiques, requested him to prepare a restoration of the cathedral. The task of the restoration continued over the next thirty-three years. Initially, the Ministry requested a written history, a visual documentation, and a proposal for reconstruction and completion of the cathedral. There were two major considerations at play. First, and most obviously, there was a campaign of reparation, for the purpose of preserving church fabric and artworks. Second, and most importantly, a program of architectural completion was involved. In the minds of most observers, the church as it stood in 1844 remained a fragment of some greater conception envisioned by the bishop Bernard de Castanet in 1277, and continued by his successors until Louis I d'Amboise completed the front tower in the late fifteenth century. Daly's major task was to resume the great work, prematurely and inexpertly halted at the beginning of the French Renaissance.

Daly's primary problem was one of historical interpretation. As stated earlier, his early work on Chartres Cathedral assumed an interpretation of the church as a symbol, a vehicle of inspiration, a paradigm serving as ancestor for all subsequent *Ile-de-France* development. This idea should not be unfamiliar to modern historians, for such authors as Robert Branner and Paul Frankl treat Chartres similarly, seeing it as a norm recognized in subsequent Rayonnant Cathedrals, despite variations and critiques.[21] There were those in the early nineteenth century who maintained a similar stand. This idea is present in the first major monograph on the church, Antoine Gilbert's *Description Historique de l'Eglise Cathédrale de Chartres* (1824), where it is discussed as a great watershed church.[22] Singular, focal, persuasive, Chartres (along with competitors Notre-Dame de Paris and Amiens) became a standard by which other thirteenth-century cathedrals were measured and evaluated.

However, no church could be more unlike Chartres than Albi Cathedral. In plan Chartres was an outgrowth of the pilgrimage church type—with nave, side aisles, transept, and ambulatory (plate 38). Albi, if anything, stood closer to the late antique Roman basilica type (plate 39). The functional planning of Chartres maintained a careful distinction between the lay and clerical realms, as well as specified areas for specialized processional movement. Albi, in its primitive state, that is, before the addition of the fifteenth century *jubé,* was nothing if not a kind of primitive, non-hierarchical universal space. In silhouette, Chartres presented a picturesque combination of volumes, masses, and details in an extruded articulation of the plan. Moreover, plan and elevation worked in concert to create a formal unity, integrating a variety of disparate formal elements into a convincing whole. In contrast, Albi was a single enormous mass of brick whose emphatic horizontality was interrupted only by the verticality of two elements—the porch structure and the tower (plate 40). Whereas plan and elevation of Chartres together integrated all disparate architectonic elements into a formal and spatial unity, Albi preserved a unitary nave against which highly idiosyncratic elements were juxtaposed. In contrast to the unified qualities of Chartres, Albi seemed an additive combination of parts.

Contrasts continued at the level of detail. Whereas Chartres was built of limestone, Albi was brick, with certain honorific elements built of limestone or imported marble. Chartres was a monochromatic church; Albi was coloristic or polychrome. Chartres displayed decoration that was distinctly architectonic—sculpture melded with structural elements of the church. Albi's major decoration was added as independent elements (porch and *jubé*), or were laid onto the architecture in terms of fresco. If Chartres' decoration could be regarded as "organic" with regard to building form, Albi's must have appeared self-conscious or artificial. Albi was very different indeed from Chartres.

Problems of interpretation might have been avoided had Albi been dismissed as an aberration. Yet the encyclopedic aspect of the antiquarian movement could not allow the dismissal of a single shred or archaeological evidence. All had to be fitted into the vast, cosmic scheme of things. Albi could be viewed as a new animal specimen, conforming to none of the qualities of other animal species. It had to be viewed as a kind of architectural mutation, its hybrid character giving rise to two questions. First, to what parentage or *genre* could the speciman ultimately be attributed? Secondly, and perhaps more importantly, what caused the physical deviation in the first place?

Moreover, Albi Cathedral could not be ignored. The enormous merit of the building was proclaimed by many influential authors. Chateaubriand called it, "Un magnifique musée."[23] Merimée lavished great attention on it in his *Notes d'un Voyage dans le Midi,* elaborately describing its most important details. About the south porch he stated:

> L'imagination ne peut rien concevoir de plus élégant, de plus gracieux que ces ogives flamboyantes, ces trèfles, ces meneaux d'une légereté inouie, véritable dentelle de pierre.[24]

> The imagination cannot conceive of anything more elegant, more gracious, than those flamboyant ogives, these trefoils, these vaulting ribs of an uncomparable lightness, true laceworks of stone.

Viollet-le-Duc stressed the singular importance of Albi. "Saint-Cécile d'Alby (sic) est...dans son genre un monument unique."[25] Many perceived Albi as significant. Why? This is the fundamental question that Daly was forced to confront. It was immediately clear that he could not apply the principles of *Ile-de-France* Gothic to this edifice, except in a very limited and specific way. Evaluation had to proceed, at least initially, on a very different tack.

Albi Cathedral and Materialistic History

The major problem for Daly in 1844 was to fit Albi Cathedral into an architectural history, at that time predetermined or dominated by then-current historical method. Within the context of French antiquarianism, there were two ways to discuss the historical artifact. Arcisse de Caumont makes the distinction:

> Deux méthodes se présentent pour décrire et classer chronologiquement les monuments. L'une consisterait à présenter, siècle par siècle, l'état de l'architecture réligieuse, civile et militaire, au moyen-âge.
> L'autre à traiter successivement et isolement chaque partie dans son entier, c'est-à-dire, à épuiser tout ce qui concerne l'architecture religieuse, avant de passer à l'architecture militaire, et ainsi de suite.
> La première méthode offre, je crois, plusieurs inconvénients dont le plus grave serait de porter continuellement l'attention sur les sujets differents, de nécessiter un plus grand travail de mémoire, et peut-être de laisser dans l'esprit quelque confusion.
> La seconde me paraît plus naturelle et moins fatiguante; on saisit mieux l'ensemble des faits, lorsqu'on étudie separément chaque object de manière à s'en former une idée claire et distincte.[26]

> Two methods present themselves in order to describe and classify monuments chronologically. One would consist of presenting, century by century, the state of religious, civil, and military architecture in the Middle Ages.
> The other is to treat successively and in isolation each part in its entirety, that is to say, to exhaust all that concerns religious architecture before passing to military architecture, and so forth.
> The first method offers, I believe, more inconveniences of which the gravest would be in continually directing attention to different subjects, necessitating an enormous work of memory, and perhaps leaving confusion in the mind.
> The second seems more natural to me and less fatiguing; one grasps better the collection of facts, while one studies each object separately so as to form a clear and distinct idea.

The first method assessed all building types within a period, broke them into their formal/structural components, and then compared them to correlative forms of other periods (plate 21). This was a posture fundamentally opposed to the functional type. Rather, it was closer to a "structuralist" posture, which assumed that all building types within a period can be constituted from the same set of components.[27] The second method assessed an individual building type (religious architecture, military architecture) through time, in order to discern continuities and discontinuities in formal elements. Moreover, what De Caumont left unstated was a typological norm which included compositional and proportional considerations, allowing for easy comparison and reconstruction. This was a posture which implied constancies of form as well as inconstancies, which could be ascribed to the historical climate of a particular period. The method was not unlike that of J-N-L. Durand's *Recueil et Parallèle des Edifices,* which sought to examine a building type in all its permutations through the ages, especially seeking formal transcendencies (plate 31). The first method concentrated upon detail, the second reinforced basic typological predispositions.

As noted above, Daly displayed idealistic tendencies in his interpretation of Chartres Cathedral. Not only was it a norm which this and subsequent *Ile-de-France* churches imitated, but it was also a symbol. In a Platonic sense, this church was a vehicle of inspiration. However, Albi could not be interpreted as imitating such a paradigm. Dealing with Albi as a pure functional type was impossible. Instead, Daly, along with many others, treated the church as a hybrid structure, part church and part fortification, the result of the play of historical forces on building fabric. Rather than treat Albi in a paradigmatic, holistic way, Daly preferred to interpret from a piece-meal, detail-related point of view. Typological purity, hence spirit, might not exist in the total building form; instead, meaning could be communicated by its parts. Rather than the typological point of view engendered by De Caumont's second method, Daly espoused the first. He later reverted to a more idealistic posture.

At the outset of his effort, Daly viewed the hybrid building form at Albi as having been affected largely by defensive considerations. Daly states:

> La conception première était d'un caractère tout militaire; l'édifice réligieux se reliait à un ensemble de fortifications comprenant l'archevêché et une muraille de tours flanqués de tours...[28]

> The first conception was of a military character; the religious edifice allied itself to a collection of fortifications including the bishop's palace and a turreted wall.

The issue of fortification is explained by the history of Languedoc during the thirteenth century: in short, the building was created by the Albigensian Wars. This interpretation of Sainte-Cécile, as a building whose fabric was shaped by momentous historical circumstances, was not a new one. Jules Michelet uses the second volume of his *Histoire de la France* to recount the history of the Capetians, and particularly these wars of religion. Charles Nodier, in his *Voyages Pittoresques dans l'Ancienne France: Languedoc,* also attempts to explain this church's form by the socio-political climate. It may be useful at this point to summarize this episode.

The Albigensian Wars were waged against a large and powerful sect of religious heretics, the Cathares. They espoused a kind of Manicheanism, which allowed for, among other things, suicide, a mortal sin in orthodox Catholicism. Moreover, the Albigensian movement was a political one, supported by the king of England, Henry II, by the king of Aragon, and by the Comte de Toulouse, against the king of France and the pope. In order to fight the heretic faction, a number of Crusades were fought against the *Cathares* during the first half of the century. The eventual victory of France and the Church in part took the form of an Inquisition, with tribunals established in Toulouse, Carcassonne, and Albi. For the town of Albi, the age was violent. Nodier writes:

> Le peuple d'Albi, d'une organisation impressionable et passionné, peut fournir par son histoire, jusqu'à des jours recens où le spectacle d'une exécution l'agite d'émotions si violentes, les tableaux les plus dramatiques pour le chroniqueur et le peintre.[29]

> The people of Albi, an impressionable and passionate organization, can furnish by its history, both distant and recent, scenes in which executions generate violent emotion, an extremely dramatic tableau for the chronicler and for the painter.

As painting and writing were affected by social history, so was architecture.

According to Nodier, art and architecture were the outcome of the socio-political situation. Historical "climate" affected the development of church form. This point of view, however, could be attacked on a number of fronts. If the historical situation had an instrumental role in shaping form, why was it that other churches in quite comparable historical situations displayed such different forms? As an illustration of this, I cite Nodier's chronicle of the commune of Laon, which in its violence and intensity sounds very much like the history of Albi.

> L'histoire de la commune de Laon est presque aussi pleine d'agitation que l'histoire d'un château féodal. Institution d'ordre et de paix, elle fût, dès l'origine, une cause de troubles et de violences, par les discussions qu'elle fît naître entre la bourgeoisie et l'évêque. Dans cette lutte, la ville fut pillée et la cathédrale incendiée. Ces actes de vandalisme provonquèrent la suppression de la commune, qui fût rétablie en 1128 et maintenue jusqu'en 1295 ... (En 1331) finît la vie civile et politique de cette ville.[30]

> The history of the commune of Laon is almost as violent and full of agitation as the history of a feudal chateau. An institution of order and peace, it was, from its origin, a source of trouble and violence on account of the heated discussions it spawned between the bourgeoisie and the bishop. In this struggle, the city was pillaged and the cathedral burned. These acts of vandalism provoked the suppression of the commune, which was reestablished in 1128 and maintained until 1295 ... [In 1331], the civil and political life of this city (effectively) ended.

For Nodier the history of Laon was no less violent than that of Albi. Furthermore, if Nodier used catastrophic historical forces in Albi to explain the form of its church, why did he not do the same at Laon? Laon Cathedral, however, bears no resemblance to Sainte-Cécile, or to any other purported fortification for that matter. Rather Laon is to be regarded as a church type, giving initial form to the great *Ile-de-France* cathedrals, and transcending non-architectural forces.[31]

Furthermore, if Sainte-Cécile as seat of the Inquisition was affected by needs for defense, why was not the contemporaneous church addition (transept and chevet) at Saint Nazaire in Carcassonne, Albi's inquisitional sister city, also fortified? Unlike Albi, this addition, built at the same time as ground was broken for Albi Cathedral, was designed in the fashionable court style of Louis IX. There are few gestures to defense. Rather, we observe the attenuated proportions, the careful traceries, the luminous glass walls inspired by the most consciously artistic work of the period, the Sainte-Chapelle in Paris. At Saint Nazaire, we see little evidence of the action of society and history on architectural form. Instead, the building is better explained by the imposition of an aesthetic norm on an artistic situation.[32]

Such inconsistencies with the prevalent historical viewpoint give rise to considerations of fashion, the imposition of stylistic norms, and typological survivals with which Daly was ill-prepared to deal in the early 1840s. Having momentarily abandoned a typological point of view for purposes of interpreting Albi, he turned to materialistic history as a means of escaping his particular dilemma. Denying the church a paradigmatic component, as Daly initially did at Albi, moved the architect to a consideration of architectural form in terms of its parts in and of themselves. This analytical method became one of dismembering the edifice, wherein structural components and details were examined at the expense of holistic meaning. The ideal part was resurrected only later, when Daly was able to recognize symbolic meaning in the church as *genre.* At such time, Daly became aware that Albi was not unique in time and space, but represented, along with a body of like structures, a shared body of intellectual and moral concern.

The Return to Historical Metaphysics

Daly's initial move away from the metaphysics of form paralleled attitudinal changes in archeological circles generally. De Caumont's rationalism left behind the idealistic stand of Chateaubriand. Developments in the realm of linguistic meaning, particularly as it pertained to iconography, were similar to those in architectural interpretation. Hugo's linguistic posture was informed by an architectural metaphor. He shifted from a spiritual, typological approach, that is, one which stressed a building's innate ideality, to a more progressive stance. He wrote,

The general characteristics of all theocratic architectures are immutability, horror of progress, strict adherence to traditional lines, and consecration of primitive types. The adaptation of every aspect of man and nature to the incomprehensible whims of symbolism. Dark and mysterious book, which only the initiated can decipher! Furthermore, every form, and every deformity even, in them has a meaning which renders it inviolable. Never ask a Hindu, Egyptian or Roman architecture to change its designs or perfect its sculpture. To it, improvement in any shape or form is an impiety. Here the rigidity of dogma seems to spread over the stone like a second casting of petrification. [33]

In preference to the implicit typologies of ancient architecture, Hugo proposed popular architectures which are modern, innovative, and expressive of the nature of the age.

On the other hand, the main characteristics of a popular architecture are diversity, progress, originality, richness of design, perpetual change. They are already sufficiently detached from religion to take thought for their beauty, to tend it, to alter and improve without ceasing their garniture of arabesques and statues, they go with the times. They have something human in them, which mingles with divine symbolism under whose inspiration they are still produced. Here you get edifices accessible to every spirit, every intelligence, every imagination; symbolic still, but as easily understood as the signs of nature. Between this style of architecture and the theocratic there are the same differences as between the sacred and the vulgar tongues, between hieroglyphics and art, between Solomon and Phidias. [34]

In short, what we observe in Hugo is a move away from the notion of building as an inviolable type, complete and unalterable, to one of building as a compendium of meaning, as a collection of symbols or decoration comprising a building's fabric. No longer empathic as a unified house of the spirit and a social generator, architecture's meaning now had multiple meanings, conditioned by the circumstantial and variable. It became a continually expanding architectural text, with meanings ultimately connected to the historical situation and artistic intention.

Architecture moved from a frame of reference where ontology was the major issue, to one where meaning was sought in its parts. Analysis sought to break a building apart. One no longer hesitated to dismember architecture for fear of destroying a life force of immutable unity. The research saw two levels. The first was the structural level, encountered already in our dealings with French antiquarians. The second was iconographic, a hermeneutic level which sought to assess the explicitly symbolic component of art and architecture in terms of "unit-ideas."

Researches into meaning gave birth to specifically iconographic research. The major spokesman for this subject was Didron l'Aîné, the editor of the archaeological journal *Annales Archéologiques*. Iconographic, like formal, research underwent idealistic and analytical periods. Generalized, impressionistic interpretations were abandoned in favor of encyclopedic compendia of symbols, which were modern-day emblem books. A useful comparison can be drawn between Arcisse de Caumont and Didron. Much as de Caumont had been the great analyzer of form, Didron l'Aîné was the evaluator of significance. As de Caumont interpreted structural order, Didron assessed symbolism.

A controversy arose between Daly and Didron centering on the issues of inviolable architectural form and progress. Their interchange over five years chronicles Daly's shift from a scientific to a more idealistic posture, especially with regard to his work at Albi. As early as 1844, Didron attacked architect Janniard for his restorations of St. Ouen at Rouen and St. Germain l'Auxerrois, particularly for his removal of gargoyles. Janniard argued that gargoyles were unsafe, that they tended to erode foundations, that they were inefficient, and most importantly, that they were gratuitous decorative elements, expressing a predilection for "picturesqueness." Although he disapproved of Janniard's actions, Daly also opposed Didron stating that all buildings, whether historic or modern, must respond to new needs, and that existing building forms can be improved by modern, innovative, building techniques, in this case, gutters and downspouts. He further buttressed his arguments for a modern formal awareness when he confronted Didron at the *Congrès Archéologique* of 1847, defending his use of wood paving at Albi Cathedral in preference to the more historically accurate black and white marble pavers. Daly stated,

> Il faut faire quelque'chose avec la science actuelle, produire de grands effets avec l'exiguité de moyens qu'on possède. Il faut tenir compte du present, et non pas vivre dans le passé; l'art est une création, et depuis six mille ans, la parole éternelle qui a tiré le monde du néant, poursuit son oeuvre, accomplit sa mission . . . il faut être de son temps, avec les moyens de son temps. [35]

> It is necessary to make something with current science, to produce grand effects by employing the means one possesses. It is necessary to take account of the present, and not to live in the past; art has been a creation for the last 6,000 years, the eternal world that created the earth from nothing, pursued its own work, accomplished its mission; [now, the creative act] must be of one's own time, using the means of one's time.

It appears at first that Daly opposes architectural paradigms in favor of progressive forms. To be sure, if a building was interpreted not as a vestige of the past but as a composite history, modernity certainly had a place in this receptacle of life's artifacts. Such a posture, however, was a relativistic one. There was an implicit contradiction in Daly's stand, for in asserting that all historical periods were equal, he implied that restoration, or returning a building to some past state, was impossible. Just as no single historical period could be seen as more important than any other, no single style could be seen as superior.

However, Daly clearly did not believe this. For him, all periods were not equal in importance. This issue was exemplified by Daly's insistence on the removal of certain latter-day rococo screens from Notre-Dame de Paris.[36] He attacked those elements within the church fabric which tended to obfuscate the logic of the original thirteenth-century structure. Didron l'Aîné, however, felt that nothing should be removed from a church, that each artifact expressed the spirit of its period. Because of this symbolic component, each piece was in itself "beautiful." Didron further argued that objects of beauty could never be contradictory, that their very nature drew them into harmony. Daly disagreed. He countered Didron's assertion, "Le beau et le beau se conviennent toujours," with the argument that a beautiful horse would be very much out of place in a beautiful chapel.[37] Daly, who earlier stressed the necessary acceptability of the progressive forms of his own period, could not perceive post-Gothic additions in Gothic churches to be similarly innovative within the context of their own day. Wholly unaware of the basic inconsistency in his own arguement, Daly argued in favor of a rarified, typological interpretation of architecture based on a period/style interpretation. Quoting Janniard, Daly asserted,

> Quand un object de détail fait un contrast très-choquant avec le caractère de l'édifice, on ne doit pas se préoccuper trop de la théorie des faits accomplis, il faut l'éloigner impitoyablement.[38]

> When an object of detail makes a very shocking contrast with the character of a building, one must not be too preoccupied with "faits accomplis" [rather] it is necessary to delete [the disharmonious detail] pitilessly.

Furthermore, he proposed uniformity of style.

> ...il nous semble (nous parlons du beau visible) que lorsqu'un objet d'art satisfait entièrement sous le triple rapport de la forme, du style, et de l'époque (il n'est pas question ici de la couleur), il doit être beau, [et tout]...se confondent,...dans une complète identité.[39]

> ...it seems to use (we are speaking here of visible beauty) that if a work of art entirely satisfies the three aspects of form, style, and epoch (it is not a question here of color)...then it must be beautiful; [all]...fuses into a complete identity.

What Daly advocated in restoration was the creation of a consistent formal identity removing all distracting architectonic elements (except his own, that is). Implicitly, the consequent formal unity must be achieved by conforming to a stylistic model or paradigm, on other words, a type.

Daly paralleled his move to formal and stylistic unity with a comparable shift toward symbolic unity. Daly's target was Didron's iconographic method. He opposed Didron's tendency to fragment a church's total meaning, in favor of a more organic, impressionistic meaning. This posture was not unprecedented, particularly in historical circles. For instance, Michelet, although acknowledging the importance of the antiquarian movement, recognized that scientific procedure had done a disservice to the objects of its investigation. He criticized analytical procedure which sought to categorize particular evidences rather than transcendent structure. He stated,

> [L'église]... c'est maintenant un object de curiosité scientifique... l'église est un musée que visitent les habiles: ils tournent autour, regardent irréverencieusement, et louent au lieu de prier... que dois-je faire?... décrire (les) églises... les comparer aux monuments analogues...? Cette description, cette comparaison même n'en donnerait qu'une connaissance extérieure, superficielle, confuse. Il faut aller plus loin, fouiller plus avant, il faut attendre le principe de leur formation, la loi physiologique que a présidé à cette végétation d'une nature particulière.[40]

> [The church]... is now an object of scientific curiosity... the church is a museum which the cunning visit, turn around, look about irreverently, and praise instead of pray... What must I do?... describe churches, compare them to analogous monuments...? This description, this comparison itself will yield only an external knowledge of them, superficial and confused. One must go further, forge ahead, one must anticipate the principle of their function, the physiological law which has presided over this growth of a special order.

Rather than scientific analysis, Michelet sought the vital principle of formation and growth.

The *Congrés Archéologique* of 1847 brought the analytic/organic conflict to center stage. Didron argued for an empirical evaluative technique paralleling De Caumont's dismembering of churches, iconographic emblem by emblem.

> M. Didron dit qu'il reconnaît beaucoup de faits, dans lesquels, on ne peut nier le symbolisme; ainsi l'orientation des églises, le plan cruciforme, l'ordre dans les sculptures, les zodiaques, les vertus, les vices, les couleurs, les vêtements.[41]

> M. Didron says that he recognizes many facts in which symbolism cannot be denied: i.e., the orientation of churches, the cruciform plan, the order of the sculptures, the zodiacs, the virtues, the vices, the colors, the vestments.

Daly implies that Didron's analytic method, though meritorious in certain respects, fails to grasp the more important notions of a building and its form, stemming from principles of unity. Daly asserts that Didron should be less analytic, and more synthetic, less scientific, and more poetic. In short, Daly draws closer to early romantic notions of organicism and poetic genius, which assumed a work of art's or building's ontology would never be wholly known by scientific method. Rather, analysis may destroy a building's inner life, thereby preventing it from performing its true function, inspiration.[42] The minutes of the *Congrès* summarize Daly's posture.

> M. Daly veut qu'il puisse y avoir harmonie entre la poésie et le bon sens et trouve que M. Didron a été trop sévere pour la poésie. Les images vraies sont souvent les plus poétiques, les mieux senties. Les belles choses, les beaux sentiments viennent de Dieu; il rend hommage au symbolisme religieuse...[43]

M. Daly wishes that it would be possible to have a harmony between poetry and good sense and finds that M. Didron has been too severe for poetry. True images are, after all, the most poetic, the best felt. Beautiful things, beautiful sentiments come from God; Daly renders homage to this religious symbolism...

With regard to the earlier dichotomy proposed by Victor Hugo, should Daly be assessed as either progressive or retrospective? From his own vantage, Daly sees the work of modernity to be an adjunct of Gothic architecture, at least in restoration. He furthermore sees himself able to contribute to the clarification of history. However, he also finds post-Gothic periods other than his own to be aberrations, and proposes that such work be removed. Hence, as formal purifier, he seeks reconstitution of the spirit of a past age. As form giver himself, he becomes the spokesman of a resurrected tradition, attempting to reinvoke not only the logic, but the social conscience of the past in the present day as well.

What are Daly's artistic standards? To draw again upon his confrontation with Didron, it would not seem to be based in conceptions governing Le Beau, but rather in Le Vrai. The introduction of truthfulness gives rise to the notion of ideality, resting on an underpinning of logic and order. Following the interpretation of Rickman, Pugin, Viollet-le-Duc, and de Caumont, Daly saw Gothic structures to be eminently logical. Nineteenth-century modernity also sought a formal end based in structural logic, and hence, seemed to be the true descendent of this orderly tradition.[44]

Moreover, *Le Vrai* invoked social order. Such order was based in social unity, achieved by community of values. In the thirteenth century, these values were communicated by the instrument of the church, by a process of idea transference, or inspiration. This is an issue that we have already encountered in Daly's work on Chartres Cathedral. In this project, reconstruction and clarification of architectural form and structure was explicit; implicit was a reconstruction of society. Daly himself was instrumental in resurrecting not only transcendent architectural values, but social ones as well. It was he who was to resume the great architectural and social task momentarily halted. Daly placed himself in the roles of both master builder and hero of society, on the one hand equated with Abbé Suger or Alberti, and on the other, with Charlemagne or Louis IX. His self-imposed duty was to clothe the idea, both physically and socially. This realization draws us to the problem of historical causality. What was Daly's role within the realm of historical forces? Was Daly merely the pawn of destiny or progress, or was he the spokesman of progress, somehow able both to finalize the past and to expedite the birth of what must be?

To respond adequately, we must return to that question initially posed in this section—how does Daly interpret history? We began this discussion by attempting to define the place of Albi within an architectural and social history. In terms of historical method, Daly began by following the anecdotal, episodic method of historical presentation exploited by Charles Nodier in his *Voyages Pittoresques,* as explanation for building form. For Nodier, human and social life was a great continuum, inflected only by certain cataclysmic and cathartic moments. Nodier attempted to tie architectural causality to social climate. Likewise, in his early discussions of Albi, Daly sought to ascribe cause to historical event.

History as a series of isolated moments paralleled architectural analysis as a collection of episodes or pieces. Fragmentation of a period or of a building permitted an analysis of discrete parts. But without an overriding historical or formal scheme, without certain implicit rules of composition, these parts had great difficulty in being reassembled into an orderly whole. This predicament might be likened to that of an anatomist, who, upon completion of a meticulous examination of some animal's remains, had forgotten whether the specimen was a vertebrate or invertebrate, biped or quadruped. In short, what Nodier's interpretation lacked was a higher historical motive by which independent events or actions might take on an internal logic. For the antiquarian intent upon architectural components or details, what was missing was a means of composition, laws of order by which disparate parts could be collected into a consummate stylistic whole.

It was Jules Michelet who attacked the problem of higher order in both historical and architectural frames. Certainly, in his discussion of the Albigensian Wars, Michelet passionately described the various battles and personalities involved in the momentous conflict. His love of description was no less than Nodier's. But beneath the surface of his chronicle, there was an immanent force which somehow organized and orchestrated the particular historical moments of France during this period. Michelet perceived this force to the be spirit of nationalism, a consciousness beginning with the Capetian dynasty and culminating with Louis IX. Like Hegel in his notion of *Volksgeist,* Michelet believed that the rise of nationalism provided the evidence of divine intervention in the thirteenth century. Daly echoed this view at Albi. Emphasizing the singular domination of royalty over the piecemeal domains of the feudal lords, he stated,

> ...le sceptre de la royauté avait brisé l'épée de la féodalite; les évêques, protégés par le couronne, avaient vu croître leur influence sur les seigneurs laïques...[45]

> ...the scepter of royalty has broken the sword of feudalism; the bishops, protected by the crown, have witnessed the rise of their influence upon lay lords.

For Daly, as for Michelet, the logic of the situation was the national unity fostered by the crown.

Michelet then made a jump from the purely historical to architectural concerns. He cited Hugo, maintaining that architecture is nothing if not the index of human history. Speaking of Notre-Dame de Paris, he asserted,

Si je regardais cette église, ce serait comme le livre d'histoire, comme le grand régistre des destinées de la monarchie.[46]

If I examined this church, it would seem like a book of history, like the great register of the destinies of the monarchy.

Michelet found Notre-Dame to be the representation of a national unity, concentrated in the crown. Even more, for Michelet, architecture became a metaphor of history. He likened details to historical events; composition was described as the "principe de formation." In historical terms, what was this formational principle? Michelet described it as

L'unique principe: aspiration d l'agrégation, de tous en un, de tous vers l'un, comme tendent vers la pointe toutes les lignes de la pyramide.[47]

The unique principle: the aspiration toward aggregation, of all in one, of all toward one, as all the lines of a pyramid converge on a single point.

Michelet implied social or national unity as the fundamental principle. It manifested itself in geometry, for example, the pyramid or triangle. This spirit of composition found a ready analogy in architecture, where geometry and allied proportion lies at the basis of form. For example, if Greek society could best be characterized by the rise of logical thought and a sense of natural order, then architecture must be similarly characterized. Michelet described the Greek temple as a collection of columns and a pediment. The pediment is a triangle, a geometrical figure, symbolizing order to Michelet. Greek political structure remained disunified. Greek architecture's trabeated structural system, with its concomitant forest of columns, implied similar factionalism, with its collection of autonomous, unintegrated stuctural elements. For Michelet these columns symbolized the Greek states, each autonomous, each founded its own set of logical principles.

Roman civilization, however, was characterized by the circle. First the circle was seen as logical, thus Roman architecture was similarly logical. Secondly, arcuated architecture was seen as unified, much as the Roman Empire, the first centralized state, was unified. Michelet expanded this discussion. Unlike the individual structural elements of the Greek system, Roman architecture turned columns into piers, each pier taking in two arches, each arch adjacent to two others. In short, individual architectonic elements were unified by the arcade. Romanesque architecture, the descendant of the Roman, expanded this system, introducing a greater number of formal elements, as well as the superposition of arcades. Ultimately, circularity implied social and political unity. Michelet described the Gothic as a synthesis of the Greek systems of Knowledge, hence logical order, and Roman political unity, defining the ogive as both triangle and circle, linking the two systems.[49]

Daly linked the issue of social spirit with architecture as early as 1847 in his "Tableau de l'Evolution des Styles," in which he paralleled stylistic geometries with social character. The spirit of the age was intimately allied with the geometric rules of composition, described age by age (plate 4).[49] Perhaps this is not the place for a lengthy discussion of historical progress. However, much as for Michelet, the triangle distilled and organized the social ideas of ancient Greece, for Daly, it is the geometry of progress (whatever that may be) which skewered through all historical periods in forming the idea of history itself. It is important that Daly did not perceive history in terms of events any more than he interpreted architecture merely in terms of its parts.

Daly's historical cause was not unlike Michelet's "loi physiologique" based in "une aspiration de l'agrégation." Likewise for Daly, there was a vital principle that activated history, that unified and ordered its events in terms of some perceptible, positive outcome. Similarly, there was a vital principle, a seed, a soul, that ordered architecture. This conception might be termed "organism," to rationalize this *modus* of organization by way of a plant metaphor. The spirit of life, the spark, the instrumentality of higher consciousness gives unity to historical events.

In the face of destiny, what is the human responsibility, the human role, in the shaping of history? Perhaps there is none. Perhaps man is merely to passively follow the course of destiny, drawn by the historical currents or moved by the strings manipulated by higher consciousness. Daly, however, did not believe this. As mentioned above, Daly perceived himself as master-builder and hero. The problem of heroism invokes the issue of consciousness or will in the face of destiny.

The modern law of destiny—progress—was created out of an analogy with natural philsophy, in short, physical science. It was progress which many believe to govern the course of history during the Enlightenment. Concomitantly, however, immanence of such natural law relieved responsibility for oneself. The issue of personal choice and self-determination was an impossibility in the progressive scheme. One was merely the pawn of history.

In theory, Daly believed in progress. In action this view became a more problematical assertion for Daly to maintain. In his role as critic, Daly was social and architectural herald. Rather than accepting a traditional view of the world, Daly shaped and propagated new ones. He acted as spokesman of an impending consciousness not yet born or much less recognized. Consequently, Daly's perceptions had an explicitly causal component. Rather than a follower of destiny, he was its shaper and form-giver. This realization deters one from the idea that Daly was a complacent law-abiding theoretician. Rather, he must be viewed as a man who wrote the laws, guided, as I have already discussed, by a prevision of things to come.

Surely, a few were more progress-fixated than César Daly. At the same time, few were more self-conscious. These two impulses resulted in the feeling that Daly could somehow supervene natural law (progress), to accelerate, to decelerate and even to deviate its course. In so doing, he implicitly brought into question his place in history. In short, Daly by virtue of his sense of self, desired to manipulate destiny, if not to oppose it. This idea forces us to return to the discussion of Daly as hero and artist, both of which involve ideas of personal genius. Daly superimposed inspired consciousness and ideology on the natural law of progress and history itself.

Michelet regarded history as a drama against which heroic action was portrayed, and in which, heroism was involved. He further rejected classical notions of Fate, maintaining that heroic action could alter history. He amplified this assertion in a discussion of art, which he defined as the imposition of consciousness or will upon nature. Michelet described art as "Nature humanisée."[50] Both Michelet and Daly saw life as not only determined by natural law, or progress, but also by heroic will, that is, by the visible signs of genius in man. Clearly, all men could not be heroes. Rather, most were merely the jetsam and flotsam of the tidal movements of history. But men of genius could function independently of destiny. In both Michelet's and Daly's interpretation of history, such men were not passive, but actively instrumental agents of things to be. This instrumentality was apparent in the manifestations of will, or in ideology. The hero's presence was especially evident, not in those logical actions which seemed to be controlled by reason and science, but in certain artistic and consciously stylistic components which appeared to be totally self-motivated.

As a result, certain special men were able to maintain a degree of control over their own futures and over history, itself moved, not by natural law, but by God himself via inspiration. For example, in the thirteenth century, Michelet's great hero was Louis IX. The author described the effects of Louis' genius:

Cette transfiguration du genre humain qui reconnût l'image de Dieu en soi, qui généralisa et qui avait été individuel, qui fixa dans un présent éternel ce qu'on avait cru temporaire et passé, qui naît sur terre un ciel; elle fût la rédemption du monde moderne.[51]

This transfiguration of the human race which recognizes the image of God in itself, which generalized what had previously been individual, which fixed in an eternal present what had been believed to be temporary and past, which gave birth on earth to a heaven; this was the redemption of the modern world.

Caesar, Charles Martel, Charlemagne, Philippe Auguste, Louis IX—all were heroes in Michelet's eyes; such men were the great manipulators of history. Even though national unity was the spirit of the age, the character of the thirteenth century could not have been established without the instrumentality of certain inspired men. For Michelet, history did not run like a huge clock, but rather needed to be manipulated, or wound up, by the intervention of men of genius equipped with *prévoyance*.

The great man syndrome characterized much history writing during this period. Napoleon I, in vindicating his own political stand, discussed Caesar, Charlemagne, and Louis XIV. Napoleon III produced a biography of Julius Caesar, and he consciously modelled himself on his great uncle, Napoleon. Historians of the arts ascribed great importance to men of taste, for it had been the case historically that enlightened patrons provided the major commissions for artists. As an example, Louis Baltard's *Paris et Ses Monuments* (1803-35) constructed a history of French architecture, focusing, not so much on socio-political conditions, as upon stylistic schools introduced by various courts. Focal personalities in his discussion included Francis I, Louis XIV, Louis XV, Louis XVI and Napoleon.[52] Perhaps more importantly, Alexandre de Laborde no longer used national boundary as the criterion for bringing architectural styles into parallel with political shifts, stating in his introduction to the second volume (1836) of *Les Monuments de la France,*

> Ces différents styles ont subi, avec les temps, de notables exceptions; mais ces changements n'ont pas de dates précises, comme la réunion d'une comté ou d'une province. Ainsi l'on ne sera pas étonné que, dans la classification des monuments, nous ne nous astreignons pas aux divisions que nous avons dû admettre en écrivant l'histoire géographique de France.[53]

> These different styles have undergone, with time, notable exceptions; but these changes don't have precise dates, like the reunion of a county or province. Thus, one will not be surprised that, in a classification of monuments, we are not confined to divisions which we have to allow in writing the geographical history of France.

He preferred instead to discuss court styles and "schools" sponsored by men of taste. About Carolingian architecture de Laborde advanced,

> L'architecture presque ensevelie dans la chute de l'empire romain d'Occident, semblera se relever avec lui, par la puissance du vaste génie de Charlemagne.[54]

> Architecture, almost enslaved after the fall of the Western Roman Empire, seems to rise again with...the power of Charlemagne.

Moreover, de Laborde noted that the French Renaissance was a fashion wholly opposed by the socio-political climate, but was fostered by remarkable men, and especially the king.

> La Renaissance...intention difficile à mettre en oeuvre que nos moeurs contrarient, à laquelle notre climat s'oppose; mais qui dût cependant céder au génie d'hommes habiles et persévérants. Ils ont à jamais consacré leur nom et le règne du prince aimable qui les protégeaient...François I.[55]

> The Renaissance...difficult intention to put into play because our morals contradict it and our climate opposes it; but which nonetheless succeeded through the genius of capable and perseverant men. [These artists] forever consecrated their names [to]...the reign of the kind prince who protected them..., François I.

In much the same way, Daly's own interpretation of French architectural history, published in 1869 in an essay "L'Architecture de l'Avenir" published in the second edition of *Motifs Historiques,* cited the importance of focal personalities and court styles rather than political or geographic situation.[56] It seems likely that Daly recognized, at least aesthetically, the need for a kind of artistic dictatorship, introduced or sponsored by a man or men of taste, or even genius. As mentioned above, Daly sought patronage in the court of Napoleon III. Injudicious political alliances in his earlier life made Daly an unacceptable candidate in official artistic circles. This failure, however, did not divert him from attempting to shape public taste by way of more popular means.

The César Daly of the representative monarchy of Louis-Philippe and democratic Second Republic knew that a new artistic despotism was unlikely. Rather, patronage ceased to be an issue in support of official style. With the decline of court styles during these periods, the role of the critic became central to the taste-making process. Daly himself could become the trend-setting man of taste, of discrimination, even of inspiration. Here, one might parallel Daly with a critic like Baudelaire, whose symbolic support of "l'art pour l'art" was an explicit argument in favor of the critic's as well as the artist's participation in higher consciousness, as we shall see in the next chapter. Daly, like Baudelaire, sought to inform the art of the future via prevision of things to come, and to set into motion the machinery of things to be.

Daly moved from a view of art history interpreted as the outcome of natural law, to one of a drama shaped by heroes, and finally, to one in which he himself became a heroic actor. As a man of genius, he desired to create forms equally inspired, imbued with the spirit of the age. This posture embodied a component which was essentially modern—mechanical, positive, and progressive. Yet, in his search for unity, Daly sought principles of higher order having a transcendental component, on the one hand, an ideality best conveyed by the architectural type, and on the other, a spiritual identity formed by his own inspired artistic consciousness.

The Restoration of Albi Cathedral

I shall begin the description of César Daly's restoration of Sainte-Cécile with a technique used earlier to discuss his work and ideas on Chartres Cathedral—an interpretation of the drawings. There were two major considerations at play in Daly's visual documentation of Albi. The first was scientific. The Conseil des Bâtiments Civils entrusted Daly with the task of analyzing and recording the existing state of the church. Moreover, it sought a proposal for the satisfactory protection of church and artworks, as well as a project for its completion.

The second consideration was didactic. As mentioned earlier, the Commission des Monuments Historiques, an adjunct organization of the Conseil, was primarily responsible for the education of the French people in subjects concerning their national architectural heritage. The subliminal motivation behind such an organization was essentially chauvinistic. The effective communication of these interests was not so much a matter of archaeological accuracy, but of persuasive articulation and style.[57]

Daly's rendition of Albi Cathedral deals with both issues. The popular, expressive component, which groped for public attention, is easily recognized in his rendering of the west front of the church (plate 41). It is especially apparent in those features already described as "characteristic," that is, the use of light, shadow, atmosphere and genre (scale) figures. Daly tied these provocative painterly techniques to new researches into pictorial form proposed by the Romantic school of painting. In 1840 he stated,

> Les dessins d'architecture sont devenus de magnifiques aquarelles, au les artistes révèlent une habileté de main et un sentiment de l'effet pictural vraiment merveilleux...[58]

> Architectural drawings have become magnificent watercolors in which artists reveal a facility of hand and a truly marvelous sentiment for pictorial effect.

Moreover, the romantic painters had become very fashionable. Daly suggested that the enormous popularity of the romantics had become an important stimulus for architectural rendering. He cited the instrumentality of the popular taste on architecture especially by means of the influential Salons. By far the most frequented part of the annual show was the painting section, and the most popular paintings were those of the young romantics. Architects tried to gain public attention by using the painterly techniques; they labored under the desire for public recognition. Daly stated,

> [C'était une]...tendence moderne à vouloir capter à tout prix l'attention du public, ce désir naturel aux artistes, jeunes et vieux, de mettre en évidence les ressources de leur talent...[59]

> [It has been]...a modern tendency to want to capture at any price the attention of the public; it is a natural desire for artists, young and old, to make evident the resourcefulness of their talent.

In short, Daly asserted that in order for architects to gain recognition, they were forced to popularize techniques so effectively exploited by their compatriots and artistic competitors, specifically the romantic painters. As a result, coloristic technique found fertile ground in contemporary architectural delineation.

Daly's presentation of the church of Sainte-Cécile is coloristic. It was surely affected by a concern with public exhibition, being presented for the first time at the Salon of 1845. The rendering of the west facade with its great tower illustrates the use of romantic light and shadow. The moody setting, the play of lights and shadows, the suggestive clouds create a strong sense of atmosphere in the *rendu*. Elements peripheral to the facade—the archiepiscopal palace, the south portal, and the main gateway—fall into silhouette in juxtaposition to the tower. Here, Daly displayed a conscious interest in evocative setting.

Still, the elevation itself avoids any equivocation or compromise by shadow. The tower is luminous, bathed ironically in a strong, direct light from the north, in direct contrast to the chiaroscuro implied by the overcast sky. There are two elements to this radiant depiction of facade. On the one hand, the description of the tower is scientific and correct. On the other, it ignores the circumstances of the situation, overcoming variations of light and shadow. By bathing it in a divine northern light, Daly interprets the elevation as an architectural feature which transcends time and place, and allows the facade to assume an almost iconic role in the reconstruction. Scientific accuracy is elevated to something more; the church as intepreted passes from the merely realistic or characteristic to the ideal.

Daly's use of color tends to reinforce this notion. Although Daly rendered the sky in a way which defies accurate description, he exploited the red color of the brick facade to define color and composition. This aspect becomes even more apparent in the transverse section of the church, included in the same suite of drawings, wherein the painted wall surfaces are used, not to fragment form, but to define planes, and to imply compositional readings (plate 42). In short, on the interior of the building, Daly viewed the existing painted surfaces as a means to clarify formal and visual relationships, not immediately visible to the eye. To use a painterly analogy, although Daly criticized the romantic colorists, attacking them on the basis of formal fragmentation and obscurity, he clearly exploited a colorism of his own. Unlike Délacroix, however, his own technique might have a greater kinship with Ingres, Delaroche, or Flandrin, who never lost a sense of line, contour, surface, and compositional logic even when composing in color. Similarly, Daly's depiction of Albi Cathedral is ambivalent. It is surely tied to certain romantic notions of atmosphere and character. Yet, it also embodies a critique of those architects who would sacrifice form in favor of the transitory, illusory, ephemeral, or evocative. Daly's Albi is, on the one hand, fragmentary, circumstantial, and romantic, and on the other reasoned and idealistic. Daly's general approach to the reconstruction project is dualistic.

Analytical drawings prepared in 1845, comprising plans, sections, and details display visualizations of the project's three major building campaigns as well as their implicit overall design intentions. I call attention to the sections (plate 43). The first of the three schemes that Daly provided is a hypothetical reconstruction of the church as it would have been envisioned by Guillaume de la Voulte at the end of the fourteenth century. The second is Louis I d'Amboise's conjectural project of the late fifteenth century. The third is Daly's own proposal. We known that Guillaume completed the church proper, roofed the nave and constructed the main tower to the height of the chancel. Moreover, Daly believed that Guillaume would have completed the building as a kind of fortification, since his reign was especially marked by warfare, stemming from English raids against Languedoc, and against the city of Albi particularly. Daly also saw Guillaume as predecessor of Bernard de Castanet who rebuilt and strengthened the city walls, completing, among other things, a city gate bearing Bernard's name.

The first of Daly's reconstructions imagined the church's completion as Guillaume would have conceived it. Daly's major evidences of the bishop's intentions included the two pinnacles and the walkway on the front of the church. Daly exploited these details to fabricate an extensive reconstruction of Guillaume's presumed project. From this evidence, Daly extrapolated Guillaume's total conception. Daly saw Guillaume as proposing a great parapet wall to surround the church, obstructing the view of the roof. Guillaume then would have planned the piers to be carried above the roof height, extending to the top of the parapet. At the rooftop level, each pier would have housed a staircase permitting freedom of access between lower and upper levels of the parapet, especially important for reasons of defense. The piers at the roof level would have been perforated, allowing for easy circulation between the tribune-like subsidiary spaces formed by the piers and covered by the overhead walkway. This walkway, establishing the upper level of the parapet, would have finally connected the turrets which surmounted the piers-cum-stairtowers. The low bulwark terminating the parapet would have been treated as crenelation.

As with Guillaume, Daly envisioned Louis I d'Amboise's completion of Albi. In Daly's view, Louis had a very different set of objectives from his fourteenth-century predecessor, conditioned by political climate and by his personality as patron. During Louis' tenure there were no wars of religion. Hence, the factor of defense at Albi was no longer considered. Furthermore, Louis' involvements were not with war or politics, but with culture. Daly, like his contemporaries, recognized the family d'Amboise as one of learning and fashion. He connected the bishop with his more famous brother, Georges d'Amboise, Chancellor to Louis XII, connoisseur and collector of Italian Renaissance art.[60] Daly's association of Louis with Georges d'Amboise intensified an understanding of the bishop of Albi, not as a man of action, but as a dilettante and a man of taste.

Hence, for Daly, Louis d'Amboise's project for Albi lacked the pragmatism and purpose of Guillaume's proposal. Daly displays the bishops' differences, especially in his rendition of Albi's tower where Louis' superstructure which displays a fanciful, flamboyant composition in contrast to Guillaume's dour base. Guillaume's lower levels present a solemn composition of brick interrupted only by the contours of structurel piers embedded in the masonry. The only surface relief in Guillaume's tower is a series of blank arches expressing the various interior levels (plate 44). In contrast, Daly displays Louis' summit as composed of a pair of distinct octagonal forms whose silhouette is complicated by flying buttresses. Surface decoration includes a complicated interplay of flamboyant elliptical with ogival arches, rinceaux, carved emblems and gargoyles. Rather than functional considerations, Daly sees Louis' achievement to be the complication of tower profile and visual effect.

With regard to the Louis I crowning of the church, the gallery and loopholes, which Daly saw to be consistent with Guillaume's design, disappear. The piers are no longer expressed above the roofline, and the towers do not articulate a vertical circulation system from parapet wall to rooftop as in Guillaume's scheme, nor do they really serve to resolve the articulation of the piers above the building proper. We are left with the feeling that turrets are retained in Louis' scheme, not so much for structural or visual logic as the picturesque effect. As in the reconstruction of Guillaume's proposal, Daly envisioned a ten meter parapet wall to be erected, surmounted by a *passerelle* connecting the lower lovels of the turrets. In the proposed reconstruction of Louis' plan, crenellations disappear, and limestone balustrades take their place, decorated with a profusion of quatrefoils interlaced with the arms of the Amboise family, the bishop of Albi, and the royal *fleur de lys*. For Daly, the points of agreement between Guillaume's and Louis' schemes are the high parapet wall serving to hide the roof, the towers articulating the structural piers in elevation (if not in section), and the *passerelle* surmounting the side walls, linking the turrets.

Daly's proposal for the restoration was a mixture of the two earlier projects. The major formal moves extended from Guillaume de la Voulte. Like Guillaume, Daly conceived the sidewalls as a ten meter parapet rising above the level of the roof. Furthermore, he articulated the piers as turrets rising above the parapet. Lastly, he surmounted the new parapet with an overhead walkway, linking the lower levels of the turrets.

His treatment of the piers in section and the decorative scheme descended from Louis d'Amboise. The piers terminated at the roof line. Their sole articulation was at their outermost extremity where piers became turrets. With regard to decoration, the exterior articulation of the corbel table duplicated Louis' similar treatment on an intermediate level of the main tower. The balustrade was treated as a carved interlace rather than Guillaume's crenelation. The gargoyles of the main tower served as model for the new ones of the parapet.

Daly's personal contribution to the church consisted of a new roof configuration, housing a carefully devised protective wrapper for the interior ceiling frescoes. The Ministry's major concern was with safeguarding the paintings from any infiltration of water. Daly's scheme comprised two independent systems—one over the nave paintings, another over the tribunes and side chapels. To protect the nave paintings, Daly covered the existing interior vaults with a second impermeable concrete vaulting system. This second skin was in turn covered with an exterior gable roof. This new roof, built on wood and cast-iron, rested on a low brick wall spanning between the piers of the nave. It was covered with the red clay tiles of the region.

The covering over the side chapels conformed more closely to the roof's original configuration. Pavers sealed with lead served as the roofing material. Permeable joints between the pavers permitted rainwater to drain into subsurface collectors, which would in turn conduct water to a trough along the perimeter of the parapet wall. This trough led to gutters and downspouts. Water from the upper roof drained in a more conventional manner. It was directed into gutters lining the extremities of this roof, conducted to downspouts, then to waterproof channels impressed into the surface of the lower roof, and finally to downspouts located at various points along the perimeter of the building. These downspouts would direct water from the roof to underground conduits at foundations of the church. Excess rainwater was relieved by rooftop scuppers masked as gargoyles.

Daly's three reconstructions give rise to certain questions. First, were towers always intended for the church? Second, is the separate articulation of nave and side chapels appropriate in this church? Third, are there formal considerations at work in Daly's reconstruction project that extend beyond the functional and visual logic of the situation? Let us begin with the question of the towers. As implied in his reconstruction of Guillaume de la Voulte's project for the church, Daly's interpretation of Albi Cathedral began on a materialistic level. As Daly saw it, Guillaume conceived the structure as a fortification rather than as a church. The gallery, *archères,* and turrets were called into existence for reasons of defense: politics caused form. Furthermore, church form was analyzed and evaluated from a functional point of view. This posture was certainly to be equated with the archaeological researches of De Caumont and Rickman, who especially appreciated Gothic architecture from a structural basis. Architecture was affected by statics, much as it was affected by society. Both types of cause could be evaluated scientifically.

For these antiquarians, all parts of a Gothic building participated in the general structural logic. A telling example of this point of view was the nineteenth century interpretation of the turret or pinnacle, and its relationship to Gothic construction. Rickman and Willis in England, and Viollet-de-Duc in France correctly interpreted the internal stresses of the buttress system fundamental to Northern Gothic structure. They realized that the compressive force resulting from the pinnacle tended to counteract the bending moment of the pier, induced by the outward thrust caused by the church wall and transmitted by the buttress itself. The flying buttress rationalized the employment of the pinnacle. However, in the monolithic, arcuated masonry system at Albi, where lateral forces were continually balanced by equal but opposite forces internal to the pier, pinnacles became a redundancy. Their structural logic was lost. The construction of turrets at Albi would do little more than to add unnecessary compressive force to the brick masonry.

Certainly, in some situations brick masonry could withstand the additional compressive load. However, at Albi, the brick walls and piers clearly could not. This fact became apparent only after Daly had built six turrets on the piers of the chevet, only to discover the foundation settling and the exterior walls pulling away from his nearly completed roof system (plate 45). In 1853 funds were requested from the Ministère des Cultes to shore up the sagging walls.[61] Work was halted for structural problems, as well as for a labor dispute which extended over the next seven years.[62] Léon Vaudoyer, *inspecteur* of the works for the Commission des Edifices Religieux, ignored the structural problems caused by the increased dead load of the new roof and recommended that the work on the towers be resumed.[63] Soon thereafter it became apparent that the towers were a problem, and work was again halted. The controversy culminated in 1866, when the motion was made in the French Senate to remove those towers already built in order to preserve the existing church fabric as well as its primitive silhouette.[64] However, Daly insisted on retention of existing towers, even if no further ones were built, and the turrets were finally removed only after Daly left his post of *architecte-diocésain* in 1877.[65]

The structural problems caused by Albi's towers were enormous. Although pinnacles are essential as counterweights for the stability of the High Gothic structural system, at Albi they were not only useless, but also destructive. Daly's justification for the ring of towers stemmed primarily from foundations of four similar towers never constructed on the south side of the church. He used this evidence as ammunition for his hypothetical reconstruction. Still, could not one suggest that these incomplete, primitive towers remained unachieved because of changes of patronage or formal viewpoint? Or perhaps these turrets were so abruptly halted in the fifteenth century for exactly the same reason as in the nineteenth. We might propose that these formal elements remained unbuilt for those structural reasons that Daly, Viollet, and others considered so important. Moreover, it would seem that early builders realized that structural elements appropriate for one constructional system were not necessarily appropriate for another. Hence, continuing this building campaign would have been wholly illogical. Yet, Daly, even though confronted with the structural inconsistencies of his project for reconstruction, continued to advocate their employ.

An explanation might be sought in areas other than structural logic. Perhaps one such area of inquiry might be what Daly earlier termed "l'effet pittoresque."[66] For Daly picturesque effect first involves a component of evocative juxtaposition of masses and irregularity of contour. Secondarily, the picturesque involves the element of imagination. As discussed above with Chartres, it is evident that Daly especially appreciated the interplay of forms and details of *Ile-de-France* Gothic churches. The play of masses, light and shadow, etc., was the result of the articulation of parts, of formal/spatial components in these churches. In elevation, Chartres could be conceived as the complete, volumetric extrusion of plan. In Daly's mind, Albi Cathedral could be something quite similar. In actuality, however, Sainte-Cécile could not have been more unlike the *Ile-de-France* churches.

What was Albi Cathedral? As Krautheimer noted when dealing with similar churches in southern Germany, it was little more than a wall-defined perimeter with a roof over it.[67] In short, it was a single volume, a universal space. It is true that there are sub-spaces within the interior—a sequence of ground level chapels and first story tribunes, which were added in the fifteenth century. Originally, chapel and tribune constituted a single vertical space of the same height as the nave. These spatial zones read less as separate volumes, than as an extension of the main space in and around the structural piers. The interior took on a single unified reading, albeit a fluid one.[68]

The early builders at Sainte-Cécile seemed particularly attuned to this fundamental spatial quality. On the exterior of the church subsidiary spaces were not indicated; they were included in the more generalized spatial envelope implied by the all-embracing roof. The brick piers, were not read as independent structural elements articulated on the exterior by pinnacles, but were treated more as building *poché,* perhaps denser than the rest of the building fabric, but implicitly establishing a continuity with the rest of the enclosure system by means of color and material. Structure and building membrane tended to be fused rather than differentiated as in the Gothic architecture of the *Ile-de-France.*[69]

Daly ignored these architectural readings. He seems to have been implicitly operating under the desire for a picturesque articulation as displayed at Chartres. He wished to treat the nave differently than the tribunes, enclosure separate from structure, surface separate from decoration. These formal components are wholly understandable within the structural assumptions of the antiquarian, but bear little relationship to the situation of schools outside of the *Ile-de-France.*

Daly's desire extended to a second, more basic level, which has little to do with the merely functional or pragmatic. Rather it has to do with visual logic. We have already observed this level of rationalization in Daly's description of the painted surfaces of the nave and tribunes of Albi Cathedral. In his transverse section, he described the walls in terms of an interplay of decorative fields. The major sections could be defined as unified fields of lozenge and diamond patterns. These fields, however, were always restrained by a different border design. The edges tended to be read as a frame, and introduced visual stability into the scheme of ornamentation. On a larger scale, this kind of framing, and the ordering system implied therein, might be equated with a schematized grid system. Unlike the romantic colorists of the 1830s, he did not use polychromy to obscure or fragment major formal systems, but to reinforce visual order.

The idea of visual order is important here, for the decorative surface treatment of Albi Cathedral does not necessarily reinforce implicit structural order. Were this the case, the decorative panelling of the piers would disappear in favor of a more generalized, indefinite, decorative field. Rather than arcuated or monolithic structural systems, the decorative scheme implied a trabeated system not unlike the classical or renaisance beam-and-column technique. Hence, we see that the painted decoration of Albi proposed a visual logic that tended to ignore the actual structure.

Since he saw no engaging visual order in Guillaume's system, Daly especially appreciated the decorative campaign of Louis I d'Amboise. Particularly instructive in this regard is a book of sketches depicting the decorative program of the porch and *jubé*, which Daly compiled before commencing the restoration of the south porch or the reconstitution of its vault. Daly's appreciation of Louis' ornamentation focuses upon the issue of the rupture between structural and decorative formal systems. The porch is supported on one side by the piers of the church, and on the other, by two buttresses which simultaneously read as clustered columns. These piers rise to support an elliptical arch, upon which tier after tier of smaller elliptical as well as ogival arches are constructed. It is clear that the major spanning device is the elliptical arch. Ogives are merely a decorative redundancy (plate 46). These distinctions between circular or arcuated systems which do the work, and ogival systems which please the eye, are especially apparent in the lower reaches of the piers, where the clustered columns manipulate and flex the pointed arch in conformity with its own contour. Furthermore, the ogives and piers are surmounted by fantastic pinnacles, the most recognizable of which are those in *fleur-de-lys* pattern. Surely, nowhere is the juxtaposition between frank and structural system and brilliant decoration more apparent than in the porch.

Daly's own work on the cathedral expresses a distinction between structural and visual logic. For example, the parapet that Daly erected over the piers to support the roof was articulated by relieving arches of Roman provenance (plate 43, detail). This masonry technique was most notably used on the Pantheon in Rome, supposedly to relieve excess compressive force on the masonry wall. Modern research has indicated that these arches at the Pantheon serve no structural purpose, and the same must be so at Albi. They do serve to inform the viewer of the new concrete vaults present behind the brick screen of the parapet. The squat pilasters which accompany them in Daly's reconstruction articulate the bay system of the interior and the calculated rhythm of the pier system beneath. Arch and pilaster, have little to do with the way in which the building is actually built, but both features have an enormous amount to do with the reading of the total idea behind Daly's restoration project.

Daly's design for a vault over the unfinished south porch *(Baldaquin)* is an even more provocative example of this phenomenon at Albi (plate 47). As a kind of prostyle *aedicule,* supported at four points, a minimal four-part vault would have been the most simple and logical solution possible. In fact, it is just such an ogival vault that Viollet-le-Duc proposed for this porch in his *Dictionnaire Raisonnée* (plate 48). However, Daly was less concerned with structural economy than Viollet, and interested more in a vault harmonious, not with the primitive structural technique, but with the innovative, consciously artistic, and willful decoration of Louis I d'Ambroise. His project was *flamboyant,* not *rayonnant.* Daly's vault was enormously complicated, a wild interplay of straight and curvilinear ribs, centering upon a hanging pendant. It was most assuredly elegant and beautiful, but it was hardly a minimal statement. Daly's fundamental interest was in stylistic consistency, not in structural efficiency. He understood and admired the fantastic character of ornament, an aspect of art existing outside of scientific or spatial consideration. Style had a life of its own.

Ultimately, the idea of artistic vitalism may give us a means to understand the use of towers at Albi. As stated above, Daly's conception of "l'effet pittoresque" invoked a component of the artistic imagination. As I argued earlier, imagination is that faculty by which the facts of nature are ordered by reason. Reason vitalized nature. Artistic creation as an especially poignant example of imagination is that wherein artistic consciousness conquers external nature, imbuing it with a soul.

Such vitalism is apparent in Daly's interpretation of the projects of Louis I d'Amboise I at Albi. Daly especially admired the *jubé* or choir screen in the nave. That element alone gave meaning to the church. The *jubé* was, iconographically, the embodiment of human and biblical history, and, visually, the seat of religion and the spirit of the church.

The *jubé* is a special object, best described as a chapel in itself, built within the nave at the end of the fifteenth century, serving as seating for the chapter of Sainte-Cécile as well as an appropriate setting for the sacrifice of the Mass (plate 49). It is an elaborate construction, whose periphery comprises an arcade of flamboyant arches, and a two-story rood screen as a facade. The exterior is decorated by a series of sculptures of the Burgundian school, representing the prophets. On the inside, similar statues depict the apostles. Both series are juxtaposed with ranks of sculpted angels, and the Madonna and child. The iconography implies a reading of the Old versus the New Testament, as well as an indication of the Heavenly Jerusalem. In short, the chronicle of religion is depicted, as well as man's just reward in the future. The *jubé* becomes the symbol of the past and the future, and, by implication, the present, i.e., of human history.

Moreover, the *jubé* is the symbol of the Church itself. Although a tiny chapel, it is to be seen as the seat of history and religion, the germ or the soul of the cathedral. Daly states, le choeur...[indique]...l'esprit symbolique, cette même alliance de la forme et de la pensée, qui anime la matière et rend l'âme visible...[70]

the choir [indicates]...the symbolic spirit, the same alliance of form and thought which animates the material and renders the soul visible.

These characteristics of the *jubé* remind us of Michelet's definition of art as "matière spiritualisée," or the domination of spirit over nature. This is exactly the process of artistic imagination—the discovery of appropriate form, not only for the effective portrayal, but also for the conveyance of an idea. Much as a seed informs the growth of a plant, and the plant creates a new seed, the vitalism inherent in the *jubé* should somehow be apparent in, or interactive with the external forms of Sainte-Cécile. The *jubé*'s composition of piers, lancet windows and pinnacles should be recognized in the form of its receptacle. Daly's love of turrets, irregular silhouette, and inventive decoration in the exterior of Sainte-Cécile may be a recognition of this notion, indicative of the play of ideology at the core of religion, and doubtless of architectural form as well.

The issue of spirit returns us to an issue discussed above—the problem of typology. Why did Daly not interpret Albi in a typological way? We have already seen that Daly was interested in the "picturesque" nature of the church, evocativeness, and imagination. He attempted to invoke these issues formally by imposing upon the church a foreign typology, that is, Chartres Cathedral, without recognizing that Sainte-Cécile might be representative of a church type in its own right. Ultimately, we feel that Daly desires to treat the church, not as it was, but as he wanted it to be.

A recurrent problem in this restoration was the continuing attempt to define Sainte-Cécile in terms of two functional types. The first was the fortification, an idea stemming from the social history of the commune of Albi. The second was the church type, epitomized for Daly by the *Ile-de-France* cathedral of the thirteenth century. Daly's immediate interpretation of Albi is as a hybrid structure, displaying characteristics of two types, but wholly conforming to neither. This tentative conclusion seems to contradict our initial assumption in this chapter that Daly tended to conceive architecture both typologically and idealistically.

Naturally, the alternative to Daly's equivocal posture would be to consider Albi as representative of a church type in and of itself, independent of the norm of Northern Gothic. If we make a closer examination of the church, we note that it contains a number of clues that might lead to such an interpretation. For example, the architects' use of brick, a common material, might pose certain suggestive questions. Traditionally, the use of brick has been explained by commentators on Albi as the outcome of practical concerns. A church serving as a fortification had little use for such an honorific material as stone. Furthermore, the building site lay a considerable distance from major quarries.

Both circumstances forced builders to depend on a locally-produced building material. Lastly, brick was economical.

Persuasive as these arguments may be for some, they do not bear up under close analysis. The use of brick as the only available material is contradicted by Albi's votive church of Saint Salvi, largely built of limestone from nearby Castres and sandstone from Carcassonne, some fifty miles away. Although some may argue that the use of stone in a votive church is an honorific application, it is clear that a cathedral is no less a ceremonial structure. Rather, it would seem the use of stone at Sainte-Cécile should be equally appropriate.

Furthermore, there was the problem of the availability of brick as opposed to the difficulty of acquiring stone. To be sure, there was no quarry on the site of Albi Cathedral. The size of the program would call for an enormous quantity of masonry, and it would have to be imported. However, what church in the north had a quarry on the site and was not at least as large as Sainte-Cécile? It was not uncommon to import stone from distant quarries for quality or density of stone. For example, the quarries of Caen, by virtue of their limestone quality, supplied stone to sites as diverse as Laon, Senlis, and Amiens, as well as to building locations across the English Channel. Why then could stone not have been imported to Albi as it had to other sites in the north?

In counterargument, some historians might claim financial limitations. However, there were few building campaigns in the whole of France as well funded as Albi. After the Albigensian Wars, Louis IX appointed the archbishop of Albi not only the religious, but also the temporal ruler of the area. As a result, the Albi diocese was one of the wealthiest in France at the time. Public works in the area were not carried out under the auspices of the local feudal lord, the Comte de Toulouse, but by the bishop. When the city walls were rebuilt in the fourteenth century, it was not with the permission of the local feudal lord, but the bishop who afforded the funds. The most lavish display of the power of Bernard de Castanet and his successors was an enormous archiepiscopal palace, which as Mâle states, was surpassed in France only by the papal palace in Avignon.[71]

Surely, at Albi economy was less an issue than at other building sites due to the sizeable resources available for the project. Rather, if brick was used, it was for reasons other than cost-efficiency or the unavailability of stone. Brick was not the only accessible material, but merely one of a number. Perhaps there was a meaning beyond such materialistic reasoning that the use of such a common construction technique represented. Perhaps brick had a historical significance. Perhaps its importance was symbolic.

Let us expand upon this symbolic component by examining, first, Albi's decorative scheme, and second, its plan. The fresco decoration of Albi's interior is unique among French churches of this status, contrasting especially with the Gothic churches of the *Ile-de-France*. In order to determine the importance of Albi's frescoes, it is necessary to examine the evidence suggesting that they were part of the architect's original intention. Whether Albi's total scheme as it now stands was planned from the outset is an open question. The uniformity of the church's broad, flat wall surfaces and its great vault, and the fact that the church's fabric per se generally lacks the shocking formal and stylistic juxtapositions that mark different building campaigns in other churches implies a comprehensive plan.[72] If, as many would maintain, Bernard de Castanet designed the building, then could one not further ask whether he also planned a distinctive kind of decoration for it? Further, did the painters, like the builders of the church, instinctively understand and carry out his intentions some three hundred years later?

At this point, a closer look at Bernard de Castanet appears worthwhile. Bernard was appointed bishop to Albi by the Roman papal court in 1277. Like his predecessors, his task included fighting the *Cathares*, hence maintaining the Inquisition, and enforcing the peace. He was a Dominican.

It is thus no accident that the Dominican involvement at Albi is well depicted in both sculptural and pictorial iconographic campaigns. For example, the sculptural decoration surmounting the gateway of Porte de Dominique includes the images of the founders of the two mendicant orders, St. Dominic and St. Francis. Furthermore, there is the figure of St. Bernard, the first Dominican missionary to confront the Albigensians during the Crusade of Louis VIII. On the interior of the church, the painted decoration, particularly the "Last Judgment" on the west wall, also displays mendicant symbolism, again depicting Saints Dominic and Francis. Clearly, the specific symbolism of these orders is important to understanding the significance of the decorative schemes at Albi.

Mendicant symbolism in pictorial composition is reinforced by the fresco technique itself. The use of common materials and low (fresco) versus high (mosaic or sculpture) art forms characterizes the new populist interests of these orders. Albi's use of painted decoration, albeit of a fifteenth-century provenance, makes a connection with the mendicant tradition with its popular and humanitarian preferences.

Moreover, the mendicant symbolism important to Albi's decorative scheme is carried into the church's plan type. This mendicant plan type might be described by turning to the great parent church of these orders, the church of San Francesco in Assissi. San Francesco comprises a pair of separate chapels, each on a different level. The lower church presents a plan configuration almost identical with Sainte-Cécile: a nave church with side chapels enclosed by the building's structural piers (plate 50). On the exterior of the church, the piers are articulated exactly as at Albi, as semicircular pilasters, or engaged columns which have somehow become embedded in the building's masonry.[73] Lastly, the church of San Francesco is characterized by the simplicity of materials and form, representational technique, and specifically mendicant iconographic programs. The same is true of Albi. Differences between the churches certainly exist. For instance, the proportions of Albi tend to be more attenuated than the horizontal San Francesco. This verticality is perhaps to be ascribed to the influence of Northern Gothic proportions.

The nave church became the great plan type of the mendicant orders. The influence of Italian prototypes is already evident in the earliest Dominican churches in France, beginning with the "Grand Couvent" in Paris at the beginning of the thirteenth century, and continuing with the subsequent Jacobin churches in Constance, Agen, and Toulouse.[74] In France, however, the type moved from a single to a double nave church plan (plate 51). This plan type is frequently compared to a monastery's refectory. The comparison is not inappropriate, for it raises questions concerning the functioning of the church. Much like a refectory, the double-nave church's function is not so much ritual as service, not so much liturgical as instructional.

The French variant of the mendicant hall plan is displayed at the church of St. Jacques in Toulouse. Like San Francesco, St. Jacques is constructed entirely of brick. Its double nave is lined by two rows of piers, and the exterior membrane of the church alternates between the inner and outer extremities of these members. This articulation results in a series of interstitial chapels, similar to those already observed by both San Francesco and Ste. Cécile. This double nave church was the immediate predecessor of the single nave at Albi. As an improvement of the shorter vaulting spans of St. Jacques, Albi's ceiling must be regarded as a supreme example of the thirteenth century's technical virtuosity. Moreover, as a single nave, Albi draws closer to its Italian than to its French relatives.

If, then, Albi Cathedral can be characterized by a distinct plan type, supported by specific mendicant iconography, why is it that César Daly refused to recognize this aspect of the church's true significance? We could postulate a number of reasons that might explain this phenomenon. First, it could be argued that Daly, along with other mid-nineteenth-century architects, failed to read plans in an iconographic way. However, this position seems untenable, since a number of Daly's contemporaries, for example Didron l'Aîné, were already developing the analytical means to evaluate plan types.

Second, we might suggest that Daly was essentially a historical materialist unable to accept any idea of architectural typology. But, as we have seen above, Daly did not hesitate to recommend certain historical building types, especially when working within an urbanistic context. Clearly, Daly's reservations concerning typology did not generate a comprehensive denial of building types, especially when considered within the appropriate conditions.

Third, we might propose that Daly could not accept mendicant symbolism because it suggested a "school" of art. As we have seen, he was opposed to institutionalized design. Yet, his hostility to artistic institutions did not prevent Daly from admiring the sixteenth-century Renaissance architectural forms of Albi Cathedral, which were clearly indebted to the court styles of Louis XII and

Francis I. Daly's hostility to institutions of art was concentrated upon the Ecole des Beaux-Arts. Others remained external to his antagonisms. We must conclude that Daly's posture to artistic institutions, as "schools" of art, was selective, and therefore, as ambivalent as was his posture toward typology.

Fourth, it might be argued that Daly was unfamiliar with other churches of the mendicant genre, most importantly, the great parent churches, San Francesco in Assissi, the "Grand Couvent" in Paris, or St. Jacques in Toulouse. Yet, we know that this cannot be the case because both Jacobin churches in Paris and Toulouse were published, the first as an engraving by Ransonnette, the second as an illustration for de Laborde's *Monuments* and de Caumont's *Cours.*[75] Moreover, during his involvement with the Commission des Arts et Edifices Religieux, Daly himself became the inspector of the diocese of Toulouse, and his reports included references to work in progress on St. Jacques. If Daly failed to consider the Jacobin church type, it must have been for reasons other than a lack of information.

Finally, we might posit that Daly failed to recognize the church's specifically Dominican iconography. Daly, however, could not have been unaware of the mendicant symbolism at Albi. In the *Revue Générale,* he reprinted a seventeenth-century manuscript entitled "Une Visite Naïve et Sensible de la Fameuse Eglise de Sainte-Cécile d'Albi" whose purpose was the identification of all components of the iconographic program, especially the elements of Dominican symbolism.[76] We must finally assume that Daly could have seen the relationship between mendicant symbolism and plan in much the same way as the manuscript associated narrative details and mendicant iconography. Yet Daly refused to acknowledge it.

I think it becomes apparent that any of the preceding explanations is insufficient to explain Daly's refusal to recognize Albi's full symbolism and meaning. I am therefore proposing an alternate explanation to account for Daly's difficulty. This proposition hinges first upon the fact that Daly regarded the church type as secular rather than religious, and second, that Daly understood Jacobinism in its eighteenth-century, rather than thirteenth-century, manifestation.

We can say that, because of this interpretation of the church of St. Jacques in Toulouse, Daly, like other nineteenth-century architects, regarded the Jacobin church type as secular. The fabric of this church had been used as an armory and warehouse since the Revolution. It is interesting to note that when Henri Labrouste began restoration of the church of the Toulouse Jacobin church, the building was maintained, not by the Ministère des Cultes, but the Ministère de la Guerre. This association with the War Ministry forced the building to be designated as "architecture militaire" rather than "architecture religieuse." For many, then, this church form as functional type seemed more appropriate for secular than for religious usage.

The Jacobin church form and other Dominican constructions became important informants to new public building campaigns in the mid-nineteenth century. Perhaps the most significant evidence of this phenomenon was Henri Labrouste's Bibliothèque Sainte-Geneviève. Labrouste used Jacobin symbolism in two ways in his project.First, the mendicant church plan was functionally well suited to the library's institutional program. St. Jacques' and Albi's universal spaces were compatible with the library's non-specific program devoted simply to book storage and study. Labrouste's double-nave reading room could be seen as a cast-iron reinterpretation of St. Jacques (plate 52). The exedral side chapels of St. Jacques and Ste. Cécile served well as book storage areas and private studies in Labrouste's project.

Moreover, the Jacobin double-nave space was important to Labrouste symbolically. For this plan type makes explicit reference to the first lecture room of the Sorbonne, the thirteenth-century "Grand Couvent" of the Jacobins, the space which could be seen as the germ of the great institution's form. By establishing a connection with the Sorbonne's history in his own building, Labrouste could be seen as substantiating the spirit that underlay the Sorbonne's physical manifestations since its beginning. In his library Labrouste corporealized the idea of the Sorbonne by exploiting the secular nature of the Jacobin church.

A second difficulty for Daly concerned the eighteenth century meaning of Jacobinism. The Jacobin party, headed by Robespierre, which controlled France between 1791-93, had a significant impact on epistemology. The Jacobin government sponsored a shift in philosophical thinking, away from academic hypothetico-deductive method to an empirco-inductive scientific system of the Encyclopedists. The latter-day Jacobins associated speculation with a metaphysical system, which they believed fostered scientific inquiry devaluing the pragmatic, progressive, and real. A number of modern authors have noted the contribution of revolutionary Jacobin thought to the positivism of Saint-Simon and Comte.[77] Labrouste's Bibliothèque Ste. Geneviève recognizes this contribution in both its plan and its decorative scheme. Neil Levine has argued for an understanding of the facades of the Bibliothèque Ste. Geneviève in terms of positivism.[78] His argument is relevant here because it leads one to entertain the notion that Labrouste might have recognized not only positivism's nineteenth-century maturity, but also its eighteenth-century nascent state as the ideology of Robespierre's Jacobinism. By incorporating an implicit growth or evolutionary analogy into his recognition of revolutionary Jacobinism, Labrouste reinforced the significance of the library as symbolization of positivist epistemology.

I propose that Daly's understanding of Jacobin imagery was similar to Labrouste's. As noted above, this understanding was appropriate to a building program as specific as the Bibliothèque Ste. Geneviève. Yet, Daly's project was not of a secular, but of a religious nature. Jacobin form and iconography as

Labrouste used it would have been inappropriate in Daly's situation at Albi. Labrouste used Jacobinism to reinforce the scientific reading of his building. Daly could not take advantage of this kind of reading at Albi Cathedral. For Daly the importance of a church was less as a symbol of scientific knowledge than as a seat of religion.

It must not be forgotten that Daly had monarchist sympathies. He viewed Jacobinism as a particularly distasteful episode in the French Revolution, the Reign of Terror. This period was characterized by complete philosophical materialism and social anarchy, caused by the eradication of traditional institutions and social structures. In 1871 Daly assaulted modern-day Jacobinism for its lack of a system of belief, describing its method as "doute timide," its epistemology little more than "rationalisme utilitaire."[79] Daly understood Jacobinism as a disorderly collection of facts and postures lacking an essential unifying component, a metaphysic. Without this spirituality, neither a philosophy nor a society could be achieved.

Ultimately, Daly was unable to recognize in the Toulouse Jacobin church an architectural entity suitable to inform the architecture of a truly religious edifice. Daly, like Labouste, might have seen a connection between the Jacobin church type and civil institutions, as in the case of the Bibliothèque Ste. Geneviève. But Daly would have argued against the applicability of the hall type church of the Jacobins as appropriate to the specifically religious program. Rather, Daly preferred to interpret the church of Sainte-Cécile as a religious aberration, the physical result of a chaotic and violent social history.

This would seem to be the background of Daly's deemphasis of specifically Jacobin references at Albi. Albi Cathedral for Daly was first and foremost a church, that is, the dwelling place of the spirit. The spirit of the cathedral rests in the non-fortified, the non-practical, or "non-Jacobin" elements of the church, especially, in the decoration of Louis I and II d'Amboise. As described above, both *jubé* and portico were clearly additions to the church fabric, and as such, were non-structural. In their disdain of the science of building, the decorative schemes of the Amboise took on a life of their own. They sought neither an understandable scientific order nor a connectedness with the church's statical component, but rather, a more self-intent spiritual order.

Daly's project for the church's completion emphasized the works of its patrons, the "great men" dominating the church's form. Their contributions provided the locations wherein the spirit of history and religion came to reside. Daly's appreciation of the Amboise paralleled his interest in the artistic and historical hero. In contrast to materialistic notions of history with their implicit reliance on progress and concomitant fatality, Daly's appreciation of the hero is based in the celebration of a single man's ability to ignore, to transcend, or even to direct the forces of history. The mission of such men is imposed upon them by a higher consciousness or purpose that is instrumental in shaping the course of history, or the future. Daly esteemed the d'Ambroise family as men inspired and directed not by natural law, but by God himself. The central theme of Albi Cathedral, as in the New Testament, was history affected by a man or men of genius. Daly perceived his own role, both in social and architectural terms in the same manner.

Although Daly had difficulty in accepting one idealistic interpretation of Albi Cathedral, that is, as a member of a distinct functional type, he countered with another. His view of the history of Sainte-Cécile is composed of series of vignettes, of very willful moves carried out by men of genius. He is likewise willful, and views his responsibility to be the completion of the work begun by his predecessors. In conclusion, we might compare Daly's stand with Michelet's defintion of art, "nature humanisée, matière spiritualisée." In likening himself with the heroes of the past, César Daly, like Louis I d'Amboise, is shaping history and nature, hence creating art.

Postscript

It would be misleading to say that César Daly remained unchanged in his interpretation of Albi Cathedral. In fact, as the fifties progressed, he came to acknowledge the typological point of view. By the time of the 1863 Congrès Archéologique in Toulouse, the idea that Albi was not a single, unique edifice conditioned by the circumstances of the region or era, but part of a larger school, became a more popular idea. The Duc de Caumont, for example, advanced the idea that Albi participated in the Angevin church type, citing the instances of both Angers Cathedral and St. Serge, Angers, as similar nave and hall churches.[80] This comprises a parallel interpretation to considering Albi as part of the succession of Dominican churches, both in France and abroad, during the thirteenth century.

Daly himself poses the question "La Cathédrale d'Albi a-t-elle fait école" in the south of France? Daly's response to this question marks his position at the crossroads of contemporary archaeological thought. One route follows the path of antiquarianism and the other of typology. Daly adheres to the Duc de Caumont's comparative and classificational method when he states:

> ...lorsqu'une science est dans l'enfance, on est disposé à trop de rigueur ou a trop de suppositions; tandis qu'après des études approfondies, on arrive à une classification... comparée.[81]

> "While a science is in its infancy, one is disposed toward too much rigor and too many suppositions; whereas after profound studies, one arrives at a ... comparative classification."

Yet, Daly comes upon an alternative method, typology, when he asserts:

> Autrefois on voyageait moins qu'aujourd'hui et on copiait de plus ou moins loin le chef d'oeuvre de la contrée qui faisait type.[82]

In the past, one travelled less than today and one copied from a greater or lesser distance the masterpieces of the region that had been designated a "type."

At that point, Daly turns from the antiquarian road, recognizing that the comparative method emphasizes parts rather than the whole and finding in classification the potential for associating incompatible architectural specimens. He asserts that an understanding of Albi Cathedral rests upon more than an analysis and catalogue of distinctive features. Rather, the building's total form and composition must be recognized and evaluated.[83]

Hence, in the intersection of two methodologies, Daly comes to appreciate Albi as an empathic instrument, a persuasive paradigm that served to inspire similar constructions in its day. Because it affected other religious buildings in Languedoc, Daly sees Albi as participating in a church type transcending any specific situation.

Daly continues his typological argument when he recognizes that in the area of Strasbourg and southern Germany there exists a number of churches surprisingly similar to Sainte-Cécile. He further notes how improbable it is that these churches derive from Albi, suggesting instead that they stem from an antique source.

Where Albi is concerned, the typological method allows Daly to address the cathedral as a unified composition. He appreciates the cathedral less as a receptacle of a number of important pieces than as a total form with a specific identity and vitality.

Some of the implications of this stand are displayed in Daly's project for the *isolement* of the church from the town fabric. There were two major considerations at work in this proposal. The first was governmental; as set out in the instructions to diocesan architects by the Commission des Arts et Edifices Religieux, *isolement* was a defensive strategy advocating removal of all parasitic fabric from the monument's flanks. The second was the creation of a setting that would recognize the importance of the church as a distinct entity.[85]

Dégagement began in the mid-1850s as a matter of course. However, by the 1860s a second phenomenon was in evidence. No longer was the city being removed from the church for its protection or defense, but now the church was on the offensive. It was almost as if the church's identity, and its implicit spirit of order, was moving outside of its confines for purposes of affecting a new order, this time at an urbanistic level. The church sponsored an enormous square, overlaid with four subreadings (plate 53). The north and south spaces spotlight the Baldaquin and a new doorway proposed on the north, opposite from the south porch in a kind of false transept reading. The west space focuses on the tower. The east space, or the market square, concentrates on the chevet and particularly the Porte de Dominique. The total reading of this enormous square housing Sainte-Cécile is reinforced by the regularization of the streets and facades alongside. For the most part, any ambiguous spatial reading caused by irregularity is abolished, except perhaps for the south side of the square, where the perimeter is momentarily broken by the edge's conformity to the medieval city wall. The total order of this space is reinforced by a new reorganized street system for the town. A new axial street, focusing upon the Porte de Dominique, traverses the city, linking the church with the town hall. Entry into the new space is further facilitated by a new street arriving from the old market square. These two incisions regularize the easternmost facade of the Square Sainte-Cécile, turning it into a great tripartite composition.

The scale of this scheme was grand. Daly had difficulty convincing the city council of the judiciousness of the project, which would have modified or destroyed portions of the archiepiscopal palace. Subsequent projects for the square alter the scale and the articulation, hence clouding the original conception. Still the idea remained. The square as executed continued Daly's interest in spotlighting the church in its entirety, rather than parts or elements. Furthermore, the final project uses the church as a seed or germ, by which a new organic unity can be given to the entire city. In general, Daly's conception of the church has moved from a piecemeal to a holistic one. Albi Cathedral as eminently persuasive paradigm is now able to exert effective control over its surroundings, in order to shape nature, the city, and history itself.

5

The City of Rhetoric

Nineteenth-century literary criticism has provided us with two potent and long lived metaphors describing the character of the city: the mechanical and the biological. Victor Considérant effectively exploited the first type; he discussed the city as a kind of machine:

> In the first level of the industrial city, a line of factories, of great workshops raises itself... the motors of the great machines deploy their forces, grind, bend and transform elementary matter under their metallic organs and they execute... a thousand marvelous operations. The city is the arsenal of the active and living creations of human intelligence.[1]

This passage from his *Description du Phalanstère* depicted the city not so much in terms of what it was, but in the positivist terms of what it did: it produced. Factories, workshops, and machines manufactured the commodities essential to human life and development. For Considérant, the city became the embodiment of the organization of labor, industry, and the physical requisites for human happiness and consequent social order.

The second metaphor, the biological, treated the city as a species of animal. Victor Hugo's *Notre-Dame de Paris* provides us with an example. Critical of artificial, rationalistic, post-Renaissance Paris, Hugo evoked an image of the city that tended toward the imaginative and impressionistic:

> Admirable as the city of Paris of to-day may seem to you, conjure up the Paris of the fifteenth century; rebuild it in your imagination, look through the middle of the immense city of the Seine, with its broad green and yellow pools that make it iridescent as a serpent's skin; divide it at the island points, send it swirling around the piers of the bridges; project sharply against an azure horizon the Gothic profile of old Paris; let its outline float in the wintry mist clinging around its numerous chimneys, plunge it in the deepest night and watch the fantastic play of light and shadow in that sombre labyrinth of edifices; cast into it a ray of moonlight, showing it vague and uncertain, with its towers rearing its massive heads above the mist... In general, the murmur that rises up from Paris during the daytime is the city talking, at night it is the city breathing.[2]

Hugo regarded the city as a living being. He speculated upon the source or center of its life. Hugo endowed the city of Paris with a soul, thus allowing it an identity of its own, an ontology. This source of life could not be understood or discovered rationally. Hugo was as critical of empirical examination or realistic consideration of the city as he was of its consciously artistic, classical embellishments. He attacked the dissection of Paris by such materialist writers as Considérant, implying that the rational dismembering of the city deprived it of its very essence. In the final analysis, an organism must defy examination.

Even more importantly, Hugo's organic perception of the city was an early attempt to regard the city holistically, rather than as a random aggregate of distinct objects, or spaces. His attitude toward the city as a being endowed it with a vitalism which orchestrated and unified the city's various parts. The city operated through a series of imperceptible relationships, with a subtlety which frustrated attempts to isolate functions. It goes without saying that the two metaphors, the mechanical and biological, tended to be not only mutually exclusive, but openly hostile as well.

There was a point of contact between the two metaphors, however, and that was in the realm of consciousness. Both recognized the city as an object worthy of contemplation. Some authorities have distinguished between two conscious faculties, one of recognition and the other of evaluation and judgment.[3] The first faculty discerns an identity in an object. The second submits the object to certain processes of analysis. It could be said that Considérant stated little about the nature of the city itself; he assumed its identity to be inseparable from its qualities and functions. He exploited certain evaluative techniques in order to understand the city, without broaching the problem of ontology. In contrast, Hugo dealt more directly with the problems of recognition and identity. He clearly perceived the city as a part of nature, like a plant or animal. For him, the city could not be submitted to analysis. Recognizing the city as an entity, he questioned man's ability to understand it rationally. For Hugo, and Considérant as well, the two sides of consciousness were separated.

Both points of view were partial in their attempts to describe the totality of consciousness. On the one hand, Hugo asserted the presence of a soul and an implicit truth and morality which lay at the root of ontology. Yet he deprived man of any means of understanding the good, at least rationally. On the other hand, Considérant allowed for the individual's participation in shaping the city, but he denied the individual any ethical or moral responsibility other than material production or liberal altruism. Hugo's point of view ignored humanity for the sake of a transcendental existence apart from contingency or human will. Considérant's point of view was essentially libertarian, allowing for man's instrumentality and analysis with regard to the city, but for no other end than production and satisfaction of human need. In artistic terms, Hugo's point of view led to an ideality and understanding which escaped final knowledge, ultimately failing to instruct man's own attempts in creating form. Considérant's point of view permitted the most elaborate artificiality, allowing man's own inventive genius to be imposed upon nature. However, it denied the possibility of ultimate evaluation, because moral norms could never enter into his judgments.

There have been few artistic and social moments more tantalizing to the modern historian than Second Empire Paris. Particularly interesting is the history of its architecture, and especially its urban form. As with the nineteenth century, modern criticisms of the city have been affected by the mechanical and biological metaphors. For example, Françoise Choay, in *The Modern City: Planning in the Nineteenth Century,* interprets the history of Haussmann's plan in essentially materialistic terms, which extended from the supposed realism of the mechanical analogy.[4] Moreover, Choay regards the nineteenth-century plan as essentially "pre-urbanistic," discussing the Paris of Louis-Napoleon as a continuity of older formal and intellectual systems shaping the city. Implicit in her criticisms of Paris' form was an objection to the pre-Marxian liberal state. Indeed, Choay contends that the term *urbanism* as neologism appears only as the result of the withering of the traditional state and the rise of socialism. In short, Paris as a discrete urbanistic   phenomenon cannot exist; because the necessary environment for its proper nurturing has not yet been called into existence.[5]

Although Choay does not regard the nineteenth-century city of Paris as an urbanistic phenomenon, but as a collection of quarters, it is apparent that both Louis-Napoleon and Haussmann wished to combat just such a reading. The two creators of modern Paris desired to regard the city as a single community, or *commune.* Both Louis-Napoleon and Haussmann focused much of their energies on the unification of Paris' centuries-old aggregate. Haussmann wanted Paris to be a kind of super-commune, within which there was not merely an overriding social unity, but a formal one as well. He first emphasized the commune as archetype of unity:

> La Commune est presque aussi ancienne que la Famille. Ce n'est pas seulement une division territoriale; c'est une collection de personnes liées par les intérêts tout à la fois moraux et matériels, presenté à l'esprit et aux yeux de chacun. C'est le principe, le point de départ de tout organisation sociale; c'est l'élément constitutif des empires.[6]

> The Commune is almost as old as the Family. It isn't only a territorial division; it is a collection of persons allied by interests at once moral and material, presented to the spirit and the eyes of each. It is the principle, the point of departure of all sound organization; it is the constitutional element of empires.

The spirituality and cohesiveness of the Commune were extensions of the sovereign will of Napoleon III—*l'Idée Napoléonienne*—which would serve to unify the new Paris.

In short, Napoleon's great idea for a Parisian community was to be compared to the spiritual unity of the family—orderly and harmonious. Napoleon I, Louis-Napoleon's spiritual father, expressed this view of Paris:

> ... à l'intérieur, ordre, autorité, religion, bien-être du people; à l'extérieur, dignité naturelle.[7]

> ... on the interior, order, authority, religion, well-being of the people; on the exterior, natural dignity.

Haussmann formalized these new social values by the implicit visual unity of his Parisian enterprise. The cohesiveness of the city would symbolize its social unity and would become the emblem of harmony to the rest of France.

> S'il est une oeuvre devant laquelle toutes les passions politiques devraient faire silence, vers laquelle une pensée patriotique devait diriger tous les bons vouloirs, c'est assurément l'entreprise immense qui fera de Paris une Capitale de la France, j'ai presque dit du Monde Civilisée.[8]

> If it is work before which all the political passions must fall silent, toward which a patriotic thought must direct all good wishes, it is surely the immense enterprise which will make all of Paris a Capital of France, ... [perhaps] ... of the Civilized World.

Moreover, in contradiction to materialist writers like Considérant and Choay, a number of authors point out that Paris was *not* comprehensively planned as a model of efficiency. Despite the importance of access and egress for all major structures and quarters in the new plans, many situations simply did not reflect that kind of concern. David Pinckney, for example, has noted the lack of utilitarian function of the new streets between the Bourse and Opera, or between the Opera and an inaccessible pavilion of the Louvre. Moreover, he has marked the insufficiency of the street system servicing certain important structures, like the Gare du Nord, or Les Halles.[9]

Others propose that although nineteenth-century utilitarians enjoyed discussing the city as factory, it is clear that Napoleon III had no such idea in mind. There was nothing that Louis-Napoleon feared more than the urban proletariat. Rather than incorporating industry into the capital, hence attracting enormous numbers of workers to the city proper, Napoleon III preferred to decentralize the factories, relegating them to the lower cost suburban lands. In so doing, the workers would be removed for the most part from the central administration of the city. Ultimately, Napoleon's idea of social unity was achieved only by compromising the functions of production in society.[10]

As an alternative to Choay's view of the city, these authors posit a kind of idealism which finds a close parallel in Hugo's organic vitalism. Pinckney's perceptions of Paris, although elaborately involved with the financing and servicing of the new city, never deny the importance of formal plan and ideology on the part of either Louis-Napoleon or Haussmann. According to César Daly, Louis-Napoleon's *Idées* were those of his uncle, who likewise tended to deemphasize the material components of Paris in favor of the ideal.

Paris ne doit être ni une vaste usine, ni un grand comptoir, mais la cité des palais, un musée universel.[11]

Paris must be neither a vast factory, nor a great sales counter, but the city of palaces, a universal museum.

For Louis-Napoleon the symbolism of a universal museum introduced into the problem of urbanism the idea of history, and the city's relationship to history. In contrast to the mechanical and biological metaphors, the city as history provided another kind of analogy, which could potentially account for the strengths and deficiencies of the other two. As noted above, the mechanical metaphor tended to discount the influence of history in ways other than the purely experiential chronicle of man's solution to problems through the ages. Alternatively, the city as plant or animal provided an image of growth, hence of a progressive historical revelation in conformity with the germinal urge. As we saw earlier, the organic analogy involved the notion of germination, the gradual development of ideology. As Michelet developed this idea, germination was associated with genius, the effects of inspired human will which finally revealed and shaped the idea.

The historical metaphor for the city may bridge the gap between mechanistic and biological views, by its association with the processes of memory. In classical notions of memory, perceptions are recognized and judged with regard to *topoi* (or symbolic types) held within the mind's eye. History then comprises a series of ideal forms as in the traditional literary mode, *historia,* a didactic genre in which ideas are linked within an appropriate, decorous, communicative structure.

In this context, history is associated with rhetoric, by which the divinity of Idea is conveyed from speaker to audience, in an act of inspiration. *Historia,* in its didactic role thus has a dual function, simultaneously ideal and utilitarian, involving the transference of truth via the neutral structure of communication. In that transfer, both the ideal and functional faculties of consciousness become central concerns.[12]

The study of history and memory mediates between the extremes of the mechanical and biological metaphors. The makers of Second Empire Paris, particularly Louis-Napoleon and Baron Haussmann, were concerned with the social well-being of Paris, formalized by the physical improvements they introduced. Yet these were the means of communicating the lofty ideals of the government to the population at large. The problems of truth, ideology, and social order of an abstract kind were important to the political conceptions of the Second Empire. This dual concern—ideas tied to appropriate intelligible and inspiring form—was of central importance to the period.

At this point it is exigent to summarize the themes with which this chapter is concerned. The first theme is the city as a metaphor for history and a repository of knowledge. The second theme deals with man's perception of the city, and his desire to understand it. Ultimate knowledge, both of the city and of time, entails an awareness of both conscious and subconscious levels of history. The conscious level of history is the realm of facts. The subconscious level of history deals with forces and ultimate causes; it can be viewed as the dwelling place of the essence of history. The third and final theme is the shift of history from a natural to a moral science. History becomes *historia. Historia* invokes the problem of rhetoric, combining the ideational basis of knowledge with the communication of these ideas to the public via purely instrumental means. The outcome of *historia* is inspiration and personal edification. The city becomes the medium by which the idea, hence truth, is communicated. Ultimately, this theme treats urban morality as *historia*'s rhetorical basis, in terms of the involvement of the city as backdrop to virtuous human life.

The Ontology of the City

For Francoise Choay, the first intimation of the city as a total entity is the appearance of the neologism, *urbanism,* a term coined by Ildefonso Cerdà in his *Urbanizaciòn* and later reinvoked by Camillo Sitte in his *Städte-Bau.*[13] Choay notes that the term became popularized with the emergence of the social sciences at the end of the nineteenth century. To state, however, that a conception of urbanism can not have existed before the means for its examination is as questionable an assertion as maintaining that space as an artistic problem can not antedate the nineteenth century neologism *Raumgestaltung.* Surely, certain important notions determining urbanism must predate both Cerdà or Sitte.

To cite three examples, perception of the city as a discrete entity was already apparent in Victor Hugo's *Notre-Dame de Paris,* Eugène Sue's *Les Mystères de Paris,* and Charles Baudelaire's "Tableaux Parisiens" of *Les Fleurs du Mal,* all dating from the mid-nineteenth century. The view of the city as something more than isolated fragments or quarters paralleled the rise of the appreciation of *grandeur* and *étendue* as fundamental to feelings of beauty and sublimity. Walter Benjamin illuminates one cultural evidence of this idea. Benjamin points to the panorama as having an important effect in cultivating a taste for vastness and in ascribing distinct visual characteristics to a city or region in a way that one might have earlier applied to a building or city quarter (plate 54). Moreover, Benjamin emphasizes the importance of panorama in raising the popular consciousness to appreciate urbanism at an enormous scale.

The idea of extended view seems a reasonable vantage point for the perception of the city as sublime experience. The taste for extended view was prevalent in late eighteenth-century gardens, where one of the most popular features was the *belvedere* (plate 55). A belvedere was a platform or terrace from which great expanses of landscape, either wild or urban, could be surveyed.[5] Alexandre de Laborde, in his *Description des Nouveaux Jardins de la France* (1808), displayed numerous belvederes, citing those of Monceaux, Méréville, St. Leu, and Morfontaine.[16] Louis-Carrogis Carmontelle lavished special attention on the view of Paris provided by his minaret at the Parc Monceau:

> Si l'on monte au Minaret, et que l'on parcoure des yeux l'horizon, on voit, en commençant par Montmartre à droite les hauteurs de Belleville, tous les monuments de Paris, finissant à l'Observatoire. Ensuite Vanvres, Issy, Meudon, Bellevue, Seve, le Mont Valérien. Les hauteurs de Marly, Saint Germain, les hauteurs de Sanois, celles de Saint-Prix, Montmorency, et au-dessus le Château de Montmorency, Ecouen et au bord de la rivière, Epernay, ensuite Saint-Denis, et puis l'on retrouve Montmartre.[17]

> If one mounts the minaret, and one's eyes travel across the horizon, one sees, beginning at Montmartre on the right, the heights of Belleville, all the monuments of Paris, finishing at the Observatory. Then Vanvres, Issy, Meudon, Belleville, Seve, Mount Valerien. The heights of Marly, Saint-Germain, the heights of Sanois, those of Saint-Prix, Montmorency, and, beneath, the Chateau of Montmorency, Ecouen, and on the shore of the river, Epernay, then Saint-Denis, and finally, one again sees Montmartre.

It is to be assumed that Carmontelle regarded such a moving sensory experience as a counterpart to the range of sublime sensations arising from the promenade around his Parc Monceau.

The conception of the vista quickly found its way into the public realm. Most notably, Percier and Fontaine very consciously exploited this notion in their most important project for First Empire Paris, the Palace for the King of Rome. In their *Résidences des Souverains* (1833), they described not only the site but also the proposed prospect from the Palace on the Colline de Chaillot:

> De là on aurait joui du coup d'oeil de la Seine qui, vers le levant, semble se replier pour laisser apercevoir les ponts nombreux qui la traversent, les beaux quais qui bordent son cours, et la longue perspective des edifices parmi lesquels brillent le château des Tuileries, ses jardins, la colonnade avec les statues de la place Louis XV, les nouvelles rues qui y aboutissent et la superbe promenade des Champs-Elysées. La Seine de l'autre coté, au couchant, en s'éloignant de Paris, offrait un autre tableau non moins magnifique et beaucoup plus riant encore. Toujours aperçue dans les differents détours, on la voyait serpenter, jusqu'au pied des riches côteaux de Sèvres, de Meudon, de Saint-Cloud, qui terminent l'horizon de ce côté.[18]

From there, one would have enjoyed a view of the Seine, which, toward the east, seems to wind in order to allow a view of the numerous bridges that cross it, the beautiful quais that border its course, and the long vista of edifices among which shimmer the château of the Tuileries, its gardens, the colonnade with the statues of the Place Louis XV, the new streets that abut it and the superb panorama of the Champs-Elysées. The Seine, on the other side to the west, in moving away from Paris, creates another tableau no less magnificent, and even more cheerful. Seen in all its turns, one would see it snake to the foot of the rich hillsides of Sèvres, of Meudon, and Saint-Cloud, which terminates the horizon on this side.

Moreover, the architects spoke of the palace in relationship to the prospect it was to dominate.

Un edifice est majestueux lorsque par son immensité il domine tout ce qui l'environne et de belle proportion l'emporte sur celle des autres productions de même sorte. Lorsq'enfin la choix et la magnificence de tout ce dont il se compose indique la puissance et la superiorité dont on veut qu'il soît l'image.[19]

An edifice is majestic when, by its immensity, it dominates all that surrounds it, [and] its beautiful proportions prevail over those of other productions of the same sort. And, finally [an edifice is majestic] when the choice and magnificence of all it is composed by indicates the power and superiority that one wants it to represent.

The view of this great domain was clearly designed to be a sublime experience for Napoleon, whose own aesthetic predispositions tended toward "grandeur... étendue... immensité... magnificence... et éclat."[20] Moreover, his Palais du Roi de Rome was a physical expression of his imperial consciousness and control over nature.

The urban implications of the vista from the belvedere were expanded by the aerial view, provided by balloon flight (plate 56). César Daly recognized the elements of sublimity in the unlimited vista provided by the balloon, in a manner not unlike either Carmontelle or Percier and Fontaine. Daly states,

C'est que rien n'est beau comme les grands horizons, les paysages immenses, les perspectives dont l'oeil est impuissant à saisir l'étendue. Les grandes spectacles retrempent les forces de l'homme, remuent son coeur et séduisent son imagination. C'est d'en haute seulement qu'on saisit bien les masses des grands monuments, qu'on lit leurs véritables dispositions, un caractère réel, qu'on reconnaît l'agencement général de toutes leurs parties... C'est en s'élevant au dessus des habitations de nos villes qu'on reconnaît leur laideur, qu'on saisit leurs voies coulés qu'on apprécie l'heureuse influence de l'ordre et d'une certaine symétrie dans la distribution des grandes masses.[21]

Nothing is so beautiful as great horizons, immense landscapes perspectives whose extent one's eye cannot seize. Great spectacles reinvigorate man's forces, stir his heart and seduce his imagination. It is only from on high that one apprehends the masses of great monuments, reads their true dispositions and real character, and recognizes the general arrangement of their parts... It is in elevating oneself above the habitations of our cities, whose ugliness one recognizes, that one sees their fleet streets and that one appreciates the happy influence of order and certain symmetry in the distribution of great masses.

Daly moved beyond mere emotionalism in this statement. Besides those attributes that he considered sublime, he also recognized in the city certain features betraying a fundamental visual order in the formal characteristics of balance and symmetry.

As noted above, Carmontelle made a visual connection between the sensationalism of picturesque nature at Monceau and the sublimity of a view of Paris. An implicit parallel was made between the landscape and architectural promenades. As the eighteenth century draws to a close, notes Antoine Grumbach, a recent commentator, there was an increasing relationship between *l'art des jardins* and *l'art urbain*. He sees an important relationship between Jean-Jacques Rousseau's eighteenth-century *Rêveries du Promeneur Solitaire,* where Rousseau wanders through the outskirts of Paris, at the edge where architecture and landscape meet, and Alphonse Alphand's *Les Promenades de Paris* of the mid-nineteenth century, where the distinctions between the garden and city vanish.[22]

The sensibility and melancholy associated with the eighteenth-century *jardin anglo-chinois* were rapidly transferred to the new urban landscape of the nineteenth. Charles Nodier, in his *Paris Historique: Promenade dans les Rues de Paris* (1838), compared physical movement around the city of Paris and the confrontation of evocative architectural tableaux to theatre. Like a dramatic presentation, Paris evoked certain sentiments by juxtaposing a variety of scenes. The dramatic work is ordered by plot and temporal unity; the city of Paris—by history. History was recounted in the facades of Paris and was the means of the city's formal unity. Nodier asserted that the plot of Paris, the unfolding drama, comprised the history of France:

> Parisiens désoeuvrés, qui mettez à profit les beaux jours pour promener vos loisirs dans le labyrinthe des rues; provinciaux avides de sensations, qui regardez comme perdues toutes les heures qui s'écoulent entre la clôture d'un musée et l'ouverture d'un théâtre, voyageurs instincts que tourmente encore le besoin d'apprendre, car le principal caractère du savoir, c'est un desir assidu de savoir davantage, seriez-vous tentés de prendre part avec nous à un spectacle sans appareil et sans frais? On ne prend de billets à la porte, on ne se presse sous les vestibules. La toile est toujours levée. La scene, c'est la ville immense avec ses colonnes et ses bruits; la décoration, ce sont les églises, les palais, les maisons auxquelles la gloire, le malheur ou le crime attachent les souvenirs ineffaçables, les acteurs, ce sont les personnages les plus illustre de la nation, dans le gouvernement, dans les armes, dans les sciences, dans les lettres, dans les arts; le drame, c'est l'histoire de la France.[27]

> Idle Parisians, who put to good use the beautiful days to promenade at leisure through the labyrinth of streets like lost souls during the time between the closing of a museum and the opening of a theater, instinctive travellers who trouble after the need to learn, because the principle characteristic of knowing is an assiduous desire to know more, would you be tempted to take part with us in a spectacle without machinery and without cost? No one takes tickets at the door; no one crushes you in the vestibule. The curtain is always raised. The setting is the immense city with its columns and its noises; the decors are the churches, palaces, and houses to which glory, unhappiness or crime attaches indelible memories; the

actors, they are the most illustrious personalities of the nation—in the government, the military, the sciences, letters, arts, drama—it is the entire history of France.

Charles Nodier provided us with an essential understanding of the city. He linked perceptions with knowledge ('savoir') and with memory ('souvenirs ineffaçables'). In another passage, he allied sensationalist theory with truth:

> Nous avons cherché la rassemblance dans nos portraits. La vérité dans nos petites sensations.[24]

> We looked for resemblance in our portraits. The truth [signalled] by our little sensations.

However, Nodier still dealt with the city of Paris on the level of the individual object, or, at most, a quarter. His perceptions concerned knowledge of single urban elements; he failed to deal with the city as a whole, as an object of contemplation in itself. It was just such a change in perception that became a central issue to the period. This enlarged order of urban perception involved knowledge on a scale beyond that of the individual urbanistic or historical event.

As emphasized above, Hugo discussed the city as a single entity, imbuing it with a soul which was its essence. Moreover, he involved a historical reconstruction of the city, giving access to that essence. The city became the externalization of the past and the repository of human experience. Yet, although Hugo identified the city in historical terms, he failed to assess adequately the nature of history itself. His historical view was incomplete, and incompatible with a unified formal articulation. As a result, Hugo avoided the possibility that history itself might have an order, potentially visible in formal terms. Hugo discarded order as a formal imposition upon the organic city, taking it instead to be an indication of man's own consciousness and will to order rather than a structure inherent in the city itself.

However, organic interpretations of the city soon became allied to immanent order. Edmond Texier's *Tableaux de Paris* (1852) resurrected Hugo's notions of the city as historical aggregate, of complex and incomprehensible total form:

> Voulez-vous la voir dans toute sa grandeur, cette fière cité étendue à vos pieds et déroulant sous vos regards son vaste panorama?... Ça et là l'ardoise, les dômes étincellent; on dirait des flots blanchissant sur le vert sombre d'un océan d'édifices. Mais cette mer, exempte de monotonie, s'entrecoupe d'îlots de verdure et de vaste oasis... Mille monuments varient à l'infini les lignes de l'horizon...[25]

> Do you want to see, in all its grandeur, this proud city extended at your feet and unfolded in a vast panorama before your eyes? Here and there the rooftop slates and domes sparkle; one might call them white wavelets upon the green ocean of buildings. But this sea, free of monotony, [is] interrupted by islets of green and a vast oasis,... A thousand monuments infinitely vary the lines of the horizon.

He juxtaposed this description made during the daytime, however, with a bird's eye view made at night. This nighttime image of Paris revealed a complex street system outlined by lines of gas lamps, comprising a comprehensible internal organization for the city.

Vus à vol d'oiseau, on dirait que ces édifices se touchent, et des lieues les séparent. Si le soir vous surprend dans cette contemplation, vous allez voir mille clartés soudaines apparaître... Les feux en suivent le cours sinueux, puis ils rayonnent sur la ligne des boulevards, étoilent l'obscurité des rues et la sombre verdure des promenades.[26]

From a bird's eye view, one would say that these edifices touch although [in reality] leagues separate them. If nighttime creeps up on you during your musings, you will see a thousand lights suddenly appear... Their flames follow a sinuous course, then they radiate along the lines of the boulevards, studding the darkness of streets and the dark verdure of the promenades [like stars].

Ultimately, for Texier, the overriding order of Paris became a system of lighted streets, boulevards, and promenades.

Both Victor Considérant and César Daly believed in the equivalence of architecture and history. Their adage, "Architecture writes history," elevated the architect to the role of scribe of the historical event, like the novelist in Hugo's view. It is apparent that both Considérant and Daly believed in an equivalence between architecture and the historical chronicle, and regarded urbanism as total historical manuscript. César Daly, like Edmond Texier, paralleled Hugo's organic understanding of the city, yet moved to a more analytical level by which historical ontology could be understood in formal structure. As with Edmond Texier, this structure relied on circulation.

César Daly provided an instructive parallel to both Hugo's "Bird's Eye view of Paris" and Texier's "Tableaux," He states:

Du sommet des tours de Notre-Dame ou des hauteurs de Montmartre, l'étranger peut voir mieux et plus rapidement Paris qu'en se promenant par les rues. Cette vue de l'ensemble de la grande cité lui permet de mieux comprendre le réseau de la circulation ainsi que la place et l'importance relative des jardins et des édifices....

L'étude des traits caractéristiques de l'architecture (et de l'urbanisme) contemporaine, détachée du tableau synthétique de son histoire, ne peut se faire ni complètement, ni clairement, ni bien utilement.[27]

From the summit of the towers of Notre-Dame or from the heights of Montmartre, the stranger can see Paris better and more rapidly than by walking in the streets. This view of the ensemble of the great city permits him to better comprehend the circulation scheme and thus the placement and relative importance of gardens and buildings...

The study of the characteristic traits of contemporary architecture (and urbanism), detached from a synthetic picture of its history cannot be done completely, clearly, or very usefully.

Daly's view stressed the constructive and ordering elements of the city. If the city portrayed history for Daly, it was not a history of an incidental nature. Rather, a chronicle orchestrated incident through historical plot, movement, or scheme, which if not entirely logical, must at least be ordered and unified. This involvement of the city with history, whose essence revealed a fundamental structure, "un tableau synthétique," resulted in a form that articulated rather than transcended order and unity. Daly's view did not vary so much from Nodier's as to allow total contemplation of the city. Unlike Nodier's approach, however, Daly viewed the city not on an architectural but on an urbanistic level. Moreover, like Nodier, he attempted to reach truth via sensation. Like Texier, however, Daly understood truth as having an apparent visual order.

History—Conscious and Subconscious

As noted above, Napoleon wanted Paris to be a "musée universel." By implication, he desired his capital to be the embodiment of consummate knowledge. For Bonaparte, as for his Neoplatonic theorists, knowledge was to be defined as awareness of the true. Total knowledge concerned the understanding of nature, as well as ourselves as part of nature. Knowledge was to be mediated by man's intelligent faculty, rational consciousness.

For Sigmund Freud, knowledge of the city was a useful metaphor of psychic life. He selected Rome to be the symbol of the conscious and the subconscious, which together comprised total self-knowledge. The modern city of Rome characterized the conscious. Ancient, medieval, and renaissance architectural fragments were seen as mixed and juxtaposed in seemingly erratic fashion.

> It is hardly necessary to remark that all the remains of ancient Rome are found dovetailed into the jumble of a great metropolis which has grown up in the last few centuries since the Renaissance. There is certainly not a little that is ancient still buried in the soil of the city or beneath the modern city. This is the manner in which the past is preserved in historical sites like Rome.[28]

Clearly, however, Freud did not regard familiarity with present-day Rome as the source of total knowledge. He juxtaposed the presentation of modern Rome with a second, subliminal city, a Rome of the imagination, in which all eras of the metropolis coexisted.

> Let us, by a flight of imagination, suppose that Rome is not a human habitation but a psychical entity with a ... long and copious past—an entity, that is to say, in which nothing that has once come into existence will have past away and all the earlier phases of development continue to exist alongside the latest one. This would mean that in Rome the palaces of the Caesar and the Septizonium of Septimius Severus would still be rising to their

old height on the Palatine and that the castle of S. Angelo would still be carrying on its battlements the beautiful statutes which graced it until the siege of the Goths, and so on. But more than this. In the place occupied by the Palazzo Cafarelli would once more stand— without the Palazzo ever having to be removed—the Temple of Jupiter Capitolinus; and this not only in its latest shape, as the Romans of the Empire saw it, but also in its earliest one, when it still showed Etruscan forms and was ornamented with terracotta antefixes. Where the Coliseum now stands we could at the same time admire Nero's vanished Golden House. On the Piazza of the Pantheon we should find not only the Pantheon of today as bequeathed to us by Hadrian, but, on the same site, the original edifice erected by Agrippa; indeed, the same piece of ground would be supporting the church of Santa Maria sopra Minverva and the ancient temple over which it was built. And the observer would perhaps only have to change the direction of his glance or the position in order to call up the one view on the other.[29]

For Freud, total knowledge could not be gained from the present-day vantage, but only by regarding the phenomenon under examination over time. Total knowledge of Rome was not achieved by natural interpretation proposed at the conscious level of the city. It also required the realm governed by the subconscious. The subconscious level of Rome could be inferred from certain clues provided by fragments of antiquity, but could not be wholly known without excavation. One's examination had ultimately to be directed toward subliminal motivations or predispositions immersed within the subconscious. Total knowledge lay in juxtaposing the conscious with the subconscious.

The expanded knowledge of man's psyche provided by the subconscious consisted in establishing primary causes. Freud discussed the subconscious, the *libido,* as the faculty which drove man to domination, hence to the pursuit of knowledge. His view of man's passion for unity and domination, his search for causes in natural laws, has frequently been compared to Fourier's Law of Passional Attraction and Sade's libertarianism.[28] The association of Freud with these early psychological empiricists implies a continuity of concern between the nineteenth and twentieth centuries, especially in the attempt to describe appearances, or nature's conscious level, by subconscious cause.

Hence, Freud implied that the present-day appearance of Rome had causes which were hidden beneath the earth's surface. Spatial configurations, formal residues, archaeological fragments were to be explained only by a kind of space-time continuum, in which the formal dispositions and motivations of the city could be determined, and the present-day aggregate explained. Likewise, causality in man's own existence was to be found in his subconscious. Much as with Rome, man's *raison d'être* lay below the surface.

The ontology of history may be approached in a similar way. There are two levels of history. A superficial level can be empirically described and defined as the historical incident or event. But, there is also a second level that deals with causality. This level, which might be called the historical subconscious, deals with impulsion and motivation, the facts which ultimately structure and explain history's externalizations. Total knowledge, like total self-knowledge, involves a combination or superposition of conscious upon subconscious. Total knowledge of history must finally deal with problems of structure and cause.

The idea of the historical subconscious originated long before Freud's metaphor. From what source did Freud's metaphor spring? Could it have been a text like Luigi Canina's *Gli Edifici di Roma Antica* (1848), which implicitly saw the importance of superposing modern upon antique Rome to provide an enlarged understanding of existing urban form (plate 57)? A plate from this work, displaying the Roman Forum, provided a *rationale* for certain formal and spatial configurations in the modern city.[29] An isolated colonnade became the resurrected Temple of Marcus Aurelius Antoninus; a square—the Forum of Augustus or Trajan. The modern streets betrayed an older logic by their association with ancient Roman arteries, manipulated in the interests of structures no longer extant. In short, Canina's urban superpositions attempted to give not only a total record of construction, but, more importantly, a sense of internal logic to the architectural dispositions of modern Rome, based upon the past.

Yet this manner of urbanistic thinking should not be limited to Rome, a city endowed with a particularly illustrious history. All European capital cities of the nineteenth century modelled themselves to a certain extent on this cradle of modern government. Rome became a model of urban performance as well as formal grandeur. Moreover, it became the great paradigm by which its descendents examined themselves, and by which they drew inspiration by comparison. Paris was no exception to this rule. Ferdinand de Guilhermy's *Inventaire Archéologique de Paris* (1855) begs comparison with Canina's Rome (plate 58). The plan attempted to be a comprehensive record of the city's monuments as well to determine the formal devices (streets, squares, walls) which shaped the cumulative form of Paris over its entire history. By using varying shades of cross-hatching and tonality, Guilhermy differentiated major eras of Parisian history and growth, almost as if the various *enceintes* could be probed like various geological substrata. The author portrayed simultaneous historical readings. New nineteenth-century streets superimposed themselves on medieval structure, ancient walls coexisted happily with modern construction. Ambivalent readings coexisted everywhere. For example, the Louvre was simultaneously the chateau-fort of Phillippe-Auguste, the enlarged country house of François I and Henry II, a palace linked to the Tuileries by Henry IV, the public embellishment of Louis XIV, the seat of the imperial power of Napoleon I and III. All generations of the building coexisted. It was likewise with the entire city at an urbanistic scale. The Pantheon and the fifteenth-century Abbaye Ste. Geneviève overlapped. The church of St. Benoît remained undisturbed by the onslaught of the newly widened Rue St. Jacques. The spectral presence of the Abbaye St. Victor continued to overshadow the new Halle aux Vins. Streets attested to fortifications no longer extant—the

Rue du Petit Lion, Rue de Seine, Rue St. Antoine, Boulevard du Temple, Boulevard Beaumarchais, as well as Haussmann's new set of *boulevards périphériques*. On an even larger scale, four cities lay one upon the other: the Paris of Phillippe-Auguste, Charles V, Louis XVIII, and Napoleon III. The history of Paris became a comprehensive chronicle of humanity as well as a series of coherent historical epochs governing the externalities of present-day urban form.

To conclude, it appears that during the course of the nineteenth century, history, both human and urban, was no longer regarded as a collection of incidents or propitious moments. History, the seat of knowledge, was regulated by subconscious laws and structure. The knowledge of history itself consisted in an awareness of these rules. As a sequence of events governed by an intelligible order, there was a scheme to history, a cause and outcome. This kind of scheme could not be separated from idealistic notions of history by which events were orchestrated primarily by the will of the prime mover. Parenthetically, the historical subconscious had numerous points of agreement with classical notions of fate, a connection to be discussed later in this chapter.

Three Plans

If we turn to visual interpretations of these ideas, the move from the view of history as empirical observation to one of history as ordering structure might be observed in three Paris plans, dating from the early eighteenth to the early nineteenth centuries. I refer especially to the Turgot plan of 1739, the Patte plan of 1765, and Percier and Fontaine's scheme for the Palace of the King of Rome of 1811. The space of a century clarifies the city's changing concerns.

Michel-Etienne Turgot, Conseiller to the Parlement during Louis XV's reign, undertook to document and inventory all Parisian buildings. His axonometric aerial view followed a tradition in city plans, especially those of Paris (plate 59). The objective of the project was to mark and identify the structures of Paris for purposes of urban statistics and property taxes. Turgot divided the city into twenty quarters and identified the major institutions and "embellissements publics" for each. Although his record of Paris was comprehensive in scope, it maintained a fundamental interest in individual landholds and separate quarters rather than in the city as totality.

Although the Turgot plan did emphasize the public embellishments that characterized each individual quarter, its major purpose was to document the private sector.[30] The Patte plan of 1765 posed new ways of perceiving the city (plate 60). Its interest was emphatically not in individual private property, but in public works. It attempted to situate and identify those elements of the city which might establish a comprehensive public realm.[31]

To a considerable degree Patte owed his visual success to his style of graphic documentation, having little in common with the more antiquated, particularistic axonometric approach. Using a technique akin to modern figure/ground plans, Patte initially deemphasized the structures in favor of larger readings of built fabric. To a considerable extent the deemphasis of individual buildings was the result of thinking about the city in terms of quarters, modulated by an explicit public realm—a square embellished by a local antiquity, or, especially in the Patte plan, by a statue of the king. The public realm tended to articulate and identify the autonomous quarter.

Yet the Patte plan was to be read on a scale that went considerably beyond the local quarter. This feature was apparent on two levels. First, he treated the street as part of the public realm, equal with the square. Streets were stressed as connections between the various public embellishments. Two situations in the Patte plan developed these features. The first comprised a spatial sequence moving along a path inflected primarily by the Place Dauphine on the Ile de la Cité. The route began in a series of squares on the Right Bank proposed by Boffrand as a public market. It moved along a fragment of coordinated street, across the Pont Neuf to Boffrand's design for a new Place Dauphine, continued across the bridge, through a new building on the Quai Conti (the site of the present-day Mint), past de l'Estrade's scheme for the Quai Malaquais, to Pétard's *rond-point* at the Carrefour Bussi, and finally into the Rue Tournon, where the sequence was terminated by the Palais du Luxembourg. A second major sequence was regulated by two of Paris' antique streets, the Rue St. Denis and the Rue St. Martin. The route involved a square stretching between the two streets in the quarter of St. Jacques de la Boucherie, across the Pont Notre-Dame to Parsin's project for a square for the Ile de la Cité, and finally down the Rue St. Jacques to Hazon's new University. It is apparent also that in his orchestration of the numerous projects for the Place Louis XV, Patte was concerned with the larger-scale issues of public utility. Most notable in this regard was the north/south street across the city of Paris, unifying the two banks of the Seine and the Cité. All these proposals involving public movement and spatial sequence tended to deemphasize the individual quarter in favor of larger scale urbanistic experience.

This shift in scale was perhaps most apparent in Patte's own proposal for the Ile de la Cité in the plan's lower right-hand corner of the plan. As noted above, a usual technique for identifying an individual quarter was the *dégagement* of a local antiquity or embellishment (the Louvre East facade, Saint Sulpice, Notre-Dame, the new church of the Madeleine) and the regularization of squares focusing upon the object. Patte's plan for the Cité continued this device. The architect joined the Ile de la Cité and Ile St. Louis. He then orchestrated a huge square at the head of the island with an implied spatial reading across the Seine linking two identical squares on the Quai Conti and the Quai du Louvre. Patte further regularized the quais on the Right and Left Banks with new uniform facades exactly as one might have done in a renaissance square. The Seine became part of the plan, setting off the island as a wholly monumental quarter. Ultimately, the object of Patte's plan was not merely to focus upon the new Metropole on the former site of the Place Dauphine, but to spotlight the now unified Ile de la Cité/St. Louis. By this single act, Patte expanded his urbanistic concerns. As an entire quarter was turned into public embellishment, with open spaces coordinated around it, the entire city would become organized into differentiated textures articulated by the dialectic between the aggregate of housing of one quarter and the character of another. Here, for the first time, the city was conceived as a totality no longer obscured by idiosyncratic particularities as in the Turgot plan. In this new holistic approach, the city was no longer thought of as a collection of isolated quarters; public places were linked across the boundaries of quarters by planned streets coordinating instead of fragmenting the city as a whole.

The third project to be discussed is the 1811 plan for Napoleon I's embellishments of Paris (plate 61). In their proposal, Percier and Fontaine exploited the same map type as Patte. The private realm or *matérielle* of the city, was depicted in black. The public realm, primarily the city squares and streets, was in white. The depiction of the project centered upon Napoleon's "quartier des monuments," housing the major institutions of the state. The Corps Législatif, the Collège des Quatre Nations and the Louvre were to be contiguous with his new quarter. The architects described the project:

... premièrement au levant, près de la rivière, les archives de l'état, le palais des arts, l'université, le palais du grand maître, les habitations des professeurs émerites, pour les savants et les hommes célèbres qui, par des services importants ou par leurs talents, ont merités les respects et la reconnaissance nationale. Secondement, au couchant, de l'autre coté des Champs de Mars, une caserne de cavalerie et des magasins pour les dépôts des sels, des tabacs, et autres marchandises d'octroi. A l'extremité, vers Vaugirard, un hôpital militaire, et en répétition, du coté des Invalides une caserne d'infanterie. Plus loin, vers le boulevard neuf, l'abattoir de Grenelle, des maisons de retraite et d'autres monuments d'utilité publique. Ces différentes édifices réunis à ceux des Invalides, Corps législatif, et aux belles habitations de ce quartier, auraient fait du Gros-Caillou et de la plaine de Grenelle, comme le voulait l'empéreur, la ville nouvelle, le quartier des monuments, au-dessus desquels devait s'élever le palais du roi de Rome.[32]

First, to the east, near the river, the archives of the state, the palace of the arts, the palace of the great master, the dwellings of the distinguished professors, of the intellectuals and celebrated men, who, by important service or talent, have merited respect and national recognition. Secondly, to the west, on the other side of the Champs de Mars, a barracks of cavalry and stores for the sale of salt, tobacco, and other taxable merchandise. In the distance, toward Vaugirard, a military hospital, and in repetition, on the other side of the Invalides, a barracks of the infantry. Further, toward the new boulevard, the stockyards of Grenelle, retreat houses, and other monuments of public utility. These different buildings, together with the Invalides, Legislature, and other beautiful habitations of this quarter, would have made of the "Gros-Caillou" and the Grenelle plain, as the emperor wished, the new city, the quarter of monuments, above which was to be erected the palace of the king of Rome.

A new quarter was to be built to house the instruments of Napoleon's imperial government. We recall that Napoleon's adage, "Fate is politics," suggested a materialization of history.[33] Material history was as much a part of Napoleon's interest in Paris as it was of Turgot's. The emperor's new political quarter was informed by an encyclopedic notion.

In addition, the existing city of Paris was to be overlaid by a higher visual order to orchestrate the ensemble. Much as with Patte's scheme for the Ile de la Cité, Napoleon's entire administrative quarter was spotlighted against a neutral urban framework. This framework was unified by a new comprehensive street system working in a way not unlike the streets of Patte's proposal. Patte's scheme maintained a comprehensive north-south street system, focusing upon his project for the Ile de la Cité which was oriented in an east/west direction. The Napoleonic project reversed this relationship. Napoleon's quarter was oriented north/south, with his major street (Champs-Elysées, Rue de Rivoli) on the east/west axis. As Patte's scheme fused built fabric and riverscape, or nature and art, Percier and Fontaine's project established an equivalence between landscape and urban fabric. The Napoleonic scheme took its form in part from the royal *Forêt de Madrid,* whose geometrical plan provided a way of coordinating the new imperial city. Patte's great motif for striating and unifying the medieval city of Paris might be seen as influenced by Paris' Roman streets, a technique which Percier and Fontaine learned from Louis XIV and the gardens of Le Nôtre.

The juxtaposition of built and planted form was a frequent motif in Napoleonic urban planning. Most importantly, the Rue de Rivoli recalled Laugier's theory of architecture which proposed that architecture grew out of landscape forms. The street's long, monotonous arcades seemed to take their form from the enfilades of chestnuts in the Tuileries, further down the Champs-Elyseés.[34] Furthermore, the same phenomenon was apparent in the Percier and Fontaine project, particularly in a *naumachia*-shaped space which enclosed the Arc de Triomphe. The space utilized urban fabric only on one side; the other was planted. The square had an ambivalent identity. On the one hand, it resembled one of the great Parisian squares of the seventeenth century. On the other, it resembled a *quincunx,* an open space terminating a vista, characteristic of seventeenth century baroque garden planning. Napoleon's fascination with the garden as a kind of subliminal ordering system was especially apparent in his new urban fabric adjacent to the east side of his monumental quarter, corresponding to the royal part which framed the site on the west.

These observations allow us to propose that the Napoleonic reordering of Paris had much to do with the garden "grand style" of Louis XIV. Napoleon I used the garden of Versailles as a great paradigm which the city of Paris might imitate.

Je condamnais Versailles dans sa création ... mais, dans mes idées gigantesques sur Paris, je rêvais d'en tirer parti et de n'en faire, avec le temps, qu'une espèce de faubourg, un site voisin; un point de vue de la grande capitale; et pour l'approprier davantage à ces objets j'avais conçu une singulière idée dont je m'étais même fait présenter le programme. De ces beaux bosquets, je chassais toutes ces nymphes de mauvais goût, ces ornements à la *Turcaret,* et je les remplaçai par des panoramas en maçonnerie; de toutes les capitales ou nous étions entrés victorieux; de toutes le célèbres batailles qui avaient illustré nos armées. C'eût été autant de monuments éternels de nos triomphes et de notre gloire nationale, posés à la porte de la capitale de l'Europe, laquelle ne pouvait manquer d'être visitée par force du reste de l'univers.[35]

I had condemned the creation of Versailles ... but, in my gigantic ideas concerning Paris, I dreamed of making use of it, and in time, making it into a kind of faubourg, a neighboring site; a focus of the great capital; and in order to adapt it even further to these ends, I conceived a singular idea whose physical program I had even presented. From those beautiful bosquets, I chased all the vulgar nymphs, the ornaments *à la Turcaret,* and I replaced them with panoramas in masonry of the capitals over which we have been victorious, of all the celebrated battles which have displayed our arms. There were to have been many eternal monuments of our triumphs and of our national glory, poised at the door of the capital of Europe, which could not miss being visited by the forces of the rest of the universe.

History was a central issue to the French garden. Napoleon noted that he wished to chase the gods and demigods from the bosquets of Versailles, and in so doing eradicate classical history. However, he sought to replace mythic existence with and eminently real one—the history of Napoleon. Napoleon desired to demystify the range of human activities, past and present. Historical destiny, he said, was merely politics. Ironically, as he deconstructed *historia,* Napoleon erected another mythical form—himself. Just as the classical gods fashioned human history as the externalization of divine will, modern history was to be the chronicle of Napoleon's ideology, vindicated by his acts of heroism and virtue. The new Paris was to become the embodiment of history as well as the home of cosmic forces, orchestrated in conformity with the Napoleonic idea.

Also implicit in Napoleon's vision was the idea of perspectives marked by monumental buildings serving as a backdrop for heroic actions, like the tragic scene so important to heroic drama in European theater.[36] This vision moved Napoleon from mere historian to moralist. To be sure, knowledge was important to the emperor. Yet, what concerned him even more were the forces behind history—the mechanism of historical operation, historical order—comprising, for Napoleon, ultimate historical knowledge, or truth. A metaphor for such a structure of knowledge could be found in the organization of the city. Two orders of inquiry were especially applicable: the order behind the unified street, with provenance descending from the tragic scene, and the totally coordinated urban plan, with sources in the garden, both Italian and French. Both the unified street and coordinated plan, and their ancestors, the tragic scene and the formal garden, had explicit idealistic overtones. The presence of order in both situations underlined thc involvement of will, either human or superhuman, in directing the organization. Such will indicated the presence of divine forces in the shaping of history, rather than a purely empirical interpretation of human progress. Moreover, the association of the garden with the tragic scene or theater, dealt not only with the problem of the appropriate imitation of nature, but also with the didactic function in communicating the essence of nature to the audience. In short, the primary objective of both constructions was the effective conveyance, by means of inspiration, of Truth to an audience. In other words, the tragic set and the garden sought not so much to instruct as to edify. Their purpose was not so much instructive, as it was moralistic.

The City in *Historia*

The description of history's subconscious infrastructure was an attempt to portray its essence. This portrayal constituted history's moral being, which could be communicated to an audience in a moment of inspiration. The ultimate purpose behind determining historical truth was a rhetorical one, and involved the edification of the observer. This didactic urge moved history from the realm of the mere study of the past to *historia* and the recounting of certain events which embodied historical truths. The events in *historia* focused upon moments of will, both human and divine. Moreover, they drew upon episodes in which virtue, or moral behavior as the externalization of will, could best portray the historical subconscious.

The problem of artistic creation, at least in the classical sense, focused upon the central problem of imitation. The objective of art lay in the artist's responsibility to communicate truths convincingly. Artistic creation confronted truth on three different levels, those of the artwork, of the artist, of the public. On the first level, the work of art functioned under the Aristotelian dictum to faithfully imitate nature. However, the goal of art was to represent not nature's appearance, but the essence of the natural situation. Moreover, in dramatic imitation, when art imitated history as well as nature, the work of art focused upon the moral dictate of virtuous will, particularly as it coincided with or deviated from divine will or fate. The work of art was to portray, and to embody, truth.

Art had a creator as well as an ontology of its own. This notion introduces the second level of inquiry. The artist, giving form to natural or historical truth, was himself involved in a heroic act, comparable with those acts of divine and quasi-divine acts of will provided by history. The artist, in imitating such action, was directed by an unstated morality. Virtuous actions for the artist lie in a personal act worthy of emulation, especially in the creation of artworks which could lead to inspiration and imitation. His art was destined for the public realm, like the speech of an orator, the dialogue of a philosopher, the law of a legislator. As with these men whose actions were ostensibly directed by virtue, an artist's acts and creations were to have a moralizing motivation. This draws us to the third level of inquiry, the public. As the artist imitated the actions of gods and heroes in his creative act, so the artwork was to move the public to imitate similar virtuous action. This imitation was accomplished by a process of inspiration. The resulting catharsis energized men to virtuous imitation of the virtue represented. By a transference of truth, and the concomitant process of moralization, art moved men to an awareness of personal responsibility and will in terms of the shaping of theirs and others' moral and virtuous lives. On the one hand, the artist, in his own imitation of the historical or natural situation, performed a heroic act in the course of his artistic creation. The work of art thus embodied essential truth. On the other hand, the artist as medium for historical truth acted as a catalyst by which truth could be transferred to the artistic audience. This resulting act of inspiration moved men to imitate acts of virtue, comparable to those accomplished by the artist himself.[38]

Plato confronted the central problem of imitation in art, and informed the artist of those situations appropriate for imitation. Those significant situations were the actions or events which would lead men on to further virtuous actions, in imitation of the virtuous portrayal in the representation. With regard to dramatic imitation, Plato stated in *The Republic:*

> For our benefit, we shall employ the poets and story-tellers of the more austere and attractive type, who will reproduce only the manner of a person of "high character," and in the substance of their decorum, conform to those rules we laid down when we began the education of our warriors.[39]

Plutarch also confronted the problem of artistic imitation. But appropriate artistic models were only those which would lead the observer to emulate the action represented in pursuit of virtue. In short, only heroic subject matter was appropriate for artistic imitation. Plutarch created numerous historical tableaux in his *Lives,* closely approximating the modern notion of *historia.* The subject matter of his portrayals were:

> ...objects we find in the acts of virtue, which also produces in the minds of the mere reader...an emulation and eagerness that may lead them to imitation...Virtue, by the bare statement of its actions can so affect men's minds as to create at once both admiration of the things done and desire to imitate the doers of them. The goods of fortune we would possess and enjoy; those of virtue we long to practice and exercise; we are content to receive the former from others, the latter we wish to experience from ourselves. Moral good is a practical stimulus; it is no sooner seen, than it inspires an impulse to practice, and influences the mind and character not by a mere imitation which we look at, but by the statement of the fact creates a moral purpose which we form.[40]

There was an implied limit to the range of artistic imitation. It was confined by the purpose of art to communicate historical truth in order to edify the observer.

It was Leon Battista Alberti who first directly addressed the problem of *historia* in painting, continuing the notions of appropriate artistic imitation discussed by the ancients. In *Della Pittura,* Alberti instructed the artist to avoid mere external nature in the process of imitation, and to search for the ideal formal essence. Truth resided in the type. He cited the example of Zeuxis, and the ancient preference for types over individuals, as appropriate means for communicating ideal nature. Correct representation of history, too, went beyond the surface. As with the imitation of nature, *historia* should attempt to determine cause, which in Alberti's thought, as in Plato's, lay in virtuous action and will. The true object of imitation, in nature and in history, was to be revealed only by scientific and philosophical investigation.[41]

Moreover, Alberti also discussed the place of *historia* in society. It was not to be a private art form, but a public one. Although historical painting gained meaning in juxtaposition to the depravity of present-day life, it was, in time, to fuse with daily life. *Historia* was to be regarded as "the common property of all citizens" like the city republic itself. In short, art was no longer a foil to life, but one with it. In imitating history man becomes history's representative, a performer of virtuous acts, and as such, the model for subsequent historical imitation. The historical idea was a vital force ultimately dominating all aspects of man's life.

Alberti valued historical painting as the stimulus for the general moralizing and uplifting of mankind. Man's city and man's institutions were to be shaped by the moralizing urge implicit in public embellishments of this nature. Its effects would be longlasting. To demonstrate the reasonance of this notion, I cite Mariette's dedication of Jacques-Louis David's historical painting, *The Rape of The Sabines.* He stated,

> Antiquity has not ceased to be the great school of modern painters, the source from which they draw the beauties of their arts. We seek to imitate the ancients, in the germ of their conception, the purity of their design, the expressiveness of their features, and the gravity of their form. Could we not take a step further and imitate them also in their customs and institutions established by them to bring their arts to perfection?[42]

The allusion is comparable to Alberti. For Mariette, the truth, sought in imitation of antiquity became the propery of modernity. Moreover, truth might extend beyond consciously artistic concerns, and move into the realm of the customary and the political. Like Alberti, Mariette and David believed the ultimate outcome of imitation to be in the shaping of man's present-day, real-life historical situation, especially in the city.

Much as *historia* and theater became art with Alberti, theater became city with Jean-Jacques Rousseau. The idea of the city as source of inspiration as well as inspiring backdrop to heroic action was articulated in Rousseau's two essays, "An Epistle to M. d'Alembert," and "On Theatrical Imitation." Like Plato, Rousseau addressed the problem of imitation, inspiration, and *historia* from the point of view of dramatic presentation. Rousseau criticized contemporary theater for its elitism, as well as for the comic, unheroic manners of contemporary theatrical. If theater was to communicate virtue (the object of all representation, whether dramatic or artistic, it should do so by virtuous means, Modern theater's appeal to sentimentalism sought inspiration utilizing the most questionable of means. Rousseau proposed the suppression of modern theater.

Moreover, Rousseau broke apart distinctions between modern life and theater. Modern life should be virtuous; modern life should participate in life's heroic dramas; modern life should be filled with moralizing events and individuals which edify the population. Most importantly, modern life should be portrayed against an appropriately solemn backdrop of epic proportions.

> Must there be then, no public show or entertainment in a republican state? There would be a great many. It was in republics that they were first introduced, and it is in them that they are celebrated with a genuine air of festivity. What people does it more become to have frequent meetings to engage in parties of pleasure and diversion, than those who have so many reasons for loving each other, and for continuing united? We have so many of these festivals already, and I should be delighted if we had more. But let us not consider those exclusive entertainments which keep a small number of people shut in gloomy caverns, there to sit for two hours motionless, silent and inattentive ... it is in the open air, in the face of heaven, you ought to meet and indulge yourselves, in the enjoyment of your own happiness. Your pleasures should be neither venal nor effeminate; impoisoned by interest or constraint; but free and generous like yourselves, the fun should enliven your innocent spectacles with its meridian beams; while you yourselves would form one of the noblest sights they ever enlightened.[43]

These mass celebrations were to be erected against civic structures befitting the moral purpose of the event. Rousseau discussed the public *fêtes* of the Greeks and Romans, assumedly performed before the backdrop of Periclean Athens or Republican Rome.

> Why should we not adopt the plan of military rewards and found other gymnastic prizes for running, wrestling, throwing quoits, and other bodily exercises? Why do we not animate our watermen to exert themselves for wagers on the lake? Can the possibly be a finer sight in the world, than to see some hundreds of boats, elegantly equipped, floating on that spacious basin, and setting off at a given signal, to seize a flag hoisted as a mark?[44]

To a large extent, Rousseau's devaluation of artistic imitation per se involved a destruction of the traditional forms of art. On a second level, however, Rousseau never escaped the primal urge of art—the will to moralize. Rather than viewing art as special object or occasion, removed from the daily experience of man, he wished to incorporate it wholly into the human situation.

As a result, the city no longer contrasted with art, but merged with it. The city as a source of edification was now an object in itself. Moreover, as men's lives further assumed a heroic existence, the city served as setting for dramatic representation. Citizens themselves were transformed into actors. Rousseau wrote:

> Whenever liberty is to be found in the midst of plenty, there is the feat of human happiness. Raise a maypole with a chaplet of flowers, in the middle of a plain; call the people about it, and their assembly will become a festival. But you may still do better; the spectators themselves may be made actors . . . [45]

The metropolis was now total artwork. As the citizens performed, city streets became the tragic scene of the classic theater. The actions of men in *tableau vivant* fashion developed into edifying representations of civic virtue.

The most significant results of Rousseau's plea for moralizing civic expression were the *fêtes repùblicaines*. Conceived by Jacques-Louis David in 1790, these tragic scenes were produced on significant days of the republican calendar, and erected at important locations in Paris and in the provinces. In Paris, the Champs de Mars, the Pantheon, and the Bastille became favorite spots for these civic presentations. [46] The *fêtes* had an urbanistic impact in expanding the significance of their sites, which were designated now as historically and politically uplifting. The outcome of this new spatial and formal awareness was the Artist's Plan of 1793, proposed by David, Quatremère, and others, where the symbolic qualities of these distinct locales were linked by ideal streets. [47]

Napoleon I paralleled Rousseau's and David's desire for public edification in the city in criticizing museums and theaters for their removal of objects of edification and emulation from the public realm. [48] As Napoleon wished to make Paris into a *musée universel,* he also wished to transform it into a total theatrical production. Like Rousseau, Napoleon was critical of modern theatre, calling its productions "les tragédies de femme de chambre."[49] True tragedy lay in heroic action portrayed against the backdrop of a great city. He cited the example of the Romans, who had no tragedies. De Las Cases, Napoleon's biographer, recounts:

> D'abord il s'étonnait que les Romains n'eussent point de tragédies puis il convenait qu'elles eussent été peu propres à les émouvoir sur le théàtre; qu'elles se donnait en réalité dans les cirques. «Les combats des gladiateurs, disait-il, celui des hommes livrés aux bêtes féroces, étaient bien autrement terribles que toutes nos scénes dramatiques ensemble...»[50]

> At first he was surprised that the Romans may not have had tragedies, then he agreed that theatrical tragedies could hardly be moving; that in reality, tragedies were given in the circuses. "The combats of the gladiators," he said, "and that of men delivered to fierce beasts, were far more dramatic than all our dramatic scenes put together."

The Romans automatically incorporated heroism into their daily lives; Napoleon, like Rousseau, recommended that Parisians do the same. By a program of public works, Napoleon hoped to turn the tide of "hideux libertinage" in the Parisian metropolis, and to encourage the moral life of the citizenry. Important to the moralizing scheme were *fêtes publics*. It should be noted, however, that Napoleon had reservations concerning the festivals. He felt that the transitory nature of the *fêtes* betrayed an insincerity concerning the role of virtue in the public realm. Heroism for Napoleon was something durable, not temporary. Consequently, constant civic virtues had to be reinforced by enduring civic settings.

> J'ai souvent combattu des fêtes que la ville de Paris voulait me donner . . . c'étaient des diners, des bals, des feux d'artifice, de quatre, de six, de huit cent mille francs, dont les préparatifs obstruaient plusieurs jours la voie publique, et qui coûtaient ensuite autant à défaire qu'elles avaient coûté à construire. Je prouvais qu'avec ces faux frais ils auraient fait des monuments durables, magnifiques . . . [51]

> I have long opposed the feats that the city of Paris wishes to give me . . . the dinners, the balls, the fireworks costing four, six, or eight hundred thousand francs, whose preparations obstruct public thoroughfares for days, and which they cost as much to take down and they did to put up. I contend that these artificial expenses should have been used to make durable, magnificent monuments.

The city was to become *historia* in a vast campaign of public works.

We have been examining the conceptions of history from two points of view—one materialistic, the other idealistic. We began our investigation by separating history into conscious and subconscious. Conscious history provided us with material to satisfy the encyclopedic urge, the need to catalogue nature. Subconscious history dealt with understanding, the drive to discern fundamental principles, primary causes, or essences. The striving to unmask subconscious history paralleled the need to attain total knowledge, or truth. Once truth became an issue, we moved from the realm of the natural sciences to the moral. At this point, the object of our investigation, history, became transfigured. It was given the name *historia,* the chronicle not of isolated events but of fundamental historical forces, of human versus divine will, or destiny.

For both ancients and moderns, the moral imperative of art was not merely imitation of nature, of history's conscious level, but representation of the truth, its subconscious level. Moreover, the object of art was to be the effective communication in an act of inspiration of that truth to an audience. The artistic imitation of nature, and man's history, began in drama. Appropriate dramatic subjects were those by which truth could be effectively communicated to an audience for purposes of instruction and uplift. Themes focused upon the virtuous actions of the gods, or of men. *Historia* moved from dramatic to other forms of pictorial representation—painting and sculpture especially. In light of the didactic imperative, it became apparent, especially during the Renaissance, that the public realm alone was appropriate for the fitting display of historical themes. Thus, the city itself was affected by *historia*. Theater and history painting became one with the city. Ultimately, the city, as backdrop for decorous pictorial action, became the *scenae frons* for the heroics of the present day. The city was to become a historical setting, which not only instructed, but also fused with the virtuous life.

Tragic and Satiric Scene

Napoleon was well aware of the comic image that the city of Paris presented at the end of the eighteenth century. He criticized the sentimentalized, trivial and sensual lives of modern Parisians. De las Cases recounted Napoleon's opinion:

> ... l'empéreur, parlant des moeurs de Paris, et de l'ensemble de son immense population énumérait toutes les abominations inévitables, disait-il, d'une grande capitale où la perversité naturelle et la somme de tous les vices se trouvoient aiguillonnées à chaque instant par les besoins, la passion, l'esprit et toutes les facilités de melánge et de la confusion; et il répétait souvent que toutes les capitales étaient autant de Babylons. Il a cité quelques détails du plus sâle et du plus hideux libertinage; il a dit qu'étant Empéreur il s'était fait représenter et avait parcouru le livre le plus abominable qu'ait enfanté l'imagination la plus depravée: c'etait un roman qui...avait revolté...la morale publique...[52]

> ... the emperor, speaking of the morals of Paris, and of the ensemble of its immense population, enumerated all the abominations, he said, of a great capital where the natural perversity and the sum of all vices are exacerbated at each instant by the needs, passions, the mind and all the facilities serving its mixture and confusion; and he often repeated that all of Europe's capitals are so many Babylons. He cited certain details of the most vile and hideous libertinage; he said that as Emperor, he was forced to present and examine the most abominable book that had ever emerged from the most depraved imagination; it was a novel which had revolted ... the public morality

Napoleon saw Parisian city life as depraved. As noted above, he tied the morality of the population to urban form. For Napoleon chaotic environment led to questionable human motivations and aberrant behavior.

Later commentators on the city operated under similar biases as Napoleon. For example, Henry Bayard, in his important work on the public health of Paris, *Mémoire sur la Topographie Médicale de Paris* (1842), stressed a lack of morality in the city, spiritual illness as well as physical. His pleas were not so much for medical improvement in the city (although he certainly did address these issues) as for uplifting physical environment by which the Parisian physical and moral health could be assured:

> C'est une verité de tous les temps, de tous les lieux, une verité qu'il faut redire sans cesse, parce que sans cesse on l'oublie: Il existe entre l'homme et tout ce qui l'entoure de secrets liens, de

mystérieux rapports, dont l'influence sur lui est continuelle et profonde. Favorable, cette influence ajoute à ses forces physiques et morales, elle les développe, les conserve; nuisible, alors elle les altère, les anéantit, les tue ... [53]

It is a truth of all times and places, a truth that one must repeat without cease otherwise one forgets: it exists between man and all that surrounds him with secret connections, mysterious relationships whose influence upon him is continual and profound. If favorable, this influence supplements his physical and moral forces; it develops and conserves them; if harmful, it alters, lessens, and kills them.

If contemporary urban form could be likened to any particular image, it was the Renaissance comic scene (plate 62). As an alternative to the comic, Napoleon preferred either the tragic or the satiric scene as particularly instructive and uplifting to the city of Paris (plates 63, 64). Initially, the tragic scene in its most easily recognizable form, the unified street, became the paradigm of responsible and moral administration. It symbolized historical will acting in people's lives, under the guise of politics. Moreover, as the backdrop to people's lives, the tragic scene became the setting for heroic action and virtuous life.

Napoleon linked both references—one of personal glory by the equation of his government with the forces of history, and the other, the drive to moralization. As noted above, Napoleon believed that the Romans had no tragedy, because they lived heroic tragedies. This allusion proposed that life and art could be one. With the ancients, men's daily heroic deeds were juxtaposed against fitting architectural settings, a kind of real tragic scene. Napoleon drew upon Greek and Roman precedents to evoke images of an appropriate realm. Plutarch, one of the most important ancient sources for Napoleon, provided important examples.[54] For instance, Napoleon, as de las Cases notes, admired Pericles, who, in fifth-century Athens used public works not merely as a means to improve the public weal, but as a kind of tragic scene designed to instruct and edify. Plutarch reminds us of Pericles' achievements.

That which gave most pleasure and ornament to the city of Athens and the greatest admiration, and even astonishment to all strangers, and that which now is Greece's only evidence that the power she boasts of and her ancient wealth are no romance or idle story, was [Pericles'] construction of sacred and public buildings... For as those who are of age and strength are provided for and maintained in the armaments abroad by their pay out of the public stock, so, it being his desire and design that the undisciplined mechanic multitude that stayed at home should not go without their share of public salaries... these vast projects... would give employment to numerous arts so that the part of the people that stayed at home might... have a fair and just occasion of receiving the benefit and having their share of the public monies... [55]

The ancient building campaign was a source of admiration. As with rhetoric, the objective of the monumental program was the communication of the truth, hence, inspiration. Plutarch himself was moved by the works.

Pericles' works are especially admired, as having been made quickly, to last long. For every particular piece of the work was immediately, even at that time, for its beauty and elegance, antique; and yet in its vigor and freshness looks to this day as if it were just executed. There is a sort of bloom of newness upon those works of his, preserving them from the touch of time, as if they had some perennial spirit and undying vitality in the composition of them.[56]

Like Plutarch and Pericles, Napoleon believed in a program of public works that would edify the population by the sublimity of their scale, the comprehensiveness of their public concerns, and by their beauty. It was the communication of his quasi-divine will which would ultimately inspire. To quote de las Cases,

C'est le représentant d'une révolution accusée vulgairement d'avoir tout détruit celui qui a refait les universités, les écoles, [mais] qui a couvert son Empire des chefs d'oeuvres des arts; C'est l'auteur des travaux les plus vastes, les plus hardis, qui aient étonné et honoré l'esprit humain...[57]

He [Napoleon] is the representative of a revolution accused vulgarly of having destroyed all those who rebuilt the universities, the institutes, [but] who has covered his Empire with masterpieces of the arts. He is the author of the most vast works, the most audacious works to astonish and honor the human spirit.

Napoleon III, like his great uncle, carried on a tradition of public works in Paris, a program by which the passions would be suppressed and social order and harmony fostered. Louis-Napoleon cited the need for public institutions, designed on the models of antiquity.[58] Moreover, he seemed almost to paraphrase the words of his great predecessor (according to de las Cases) in the moralizing influence of the city of *historia*:

Cette mission consiste à fermer l'ère des revolutions en satisfaisant les besoins légitimes du peuple et en le protégeant contre les passions subversives. Elle consiste surtout à créer des institutions aux hommes et qui soient enfin des fondations sur lesquelles on puisse asseoir quelque chose durable.[59]

This mission consists in closing the era of revolutions while satisfying the legitimate needs of the people and protecting them from subversive passions. It consists above all in creating institutions for men which finally become the foundations upon which can be set something durable.

Les Halles was the first piece of his monumental program undertaken during his Second Republic presidency. It was to be a great symbol of social welfare, as well as the germ of the luxury ultimately seen as characterizing the Second Empire. Napoleon III stated at Les Halles' dedication,

En posant la première pierre d'un édifice dont la destination est si éminemment populaire, je me lève avec confiance à l'espoir qu'avec l'appui des bons citoyens et avec la protection du ciel, il nous sera donné de jeter dans le sol de la France quelques foundations sur lesquelles s'élevera un édifice sociale pour offrir un abri contre la violence et la mobilité des passions humaines.[60]

In placing the first stone of an edifice whose destination is so eminently popular, I rise with confidence to the hope that with the moral support of good citizens and with the protection of heaven, it will be bestowed upon us to thrust into the soil of France certain foundations upon which will be erected a social edifice offering a shelter against the violence and the instability of human passions.

In summary, the tragic scene was important on two levels, the pictorial and the ideal. On the pictorial level, it proposed a scheme of public works and created an artistic public realm, by which the public could be edified and against which virtuous action could be poised. However, on a structural level, it proposed a historical subconscious, the idea of history, which was ultimately the source of inspiration. Individual amusements were to be orchestrated and unified by the comprehensive perspective scheme of the tragic scenes, but the harmonious urban realm was fused by will, be it human or divine. The action of will, of ideology articulated in the grandeur of the comprehensive urban scheme, provided the key to inspiration. The action of poising man against the edifice of history, of juxtaposing him with the scheme of things, led him to sublime experience.

As *topos,* the coordinated street organized by a perspective system provided an image of external order or will imposed upon the various functions of everyday life. The problem set by theatrical imitation was urban life orchestrated by a mathematical system. The major formal outcome of the tragic scene dealt with a street facade, unified by the mathematics implicit in the perspective grid, creating an implicit order in elevation. The straightness of the tragic street did imply a mathematical reading on an even more fundamental level—in the plan. In this regard the geometry of the vertical surface provided by the perspective scheme prefigured the geometry of the horizontal.

It was in the realm of the ideal city that this formal implication was to be examined. Mathematical city planning, like the mathematical street facade, became a focal issue of Renaissance and post-Renaissance architectural theory. The treatises of Alberti, Filarete, Leonardo, Fra Giocondo, Serlio, etc., devoted considerable attention to the problem of the city mathematically conceived. However, despite profuse theorizing on the nature of this tragic city, built manifestations were infrequent. Holistic considerations of the city from this point of view were by and large limited to an ideal set piece, street, or perhaps a quarter. Ideal cities like Palmanova and Richelieu were the exceptions that proved the rule.

Perhaps their infrequency was due fundamentally to the paradox of ideality. Once any city, even an ideal city, becomes built, it necessarily becomes real. It must by necessity house certain inglorious, even sordid, functions necessary for human life. It must concern itself with banal life issues, such as food, water, and defense. An ideal city in a real world is an impossibility. Perhaps it was just such a realization in this regard that limited the extent of optimistic urban experiment.

Yet, perhaps, one should look into another realm entirely to observe the implications of ideal urban theory. Perhaps the ideal city—the seat of harmony and social order—should be sought in a situation other than the physical reality of the city. Perhaps ideal cities were not built at all, but, at least initially, fashioned of other materials at once more durable and more transitory. Perhaps they were gardens.

As mentioned above, the scenic alternative to the comic were the tragic and satiric scenes. The satiric scene, or the garden, was an important paradigm for France in the eighteenth and nineteenth centuries. Laugier, Blondel, Patte, Le Camus de Mezières all recommended an observation of the principles of classical garden design to combat the depraved, or comic, character of the city.[61] As noted above, Napoleon was no less influenced by such reasoning in his admiration of Versailles. Although Bonaparte criticized the palace and gardens for their monotony, he valued the ensemble for its enormous scale, comparable only to a city like Paris in the sublime feeling evoked by its grandeur, and perhaps more importantly, as its expression of artistic will betraying the force of ideology, apparent in the imposition of geometric order on nature.

The plans of the garden and the town of Versailles make a useful comparison with Napoleon's monumental quarter of 1811 (plate 65). Like the palace, the quarter is an autonomous formal element, mediating between the garden and the city. Moreover, as garden and city are unified by a series of orthogonal and oblique striations, Napoleon's new realm is similarly organized by a dialogue between *allées* and streets. No longer antithetical elements in a formal dialectic, Louis XIV's landscape and Napoleon's new city are synthesized by shared formal concerns. Distinctions between man and nature vanish.

The meaning of the new city benefited by the intellectual history of the garden. The ideal landscape, or *locus amoenus,* in both classical and Christian literatures symbolized a place of fecundity and repose, a place signifying spiritual birth, Eden, while it also symbolized death and rebirth, a New Jerusalem. The life cycle, or human history, was fundamental to the iconography of the garden.[62] Furthermore, it was the symbol of an idyllic existence, where men lived in harmony with the gods. The Renaissance garden especially overlaid the idea of idyll with notions of history, using allegorical imagery to evoke the classical epochs. In addition, these gardens were organized by consciously prescribed circulation sequences which were designed to describe the various classical ages of humanity.[63] Hence, the author of such a garden placed the observer in the dualistic situation of first, experiencing time as history, and second, manipulating, controlling, and transcending history. Ideal human existence free of the need to dominate nature in search of knowledge was balanced by the presence of history, understood as the chronicle of man's progress and accumulated knowledge through the ages. This realm exploited notions akin to Freud's ideas of superego and libido—the desire to be one with nature in dialectic with the desire to dominate nature. The natural successor to the Renaissance *topos* was the "jardin anglo-chinois" of the late eighteenth century, both in England and France.

A particularly important garden in the shaping of late eighteenth-century taste in France was the Parc Monceau, a country seat of Louis-Philippe-Joseph d'Orléans (Philippe Egalité), father of Louis-Philippe (plate 66). Designed by Louis Carrogis Carmontelle, one of the period's important dramatists, the garden introduced a number of iconographic features important for the allegorical reading of landscape for the period. On a basic level, the garden was to be a *locus amoenus,* intended to "move, interest, and amuse by the choice of special images."[64] At the same time, the garden was to be the receptable of human civilization, both ancient and recent. It memorialized the saga of mankind—man's failures, successes, wars and death. The garden was to be an allegory of history. Carmontelle stated,

> What we wish to do here at Monceau is to reunite all times and places in a single garden. It is a simple fantasy, the desire to have an extraordinary garden.[65]

Carmontelle symbolized history in two ways, by allegorical backdrops and by the style of plantings. The various locales represented in the garden served two functions. First, Carmontelle's and Louis-Philippe's encyclopedism was apparent in the confrontation of conscious exoticism and vernacular elements, the juxtaposition of nature and science, the contrast of antiquity with modernity. Second, the garden's plantings juxtaposed a "jardin regulier" with a "jardin agreste," unified in what the mid-eighteenth century termed a "jardin mixte." The "agreste" or wild section of the garden was characterized by ruinated elements, particularly a scarred Gothic battlement, a collapsed Temple of Mars, and a decomposing Naumachia. The three features allude to a period of warfare. Yet, it is important to realize that the landscape has intruded upon these elements, eroding their original completeness, and subverting their original meaning. For example, the battlement served the garden not defensively, but as pumping stations for the site's waterworks. The Naumachia, an ancient institution where Romans would divert themselves by watching mock sea battles, is further deprived of its militaristic overtones in the garden, where it is merely a pleasant spot for boating.[66]

The ordered part of the landscape was entered from the street via the Duc d'Orlean's pavilion, or from the garden, past the so-called Temple of White Marble. As gateway, the temple is important to the garden's formal structure.

Its furnishings are important to the garden iconographically. Inside the temple stands a sculpture of the Greek hero, Achilles, and a frieze depicting the hero during one of the battles of the Trojan War. The monumentality of the temple and of its artworks again allude to the theme of warfare. Yet, the portrayal of war is markedly different than that of the wild section of garden. Here, war in its completeness is attached to the most artistic and most orderly component of the site plan.

The two sections of the Parc Monceau concentrate upon different treatments of the same theme: the memorializing and the passing of warfare. This duality is not unlike one which characterized many Italian Renaissance gardens. At the Villa Lante, Bagnaia, for example, the central, ordered portion of the garden was meant to represent man at the apex of his intellectual powers. Art, and unfortunately, warfare as well, were regarded as two significant indices of man's heightened mental and degraded moral faculties. A historical dimension was also attached to this portion of the garden: it was designed to represent the Iron Age of classical history. The ordered section of the villa's garden counterpoised the wild, where ruins, primitive structures, and peacefulness were seen as representing a Golden Age, the first of classical history's major periods.[67] At the Parc Monceau, the two species of landscape, and I suspect the two periods of time, are also juxtaposed: the orderly, yet aggressive *parterre* next to the main house, and the disorderly, but peaceful landscape some distance away.

As at the Villa Lante, the two spatial and temporal frames did not merely coexist at Parc Monceau, but were drawn together by a system of controlled movement. At Villa Lante, a progress was clearly marked by a "preferred route" which sequentially moved the visitor from wild to ordered sections of the site, thereby allowing him to trace a path analogous to the march of classical time. In the Parc Monceau, the "preferred route" was replaced by a "promenade," which was not so much uni- as multi-dimensional. Movement in the garden could be from ordered to wild, or wild to ordered landscape, depending upon where one entered the site. The strictly linear progress of the earlier garden is replaced at Monceau by a cyclical narrative scheme. Such cyclical narrative structure derives less from classical sources than eschatological, specifically Biblical notions of progress.[68]

Carmontelle, it appears, realized this provenance in naming the "promenade" of the garden, "Vigne de Judée." This designation refers not simply to Judaic history, but more specifically, to the history of the life of Christ. The cyclical notion of progress is recalled here both in Christ's life, which focused upon resurrection, and in the relationship of Old to New Testament, in which the former serves to foreshadow the latter. Lastly, the entire progress of the New Testament culminates in the apocalyptic moment when Christ returns for still a third time, bringing with him to the Last Judgment man's entire history.[69]

The garden was designed as a piece of theater, or as Carmontelle proposed, an opera with sets erected at strategic locations to give clues of historical readings. Carmontelle stated,

> ... transportons, dans nos jardins, les changements de scène des Opéra; faisons-y voir, en réalité, ce que les plus habiles Peintres pourroient y offrir en décoration, tous les temps et tous les lieux.[70]

> ... let us transport into our gardens the set changes of the Opéra; let us there make visible in reality, that which the most capable Painters would be able to offer by way of decor at all times and places.

The pageant of history was recreated in all its diversity. The visitor was to become actor in the scenario. His actions, however, were not meant to be free ones. Rather, they were to be modelled upon the heroism of a man who passed through history before him—Christ. The conscious level of the garden provided him with an encyclopedic work. More importantly, the subconscious level dealt with the interaction of the forces of history—an undercurrent of fate, determined by the gods yet foiled by the personal will of a man whose will was the equal of the divine. Moreover, in the association of the visitor with the tragic journey of Christ, moved by the force of his will, one was edified by this most careful example of *historia*. The total outcome was tragedy of the most subtle variety, wherein human will was pitted against history itself.

History, destiny, and will—these were the forces behind *historia*. They were also the forces to be represented and communicated in the form of the city at the beginning of the nineteenth century. The city's involvement with the essence of history moved its responsibility from the merely narrative to the moral. The tragic scene, as the ready example of the city's moralizing intention, attempted to represent an appropriate backdrop for the virtuous life. Moreover, the formalism of the scene indicated the presence of higher will in action, especially in the shaping of the city.

The garden took this idea of order to a more comprehensive level. Not only did the garden attempt to orchestrate individual dramatic scenes (or historical moments), it also imbued the city with a richer sense of history and a plot, by which man proceeded through history. If history was ordered by the underlying forces of fate and destiny, then plot was determined by the force of human will, evoking an image of heroic life.

The *Revue Générale* and the City

In César Daly's major writings on both public and private architecture, typified by such works as *L'Architecture Privée au Dix-neuvième Siècle* (1863), and *Les Théâtres de la Place du Châtelet* (1874), the architectural scale was stressed more than the urbanistic. Urban design issues were addressed indirectly. However, within the course of its publication, the *Revue Générale* lavished considerable attention on the city itself. This interest was characterized from an early date in an important series of articles prepared by A. Perreymond entitled "Etudes sur la Ville de Paris" (1842-43) and continued in Albert Lenoir's "Théorie des Villes" (1859), and César Daly's "Panorama du Mouvement Architecturale du Monde" (1862), and "Promenades et Plantations" (1863).

I intend to trace the themes introduced in the preceding pages through the *Revue Générale* in general, and through the writings of César Daly in particular. Perhaps a logical starting point in this examination would be A. Perreymond's evaluation of and proposals for the city of Paris. The personality of Perreymond is an obscure one. He was a disciple of both Saint-Simon, and later, Fourier, and he became involved with the Considérant circle. Later in his life, he, like Daly, followed the Fourierists to Considérant's experimental colony in Texas, La Réunion. Little is known beyond this. Generally speaking, his proposals for the city of Paris have been considered utilitarian.[71] Yet it is also apparent that beneath the surface of his Paris proposal Perreymond betrays certain idealistic concerns, extending late eighteenth- and early nineteenth-century intellectual involvements.

Perreymond was fundamentally concerned with the perception of Paris as a unified entity, one with a distinct ontology. To determine this, he observed Paris in history. Perreymond initially stressed the importance of formal unity in the establishment of identity. His historical analyses noted that in its earlier form, Paris extended no further than the Ile de la Cité, the germ of its subsequent growth. The Romans extended the city to the right and left banks. Although individual quarters multiplied, unity was maintained by the judicious incorporation of major north/south traffic routes traversing the entire city fabric. Moreover, under the Romans, the city underwent a separation of functions, which increasingly distinguished the three quarters with distinct activities. Perreymond did not regard this factor in the city growth to be detrimental, so long as adequate circulation permitted the easy movement of goods and people. As time passed, however, the number of quarters multiplied. As they proliferated, the simple formal organization of Roman Paris proved to be insufficient, and the quarters grew increasingly isolated in terms of function and movement.[72] This phenomenon became especially apparent under François I, when the Cité, and Right and Left Banks became largely tied to governmental residential and educational institutions respectively. From this time onwards the quarters of the Left Bank had difficulty in maintaining resident population.[73]

The dilemma of Paris, according to Perreymond, was more the loss of formal unity than it was Paris' inadequate means of circulation.

Paris n'est plus homogène; il forme plusieurs villes sous une désignation collective.[74]

Paris is no longer homogenous; it is formed of a number of cities under a collective designation.

He opposed the multiplication of new quarters and especially the suburbanization process in Paris. Moreover, he viewed the problem of Paris as the increasing autonomy and alienation of each quarter. His perceptions presaged those of Albert Lenoir who asserted that the disintegration of Parisian urban form was due to the factionalism caused by *intérêt privé*.[75] For Perreymond such special interest was characterized by the city's growing lack of coordination between quarters. He wished to sponsor in the city a new spirit of community, manifested by the formal unity of Paris.

> La prosperité normale de Paris, aux différentes époques de l'histoire de cette capitale, dépend toujours de la plus ou moins parfaite coincidence du centre de configuration de cette ville, avec le foyer de tous ses monuments qui s'accomplit dans son sein.
>
> Chaque fois l'action vitale s'est fractionné en plusieurs foyers l'existence de Paris a été d'autant plus irrégulière que foyers divers ont été éloignés les uns des autres, et que leurs rapports matériels sont devenus plus difficiles. Dès lors la prosperité de chaque quartier a été en raison directe de l'importance du foyer qu'il possédait, et en raison inverse de son éloignement rélatif aux autres foyers existants et des obstacles intermédiaires.
>
> Enfin, si une seule fonction est devenue prééminente dans une époque, et si une partie excentrique de la ville, fortuitement, ou par suite d'une influence quelconque, possède à elle seule le foyer de cette attraction, cette partie a dû prendre une développement exubérante; elle a dû attirer à elle toutes les forces de la commune, et paralyser plus ou moins complètement les autres membres.
>
> Donc, le foyer principal de Paris doit être UN, STABLE, CENTRAL et ACTIF PAR LUI-MEME.[76]

> The normal prosperity of Paris, during the different epochs of the history of this capital, always depends on the greatest or least perfect coincidence of the center of this city with the core of monuments erected in its bosom.
>
> As the vital action of central Paris broke into a number of cores, and as the distance between the cores complicated their material servicing, Paris' growth as a whole became irregular. From that point, the prosperity of each quarter became the direct consequence of the core that it possessed and was inversely related to the distance between itself and other cores, as well as obstacles in between.
>
> Finally, if a single function has become pre-eminent during an epoch, and if an eccentric part of the city, as the result of some consequence or other, fortuitously possesses exclusively the core of this attraction, then this part must experience an exuberant growth; it comes to attract all the forces of the commune and more or less paralyzes the other members completely.
>
> Therefore, the principal core of Paris must be ONE, STABLE, CENTRAL, and ACTIVE BY ITSELF.

Perreymond's allusion to *action vitale* invoked the notion of organicism. The city was to function as a species of animal or plant. Physical improvements to the city of Paris would concentrate upon linking all quarters of Paris into a visual and functional unity, as well as to center the whole on the spiritual core of the city, the Ile de la Cité. The final result proposed a new Paris conceived as an organic unity, with streets as arteries and the Cité as a heart. This system involved a duality, readily apparent in Perreymond's treatment of the city. As in Roman Paris, the city was a collection of discrete, independent social elements, non-hierarchical and equal. Simultaneously, however, by virtue of its street system, the city was focused and dependent upon the life-giving source or essence of the city, the Cité. The Cité was the animating force by which the city received its ontology.

The unified identity of the city was recognized in its overall organization: his emphasis on structure differentiated Perreymond's idea of organicism from that of Hugo. As previously noted, Perreymond regretted the loss of Paris' recognizable urban form. In the past he observed the existence of a kind of psychological boundary to Paris, encompassed by the Place de l'Etoile, the Place du Trône, and the Collines de Montmartre and de Montrouge.[77] Generally speaking, these were the limits set by the city walls of Louis XV and XVI, the "murs d'octroi," embellished by the *barrières* of Ledoux.

For Perreymond, discernible urban form was thus created by a program of comprehensive public works. However, as a *Saint-Simonien,* Perreymond was opposed to any public expenditure which was not productive or positive. Both he and César Daly disapproved of the new city fortifications built under Louis XVIII and Louis-Philippe. Rather, both concentrated on a comprehensive scheme of public works, focusing on buildings, canals, railroads, and especially streets.[78] Daly discussed such improvements for the city of Paris as:

> Le développement et la prospérité de l'industrie et du commerce français...appliqués à l'achèvement de notre systeme de navigation intérieure, à l'exécution de nouvelles routes, de chemins de fer...[29]

> The development and prosperity of industry and of French commerce applied to the achievement of our system of interior navigation, to the execution of new roads and railroads....

Such a campaign of public works would succeed in linking all quarters into a visual unity, as well as in centering the whole on the spiritual heart of the city, the Ile de la Cité. The ontology of Paris, the spirit of the city, would thus be recognizable in the material means of its formal cohesion.

It goes without saying that the *Saint-Simonien* Perreymond discussed at great length the public works for the city of Paris.[80] Streets, canals, railroads, sewers were not dismissed in his proposals. Furthermore, he constructed a political structure allowing for condemnation and expropriation, as well as a credit banking system prophetic of that established under Louis-Napoleon by fellow *Saint-Simoniens,* Fould and the brothers Pereire. Perreymond provided a reasonable idea of the range of his proposals in his "Plan du Centre de Paris" appearing in 1843 in the *Revue Générale* (plate 67). Immediately apparent was a dominant structure of circulation "arteries" overlaid onto the existing urban fabric. The designation of street as "artère" in contrast to "rue" or "boulevard" encouraged the organic analogy observed earlier in Perreymond's perceptions of the city. These new streets included the Artères du Centre, de l'Est, du Nord, and du Sud. A fifth artery, the Artère de l'Ouest, occurred on a line perpendicular to the Place de la Concorde, positioned outside of the range of the illustration.

Although Perreymond's scheme will never be commended for its sympathy to the historical city of Paris, certain important features draw it into the context of plans already discussed. First, it attempted to establish an order rising above the concerns of the individual dwelling or quarter, exemplified by the Turgot plan. This interest was especially important to Perreymond's graphic technique. His primary emphases were streets and historical or institutional structures. Important buildings were noted in *poché* depiction. In general, Perreymond ignored the particularities of the urban fabric, treating it as a series of neutral zones captured within a matrix of significant streets. The area of the plan directly to the north of the Seine, enclosed by the East facade of the Louvre and the Hôtel de Ville, provided important evidence of Perreymond's urbanistic interpretation. He described this zone as a series of discrete pockets of housing, defined by the Rue St. Honoré on the north and the quai on the south. These pockets were to be defined on the east and west by a series of north/south striations comprising the Rue du Louvre, Rue de la Monnaie, Rue St. Denis, Rue St. Martin (des Arcis), Rue des Coquilles. Perreymond recognized the autonomy of these quarters, implied by the homogeneous treatment of their interiors (in a way similar to Patte's figure/ground treatment), and by their perimeter determined by streets. He then shifted scale and unified this accumulation of neighborhoods into a larger reading. Using a technique of peripheral demarcation by streets, comparable to that by which he initially interpreted the neighborhood, he magnified the conception to describe mega-quarters utilizing a framework of *artères*. A new scale of urban organization was apparent, transcending the local or contingent situation. It was a scale first encountered in Pierre Patte's plan, where the architect dealt with a magnified conception of the city. This was a scale of experience which transcended the personal experience of perambulation or promenade. Moreover, it was a scale which escaped human perception, understood only from the omniscient point of view, or *vue aérienne*. For the citizen, such a perception of the city could be appreciated only in the mind's eye.

Second, Perreymond took into account the city's institutions, apprehended only within the historical situation, in the manipulation of his great arterial plan. Perreymond viewed the city of Paris as the embodiment of the three estates—aristocracy, religious, bourgeoisie—manifest in the institutions and associated quarters devoted to the government, the school, and the city. Moreover, his street system focused upon Paris' three symbolic centers—Louvre, University, and Hôtel de Ville. For example, the Artère du

Sud centered upon the Sorbonne, the Artère du Centre on the Louvre. The Artère du Nord linked the Louvre and the Hôtel de Ville. The Artère de l'Est was ordered by the Hôtel de Ville and the University (Bibliothèque Ste. Geneviève and Ecole Polytechnique). Like the Romans, Perreymond linked various *foyers* of activity by streets.

Third, although Perreymond's treatment of antique and medieval architecture remains subject to certain criticisms, it is apparent that he used history as an important referent. As noted above, his lattice of streets was restrained by certain symbolic institutions—the Louvre, Hôtel de Ville, etc. Moreover, Perreymond utilized Paris' historical structures, as embodied in streets and squares, to inflect his somewhat schematic project whenever possible. For example, he drew the churches of St. Germain des Prés and St. Merry as well as the Palais Royal into his street design, creating squares around and before them for *dégagement,* as well as for inflecting what otherwise might be seen as monotonous streetscape. Similarly, the squares of St. Sulpice and the Place des Victoires (the latter sadly altered), were likewise exploited as centers of activity by which the whole could be orchestrated. Only one of Perreymond's new streets possessed an explicitly historical provenance: the Artère du Nord expanded the Rue St. Honoré, laid out under Charles V. However, great north/south arteries, particularly the Artères de l'Est et du Centre, performed in exactly the same way as the Roman Rues St. Denis and St. Martin, skewering the three major parts of Paris (Right Bank, Left Bank, Cité) into a comprehensive whole. Like the Artère du Nord, these new streets were based in an antique typology, expanded to a new scale, in exactly the same way as Perreymond's notion of *îlot* was magnified in his new conception of the unified *quartier.*

Fourth, the three arteries—Nord, Est, Centre—comprised a great formal focus for the city of Paris in exactly the same way as the Rues St. Honoré, St. Martin, and St. Denis performed for Charles V. Here, Perreymond resurrected the "Grande Croisée," the subliminal center for the city of Paris during the Middle Ages, now reinvoked on an even greater scale for the urbanism of Louis-Philippe.[80] Moreover, the creation of a new Artère du Sud implied the establishment of a formal structure on the south bank, not unlike that on the north.

Perreymond used history on three levels. The first was of purely local interest, introducing picturesqueness and variety into his formal strategy. Second, the vestiges of antique formal structures and circulation were recognized and admired. The forms themselves were resurrected and manipulated in an expanded, topological way. Although the ancients provided an explicit precedent in only one instance in a more comprehensive, although less liberal, way, they suggested strategies to be followed on a new scale. The third level was an application of a more fundamental, though less explicit nature. Historical structures symbolized institutions, which lent character to enormous sections of the urban fabric. Social unity was established by an equivalence and balance among these institutions, symbolized by a matrix of streets. The autonomy of individual institutions with their associated quarters thus vanished, and a new unity arose, synthesizing all into a single physical and spiritual entity.

I turn again to the problem of the shift in scale. As noted above, the recognition of a distinct ontology for the city of Paris was linked to a love of sublime sensory experience. It was particularly the notion of sublimity which accompanied the cathartic moment of inspiration. Expansiveness and grandeur were the most important formal catalysts.

It is apparent that these issues were central to Perreymond's ideas concerning the reorganization of Paris. Perhaps nowhere was the shift in urban scale more apparent than in his proposal for the Ile de la Cité and the Ile St. Louis. Perreymond planned to join the two islands in a tactical move akin to Delamaire's and Patte's projects of the mid-eighteenth century.[82] Moreover, he intended to cover the south branch of the Seine, turning it into a kind of subterranean canal, and creating on the surface an enormous public square serving in part as embarcadero for merchandise and site for marketing. Perhaps most importantly, this square was to be the location of an enormous honorific facade for the Cité, designed for public embellishment and contemplation. The Ile de la Cité and the Ile St. Louis would be unified as a single autonomous physical element, which would be physically linked to the left bank by the new esplanade on the south, and isolated by the river on the north. The next result would be the isolation of the Ile de la Cité and Ile St. Louis by both physical and natural means. The newly reorganized perimeter of this urban ensemble—river and square—treated the island much as in the Patte proposal, as a single monument, *dégagé* from ordinary urbanistic interests, in turn becoming a public object of admiration. At the same time it established a dialogue between nature and architecture, in the reciprocity between square and river, a feature earlier discussed with regard to the Patte plan for Paris.

Perreymond's intention for the new Ile de la Cité was explicit. The Cité was to become the heart of his new organism, embellished with monuments. The ensemble was to be called "La Nouvelle Lutèce," an allusion to the Roman settlement on the site of present-day Paris. The architectural grouping included "établissements d'art, de science, et d'administration": a Hôtel de Postes, an archiepiscopal palace, the Palais de Justice, the Cour de Cassation, an Opéra, a Théâtre Français, the Royal Library, and a Palace of Industry.[83] The range of public institutions closely resembled Napoleon's own "quartier des monuments" in the Percier and Fontaine project for the Palace of the King of Rome. Moreover, Perreymond stressed the *dégagement* of this quarter as essential to his fundamental interest in public morality, comparable to the edifying ensembles of the Athenian Acropolis, the Roman Forum, the Venetian Piazza San Marco, and Paris' own Place de la Concorde.

It is apparent that Perreymond viewed the ultimate objective of his scheme to be the uplift of the Parisian population. This interest rested on three primary considerations. First, the encyclopedic realm of institutions symbolized a compendium of architectural interests. The very name of the new quarter, *La Nouvelle Lutèce,* placed it into a historical frame of reference, and the ideal history of this urban set-piece implied an embodiment of consummate knowledge. Second, the scale of the enterprise moved it from the merely idiosyncratic or picturesque to the sublime. The vastness of the project was designed to move the spectator to wonderment, and to inspiration. Third, *La Nouvelle Lutèce* was intended to move spectators to moral action, and other cities to imitation. In this imitation rested the ideal nature of urbanity.

Perreymond's argument focused upon classical notions of sublimity—or recognition of beauty and truth—and imitation. He stressed that Paris' grandeur, size, and holistic conception were to be designed to move the spectator. Moreover, the city's highest interest transcended the realm of pure utility to that of *Le Beau.* This interest was communicated by the sublime experience.

> Servons-nous de l'amour du grandiose, inné chez la nation française, pour la poussée vers l'utile; établissons l'utile sur une échelle assez grande pour qu'il s'élève jusqu 'au Beau.[84]

> Let us use the love of the grandiose, innate within the French nation, for the thrust towards the useful; let us establish the useful on a scale grand enough to lift it to the Beautiful.

Recognition of these qualities, particularly of *Le Beau* would have the effect of communicating truth, thereby sponsoring the morality and spiritual unity of the Parisian population.

> Qu'elles n'oublient qu'il est une voix plus puissante que celle des défamations, celle de la vérité; que, par son organe, ils puissent ressorter surtout *les conséquences morales de leurs projets,* ce sont les plus propres à provoquer *l'Assentiment Universel*...[par]... la justice ou l'égalité, et l'amour du grandiose, de la magnificence monumentale.[85]

> May they not forget that there is a voice more powerful than that of defamations, that of truth; by its organ they can make especially evident the moral consequences of their projects, which are the most appropriate to provoke *Universal Assent*...[by means of]...justice or equality, and by the love of the grandiose, of monumental magnificence.

Ultimately, Paris as the embodiment of truth would serve as a model and source of edification for its population as well as become an object of imitation for other cities. It was Perreymond's fondest hope that "la ville de Paris devienne la reine des cités, le modèle des capitales..."[86] The visual effects of Paris, the vastness of its scale, the comprehensiveness of its conception, of its sublimity and beauty, would not only inspire its population to a reasoned, orderly, and controlled public life, but would serve as models for other cities' appropriate form.

To conclude, although it seems likely that Perreymond's proposals for Paris were initially directed toward certain physical problems, it is also apparent that his ultimate intentions were metaphysical. These concerns focused upon social unity sponsored by communal spirit, beauty as the externalization of truth, and morality. It was physical form which he felt not only nurtured but also embodied the ideality of these notions. Perreymond's proposals for Paris were purposefully generalized and schematic. His was speculative interest, dealing more with strategies than with concrete physical proposals on an architectural scale. César Daly maintained Perreymond's speculative interests. However, unlike his collaborator's strategic ruminations, Daly's approach tended to be more tactical; his interests were on a more architectural level. César Daly concentrated his attention specifically upon the city's physical form.

César Daly and the City

The City and Monumentality

César Daly avoided directly addressing the formal problems of urbanism. Daly never specified, like his colleague Perreymond, a comprehensive campaign of improvements for the city, by which its unification would be assured. Generally speaking, Daly's formal interests for the French capital concentrated upon the architectural rather than the urbanistic scale. Nonetheless, he did speculate, in word if not in drawing, on the nature of the necessary urban improvements. Moreover, Daly did learn from his predecessors, especially from Perreymond, to link urbanistic features and strategies, both actual an envisioned, with a metaphysic. Daly's basic predispositions concerning the city paralleled some of the most overtly idealistic formal positions heretofore discussed.

Initially, he treated the city of Paris as a single entity, based in unified urban form. As noted above, Daly exploited the idea of aerial view to characterize the fundamental unity in which urbanistic ontology resided. He elaborated upon this idea in his *L'Architecture Privée au Dix-Neuvième Siècle* (1863), recognizing in the Second Empire Paris of Louis-Napoleon a total urban orchestration, in which all quarters are unified, perceiving Paris as unified *ensemble*. Daly criticized piecemeal planning in favor of Haussmann's holistic approach.

Il était donc indispensable de renoncer au procédé ruineux des études et des rénovations partielles, au système des entreprises décousues, sans vue d'ensemble, et par suite, contradictoire souvent. Au morcellement, il fallait substituer l'unité; à l'hésitation, la décision; à la lenteur, la rapidité. Il était temps d'étudier d'abord, et de remanier ensuite partout où la nécessité s'en faisait sentir. La grande cité dans l'ensemble de son économie architecturale, en considérant la ville entière comme un seul monument dont toutes les parties fussent solidaires.[87]

It was therefore indispensable to renounce the ruinous procedure of partial studies and renovations, of the system of disconnected and consequently, often contradictory, enterprises, without a view of the whole. For the parcelling of land, it was necessary to substitute unity; for hesitation, decision; for slowness, rapidity. It was time first to study and then to rebuild in all places where necessity was making itself felt, the great city—in the whole of its architectural economy—by considering the city as a single monument whose parts must be interdependent.

Daly perceived the new unity of Paris as a kind of monumentality. His consideration of Paris as a monument introduced two issues. First, the medieval city, composed of quarters and isolated public embellishments vanished. In its place stood a city which was in itself a comprehensive public realm, a total embellishment. Second, monumentality called forth notions of symbolism. The public embellishment of the city was counterposed to the private realm as well as to purely contigent concerns. Rather than the shelter of individualistic fancy or public utility, the monument was the recipient of ideology.

A recurrent theme in Daly's *oeuvre* was the conception of monumentality. Most importantly for Daly, the monument had an idealistic basis. For example, in 1841, he discussed Louis Duc's July Monument from this point of view. With regard to this structure especially, Daly stated, "... il existe une liaison intime entre certaines formes et certaines idées."[88] Moreover, the monument was important from the point of view of perception and psychology. There should be an intimate relationship between structure and spectator. The monument should move the spectator to a sublime experience. Daly advanced,

[Un]... monument perdu et isolé dans l'immensité... pourrait nous frapper par sa grandeur matérielle.[89]

(A)... monument, lost and isolated in immensity... should be able to strike us by its physical grandeur.

Speaking of the emotional response by which perception of this monument should be accompanied, Daly continued:

L'oeuvre d'art qui n'a conquis que l'intelligence du spectator a perdu sa cause; car, avant tout, elle s'adressait à sa passion... [90]

The works of art which conquered only the intelligence of the spectator has lost its cause; because, before all else, art addresses itself to his [the spectator's] passion.

It is not the intelligent faculty, but the passional, by which the idea was to be recognized. This view of perception paralleled those advancing catharsis as the accompaniment of inspiration.

Daly considers this monument as a word—*une parole*. This word was seen as the embodiment of an idea, a fragment of the truth. For example, in discussing the July Monument, Daly states:

> Le Monument de Juillet est un bronze commemoratif destiné à rappeler un grand evènement; c'est une belle, parole éloquente, qui doit raconter en beau langage le fait qu'il consacre en le regardant, chacun doit le comprendre sans interprète.[91]

> The July Monument is a commemorative bronze destined to recall a great event; it is an eloquent and beautiful word which, upon seeing it, must recount in beautiful language, the fact to which it is consecrated; each [of us] must understand it without an interpreter.

Moreover,

> Le rapprochement qui existe entre certaines formes qu'affecte la matière et certaines idées, en créant le symbole, n'a fait qu'ajouter à l'art une nouvelle énergie d'expression, un moyen puissant d'atteindre le coeur à travers l'intelligence, en rappelant à volonté un ordre quelconque d'idées.[92]

> The connection that exists between certain forms assumed by matter, and certain ideas, in creating a symbol, can only add to art a new energy of expression, a powerful means of reaching the heart across the intelligence, while voluntarily recalling some sort of order of ideas.

Ultimately, Daly linked form with ideology and aesthetics with the moral sciences. He proposed an architectural system in which form became the externalization of ideas, much as poetic language was imbued with a vital principle by which inspiration took place.

> L'étude des analogies du monde physique et du monde moral offre une mine précieuse à l'artiste; les anciens y ont cherché leurs plus belles inspirations, et encore n'ont-ils creusé qu'à la surface. L'étude de ces analogies s'étendrait au domaine de la symbolique dans l'art, et créerait une langue d'une expression, d'une richesse et d'une variété immenses, compréhensible dans tous les siècles, à tous les peuples.[93]

> The study of analogies between the physical world and the moral world offers a precious mine to the artist; the ancients look there for their most beautiful inspiration, and still they scarcely scratched the surface. The study of these analogies could extend itself into the realm of the symbolic in art, and could create a language of expression, with an immense richness and variety, comprehensible in all centuries, to all people.

In 1861, at the moment that Daly's energies were being directed primarily toward the city, these ideas concerning monumentality remained largely unchanged. Monuments continued to be the symbols of culture, and especially of national ideology. When speaking of the proposed Paris Opera, Daly noted the focal importance of honorific structures in the spiritual and intellectual life of a people.

> On pourrait l'affirmer sans crainte *a priori.* Sans entrer dans un détail justificatif qui nous mènerait trop loin, il suffira de rappeler les pagodes de l'Inde, les pyramides et les ruines de Karnac, en Egypte, le Parthenon d'Athènes, le Colisée de Rome, pour montrer avec quelle puissance et quelles vérités l'artiste de l'antiquité a formulé les croyances ou les moeurs de sa nation.[94]

> One should be able to affirm it without fear of *a priori* assumptions. Without entering into justifying detail that would lead us too far astray, it will suffice to recall the pagodas of India, the pyramids and ruins of Karnak in Egypt, the Parthenon of Athens, the Colosseum of Rome, in order to show with what power and what truths the artist of antiquity formulated the beliefs or morals of his nation.

He moreover imbued the monument with a soul not unlike the poetic program of organicism which he earlier proposed with regard to the Colonne de Juillet. In referring to the Opéra, Daly switched from his customary third person narrative exposition to a second person dialogue. He addressed the building as a being capable of hearing and of being heard. Moreover, Daly spoke to the Opéra, not so much as one person to another, but as creator to one of his creations. Daly's apotheosis of the artist was complete when he addressed the artwork in the manner of God speaking to his creatures in Genesis:

> Ton nom . . . est l'Opéra. Il signifie que l'intelligence humaine a fourni tout son effort pour te créer. Tu sera le piédestale du génie, la mise en scène et panorama de ses merveilles, l'épanouissement de toutes ses puissances. Tu seras hantés de célestes apparitions, et l'archet d'or des sphères te remplira de ses harmonies. Tu enchanteras les yeux et les oreilles de l'homme, son esprit et son coeur.[95]

> Your name . . . is Opéra. It signifies that human intelligence has supplied all its effort in order to create you. You will be the pedestal of [its] genius, the setting and panorama of its marvels, the blossoming of all its powers. You will be haunted with celestial apparitions, and the music of the spheres will fill you with harmonies. You will enchant the eyes and ears of man, his spirit and his heart.

Likewise, the city was to be understood as a single monument. It was the embodiment of an idea, like the Colonne de Juillet or the Opéra. In his article of 1862 "Panorama du Monde Architecturale," Daly discussed the unified Paris in much the same terms as those he used to describe Duc's monument. He emphasized that there must be an equivalence between idea and form, philosophy and art.

> Pour que l'Idée soît accueillie avec empressement, il faut la revêtir des charmes de la forme: Solidarité entre la science et l'art.[96]

In order that the Idea may be readily received, it must be clothed with the charm of form: Solidarity between science and art.

The city, he continued, must be composed on the basis of a single idea, although he denied that its appropriate form was the type, *bête noire* of the nineteenth century romantics.

Nous faisions ... la part des lieux et des circonstances; nous demandons l'ordre, mais non pas un degré de prévoyance impossible à l'homme; notre ville n'est pas un type, c'est une idée flexible qui obéit à toutes les nécessités variables des lieux et des intérêts ... [97]

On the contrary, we have taken into consideration places and circumstances; we are demanding order, but not to the degree of foresight impossible to man; our city is not a type, but a flexible idea which obeys all the variable necessities of places and interests ...

Although not typologically ordered, the city was based in ideology. In keeping with organic aesthetic theory, the city was to be considered primarily as the outcome of epochal and national will as well as a creation of an artistic, hence super-human consciousness, which participated in and spoke for the historical spirit. This assertion introduced a problem which will be discussed later at greater length.

The city was no mere receptacle of certain special buildings tagged as "public embellishments," but came to be seen as a monument in itself. Contemplation of the city in its immensity would give rise to a sublime experience:

Mais l'oeil matériel n'est pas seul sensible à la grandeur; l'esprit et le coeur de l'homme en sont également avides ... un sentiment inconnu la révèle un ordre plus grand et la fait pénétrer dans les accords plus généreux. [98]

The physical eye is not solely sensitive to grandeur; the spirit and the heart of man are also avid to it ... an unknown sentiment reveals an ever larger order and penetrates into the most noble kinds of relationships.

In *L'Architecture Privée*, Daly noted the psychological effects concomitant with inspiration caused by the *grands travaux* of Paris:

Quelques personnes reprochent à l'administration d'avoir fait, dans les nouveaux travaux, de trop grands sacrifices à de pures considérations d'art; je voudrais, pour ma part, que ce reproche fut encore plus merité: répandre largement l'art sur les places publiques et dans les rues, n'est-ce pas faire l'éducation du peuple par les yeux, faire pénétrer dans les masses le sentiment du beau par un spectacle qui chaque jour polit les moeurs en élévant les esprits. [99]

Certain persons criticize the administration for having made in its new works too many sacrifices to the pure consideration of art; I would wish, for my part, that this protest were more merited: to pour out art largely on the public squares and in the streets—isn't this a way to educate the people through the eyes, to permit a sentiment of beauty to penetrate into the masses by means of a spectacle which daily polishes their morals while elevating their spirit?

If the idea behind the city was unity, both social and architectural, what, then, was its necessary form? Daly was especially concerned with the structure of the public realm. His own views were drawn from a series of articles prepared by Albert Lenoir "La Théorie des Villes," dated 1854. In this study Lenoir addressed the problem of the proliferation of residential quarters, the fragmenting of property, and Paris' chaotic urbanscape. He structured his perceptions and program by the history of the city. In the past, the shape of Paris had been determined by two conflicting forces, public and private interest. While Paris was governed by the aristocracy and the religious estates, its form was shaped by superindividual institutions manipulating the public realm. The rise of the bourgeoisie in the Middle Ages signalled the rise of private interest, and the gradual erosion of the public realm and of comprehensible urban form. The emergence of the third estate paralleled a decline in urbanity, a situation which Lenoir felt existed to the present day, with only brief interruption by the architectural interventions of Henry IV and Louis XIV.

Moments of order were invoked by the action of explicit public interest in opposition to private. Daly recognized the public interest primarily in unified cityscapes—facades, squares, streets, and particularly, in monumental housing. London squares, for him, were great paradigms by which the public realm maintained an important component in design. London's Eaton Square was a model of superindividual unity. Daly commended the square for "un aspect monumental... présentant les singuliers spectacles de l'architecture à tous le pays appropriés."[100] Eaton Square for Daly was not merely an English housing variant, but a potential model for any locale wishing a unified urbanscape. In Paris he especially admired the Palais Royal, the former palace of the Duc d'Orléans, and in Daly's time, a variant of the town house strategy seen in the eighteenth-century English squares. Moreover, the Palais Royal, with its shops and arcaded promenade, made an explicit gesture to the public realm, even though the ensemble itself was devoted to middle class housing:

La galérie qui circule autour du jardin et abrite les promeneurs en toute saison est une des plus belles conceptions qui aient jamais été réalisées dans un monument d'architecture privé.[101]

The gallery which circulates around the garden and shelters the walkers in any season is one of the most beautiful conceptions ever realized in a monument of private architecture.

Eaton Square's ensemble of monumental facades and the enclosed regular space spoke to the public realm. At the Palais Royal, the arcade and circulation sequence moved the Parisian population to a *promenade architecturale* which deemphasized merely private interests.

Later, Daly concentrated his attention upon monumental facades and circulation systems marking a shift from an architectural to an urbanistic level. By this shift in scale, he translated the concept of public realm from individual monuments and buildings to a holistic and comprehensive order. Daly's sources were historical, and he focused upon the nature of the street. He saw that the street was addressed as an explicitly public realm only once before in Paris history—during the Roman era.

Roman Paris, a city unified through its street system, was a model of comprehensive urban thinking, particularly persuasive to both Lenoir and Daly. Daly opposed a wholesale resurrection of the street system of the Romans, symbol of order and imperial will, but he did advocate a comprehensive public realm whereby squares and monuments would be linked by streets.

> Nous avons assez dit, ce nous semble, pour justifier notre protestation contre la resurrection, de nos jours, soît de l'échequier antique, soît de la confusion du Moyen-Age. Nous faisons au contraire la part des lieux et des circonstances; nous demandons l'ordre. Mais non pas un degré de prévoyance impossible à l'homme.

> We have said enough, it seems to me, to justify our outcry against the resurrection, in our time, albeit of the antique gridiron or the confusion of the Middle Ages. Instead, we have argued for places and circumstances; we demand order. But not a degree of clairvoyance impossible to man.

It was at this point that Daly asserted that Paris should be a "flexible idea," implying a kind of ambiguous ideology modifiable by the idiosyncracies of situation and circumstance.

The conception of the city as monument had to do fundamentally with issues of sublimity and coincident inspiration. Monumentality became the definition of the city, the source of its ontology, and vehicle of inspiration. Moreover, monumentality introduced the issue of poetic form, wherein ideology might inform the shape of its material. Hence there was a synthesis between idea and the means of its conveyance. Last, monumentality implied a cognitive structure by which its great notion could be recognized. Most important, this concern involved a collection of attributes which addressed the public realm. Monumentality in the city was especially recognizable in unified public facades and open spaces, persuasively linked by its streets.

César Daly and Urban Theatricality

Having addressed the problem of ontology, César Daly subsequently concerned himself with the problems surrounding the communication of ideology to the urban audience. As noted above, the violent response of the viewer to sublimity linked the issues of psychological sensationalism and inspiration. The transference of the spirit, or idea, was accompanied by violent emotion. Daly frequently addressed the problem of inspiration, catalyzed by physical form. Like both Plato and Rousseau, Daly approached the problem by way of the theater. Theater was to be incorporated into the city by *fêtes publiques* and monumental painting, or *historia*. He cited the need for the public festival as a means of fostering public sentiment and uplift. His stand paralleled Rousseau's and David's in its praise of both popular and edifying diversion:

> Faut-il des fêtes publiques? Oui. Il y a fête là où il y a joie inaccoutumée. Or, comment constater qu'une même émotion remue toutes les âmes, sans une manifestation extérieur et publique, à laquelle tous prennent part?[103]

> Are public festivals necessary? Yes. Such feasts are moments where there is uncustomary joy. Now, how does one establish that same emotion which tires our souls without an exterior and public display in which all can partake?

In a manner betraying the person of the architect rather than the philosopher, Daly cited the need for these theatrical settings to become one with the city. He made a distinction between temporary and permanent backdrops. Temporary settings were to be allied with the momentary and transitory nature of man's interests. Permanent public settings were seen as those which reflect man's continuing concerns and ideas. It was this second type of setting which was particularly suitable to the architecture. These displays were to become public monuments. The city was to be transformed into a perennial theatrical backdrop.

Furthermore, as catalysts of inspiration, the monuments became actors themselves. City became total theater, a metaphor of life and history. Daly advanced,

> Faut-il des monuments durables pour témoigner de la joie publique? Certainement; mais nous le répétons, un monument durable ne peut exprimer qu'un sentiment continu, qui reste éternellement indifférent à la marche des temps, aux jours qui s'écoulent. La colonne Vendôme consacre le souvenir de la campagne d'Allemagne, souvenir sans anniversaire... Et quant à la *mise en scène* d'une telle fête de commemoration aux splendeurs que les architectes pourront imaginer pour que toutes les choses extérieures à nous rayonner la joie et répondent à l'émotion publique, évidemment elles devront différer essentiellement de tout ce qu'on s'imaginerait pour célébrer un mariage impérial ou un traité de paix universel.[104]

> Are durable monuments necessary to testify to the public joy? Certainly, but to repeat, a durable monument can only express one continuous sentiment which rests eternally indifferent to the march of time, to the flow of the days. The Colonne Vendôme consecrates the memory of the German campaign, history without exact anniversary... And according to the *mise en scene* of such a commemorative feast, according to the splendors that

architects would be able to imagine, in order that these external things shine with our joy and respond to public emotion, evidently they would have to differ essentially from all that one would imagine necessary to celebrate an imperial marriage or a treaty of universal peace.

Daly's stress upon theatrical, public art forms extended to a discussion of exterior monumental historical painting which both instructs and enlightens. He criticized realistic and romantic artists for an overemphasis on naturalism, claiming that appropriate painting for a public realm was *historia,* that genre intent upon the moral effect caused by the communication of truth. It was the historical painter who would inspire, hence encourage the progress of civilization.

> Il y a trop de peintres d'histoire qui, à défaut de génie, se trouvent à les recherches de la nature matérielle, comme pour demander à nos sens blasés et à notre corruption l'encouragement et la recompense qui seraient refusés au même talent traitant des sujets sobres et honnêtes...
> Si nous avions des titres pour parler au pouvoir de pareilles matières, nous aurions long à dire sur les moyens de faire rayonner Paris sur la France et de répandre sur les départements, par la voie des arts, un peuple de cette vie intellectuelle et morale qui élève l'âme et facilite le vrai progrès de la civilisation. [105]

> There are too many history painters who, lacking genius, get involved in researching nature as if to ask of our blasé senses and our corruption, the encouragement and compensation that would be refused to the same talent treating sober and honest subjects.
> If we had the right to speak of such matters, we would have much to say as to the means of making Paris shine across France and of spreading across the departments, through the voice of the arts, a people of such an intellectual and moral life as to elevate the soul and encourage the true progress of civilization.

The means of moral instruction were to be addressed on three levels: facade, street, and urban plan. *L'Architecture Privée,* César Daly's handbook of domestic architecture for Second Empire Paris, dealt with both individual and apartment dwellings. Generally speaking, the focus in *L'Architecture Privée* was upon housing in which the client was also the resident. But his interest extended to entrepreneurial development when the client's program had little to do with the specialized needs of the residents. The program of the book distinguished clients and buildings in terms of social class and building types, providing a number of examples for each. For the most part, Daly discussed and illustrated the single building, but the implication was for a larger reading, transcending the architectural level. The program of the book focused upon urbanistic rather than architectural issues.

Daly, like Lenoir, first addressed the distinction of private and public realms. With regard to housing, the private realm concerned the plan, and the accommodation of the individual client's needs. The public realm, however, dealt with the relationship of the building and the street, and the property owners' responsibility to recognize rules of decorum in order to assure the public taste and morality. These twin concerns—personal need and fantasy, and public responsibility—met in the facade.

The facade responded to both public and private considerations. Daly's interest in exterior detail, beginning with *L'Architecture Privée* (especially the third series) and *Motifs Historiques* recognized the architectural forces of personal display, choice, and imagination. These were seen as the reflections of private interest. Daly stressed the importance of public responsibility via *ordonnance*, linearity, and formal unity arising from compositional principles. In these ways, the elevation would respond to private intention and aspiration as well as to public responsibility.

To understand the ideological component of *L'Architecture Privée*, it becomes useful to place it into the context of similar works. The provenance of *L'Architecture Privée* places it into a line of work including Krafft and Ransonette's *Plans, Coupes, Elévations des Plus Belles Maisons et Hôtels Construits à Paris* (1801-3) Legrand and Landon's *Description de Rome* (1806), Percier and Fontaine's *Choix des Plus Célèbres Maisons de Plaisance de Rome* (1809-24), and P. Letarouilly's *Edifices de Rome Moderne* (1840-57). The expression of public interest with regard to morality was central to all these works. In their introduction, Percier and Fontaine asserted that art must ennoble life, and that the process of elevating nature should give impulse to art. Moreover, the architects implied that much as art should ennoble nature, it should similarly do so with man. They stated,

> Nous croyons que l'art, dont le but est d'ajouter à nos jouissances en rapprochant de nous les beautés de la nature, et en les faisant servir à nos besoins, que l'art doit tout ennoblir: dès qu'il dégrade, il cesse d'être un art; ce n'est plus que le désordre de l'imagination et l'oubli du bon goût.[106]

> We believe that art, whose goal is to add to our pleasure while drawing to us the beauties of nature and making them serve our needs, must ennoble all: as soon as it degrades, it ceases to be an art;... it is then nothing more than disorder of the imagination and an oversight of good taste.

Finally, the object of art was to embody and to communicate *le Beau*.

Letarouilly's handbook of plans and facades was similar to Daly's, although his attention was focused upon Rome rather than Paris.[107] Initially, he cited the responsibility of art to communicate sentiments of nobility, dignity, morality—to communicate the ideal to the viewer. The architect's great mission was to characterize and communicate truth.

> Il faut que les citoyens, qui souvent confient à l'architecte les intérêts les plus graves, trouvent en lui des gages certaines de talent. Cette condition accompli, presque toujours ils pourront compter sur des garantis non moins essentielles, celles que donne la moralité: car l'étude des beaux arts a le privilège d'élever l'âme et de communiquer aux sentiments de la noblesse et de la dignité.[108]

It is necessary that the citizens, who often confer upon the architect the most serious matters, find in him certain marks of talent. This condition accomplished, they will almost always be able to count upon no less essential guarantees; those which will ensure morality, because the study of the   fine -arts has the privilege of elevating the soul and of communicating to the sentiments both nobility and dignity.

Architects should strive to create models of such "moral" architecture, just as historians and dramatists have provided mankind with portrayals of virtuous action in *historia*. Letarouilly drew especially upon Plato's views on theatrical imitation in advocating artistic models suitable for emulation.[109] He drew a comparison between men of virtue and their dwellings. Their houses, like their lives, were imitated in all social strata.

Aujourd'hui comme autrefois, l'habitation du riche se modèle sur celle des princes, et, dans la demeure du simple citoyen, on retrouve encore un reflet de celle des autres.[110]

Today, as in other times, the house of the wealthy models itself upon that of princes, and even in the dwelling of a simple citizen does one still find the reflection of other [models].

Letarouilly, as a member of the idealist school surrounding Quatremère de Quincy, frequently echoed the theorist's ideas concerning imitation.

Quatremère himself prepared the section on "Palais" in the *Description de Paris* of Legrand and Landon. He asserted that it was the palace type that particularly embodied the social and political spirit of the age. As a kind of ideal type, it would automatically become the model which dwellings of all classes must emulate.

...c'est dans la demeure du souverain que se peint avec le plus de vérite la puissance de chaque nation et le goût de chaque siècle...[111]

...it is the dwelling of the sovereign upon which the power of each nation and the taste of each century is painted with the greatest truth.

The royal palace was a type "conservé dans tous les palais dans un siècle..." As such, it was the object of emulation.

Toute maison prétend à être un palais, et tout palais affecte l'air d'un monument publique.[112]

Every house pretends to be a palace and every palace affects the air of a public monument.

César Daly also implied the imitation of types and its moral implications in his own handbook of architectural models, *L'Architecture Privée*. Despite its title, the book especially addresses architecture's public responsibility to provide an event of edification, as well as suitable models for imitation. The architectural handbook was thus conceived in the idealistic tradition. Daly's plans and facades were not merely patterns for ready reference, but paradigms, to be contemplated as instruments of inspiration. The prototypes provided by Daly had a moralizing responsibility.

As already mentioned, Daly began his discussion of housing by considering both its private and public interests, in terms of plan and facade respectively:

> ... par son *plan* elle répond au mode d'existence que le climat et la civilisation imposent, par son *aspect* elle fait entrevoir le sentiment d'art qui domine.[113]

> ... by its *plan,* it responds to the style of existence that climate and civilization impose, by its *appearance* it allows one to glimpse the sentiment of art that dominates.

This distinction made even private architecture responsible to the public realm. The facade must take on certain of the formal and moral attributes of monumental architecture.

> Depuis trois ou quatre ans, l'architecture privée de Paris accuse un progrès notable: la maison actuelle semble devoir participer, en quelque sorte, aux qualités de l'édifice public. Il n'y a pas complètement erreur, en effet à la considérer ainsi, exposée comme elle l'est aux regards de tous, bordant les rues, les boulevards, dominant les places publiques, appelant, pour ainsi dire, l'approbation ou bravant la critique embellissant ou élargissant la cité, la demeure de tous.[114]

> For the past three or four years, the private architecture of Paris has displayed a notable progress: the contemporary house seems to have to participated, in some way, in the qualities of a public edifice. It is not completely incorrect, in effect, to consider it as such, exposed as it is to full view, bordering the streets, the boulevards, dominating the public squares, calling for approval, so to speak, and braving criticism, embellishing or enlarging the city, the dwelling of all.

The facade had to do with the ontology of art, especially with the conception of *Le Beau* to be found in order, particularly in composition. Daly allied aesthetics, a moral science, with truth and beauty. As the embodiment of the ideal, the facade had a moralizing and edifying effect,

> Réaliser le beau, c'est dans l'ordre de l'art *une vertu,* comme de pratiquer la charité dans l'ordre moral, ou de promulguer la verité dans l'ordre scientifique, mais la part que chacun fait ou doit faire dans sa vie à la pratique de la vertu est une question étrangère aux législations humaines; le respect ou le mépris, c'est à dire la sanction de la conscience publique, voilà en dehors des jugements formulées par la religion, la récompense ou le châtiment de l'artiste, du savant, de l'homme riche ou puissant, suivant qu'il a defendu ou abandonné les intérêts du beau, du vrai, et du bien, dont la sauvegarde lui appartenait. Le public a un vague sentiment qu'il n'est pas plus permis à l'artiste de vulgariser le spectacle de la laideur, qu'il n'est loisible au savant d'enseigner l'erreur, au prêtre de prêcher la vice. L'art, en effet, a sa moralité.[115]

Realizing the beautiful is, in this realm of art, *a virtue,* as is practicing charity in the moral realm or promulgating truth in the scientific realm. But the part that each person makes or must make in his life of the practice of virtue is a question foreign to human legislation. Respect or contempt, that is to say, the sanction of public conscience, falls outside of judgments formulated by religion, reward, or punishment of the artist, the intellectual, the rich or powerful man, but have to do with the extent to which the artist has defended or abandoned the interests of the beautiful, which it is the artist's responsibility to protect. The public has the vague feeling that it is no longer permissible for the artist to exploit the spectacle of ugliness, just as it is not permissible for the teacher to propagate an error, for the preacher to preach vice. In effect, art has its morality.

Daly noted that this morality was perhaps best displayed in the monument, a building type especially related to public interest, serving public needs. The moralizing effect of this building stemmed from the national spirit by which its form was fashioned.

La beauté d'un monument public doit être une émanation éclatante et directe du génie vivant de tous et une profession de foi esthétique de la race.[116]

The beauty of a public monument must be a brilliant and direct emanation of the living genius of all and a profession of the esthetic faith of the race.

Moreover, the residences of the population imitated such buildings, seeking to grasp the spirit embodied therein. Daly's position paralleled Quatremère's assertion that models should be provided for fitting imitation and uplift. These models should come from the range of public monumental structures, as well as from new examples of private domestic architecture, now elevated to a distinctly public status.

Il y a de ces demeures comme le palais du souvérain, les hôtels des ministres et des grands personnages d'Etat, il y a de ces vastes châteaux et résidences sur lesquels se projette l'éclat des noms historiques soutenus par d'immenses fortunes, et qui ne soît plus de simples habitations; ces édifices forment comme un lien de transition entre l'architecture publique et l'architecture privée. Moralement, par le rang et les fonctions de ceux qui les occupent, par les grandes réceptions qui s'y font, ces demeures peuvent être considerées comme des sortes de dépendances de ce grand théâtre où se développe la vie publique. Donc aux palais royaux, et aux résidences princières ou seigneuriales, le devoir de l'homme est de concilier ce qui caractérise le génie national de l'art, avec cet usage modéré de la liberté qu'il appartient aux grands d'offrir toujours en exemple à la foule.[117]

There are such dwellings as the palace of the sovereign, the hotels of ministers and of great statesmen; there are such vast chateaux and residences upon which are projected the sparkle of historical names sustained by immense fortunes, and which may no longer be simple habitations; these buildings comprise a transitional linkage between public and private architecture. Morally, by the social rank and the function of those who occupy them, by the great receptions that they hold there, these dwellings can be considered as the dependencies of this great theater where public life develops. Thus in the royal palace, and in princely or seigneurial residences, the responsibility of man is to conciliate what characterizes the national genius of art with the moderate use of liberty which belongs to great works and offers an example to the crowd.

As noted above, Daly saw an important relationship between such uplifting architecture and theater. From the preceding quotation, we note that he regarded the great men of state—leaders, legislators, men of affairs—as *dramatis personae* worthy of a citizen's emulation. Moreover, he implied an equivalence between men of virtue and their architecture. their buildings should be considered not merely as backdrops against which honorable lives are led, but as symbols of those lives themselves as well. Consequently, Daly's housing must be viewed as both stage set for dramatic action as well as the dramatic action itself, the embodiment of *historia*.

L'Architecture Privée *and the Architecture of the Stage Set*

Daly provided us with an illustration of these dramatic concerns in the architectural view provided by the frontispiece of *L'Architecture Privée* (plate 68). The frontispiece presents a species of facade which must simultaneously be read as a *scenae frons*. This architectural fantasy seems to combine fabric with tectonic elements. Two planes are superimposed: a frontal plane, resembling a stage flat or curtain, is broken at the bottom, revealing a kind of diorama. This view overtly depicts urban domestic architecture, itself the *scenae frons* against which the theatrical action of the city is to be posed. Yet, instead of the human activity which supposedly composes the subject matter and *modus* of drama, we find architecture under the spotlight. Portrayed between the columns of Daly's specious facade are the three major architectural types with which *L'Architecture Privée* is concerned: the *hôtel privé* or the single private house, the *maison de rapport* or apartment house, and the suburban villa. From the dual reading provided by Daly's frontispiece, we can conclude that Daly wishes the domestic architecture of the Second Empire to become not only the setting for human life, but also the actor in human life and history itself. Its identity has become elevated and vitalized. Furthermore, the implication of architecture as *dramatis personae* is that a building form no longer acts in isolation, but interacts with others in accordance with a script or plot. Each building has a responsibility to and involvement with all others within an implied dramatic unity which transcends all of its parts. The formal order imposed by the *scenae frons* becomes a metaphor for the dramatic presentation itself. The composition of the frontispiece becomes emblematic of the dramatic unities to be sought in the city as well as theater. As a frontispiece, it stands for the literary unity of the book. But it also represents the unifying principles which transcend the variety of its architectural citations and examples.

Daly's frontispiece provides us with a number of important formal devices by which facades could be organized. Most important is the distinction between frontal planes and deep penetration. Layering is implied by the superimposed readings of fields resembling fabric, broken only by the apertures in which the action of the architectural types takes place. The lowest moulding of the cornice resembles a curtain rod over which bands of fabric are looped, creating a scalloped zone. This scalloping introduces a fabric field which is contradicted by the representation on it of arches in relief. Those arches, in turn, frame a second fabric field decorated with rosettes, ferns, and twigs. Against this lower fabric zone, the title is posed. Below what seems to be an architectonic balcony, three smaller *proscenia* occur also framed by curtains. The lowest subdivision of the setting breaks open to reveal the stage within which Daly's architectural characters perform. The entire setting dissolves into waves at the bottom, upon which the boat symbolizing Paris lies moored.

Although spatial ambiguities abound in this piece of architectural fantasy, certain basic rules of composition are never lost. The composition is strongly centralized. A triple opening wherein Daly's three building types perform is reinvoked in the tripartite balcony, and by the three arches of the upper proscenium. An implicit grid, although warped and elaborated toward the center, controls the formal inconsistencies, ambiguities, and idiosyncracies of detail.

Such architectural interests find parallel in the period's professional practice. For example, Ruprich Robert explores a number of these formal issues in his proposed *hôtel privé* of the second class, included in Daly's *L'Architecture Privée*. The facade is especially planar, with smooth ashlar masonry interrupted only by the projection of cornices, incised mouldings, and moments of applied decoration (plate 69). The cornices divide the facade into three floors. The lowermost cornice is underarticulated, reading more as a graphic horizontal datum than as a projection. The upper two become more emphatic. The uppermost, heaviest cornice can be read similarly to the drapery rod on which Daly's frontispiece is suspended. Daly's scalloped frieze is reinvoked by Robert's inventive window pediments which undulate across the face of the *hôtel*, slipping beyond the edge of the cornice. This feature introduces a spatial ambiguity parallel to those of Daly's stage set, giving the impression that the entire building facade is attached to the uppermost cornice. Moreover, the second floor displays similar properties. Much as Daly's facade proposes the idea of a curtain within a curtain, Robert's facade implies a similar superposition. The lower planar reading is interrupted by a series of stencilled, decorative panels creating *appliqués* upon the facade. Moreover, these panels overlap the intermediate cornice to which they are attached. They mediate between cornice and ashlar masonry, grabbing it, and articulating its supportive role by rosettes. By this single decorative feature, the relationship between cornice, panel, and wall is formalized. Below this level, on the ground and first floors, the wall surface is wholly neutralized. Incised decoration around the windows duplicates the treatment of the first story string course. An equivalence is therein established, and a consistent planar reading for the two floors is reached.

Despite the facade's multiple visual readings, certain formal characteristics remain constant. One is never allowed to forget the basic ordering structure of the ensemble. The house presents a four-bay facade, where windows, mouldings, panels, and rondels serve to reinforce consistent vertical and horizontal readings. Details inflect the facade, add variety and interest, but never distort the primary formal intention.

Although Robert's facade has developed certain of the formal devices proposed in Daly's project, unlike the latter, the Robert project could be seen as lacking explicit ideological content. The flamboyance of the wealthier classes might be absent here, but the scheme is nonetheless a witty, careful, intellectual conceit, playing with dualistic formal and spatial devices, creating a dialectic between orderly severity and artistic play. In their range of purely formal manipulations, both Daly and Robert have acknowledged an imaginative component so important to architecture of the private realm. However, in their conscious retention of order, and in their facades' unmistakable emphasis upon restraint in vocabulary. The architects have also made a concession to the public realm. Generally speaking, Daly and Robert have emphasized that such buildings be controlled by idea of "grandeur" and "durée," notions akin to the Albertian notion of "gravitas" by which the work of *historia* is formally governed.

Moreover, a system of order meant more for these urban dwellings than mere restraint. Composition became an increasingly important issue in even entrepreneurial development, where client and occupant were no longer the same. In such a case, the client's personal intention might have nothing whatsoever to do with the needs of those who are ultimately to live in the building. Patron and user could have nothing in common. Personal imagination must disappear in these buildings. Only assumptions of the most general nature could be made concerning architecture, in both facade and plan. The architectural program must be concerned with schematic rather than individual requirements, emphasizing at most the social status or class status of the *locataires*.

Such buildings raised the issue of social stratification. In a series of articles which preceded the publication of *L'Architecture Privée* entitled "Maisons de Paris" (1859), Daly schematized his approach to rental housing. His considerations were primarily sociological. He divided society into three classes—aristocracy, bourgeoisie, proletariat—and discussed appropriate urban housing for each. Aristocrats occupied *hôtels privés*. The bourgeoisie lived in rental property or *maisons à loyer*. Workers resided in low-cost housing projects, or rustic cottages external to the city.

(1) L'Aristocratie occupe les hotels.

(2) La bourgeoisie, plongeant par ses extrémités dans les couches supérieurs et inférieurs de la société, tient à la fois à l'aristocratie et à la classe ouvrière par les liens de transition; une bourgeoisie aristocratique et une bourgeoisie ouvrière. La classe bourgeoise occupe toute la série des maisons à loyer proprement dites.

(3) Les habitations de la classe ouvrière commencent à former une branche spéciale de l'architecture privée moderne...[118]

(1) The Aristocracy occupies the *hôtels*.

(2) The bourgeoisie, whose class boundaries are immersed in the superior and inferior strata of society, pertains at once to the aristocracy and the working class by transitional linkages—an aristocratic bourgeoisie and a working bourgeoisie. The bourgeois class occupies the entire series of apartment houses, as they are called.

(3) The habitation of the working class begins by forming a special branch of modern private architecture.

Each social class was to have its own building type. Yet, Daly subsequently proposed a hybrid species of domestic architecture called "l'architecture mixte," where the various classes would cohabit in a single structure. In this subtype, the facade of the "maison à loyer" confronted the problem of depicting the various social strata.

La maison à loyer de première classe doit comporter des cariatides représentant de personnages engaînés qui montrent toute la partie supérieur du corps; celle de deuxième classe laisse passer le buste seulement; pour la troisième classe et naturellement celles qui suivent, la statuaire disparaît, profit d'ornements plus économiques...[119]

The apartment house of the first class requires caryatids representing engaged human figures who display the upper part of the body; that of the second class permits the bust alone to appear; for the third class and naturally for those that follow, naturally the statuary disappears and more economical ornaments are used.

Class structure which had already been analyzed in plan and building type, also had to inform the facade. This situation was especially apparent in an apartment house designed by M. Lecomte, and included in *L'Architecture Privée,* in which the first floor (premier étage) carried caryatids, the second floor composite order, the third, *Néo-Grec* pilasters, and the fourth, decorative panels (plate 70). With the transformation of the client-architect relationship, the designer now created for an anonymous user. Schematized class structure took the place of the personality and idiosyncracy of the individual patron. Plan, although still considered a part of the private realm, was now standardized and stripped of personal imagination. The architect designed for an abstraction. Educated conceit or fancy vanished from the facade, to be replaced by the social schematic. Not individual, but class consciousness was now portrayed in both plan and facade. The elevation took on a distinctly analytical tone. Moreover, explicit connectedness between the prototypical, multiplicative plan and elevation appeared. The importance of facade moved beyond the realm of mere *gravitas*, to a complex allegory by which social order and generalized life style was to be portrayed. The mathematics of the minimal plan type was hence translated to the composition of the elevation. Total unity in the public realm was never lost due to the careful manipulation and continuity of vertical gridding. Daly maintained order in facade by careful and consistent *ordonnance*.

Returning to the frontispiece of *L'Architecture Privée*, we repeat that Daly indicates that individual buildings are to be orchestrated and interrelated by a higher, more comprehensive ordering system. Daly proposes this by invoking the ordering system inherent in the dramatic unities. In a visual way, the architect proposes such an order for his building types by the composition of the *scenae frons*. That form also implies that the city can be turned into total theater.

The tripartite facade of the frontispiece calls to mind another more famous tripartite *scenae frons*. In Palladio's setting at the Teatro Olimpico, the three openings frame deep urban vistas (plate 71). There are important similarities between the two settings. Daly's facade, like Palladio's, never escapes mathematical order in composition. Second, Daly's project, like Palladio's, alludes to mathematical order on the horizontal surface as well as on the vertical. Third, the connection between the two planes implies perspective construction. The perspective implications of Daly's interests might best be seen in the Renaissance tragic scene, where individual, mathematically composed facades are coordinated and integrated by the use of overriding perspective recession and three-dimensional gridding (plate 63). The net outcome of Daly's *L'Architecture Privée* was a proposal not only for a series of appropriate urban backdrops for modern life, but also for the city as total theatrical setting coordinating individual facades. The scale of the work is explicitly architectural rather than urbanistic. However, the urbanistic component is implicit, primarily due to Daly's means of surface construction, the implied integration of facade and plan, and the transference of formal issues from horizontal to vertical plane, ultimately realizable in the perspective construction of the tragic scene.

Landscape and Morality

The major difference between Daly's article, "Maisons de Paris" (1859) and his *L'Architecture Privée* (1863) rests in his consideration of the suburban house. The earlier article tied the picturesque dwelling to Letarouilly's notion of the

peasant "cottage," inappropriate for the wealthy and aristocratic. Daly
subsequently treated the suburban dwelling more in the frame of reference of
the Italian villa than of the *cottage orné*.

Daly was initially hostile to the cottage. His feelings probably stemmed
from the stand of such a compatriot as Perreymond, who explicitly opposed
the suburbanization of Paris and the proliferation of such dwellings. Like all
Saint-Simonens, Perreymond stressed a move toward social and political
centralization. This bias had urbanistic implications. By the mid-nineteenth
century, however, suburbanization as an architectural phenomenon of modern
life could no longer be ignored. Rather, it was the legitimate outcome of the
decentralization caused by railroad travel, another of the *Saint-Simonian
causes célèbres.* By the time of the publication of *L'Architecture Privée,* Daly
acknowledged the new issue of the suburb, and its most characteristic
architectural manifestation, the detached cottage. He treated the suburban
dwelling with considerable attention. Life in the country was to result in
edification from the relationship of man and family to nature. Landscape, like
the theatrical city, should have an uplifting effect. Daly invoked an image of life
within the satiric scene, an existence at once reposeful, pleasureable and
carefree:

A l'idée d'une existence champêtre s'associe naturellement l'idée de tous les plaisirs de la
campagne, la chasse, la pêche, les réunions d'amis, les promenades dans les parcs, dans les
prairies et les grands bois, les parties en bateau sur les rivières et sur les étangs, etc. La
campagne nous attire par les promesses de la santé, du bon appetit, de l'abondance et de la
delicatesse de la table, en un mot, par la perspective d'un régime un peu sensuel, accompagné
d'une honnête paresse d'esprit... c'est, il faut l'avouer, une existence plutôt de jouissance
matérielle et de détente de l'âme, que de description et de l'effort intellectuel.[120]

The idea of country existence associates itself naturally with the idea of the pleasures of the
countryside, hunting, fishing, parties with friends, walks in parks, in fields and in forests,
boating parties on rivers, lakes, etc. The countryside attracts us by promises of health, hearty
appetite, abundance of delicacies for the table, in a word, by the prospect of a somewhat
sensual diet, accompanied by an honest laxity of spirit... it is, I have to say, an existence
more of material joys and relaxing of the soul than of intellectual exercise and effort.

Beside the joys of life in nature, he recognized its moralizing effect, and its
salutary effect on the family. Speaking of the phenomenon of English
suburbanization, he noted,

Le commerçant ou l'industriel anglais... a pu ainsi dédoubler son existence, transportant au
milieu de la verdure et sous les arbres le foyer de ses affectations, sa femme et ses petits
enfants... pour assurer sa propre santé, le bien-être moral et physique de sa famille.[121]

The English industrialist or businessman... has thus been forced to double up his existence,
transporting to the green countryside under the trees, the abode of his affections, his wife and
his children... in order to assure his proper health and the moral and physical well-being of
his family.

In contrast to the utilitarian city, life in the garden espoused a moral existence.

What was Daly's conception of the natural order, an understanding of which was central to morality? It seems unlikely that it was the "nature agreste" or wild landscape of which Rousseau spoke so eloquently in *La Nouvelle Heloïse*. Although unrestrained nature might have been a moving experience for Daly, especially through the period in which he was involved with the romantic writers of the various picturesque voyages, it is clear that his feelings shifted after his return from the new world in 1857. After his encounter with the natives of Central America, particularly during a bout with yellow fever, Daly became quickly disillusioned with the idea of natural man. By the 1860s, the nature of which Daly spoke was that of philosophers, not of savages, a nature wherein thought and culture abounded, a nature manipulated by the drive to knowledge, and shaped by will whether divine or human.[122]

Daly proposed a polarity between ordered and free landscape, symbolized by the type of country house placed therein. He distinguished between *villa* and *cottage:*

> La villa, c'est l'ordre exprimé par la symétrie, c'est le style, c'est le beau, c'est la réglementation, la contrôle incessant de l'homme sur la nature. Le cottage, c'est la liberté, exprimé par l'irrégularité commode et pittoresque. La villa c'est donc l'amour de l'art; le cottage, c'est l'amour de la Nature ... La villa est classique; le cottage est romantique ... [123]

> The villa is order expressed by symmetry, style, beauty, regimentation and the incessant control of man over nature. The cottage is liberty, expressed by commodious and picturesque regularity. The villa is therefore the love of art; the cottage is the love of nature ... the villa is classic; the cottage is romantic.

The villa is rational and composed, the cottage imaginative and idiosyncratic.

Although Daly saw these suburban types as viable formal alternatives, he makes clear his own formal preferences in his own country house at Wissous, a village just outside of Paris. Daly purchased the property in 1860, at the time that this first son, Marcel-Robert, was born. It included a sizeable piece of ground, and a moderately-sized, rectangular, five-bay dwelling, a rustic variant of the Palladian type. Over the course of the next twenty years, Daly modified and embellished the existing buildings and confines.[124]

Rather than emphasize the potentially picturesque character of this house in landscape, Daly stressed its explicitly formal nature. Primarily, Daly underlined the importance of frontality in the complex. As one moved from the gates, across the "cour d'honneur," and ultimately through the house itself, one became increasingly aware of an implied series of layered, vertical planes, which integrated interior and exterior spaces (plate 72). Daly added a pair of pavilions, one on either side of the main entry to the property, housing stables, *gardien's* quarters and subordinate services. These symmetrical pavilions defined a forecourt directly before the front facade of the house, establishing a frontal view of the house (plate 73). The site was steeply sloped, but striations were maintained across the front section of the property by *parterres,* retaining walls, and reciprocal arrangements between ancillary buildings. The drive moved obliquely across the slope, providing the opportunity to perceive the house volumetrically. Upon arrival at the crytoporticus, which once served as Daly's wine cellar, the visitor was led to the front door. One entered a dark foyer, a part of the service *poché* traversing the front of the house, which in turn led to the main *enfilade* of reception rooms (plate 74). The ground floor plan of the house comprised six rooms, kitchen and bedroom on either side of the foyer, and dining room, salon, and study opening onto the garden. Pavilions, forecourt, outbuildings, and house plan itself working in concert presented the visitor with a series of frontal planes and controlled views by which to experience the public portion of the property.

The now-modified landscape was organized as a kind of *jardin mixte,* in which regular elements were juxtaposed to irregular. The most important features of Daly's landscape were the *jardin anglais* and the *potagier.* The English garden, like others of the period, provided a locale for promenade, a terrain of illusion and imagination. The *potagier,* however, was a gridded, geometrical garden, serving the primarily utilitarian function of kitchen garden The regularity of this section was ensured by a masonry enclosure. In this section of the property were greenhouses and starting frames, still innovations in the garden, and expressions of the practical concerns of the French agricultural industry.[125]

Daly's personal landscape at Wissous was dialectical. Disorder was foil to order, whimsy confronted pragmatism, imagination contrasted with reason. The balance was not complete, however. For order appeared in the English garden as well, especially in the vista that sliced across the landscape, centering upon the garden facade of the house. Whereas in the Parc Monceau, it seemed as if the irregular, primitive English garden was about to supplant order, the reverse seemed to be the case Daly's landscape. The utilitarianism of the *potagier* and the composition of the main house appeared to be mounting a full scale assault on the romantic landscape. We are forced to recall Daly's distinctions between villa and cottage. As noted above, the villa is the embodiment of human control, or will, over nature. In his manipulation of rational architectural means at Wissous, Daly attempted to dominate nature via both pragmatic and consciously artistic compositional techniques.

At any rate, Daly's own suburban preserve modulated between poles of reason and imagination which were synthesized only by means of Daly's artistic will. At the Parc Monceau, we encountered an earlier example of such a fusion, mediated by an explicit reference to divine will, as represented in the journey of Christ. At the Villa Daly in Wissous, the ensemble was orchestrated by a human, albeit an artistic, will, the primary means by which a dialectical landscape was unified. Moreover, Daly's allusion, at least in his own country house, was not so much to the achievement of morality by an association with nature, as to the exercise of consciousness and reason within nature. Ultimate truth was realized only by the recognition of will in nature, whether that will was human or divine, or the artistic will which mediated between the two extremes. Daly's own artistic will became the subconscious organization of his dialectical landscape.

The City and the (Theatrical) Garden

In a series of articles, "Promenades et Plantations," César Daly continues the tradition of urban contemplation sponsored by the pictureseque movement in landscape. His own interpretations of the city parallel those of Alexandre de Laborde, who equated his "Nouveaux Jardins" with his "Monuments de la France," or especially of Charles Nodier whose "Voyages Pittoresques" in the French countryside became quickly associated with "Promenades dans les Rues de Paris" in his *Paris Historique*. For all three men, the point of commonality between natural and architectural form was the theater.

On two occasions, Daly cited the need for regarding the city as a collection of views or *tableaux* giving reason for contemplation and cause for inspiration. In his "Panorama du Mouvement Architectural," a series of articles dating from 1862, Daly noted the connection between the landscape promenade and the urbanistic situation:

> On comprend d'avance que notre tableau ne pourra être qu'une marquetterie épaise, dont nous ne songeons point à dissimuler les lacunes ... Notre esquisse sera donc sans proportions regulières; elle reproduira des aperçus détachés et rapprochés entre eux et rappelera ces paysages entrevus à travers les dechirures du brouillard ... Ce paysage comme le sera notre tableau—est un composé de fragmens, mais il importe au brouillard même qui le voile une harmonie que nous ne saurions trouver pour notre oeuvre dans nos ressources littéraires, c'est-à-dire pour un plan dont toutes les parties ne peuvent être éclairées à la fois.[126]

> One understands in advance that our tableau will only be able to be a dense marquetry, free of seams. Our sketch will be without regular proportions; it will reproduce both detached and connected perceptions and will recall those landscapes glimpsed across rents in the fog. This landscape will be like our tableau: it is a composition of fragments, but it brings to the fog that veils it a harmony not unlike the one we should know how to find in our literary work resources, that is to say, a plan whose parts need not all be illuminated at once.

Moreover, Daly reinvoked Rousseau's *Rêveries du Promeneur Solitaire* when in his "Promenades et Plantations" he discussed how suburban landscape, with its fusion of tectonic and natural features, had become the city. He, like Rousseau, cites that along the outskirts of Paris, the *ad hoc* theatrical garden had been eternalized in stone:

Déjà disparaissent de cette voie grandiose les établissements interlopes qui contribuaient à déshonorer les anciens boulevards extérieurs. Nous assistons ici à un veritable "changement de vue" théâtral, qui nous rappelle ces figures des vieilles mendiantes subitement transformées, par les vertus d'une magique baguette, en de charmantes princesses rayonnantes de beauté de soierie, d'or et de pierreries. Qui nous dit que cette admirable promenade des anciens boulevards extérieurs, avec ses belles chaussées, ses frais ombrages, ses fontaines brillants, ne sera pas, avant vingt ans, le rendez-vous de Paris élégant, trop resserré entre les boulevards actuels des Italiens et de la Madeleine.[127]

From this grandiose thoroughfare, all the unauthorized establishments which contributed to dishonoring the ancient exterior boulevards are disappearing. We are participating here in a true theatrical "set change," which reminds us of the figures of old beggars, suddenly transformed by the virtue of a magic stone into princesses dazzling with the beauty of silks, gold, and precious stones. Who tells us that the beautiful promenade of ancient exterior boulevards, with its beautiful carriage pathways, cool shadows, and brilliant fountains, will not in twenty years be the rendezvous of elegant Parisians, too restricted today between the Boulevards des Italiens and de la Madeleine?

The city, like the theatrical garden, presented a series of images or episodes related to man's history. As such, it was the receptacle of man's experience, as well as the purveyor of knowledge, both present and past.

Nous avons des monuments de tous ces Vieux Paris et nous y thronons. C'est une richesse, une gloire, ce sont les parchemins, nos titres de noblesse. Ils disent aux etrangers qui nous visitent et ils nous rappellent à nous même depuis combien des siècles Paris contribuait au progrès de l'intelligence humaine . . . [128]

We have monuments representing all these old Parises and we are enthroned there. They have a richness, a glory; they are the parchments, the titles of nobility. They speak to the strangers who visit us and they force us to recall the many years that Paris has contributed to human intelligence . . .

As already discussed, the theatrical landscape had been regarded simultaneously as the seat of sentiment and metaphor of knowledge. Eden, the *topos* at the source of all variants of the *locus amoenus,* was the seat of both the "Tree of Life" and the "Tree of Knowledge."[129] As repository of man's experience, the garden could be seen as a metaphor for history. Yet this view of history, like the theatrical presentation which is its medium, was not merely a collection of isolated, independent episodes or events. Rather, the drama of history, like the theatrical presentation, had a fundamental unity akin to a plot. With regard to history, Daly discussed this order in terms of progress. As historical incident became reified in the city, so did the cause for that incident, in this case, historical progress. Like the historical episode, this structure could be observed in the public realm. Unlike the individual set-piece, however, this structure sought not so much to disengage as to unify the various historical moments of the city. The unifying principle, which we have earlier discussed as a historical subconscious, manifested itself in a comprehensive way upon the urban fabric.

We can observe an architectural application of this phenomenon in Henri Labrouste's Bibliothèque Sainte-Geneviève. The public realm of this building was introduced in the ground floor vestibule, treated as a garden. This foyer, lined with the busts of French men of letters, was to be interpreted not so much as *locus amoenus,* or satiric scene, as a grove of the philosophers, where one might encounter knowledge within the context of landscape. Hence, this false landscape was a metaphor for the truth revealed over history, an assertion realized only upon ascent to the first floor reading room. The facades of the library dealt with the issues of both theater and knowledge. Labrouste invoked the theatrical landscape of philosophy by interpreting the facades as a kind of a-tectonic stage curtain.[130] The stage set as a kind of didactic *scenae frons* was important here, not so much for its structural integrity or logic, as for its emblematic system of ideas. These ideas were explicitly historical.

Neil Levine has interpreted the library as an allegory of positive epistemology, a neutral frame upon which the ciphers of momentous historical moments were displayed. However, as Levine insists, not only was historical knowledge portrayed, but the structure of history as well. This might be inferred from an association of facade with Auguste Comte's *Calendrier Positiviste ou Système Générale de Commemoration Publique Destiné Surtout à la Transition de la Grande République Occidentale,* designed in 1849. Human history was presented here in terms of a great calendar, each month and day ascribed to an important historical personality.[131]

Landscape as architecture's source was important in this building for two reasons, as seat of theater and seat of knowledge. Moreover, this dual function was depicted on the exterior of the building, in its interpretation as a stage set as well as in its allegory of history. Lastly, not only was history allegorized, but it was systematized as well, by means of the building's bay system, and by the horizontal and vertical striations of the facade. History moved from mere chronicle to *historia,* where history was imbued with the historical idea. With Labrouste as with Daly, this idea was progress. For Labrouste, the effect of communicating this idea was edification and, finally, inspiration. Man's recognition of the truth of history would lead humanity as Comte said, to "a more moral understanding of man's own divine nature."[132]

Like the Bibliothèque, the city also allegorized history. Daly articulated this interpretation of Parisian urbanism:

... [les bâtiments historiques] nous disent à tout bout de rue: noblesse oblige; ce sont donc les *mementos* aussi utiles moralement qu'ils sont interressant pour l'esprit glorieux pour notre race.[133]

... at the end of every street, historical structures say to us: "Noblesse oblige"; they are mementos as useful morally as they are interesting for the glorious spirit of our race.

For Daly, the city presented men with a series of memories, giving rise to an encyclopedic vision of historical events. In his recognition of morality present in the city's architecture, Daly also noted that the implicit historical event was informed by a deeper historical truth. He thus implied a conception of subconscious historical structure.

In what did this historical subconscious reside? As seen in the Parc Monceau, the *modus* of history was related to a *promenade* sequence referring to both human and divine will, the personal history of Christ. Within Daly's view of the city, the historical subconscious also lay particularly in a circulation system comparable to the *promenade* sequence, and within the system of public works.

Daly admitted his predispositions in his historical analysis of the city of Paris. Initially, Daly admired the public works of the Romans by which the ancients ordered their cities. In this regard, he quoted Baron Haussmann, the Prefect of the Seine:

> Dans l'ancienne Rome, les grands travaux d'édilité publique ont, de tout temps, été comptés au nombre des titres les plus importants des chefs de l'Etat, rois, consuls et empereurs, à la reconnaissance publique.[134]

> In ancient Rome, the great public works have at all times been counted, by public acknowledgment, in number equal to the most important titles of the chiefs of state, kings, counsels and emperors.

He felt modern Paris could benefit by imitating Roman civic sense, as depicted in its monumental projects. For present-day France, this responsibility might consist of the resurrection of antique urban forms. Daly admired Davioud's Place du Châtelet as the receptacle of the Roman Rues St. Denis and St. Martin, as well as the Rue St. Honoré of Charles V. This square was to function as the spatial anchor of the Right Bank, becoming a symbol of formal unity as well as artistic will. Moreover, the Place du Châtelet was to function in the same way as a more modern prototype on the west side of Paris, the Place de la Concorde.

> La situation des deux monuments présente ici une grande analogie avec celle de la Marine et du Garde-Meuble placés également de chaque coté d'une grande voie dont ils annoncent l'entrée et ayant devant eux un large espace.[135]

> The location of the two monuments [the Théâtres du Châtelet and Lyrique in the Place du Châtelet] presents here a great analogy to that of the Marine and the Garde-Meuble [in the

Place de la Concorde] placed symmetrically on either side of a great street where they announce the entry to the city and where a large space opens out before them.

He then urged the revival of certain great ideas by which the old Paris had been orchestrated, preferring to impose other significant architectural moments today in ways comparable to those which had made the city intelligible in the past. This intelligibility alone could provide the present city of Paris with an amenity and edification comparable to that of the past.

Yet, it was more than a program of isolated projects which Daly recommended for Paris. Rather, he proposed a comprehensive, concerted pageant of public works which would recognize the importance of past historical moments as well as acknowledge the present. With regard to both past and present planning moves, he especially admired the will to give comprehensive order the urban fabric. He stressed the connection between Louis-Napoleon's works and those of the Romans and of Napoleon I. He found the former comparable in terms of vision and ideology, resulting especially in a sweeping circulation system. By his interpretation of Paris' historical fabric, Daly stressed that the city must be shaped by acts of will comparable to those of the past if it wished again to be unified.

Daly's objectives in his "Promenades" were twofold. They emerged not only from his explicit architectural interests, but also from the literary form of his writings. Daly's first objective was to applaud Paris' new urbanistic unity through public embellishment. He noted that these projects have both utilitarian and symbolic significance. His perceptions focused upon the imperial palaces, honorific monuments, museums, libraries, administrative buildings, markets, military buildings, and theaters of Second Empire Paris. These buildings serviced and orchestrated the new Paris. Yet these buildings also had an emblematic function. This symbolic component was perhaps most apparent in Daly's discussion of imperial palaces.

A tout seigneur, tout honneur: Commençons donc cette revue des Palais impériaux par le plus vaste et le plus important de tous, non seulement parce qu'il est la résidence habituelle du souverain; mais aussi parce que tout Français y voit une sorte de représentation architecturale de l'unité national, d'où, depuis la dynastie des Valois, le développement des beaux-arts s'est certainement associé à l'éclat du government.[136]

To each lord, all honor: let us thus begin this review of imperial palaces by the vastest and most important of all, not simply because it is the customary residence of the sovereign; but also because each Frenchman sees there a sort of architectural representation of national unity, from which, since the dynasty of the Valois, the development of the beaux-arts has certainly been associated with the brilliance of the government.

The royal palace, as symbol to the city population, was the embodiment of increasingly centralized government, focused upon the king. Moreover, the palace was symbol of national and social unity, created by the king by virtue of his spiritual role as personification of France itself. The semi-divine nature of the monarch was made manifest, or reified, in acts of will, most apparent in the architectural realm.

The literary style of the "Promenades" proposed still a second reading of Paris. Daly's individual perceptions of Paris were not merely isolated architectural events, but rather were unified by his physical and figurative perambulations. The literary form of Daly's tableaux comprised a higher unity. Although individual architectural events might be disharmonious, fragmentary, or contradictory, an inherent cohesiveness was proposed by Daly's own sequence of perceptions made concrete in literary form. Daly's own writing postulated literary unity via poetic license, imagination, and personal consciousness. In short, historical and architectural events were fused and ordered by Daly's literary point of view and personal consciousness.

Much as Daly unified events by means of the literary promenade, so too could he perceive unity by his real promenade in the city. He not only united Paris by his own powers of perception, but also sought a more accessible visual unity in the city by means of the architectural and urbanistic sequence. The promenade itself was to be the ultimate public embellishment, by which a total reading and understanding of the city could be accomplished. In its comprehensive monumental role, it was symbolic of national will—or all-embracing idea—in much the same way as the civic structure was a symbol.

The sources of the "promenade" were both historical and dramatic. Its provenance extended both from the straight streets of the Romans and Charles V, along which the ancient and medieval buildings of Paris clustered, and from Le Nôtre's gardens at Versailles. The Parisian townscape was ordered by a superimposed rectilinear geometry provided by the *Grande Croisée,* much as the garden was controlled by a gridding system stemming from the imposition of perspective construction onto landscape. Daly would surely have interpreted the imposition of a visual order onto nature as central to Le Nôtre's intention. Similarly, he would have perceived the theatrical straight streets as the imposition of a visual order of an imperial sort on the city to establish an urbanistic unity. Daly admired the action of artistic intention and the externalization of will in the drive toward visual order in both the natural and urbanistic situation. Both situations exemplified ideology's drive to shape the physical environment, the forming presence of a consciousness over and above the realm of private interest.

Moreover, Daly made an implicit connection between the underlying order of history on the one hand, and both the personal and the historical subconscious on the other. Louis XIV's landscape presented an allegorical history of Versailles, not in the isolated allegorical event, but in the geometry and structure of the promenade, beginning and terminating at the palace. The two sections of landscape and city focused upon the palace as the site's source of order (plate 76). Ultimately, the order of history might not be ascribed so much to divine as to royal will, which in its power to unify, consolidated not only the landscape, but the French people, and history as well. Daly's appreciation of Napoleon I transferred these notions to the city of Paris. Daly, who called the emperor "la plus grande figure des temps modernes," shared the romantic preoccupation with turning Napoleon into a quasi-divine personality. [137] As Napoleon memorialized his personal history in the names of his new Paris streets, he celebrated his own will. Daly saw the projects of Napoleon I as revealing not only the logic of Napoleon's history but the emperor's psychologic as well. He focused upon creative consciousness and artistic will as the ultimate *modus* of history.

In the physical manipulations of willful men of vision Daly saw not only the presence of ideology's action, but the basic forces of history as well. These were especially apparent in the geometrical orderings of the city and of nature. Albert Lenoir, writing in the *Revue Générale,* recognized in the geometrical colonial towns of antiquity, the operations of an imperial will:

> Enfin, l'autocrate et le conquérant . . . , imposant leur colonie aux habitants, fondent les villes sur un système [de] . . . la géométrie . . . [qui] . . . leur sert de base pour tracer les formes générales et leurs subdivisions . . . [La] regularité leur semble le meilleur mode pour bien établir tous les services, et satisfaire en tous points à la symétrie. [138]

> Therefore, the autocrat and the conqueror . . . imposing their colony upon the inhabitants, founded their cities on a system . . . of geometry . . . which served as a basis for tracing general forms and their subdivisions. Regularity seemed to them the best way to establish all services and to meet the conditions of symmetry at all points.

The form of the city found its unity in the externalization of consciousness, and especially of the consciousness of France's great men, geniuses who could shape the city, and make it the embodiment of their own ideology. These great men's works would be vindicated in as much as they were repositories of "the Spirit of the Age." In subscribing to their actions as informed by the historical spirit, Daly celebrated the "man of action," or "genius," as one with the superhuman forces of history which formed expression of his own will.

César Daly and Will

César Daly's attitude toward human will was dualistic. He addressed the issue only in the later years of his career, particularly in his articles concerning "Les Hautes Etudes en Architecture." In one study "Les Concours des Hautes-Etudes" appearing in *La Semaine des Constructeurs,* he approached the problem speculatively rather than critically. He first ascribed to will an animistic component, linking it to the idea of prime mover. In his article, he

especially addressed the problem of divine will as ultimate cause, in a campaign
of scientific demystification. He approached the problem from the point of
view of the natural sciences, relating it to notions of scientific classification and
evolution. Thus he criticized the vestigially metaphysical, natural conceptions
of Linnaeus and Cuvier:

> La grand naturaliste Linné, lorsqu'il fait connaître au monde sa classification des
> productions végétales et animales de la terre, disait: les espèces ont été créés par Dieu; elles
> sont inaltérables, invariables, et il ne dépend ni de l'homme ni de ce qui en dehors de Dieu de
> les modifier.
> Cette théorie était bien absolue, mais elle était orthodoxe. De notre temps, Cuvier, notre
> grand Cuvier accepta la même doctrine. Il déclara très nettement qu'à telle epoque la flore et
> la faune qui existaient alors ont disparu à la suite d'un cataclysme. Et alors, comment la
> nature a-t-elle reproduit une faune et une flore nouvelles? Par la volonté divine.[139]

> The great naturalist Linnaeus, while he popularized his classification of the vegetable and
> animal productions of the earth, said that species have been created by God; they are
> unalterable, invariable, and they do not depend on man nor on that which is outside of man
> to modify them.
> This theory was quite absolute, but it was orthodox. In our times, Cuvier, our great
> Cuvier, accepted the same doctrine. He declared very clearly that in such an epoch, the extant
> flora and fauna disappeared following a cataclysm. And then, how did nature reproduce new
> flora and fauna? By divine will.

Daly's argumentation dismissed the idea that all life was created in an
unalterable state by God. He subscribed to the notion of transformism in
species, an idea introduced by Lamarck's and Darwin's doctrine to explain the
proliferation of animal species. His conclusion supported evolution as the
fundamental law governing nature.

Although this conclusion failed to consider adequately the problem of the
prime mover, the law of evolution did take the idea of generic transformation
out of God's hands. Moreover, Daly turned Darwin's discovery into an end in
itself, not unlike the eighteenth-century deification of Newton's law of
gravitation. God was deposed as ruler of natural sciences, but Darwin was
enthroned in his stead. The fruit of Darwin's vision, his particular insight, was
apotheosized, now made an equal of God himself. A paradox was herein
apparent. Although divinity in Daly's view was left demystified, humanity,
particularly human genius, became the new fetish.

Daly's devaluation of God counterbalanced his appreciation of personal
consciousness. *Volonté diviné* was replaced by *volonté humaine*. Daly
amplified his discussion of *Hautes-Etudes* by raising the issue of history,
distinguishing between unconscious and conscious progress. It was
unconscious progress by which history was structured and revealed. This
system might or might not be recognized by the human consciousness. Men
like Lamarck and Darwin were able to grasp and control a section of *progrès*

inconscient, turning it into *progrès conscient. Progrès conscient* was that portion of the historical subconscious which could be grasped by the human mind and manipulated by man's intervention.

> Certaines esprits distingués s'imaginent que, si nous devons avoir un style nouveau d'architecture, un style moderne, il viendra tout seul sans qu'on aît besoin de s'en préoccuper. C'est le progrès mécanique accompli en dehors de tout intervention humaine, qu'on préconise ainsi; c'est la marche hasardeuse dans les ténèbres que, sans en apercevoir, on propose, en plein jour, de facon à voir et à apprécier les obstacles qu'on peut rencontrer. Sans nier l'action du progrès inconscient, c'est cependant le progrès conscient l'instrument principal du progrès humain, la force créatrice des civilisations et des styles historiques d'architecture.[140]

> Certain distinguished minds imagine that if we must have a new style of architecture, a modern style, it will come all along without our needing to be preoccupied with it. It is mechanical progress accomplished externally to any human intervention that they thereby advocate; it is the hazardous walk in the shadows that they propose, without realizing that it is possible to advance in the daylight so as to see and appreciate obstacles that one might encounter. Without denying the action of unconscious progress, it is nonetheless conscious progress which is the principal instrument of human progress, the creative force of civilization and historical styles of architecture.

Daly contrasted unconscious progress or the mechanical laws underlying history to conscious progress, or man's awareness of these laws as well as his vision of the future. Daly elevated personal consciousness to the level of divinity, using a popular allusion for mind, *ésprit.* Consciousness discussed in terms of spirit was a reference particularly potent to the German idealist philosophers, and was later invoked by Baudelaire in his discussions of mind and the creative or artistic consciousness.[141] Initially, Daly equated knowledge accessible via human consciousness to the basis of truth. Moreover, it was this level of history, understandable to man's perceptive abilities, which was to be the one leading to an envisioned future, *préconçu* or *prévu,* the scientist who grasped the conscious level of history was seen as imbued with the gift of second sight. He was clairvoyant, able to prophesy the future, as well as cognizant of the rational means by which the future could be achieved. Although the scientist's knowledge was fragmentary, his own inspired perceptions and vision were still able to grasp the "constituent facts" of the situation. Moreover, his action was able to catalyze the action leading to tomorrow. Ultimately, Daly's demystification of divine will led only to a mystification of the human. Perception, consciousness, and reason, all were apotheosized in his view. Imagination and logical inquiry were fused, a synthesis especially tied to Daly's own artistic consciousness.

Daly's dualistic stand concerning historical forces, the future, and human mediation idealized the role of the architect. It was the influence of inspired consciousness and artistic will which allowed man, not only to perceive, but also to manipulate the historical subconscious. We can find a useful parallel to this idea in Baudelaire's poetic view. He confronted the issue of the poet's inspired perception as well as its articulation in poetic form via the processes of imagination. The role of the poet, he believed, is Godlike. Baudelaire's "Rêve Parisien" is enlightening:

> Nul astre d'ailleurs, nuls vestiges
> De soleil, meme au bas du ciel,
> Pour illuminer ces prodiges,
> Qui brillaient d'un feu personnel:[142]

> I saw no star, nor sign of late
> Sunshine along the rim of night,
> The marvels to illuminate
> That shone of their own inner light!

The poet's perception was seen as enlightened. Moreover, the poet sought to create an artwork which would similarly illuminate an audience.

Daly's own artistic stand paralleled Baudelaire's. He compared architecture with poetry, likening the poet to a divinity himself. Moreover, he saw the architect as a kind of artistic vanguard, calling society to action, on the basis of his own inspired vision. Likewise, architectural form was to share in the process of inspiration.

> Est-ce a dire que l'art, le sentiment, l'idéal doive être négligé infiniment... Nos meilleurs architectes sont comme les grands poètes, inspirés sans le savoir, ils sont comme les trompettes qui sonnet la bataille et qui ne s'entendent pas, comme les prophètes qui parlent la parole de Dieu sans en comprendre toute l'incomprehensible profondeur.[143]

> Can it be said that art, sentiment, the ideal should be infinitely neglected?... Our best architects are like great poets, inspired without knowing it, they are like the trumpets that sound the battle cry, yet they do not hear the sound themselves, like prophets who speak the word of God without understanding all the incomprehensible profundity.

The poetic experience of the promenade as garden experience survived in both Daly and Baudelaire, even though, as A. Bartlett Giamatti has pointed out, this paradisiac idea had been eroded in eighteenth- and nineteenth-century literature. Giamatti argues that the demystification of the *topos* resulted from its application to real life situations. In the process, the garden became a kind of false paradise. In the nineteenth century, this idea was transferred to the city itself, a land of dalliance, and of loss of virtue. Gustave Flaubert provides us with an example of such a transference in *Madame Bovary,* when he has the notary Homais advising Léon to beware of the evils of Paris as a kind of garden of earthly delights. "You are constantly obliged to keep your hand in your pocket there. Let us say... you are in a public garden...[144] Generally speaking, the realism of the mid-nineteenth-century novel demystified the garden as terrain of the imagination and enchantment. Idealistic poetry like Baudelaire's, however, resurrected the urban garden as a land of mystery and spirit by exercise of the poet's own semi-divine consciousness, and, more importantly, by his creative will, by which he externalized his perceptions and feelings.

Baudelaire, like Daly, continued the fashion for "urban promenade," so much a part of imaginative literature in both England and France. His "Tableaux Parisiens" from the *Fleurs du Mal* reinvoked the problems of inspiration and creativity. Unlike Nodier, however, who had used the city merely as a device for inspiration, hence making it the mere recipient of the spirit of nature, Baudelaire reversed the process, projecting his own perceptions and consciousness onto the city's form, using the poem as both means and embodiment of ideology. His poem, "Paysage," applied imageable landscape to the city

> Je veux, pour composer chastement mes églogues,
> Coucher auprès du ciel, comme les astrologues,
> Et, voisin des clochers, écouter en rêvant
> Leurs hymnes solonnels emportés par le vent.
> Les deux mains au menton, du haut de ma mansarde,
> Je verrais l'atelier qui chante et qui bavarde;
> Les tuyaux, les clochers, ces mâts de la cité
> Et les grands ciels qui font rêver d'eternité.
>
>   .   .   .   .
>
> Des baisers, des oiseaux chantent soir et matin
> Et tout ce que l'Idylle a de plus enfantin.
> L'Emeute, tempêtant vainement à ma vitre,
> Ne fera pas lever mon front de mon pupitre;
> Car je serai plongé dans cette volupté,
> De tirer un soleil de mon coeur et de faire
> De mes pensers brûlants une tiède atmosphère.[143]

> My chaste eclogues composing, I shall lie
> Stargazer, on the rim of the evening sky,
> And, near, the belfries dozing at my ease,
> Shall hear the solemn hymn borne on the breeze.
> My chin on both hands I then shall prop
> To hear them laugh and sing down in the shop.
> Chimneys and spires that spring like masts I'll see
> And Skies where float bright strands of things to be.
>
>   .   .   .   .
>
> Kisses and birdsong, long repose and idle.
> And all the childlike beauties of the Idyll.

No strife that storms my window shall be able
To make me raise my head up from the table,
For I'll be trembling with the magic thrill
Of calling forth the Spring by force of will,
Of launching suns with my hot heart wrought,
And warming worlds with incandescent thought.

The force of *volonté* introduces the notion that ideology can transform unpleasantness into an object of contemplation and beauty, by the erection of a new poetic around it. In a poem entitled "Le Soleil" also taken from "Tableaux Parisiens," Baudelaire invoked the Platonic dialectic by which truth supersedes external reality. The sun was the image of the truth in nature, and Baudelaire compared its function to that of the poet. The poet's consciousness participated in that truth; his forms described it.

Quand, ainsi qu'un poète, il descend dans les villes,
Il ennoblit le sort des choses les plus viles
Et s'introduit en roi, sans bruit et sans valet,
Dans tous les hôpitaux et tous les palais.[144]

He goes down into cities, poetwise,
Where what is most abject he glories;
And as a king, alone, without a sound
Through hospital and palace makes his round.

In this protracted simile, Baudelaire compares himself to a king, able to reify his will in verbal form. In so doing, he was able to transform an abject city into a new, morally uplifting realm. Baudelaire's poet was the counterpart of Daly's architect in fact; he compared his own poetic forms to architecture. Whereas Daly likened the architect's creative act to that of "an inspired poet," Baudelaire personified his creative drive as the "architect of my fantasies."[145]

Whereas Baudelaire exploited an architectural analogy to illuminate the problem of form-giving, Daly used a poetic simile to discuss the issues of artistic consciousness, inspiration, and ideology. Like Baudelaire, Daly's perceptions of Paris as a "promenade" extended from a literary and dramatic tradition, especially well portrayed in Carmontelle's theatrical landscapes. Like Baudelaire, Daly regarded the city as a series of "tableaux" or vignettes upon which one might produce a commentary or critique. Such commentary might take a form having to do not with the thing perceived, but with the cognizing behind artistic perception. Such commentary might produce forms which in themselves combatted depravity, attempting inspiration by their own internal beauty.

Daly himself commented upon the two Parises—old and new. The new Paris in turn was a commentary upon the old, emerging gradually from the rubble of the past, and like a new *tableau,* giving cause for sublime feelings:

L'étonnant panorama du nouveau Paris émergeant graduellement aux yeux de tous, comme
d'un brouillard, tandis qu'y rentrent successivement et à jamais toutes les parties
physiquement et moralement malsaines de l'ancienne ville, ce beau tableau est bien propre
assurément à pénétrer le spectateur du sentiment profond du bien accompli.[146]

The astonishing panorama of the new Paris, emerging gradually to the eyes of all, as though
from a fog, while all the physically and morally unhealthy portions of the city retreat to
penetrate the spectator with the profound sentiment of the accomplished good, as well as the
intelligence and will necessary to realize it.

Daly especially admired Louis-Napoleon and his Prefect of the Seine, Baron
Haussmann, for the scale of their enterprise. The new Paris was the
embodiment not only of Napoleon III's critical posture towards Paris, but his
Idée Napoléonienne for a new one as well. It was this combined artistic
consciousness as well as the great creative act which Daly especially admired.

The transcendency of personal consciousness was that faculty which Daly
found most significant. The omniscient awareness by which Paris' individual
architectural events were coordinated and orchestrated was comparable to an
increasingly popular literary form which Daly also drew upon—the novel. He
compared the willful organization of Paris to the omniscient third person
narrative, popularized by such authors as Flaubert and Zola. In narrative
form, the author becomes a semi-divine viewer, external to the action,
commenting upon individual events. Moreover, the author draws individual
personalities and situations into proximity, establishing connections and
relationships between incidents. The author knows a character's history,
psychology and context. The orchestration of the whole takes place in form.
When Daly stated that he perceived the city of Paris as "a veritable novel," he
implied the ascendancy of the omniscient narrator who makes not only
realistic, critical or ironic commentary, but also organizes and unifies the
events of man. The author not only perceived; he formulated and formalized as
well.

In architecture, form and ideology were complementary. On the one hand,
Daly's attempts to idealize the architectural form were counterparts to
Baudelaire's attempts to formalize the ideal. For Daly, ideology vitalized form.
He especially recognized ideology in man's critical faculty—in the relationship
between the artist and his context that obtains in his personal artistic
consciousness. Interpretation became formalized in an expressive act of will.

Conclusion: César Daly and the City of Rhetoric

Baudelaire's "Tableaux" provide us with a series of careful vignettes of life in
Paris. These moments are separate in time, discrete in event, unique in
personality. Baudelaire, however, is involved with the production of a lyric
narrative with a distinctly modern cast.[147] His purpose is to convey the passage

of time and the structure of life in literary form. Two of his formal means are significant here: Baudelaire's sense of composition and his use of metaphor.

Baudelaire's composition transforms the sordid into the beautiful. As noted earlier, he establishes a relationship between the kind of self-composition exemplified by his dandified appearance and the composition of his poetry, which is similarly crafted. Baudelaire's privileged consciousness can be seen as expanding outward, shaping all with which it comes into contact. Writing style, like style of dress, seeks to convey the inner workings of the mind and its ideology.

This view of Baudelaire's work allows one to assert that his cognition is of a distinctly logical order. His use of metaphor, however, argues otherwise. As Baudelaire uses it, metaphor seeks a rationale of an order distinct from logic. Metaphor marks kinships between oppositions, physical and metaphysical. The passages previously cited provide numerous examples. Among them is Baudelaire's association of the sun with the poet in "Le Soleil"; it forces a comparison between two distinct literary figures, citing illumination as the significant point of their coincidence. In this way Baudelaire describes a meeting of forms, proposing literary unities that escape the syllogistic system. Thus, by forwarding a literary mode which takes its substance from differences, Baudelaire calls into question the value of logical epistemology.

Rhetoric as the formalization of discourse draws upon similar themes. Classical philosophy cites rhetoric's essential basis in logic. It is this logic which Frances Yates, in *The Art of Memory*, recognizes as central to the mnemotechnical pictorial form. Yates describes the process of rhetorical formalization as follows. The speaker composes discourse by drawing upon a logical, argumentational structure in which he positions symbolic images which are stored in the memory. Yates visualizes such rhetorical form in terms of "architecture" comprising a series of locations (*loci*) unified by a comprehensible promenade sequence in which symbols (*topoi*) are found. Yates further argues that this architecture of the mind is externalized as pictorial and built form.[148]

It is important to note that Yates' view of rhetorical construction is limited to discourse that is purely instrumental, i.e., comprised of ideas immediately communicable to an audience. This view of rhetoric is essentially classical, and appropriate to the character of the artforms she interprets.[149] Yet, abstract discourse of an instrumental order is relevant only when the audience is equally abstract. In most rhetorical situations, however, the audience is a known variable. The audience, the receiver of information, has an impact upon the shaping of discourse. The issue of style and form arises as central to rhetoric's concerns.

As we have already observed in Baudelaire, such questioning of purely instrumental discourse, and the logic that is its underpinning, introduces the possibility of literary forms which use alogical means to order. In place of

244 The City of Rhetoric

discourse that seeks to establish a one-to-one correspondence between the idea and its literary form, alternative modes employ linguistic structures which are ambiguous and multiply significant. Metaphor is one of these.[150]

We have already noted that Daly's interpretations of the city reveal ambiguous ideological readings. As we approached Daly's perceptions of urbanism, we noted his analytical attack upon the city. Daly lavished untold time and attention upon the problems of the street, circulation, water supply, hygiene, public buildings, housing, etc. His posture was distinctly involved with an appreciation of the city as well as a will to understand and improve upon its form. Yet, Daly was simultaneously moved by the city. His estimation of its scale and sublime nature forced him to acknowledge Paris as a complex entity having significance above and beyond its many parts and functions. Here, Daly's stand was ambivalent. On the one hand, he wished to dissect and operate upon the city, regarding it in a coldly analytical way. On the other hand, he was passionate about the city, appreciating it as a moving experience, whereby its ontology transcended its parts. Consequently, piecemeal proposals for Paris did not much interest Daly, for improvements had to recognize the city as a totality. Such projects had not only to be comprehensive; they also had to be on a scale that was in keeping with the city's sublime character. Only in that way could they appropriately realize the city's vitality.

Second, we have seen that Daly addressed the city from the point of view of theater. As noted above, he saw the need for all architecture, both public and private, to participate in the public realm. The public nature of architecture existed on two levels. On one level, the architectural facade was a decorous backdrop or stage curtain against which a citizen's public life could be responsibly portrayed. The human drama was orchestrated by the fatality of culture, custom and law. On another level, the facade itself became a metaphor of human action and history. Not merely did building elevation confront the public realm, but it fused with it as well. Much as man's actions were manipulated by the forces of destiny, historical or cultural, so were the facades. As indicated earlier, the class structure of society was memorialized in the facade of the *maison de rapport*. Much as elevation substantiated these positivistic hierarchies, so did the city. City form, like the citizen's life, was itself manipulated by the social structure of the day. Ultimately, the city of Paris reified the values, the predispositions, the economic and social substructure of the Second Empire. Much as man was diminished in the face of these superhuman forces, so was the city. The city merely externalized his action in society. We must conclude that for Daly, as for others in the nineteenth century, the fatality of Greek tragedy became the sociology and politics of mid-nineteenth-century Paris. Art now really did imitate life. Although superhuman destiny was demystified to a degree by the laws of evolution, or other progressive theories, individual consciousness remained equally subordinated to similarly immutable historical forces.

Third, we have addressed the problem of history in Daly's perception of the city. This is perhaps most apparent in his assessment of Paris' urban history. Daly's evaluation of the city was involved primarily with works of a public nature—monuments, churches, institutional and governmental structures. Such constructions most effectively portrayed the spirit of the age. More importantly, Daly addressed himself to the history of Paris' public realm, appreciating especially the antique road, the medieval wall, the renaissance and baroque square. Moreover, he admired the creators of these works—rulers, leaders, saints and architects—as inspired men of affairs who, by virtue of *volonte,* shaped the total image of the city. Emperor Julian, Louis IX, Charles V, Francis I, Louis XIV, Napoleon I are among these. It was the fusion of their consciousness with the spirit of history that gave Paris a distinct and recognizable form in each major historical epoch. Moreover, it was by acts of will motivated by the force of history that the city was imbued with an ontology evidenced by the public realm. The city was simultaneously the externalization of history and the will of the geniuses who implicitly understood the spirit of the age.

For Daly history moved from an encyclopedic collection of events to a series of ages growing one upon the other in conformity to an internal logic, understood by men of genius and formalized by their will. History governed by such a formalizing will was *historia,* made manifest in he city by the range of public works. The resulting vastness of form, the grand extent of conception, and an image which escaped rational definition led to a sublime experience, the cathartic moment that is the accompaniment of inspiration. The city as repository of history was no longer the sole issue.

To summarize, Daly's discursive prose exhibits certain fundamental antagonisms: facts counter ideology, historical events contrast historical plot, action is juxtaposed to destiny, positive contends with idealistic philosophy. These dichotomies, however, all mark a common relationship. They juxtapose figurative means to logical structures. This factor is significant, for it coincides with the basic, classical structure of rhetorical form: the positioning of ideal *topoi* within a rational plan.

However, the character of these antagonisms derives not so much from Daly's instrumental predisposition as it does from his use of metaphor. Metaphor not only provides the means of accommodating structure and imagery, but permits the coexistence of previously irreconcilable philosophical points of view as well. Hence, the metaphorical quality of rhetoric substantiates intentions which are implicitly conciliatory.

Metaphor mystifies that discursive mode which initially hoped for a clear, rational transmission of ideas from speaker to audience, and in so doing, allows for a variety of interpretations. A curious inversion of linguistic values is the result. Metaphor first debunks logical epistemology which assumes that language is the pale reflection of the truths held in man's mind. Second, metaphor takes its place as the new rhetoric, which holds form to be the shaping power of man's psychic life.

As metaphor superseded the logic in rhetoric, the structures of pristine ideologies collapsed. Metaphorical form now permitted the author to graft diverse points of view onto the city's form. The city behaved as a species of *mandorla,* a vital image no longer representing, but causing a range of ideas in men's minds. Daly came to see the city as alluding to all ideologies, hence, as a microcosm of knowledge. It was a being in its own right, not merely externalizing its own ideas, but shaping the world external to itself. It was not merely the creation of God and man, but their creator. In its streets, squares, public buildings, personal and divine consciousness casually met. There, the figures of Goodness, Truth and Beauty could greet each other and shake hands.

Conclusions: History, Rhetoric, Self

Louis Duc's Palais de Justice, on the Ile de la Cité, is the most significant mark made by the eclectic philosophy and art of César Daly's era (plate 75). Completed at the moment of Louis-Napoleon's decline from power, this building summarizes the major architectural issues of half a century. The result of a building campaign that spans the political periods of the July Monarchy, the Second Republic, and the Second Empire, the Palais de Justice fuses styles of both art and thought. This movement, portrayed as a series of formal leitmotifs, is best observed in the building's Harlay facade, an elevation which terminates the axis of the Ile de la Cité's Place Dauphine. Arthur Drexler points to the workings of a program of ideological conciliation when he describes the elevation as "a Romantic translation of the classical orders."[1] Thus Drexler claims that in this facade, the figurative system of Romanticism and the instrumental language Classicism overlap.

A giant order of Choragic Corinthian columns and a decorative vocabulary of naturalistic motifs are the organizing features of the Harlay facade. The two systems are juxtaposed and unified by compositional means of sixteenth-century Italian provenance: heavy rustification, garlands, consoles and rondels. The combination of Italianism and naturalism recalls Henri Labrouste's Bibliothèque Ste. Geneviève (plate 76), and the similarities between the two buildings are provocative. Labrouste's careful facade arcading is recapitulated in the explicit bay system of Duc's elevation, although round headed thermal windows yield to more Daly-esque, elliptical, flat arches. In addition, the horizontal banding of Labrouste's upper story, articulated by string courses, by the edges of flat panels filled with *Néo-Grec* decoration, and by the incised calligraphy of a Positivist Calendar, intertwines with the strong verticals of the facade. The result is a kind of formal basket-weave of architectonic and decorative devices. Duc's invocation of this complicated device of strapping and banding betrays his debt to Labrouste. The strong vertical accents are countered by the persistent presence of the horizontal. Bosses, dados, string courses, and window mullions consistently traverse and interact with the vertical musculature. Whereas the simultaneous emphasis on the horizontal and vertical in the Labrouste facade is discontinous and phenomenal, the interaction of the two in Duc's is articulate and literal.

Turning to Labrouste's decorative devices, I call special attention to the corner spandel detail of the library's main facade (plate 77).[2] The garland draped between a tiny decorative colonnette and the rondel capping the interior tie bar is especially important, because it marks a middle ground between compositional means and physical structure. It thus creates one of several moments in which the building uses decorative language to develop thematic ambiguities between the artificial and the real, the scientific and the natural. Another example of this ambiguity is provided by the cast-iron structural system of the main reading room. It is illustrative of rational language, and is contrasted by the explicit poetic of the range of herms and painted landscape which provide the setting for the "Garden of the Philosophers" in the entry foyer.

In the Harlay facade, Duc makes an even greater attempt than Labrouste to fuse these antagonisms. Like Labrouste, he uses a metaphorical decorative system in his allegory of justice across the facade. Yet Duc moves between instrumental and natural languages, particularly in the impost blocks of the architrave where the supportive function, abstractly treated in the columns below, is naturalized by the use of herms. In this way, the move between natural and instrumental languages results in a program of anthropomorphism, where structural and didactic functions are simultaneously articulated by natural form.

Duc's play with decorative, a-structural form is contradicted by the Harlay front's insistent use of colonnade. Certainly, Duc's use of this compositional feature is intended to invoke a sense of architectural pragmatism and structural solidity markedly absent in the internalized rhetoric of the Bibliothèque Ste. Geneviève. The physicality of the structure of the Harley facade is a response to an aesthetic system absent in Labrouste's work. If any architectural system other than a realistic one is at play in Duc's work, it is probably a preromantic one, and more specifically, the idealism of the schools of Quatremère de Quincy and Victor Cousin.

The Harlay facade might thus be compared with Antoine Brongniart's Paris Bourse of 1808 (plate 78). More than any other, the Stock Exchange can be seen as the embodiment of Quatremère's architectural idealism. Influenced simultaneously by the architectural poles of Neoplatonic typology and structural rationalism, this building—simple, cubic, ordered—is a study in instrumental language. Stripped of any natural ornamentation, the Bourse deals with formal articulation on a purely cognitive level, especially in its straightforward use of clearly stated structure. Deriving from Laugier's and Cordemoy's typological and structural rationalism, Brongniart's building expresses an ideology in which the poetic that is manifested in both Labrouste's and Duc's decoration is supplanted by an instrumental, architectural grammar.

Hence, the Palais de Justice represents a fusion of ideological systems. On the one hand, we observe a romantic interest in history, imagination and poetic, formal language. On the other hand, we perceive an involvement with scientific inquiry, instrumental formalism based primarily in structure, and an explicitly cognitive architectural language which stresses the instrumentality of both architectural and linguistic structures. The Palais de Justice is a work of that eclectic, middle ground which is concerned with the formal considerations of objective reason and subjective imagination, history and progress, contingency and principle, nature and abstraction. The resulting artistic effort is implicitly conciliatory and *laissez-faire*.

The reverberation of the formal and esthetic chord lingered. Its survival is evidenced by Julien Guadet's "Hôtel des Postes" (1882), which likewise fuses ideal and romantic means of articulation (plate 79). The spare, meager *Néo-Grec* vocabulary, the use of space-defying cartouches, the interest in naturalistic decorative play, all indicate Guadet's continued involvement with romantic formal devices. Furthermore, visual composition becomes a means by which the differences encountered in the elementary build-up of forms is obscured. The compositional basket-weave encountered above becomes an issue when facade is conceived in terms of orthogonal gridding, articulated as an interaction between vertical structural emphases and horizontal straps comprising rustication, entablatures, capitals and incised fenestration.

Yet the regulating lines do not run across the facade uninterruptedly. Rather, both verticals and horizontals are varied and manipulated by their interaction with the structural skeketon composing the major street facade, articulated as a hybrid pier/column system. As in the Palais de Justice, the provenance of this feature is indisputably classical. As noted earlier, the sense of musculature and skeleton of the structural feature ultimately derives from the typological/rationalist détente seen in Brongniart's Bourse and having its sources in Quatremère's aesthetics. Like Duc's juxtaposition of architectural systems, Guadet's work falls into that eclectic, middle ground which stresses the conciliation of form with ideological oppositions. Moreover, in both formal and aesthetic preoccupations, Guadet is perhaps the most visible and certainly the most articulate inheritor of that architectural system which César Daly fathered.

It is interesting to note that Guadet began preparing his famous course comprising *Eléments et Théorie de l'Architecture* (1902) in 1894, the year following César Daly's death. It is also significant that Guadet's publisher, Paul Planat, was Daly's former co-editor of *La Semaine des Constructeurs*, and current head of the periodical, *La Construction Moderne*. Guadet's title gives important indications of the author's predipositions. *Eléments* were juxtaposed with *Théorie* in much the same way that Daly contrasted *Motifs* with *Composition*. As Guadet's title suggests, his campaign was one of generalization, moving from the specific to the general and from the idiosyncratic to the coordinated. Moreover, his work contrasts the faculties of imagination and reason. As for Daly, reason provides Guadet with a scheme by which works of artistic spirit are controlled, and beauty assured. In this way, Guadet's program reinvokes the adage Daly frequently used, "Ordre et Liberté," in order to indicate that free, artistic activity was to be restrained by mental and moral norms.

Like Daly's, Guadet's method was an outgrowth of the Encyclopedic and utilitarian schools that both architects exploited. Ostensibly, these schools were value-free and rational, as Guadet suggested when he stated:

> ...j'aspire à montrer que dans l'architecture, tout procède de la déduction. L'étudiant doit refaire ce qu'a fait avant lui le labeur des siècles: connaître d'abord les premiers besoins, les premiers moyens, les premiers témoignages d'art.[3]

> ...I aspire to show that in architecture, all proceeds from deduction. The student must redo all that the labor of centuries has done before him: thereby to know the first needs, first means, first testimonies of art.

Moreover, Guadet's method strove to be all-inclusive. Guadet reinvoked this liberal vantage in asserting,

> Une pareille méthode ne saurait être exclusive. Je puis avoir comme tout artiste mes préférences et mes aversions, mais je n'ai jamais compris professer la propagande étroite ni l'excommunication.
>
> Je ne conçois ni l'enseignement qui au nom de l'antique exorcise le moyen âge, ni celui qui, au nom du moyen âge, se renferme entre deux écrans ou deux murailles de la Chine, dont l'une lui cache le passé, l'autre l'avenir... rien d'artistique ne doit rester hors de nos études.[4]

> A comparable method would avoid being exclusive. I may have, like any artist, my preferences and my aversions, but I have never understood those who profess a narrow propaganda or a means of excommunication.
>
> I conceive neither instruction which, in the name of antiquity, exorcises the Middle Ages, nor that which, in the name of the Middle Ages, confines itself between two screens or two walls of China, one of which hides the past, the other, the future... nothing artistic must reside outside our studies.

The final means of Guadet's epistemological organization resided in the study of history. Guadet, like Daly, in citing the Lamarckian system of filiation of the natural sciences, invoked the idea of transformism, in which all natural history was united in a universal, evolutionary program. According to this scheme, history moved through a succession of spatio-temporal layers of increasing complexity and simultaneous perfection. Guadet stated,

> ...je chercherai à passer du simple au composé... [L'étudiant] voit qu'entre ces éléments simples et composés il y a un enchaînement, un progrès graduel qui sera aussi le sien; il verra ainsi le développement logique de son art, il comprendra la marche séculaire de cette oeuvre à

laquelle toutes les civilisations ont coopéré et qui continue à obéir à l'éternelle loi du mouvement et de la transformation...je dirais que notre méthode doit être la vérification due au progrès expérimental.[5]

...I seek to pass from the simple to the composed [complex]...[The student] sees that between these simple and composed forms there is a linkage, a gradual progress which will also be his; he will thus see the logical development of his art; he will understand the secular march of this work in which all civilizations have cooperated, and which continue to obey the external law of movement and transformation...I would say that our method must be the verification owed to experimental progress.

Like Daly, Guadet chose to organize his campaign of total knowledge and progress through a purported biological structure. This was the outcome of an elaborate, organic, vitalistic metaphor. Guadet's intellectual eclecticism straddled the gulf between the empiricism of the positivists and the transcendentalism of the idealists.

As in biological transformism, Guadet's architecture and writing might be viewed as the pinnacle of architectural eclecticism's implicit philosophical pyramid of increasing complexity. This was the definitive liberal epistemology in wich all philosophical vantages, viewpoints, and ideologies could reside alongside each other without fear of confrontation. Like a Second Empire architectural composition, the philosophy of eclecticism was composed of a series of mutually exclusive pieces held together with little more than the rhetorical glue of good intention. Implicit philosophical antagonisms were never really resolved. Not unexpectedly, this architectural and ideological synthesis was short-lived.

Almost as soon as Guadet made his culminating statement, the formal and ideological synthesis began to falter. The products of the Guadet/Laloux *atelier* increasingly sought to separate rather than to interweave the ideological influences present in the Ecole's official doctrine. On the one hand, students like Auguste Perret and Julien Guadet's son, Paul, moved toward a rarified, instrumental, formal articulation reflecting the idealist forces at play in eclectic theory. On the other hand, other students, like Paul Bigot, attempted a formal posture seeking to emphasize not so much the constructive or typological nature of architecture as the situational and characteristic.[6] Such formal polarizations presaged the ultimate collapse of eclecticism in both theory and practice.

Guadet's eclectic theory is an architectonic, an imaginary edifice at once incorporating the column grids of the classical school, the flying buttresses of the romantics, and the cast-iron and steel frame of the rationalists. The enclosure system of this metaphorical Ecole emphasizes carefully composed facades built up of archeological fragments so dear to historians of all persuasions, while seeking those *tracés régulateurs* of the aesthetically-minded, to give the elevations order and unity. This structure is a heterocosm. In addition, this illusory building is a museum of diversity, a menagerie of points of view, self-complete and immutable. At the same time, it is an expandable library of both the acknowledged past and the unforeseen future. This heavenly mansion is an abode where all ideas can find a resting place, where all things are equal, and all antagonisms cease.

Like the formal structure described above, the ideological structure is fusive and inherently unstable. Not only does this architectonic falter because of its inability to conciliate or arbitrate antagonisms commensurate with the number of oppositions raised; it suffers at the hands of external agents as well. As increasingly numerous critics of the Ecole level their attacks upon the ideological edifice, various pieces begin to fall. Proponents of program assault typology. Advocates of science oppose decoration. Apologists for character combat composition. Spokesmen for modernity fight history.

Under the combined force of the attack, the superstructure of the Ecole, held together so tenuously by the liberal impulse formalized by rhetoric, succumbs. In the daylight, critics rejoice. Yet, under the cloak of darkness, all return to the rubble, furtively creeping into the ruins and stealing those fragments which subsequently serve as the foundation for their own ideological structures. As each critic fabricates his own point of view, he silently incorporates those fragments of an older system into his own.

In other words, whereas the old academic system sought an epistemology that fused all of man's faculties—history, reason and imagination—the modern campaign resulted in psychic fragmentation. One group, including Paul Bigot and André Bloc, emphasized imagination. Another group, including Auguste Perret and Paul Nelson, stressed man's reason. As the psychic triad was fragmented, reason and imagination became singly glorified. History, however, found few supporters. As proponents of the two camps erected their own mutually exclusive architectural theories, they found a point of commonality in their disdain of history.

Generally speaking, this rejection of history has led to an existential *cul-de-sac*. History is that life force which gives unity to the eternal distinction between other and self. That unity is defied by advocates of science, who deny self when faced with progressive forces sponsoring a golden tomorrow; that unity is also defied by proponents of imagination, who value personal consciousness over any sort of extra- or inter-subjective concerns. Neither the fiction which science offers, nor the poetic which imagination provides, can regiment consciousness. Both ignore the subconscious domain of man's psychic life, the realm of history and its traditions. The absence of this historical subconscious, comprising a system of valuation and existential norms of action, is the one stumbling block of all liberal philosophies, eclecticism included.

A *crise de conscience* of mammoth proportions is the outcome. Both Emile Durkheim and Friederich Nietzsche speak to this problem. Durkheim terms the crisis of consciousness, *anomie,* or the alienation resulting from man's separation from society's traditions and values. In Durkheim's view, alienated man is external to history. Only via congruence with history as value system does man become situated within a social context, where he ultimately gains personal value by a union with the workings of history. As discussed in the introduction to this book, Nietzsche insistently expressed the importance of man's personal value, especially as it is described by his place in history. Nietzsche's parable of the cows in *The Use and Abuse of History* portrays man as satisfied, yet unwittingly deprived of a sense of self. In *Ecce Homo,* Nietzsche advocates self-consciousness only insofar as it is part and parcel of history. His posture toward history is, therefore, dualistic. On the one hand, he claims that history dominates self; on the other hand, he asserts that self must make history. Personal value is tied to self-expression and manipulation of events, but this manipulation is the measure of man's awareness of his contribution to the tides and climate of his age. It is only in tomorrow's history, and the historical figure's participation in that history, that man's value is ultimately decided. In *Ecce Homo,* this notion is poetically portrayed by the author's denial of his own name in hopes that posterity will resurrect it, thereby giving it value. For Nietzsche, then, man is worthwhile as historical generator and relic.[7]

César Daly recognizes the importance of history to man's psychic life when he criticizes the denial of history, albeit the outcome of liberal or positivist philosophies, or mere ignorance. He gains a sense of place as well as personal value from history. Daly states,

Négliger l'histoire, négliger le souvenir, ce qui est due aux ancêtres, c'est donc se nier soi-même, c'est commencer le suicide.[8]

To neglect history, to neglect memory, that which is owed to our ancestors, is then to deny oneself; it is to begin suicide.

The assertion of self evidenced here resulted in form-giving, in the creative act, in writing and building. Daly's rhetoric worked in two ways. First, as a writer fusing differences and antagonisms, Daly occupied a middle ground between discourse and poetry, between expression and inspiration. In the same way that his architecture linked so many different decorative pieces, Daly's rhetorical acts manipulated ideologies loosely, playfully deploying useful continuities, omitting discontinuities, and fusing all. Second, as an artist, form-maker, and life-giver, Daly juxtaposed the principles of thought as a divinity might employ the elements of life to create a physical entity having its own vitality. In his rhetoric Daly culminated his own history and spawned a future. In his architecture he ensured that tomorrow's history would vindicate him. Both his written and built *oeuvre* thus give him his identity and temporal situation.

To compare this position with our own situation: the period following the Second World War has been torn between special interests of both future- and ego-fixation. Our parents surrendered their personal concerns to posterity. Unfortunately, on too many occasions, we, as their progeny, have been only too willing to oblige their interests, concentrating our attentions exclusively upon ourselves. With our generation, posterity ceases. Our interests too frequently seem little more than the ministerings of gratification. Ours, as well as our parents' lives, might be tempered by something more than concern for posterity or for self. Life's missing coefficient could be sought in a realm transcending our own personal situations, in a sphere moving beyond physical and personal contingencies, in a sense of place and purpose articulated by the things we do to provide life with its ultimate meaning. Perhaps it is in a program not unlike César Daly's—explicitly formalistic, conciliatory, rhetorical—that a mechanism for expression of this coefficient might be found. So too might we discover a scheme of history and a place for ourselves within that scheme.

Plates

1. Portrait of César-Denis Daly and family, circa 1867.
   From the Considérant family album.

2. "L'Architecture Contemporaine." Engraving designed by Ruprich Robert, 1849. Tableau inspired by César Daly's manifesto "De la Liberté dans l'Art." From César Daly's *Revue Générale* VIII (1849).

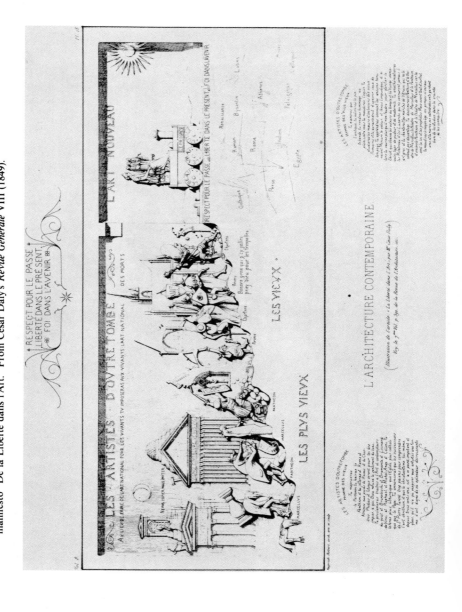

3. The Three Graces. By Antonio Canova, 1799.

4. "Table of the Evolution of Styles of Architecture with Regard to the Evolution of Corresponding Civilizations." By César Daly, 1847.

TABLEAU DE L'ÉVOLUTION DES STYLES D'ARCHITECTURE
EN REGARD DE L'ÉVOLUTION DES CIVILISATIONS CORRESPONDANTES

DOCTRINES SOCIALES — Religion | Propriété | Famille | Politique | Etc.

STYLES HISTORIQUES

EVOLUTIONS / Eléments géométriques des STYLES

Évolution	Civilisation	Religion
1re Transition (Germe) — *Evolution du*	Préhistorique Sauvage (Gestation)	Fétichisme
1er Degré Rectiligne *(Simple et complexe)* — *Evolution du*	Egyptiens / Grecs	Polythéisme
2e Transition (Mixte) — *Evolution du*	Romains	
2e Degré Curviligne *(Simple et complexe)* — *Evolution du*	Epoque du Moyen-Age	Monothéisme
3e Transition (Mixte)	Renaissance et Epoque Contemp.	
3e Degré Curviligne *(Supérieure)* — *Evolution du*	?	

Famille: Promiscuité — Polyandrie — Polygamie en Orient — Polygamie — Monogamie en Occident

en Orient — en Occident
Byzantin / Ogival — Roman / Ogival

5. "The Bishop of Paris, Accompanied by His Clergy, Comes to Bless the Handiwork of Men." From Louis-Antoine Garnier-Pagès' *Histoire de la Revolution de 1848*, 1871-78.

SYSTEME FIGURÉ
DES CONNOISSANCES HUMAINES.

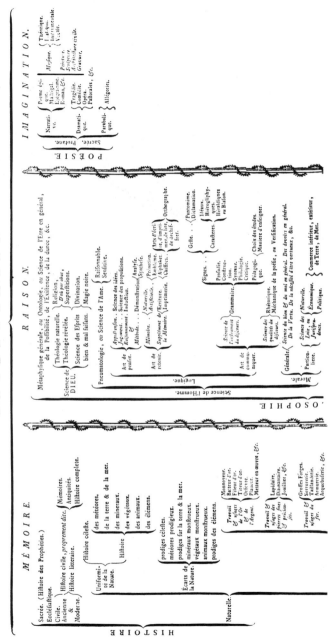

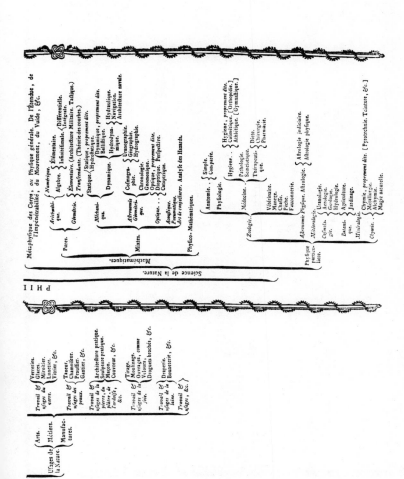

6. "A Figured System of Human Knowledge." From Jean Le Rond d'Alembert's and Denis Diderot's *Encyclopédie*, Supplement to the Discours Préliminaire, 1754.

7. "Table Synoptique—Reptiles." By George Cuvier. From the *Encyclopédie Méthodique*, vol. 188, 1792.

TABLES synoptiques de la MÉTHODE ERPÉTOLOGIQUE DE M. *le professeur* GEORGES CUVIER.

Nº. 1.

ORDRES DE LA CLASSE DES REPTILES.

CŒUR A OREILLETTE { double; membres { existant; mâchoires { sans dents......... CHÉLONIENS.
                   armées de dents...... SAURIENS.
           nuls................................ OPHIDIENS.
        unique.. BATRACIENS.

Nº. 2.

ORDRE DES CHÉLONIENS EN PARTICULIER.

                   GENRES.   SOUS-GENRES.

CARAPACE { dure; mâchoires { cornées; pattes { en moignon... TORTUE DE TERRE.
                 à doigts séparés. TORTUE D'EAU DOUCE. *T. d'eau douce. T. à boîte.*
              en nageoires... TORTUE DE MER.
          non cornées........... CHÉLYDE.
    à bords mous....................... TRIONYX.

8. "Tree of Knowledge." From the *Encyclopédie*. German edition published by Roth of Weimar, 1780.

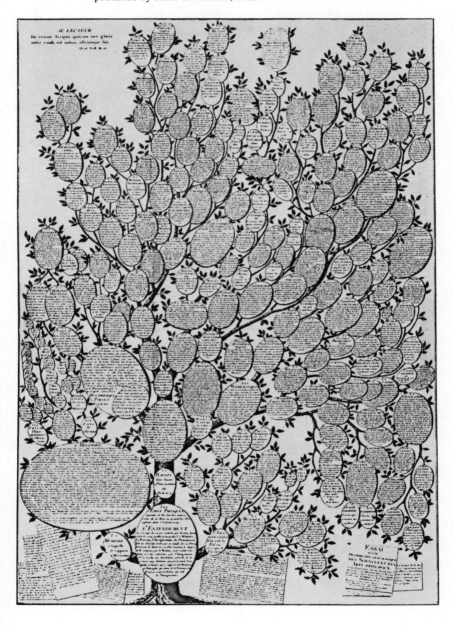

9. "L'Abri du Pauvre." By Claude-Nicolas Ledoux. From Ledoux' *L'Architecture Considérée...*, 1804.

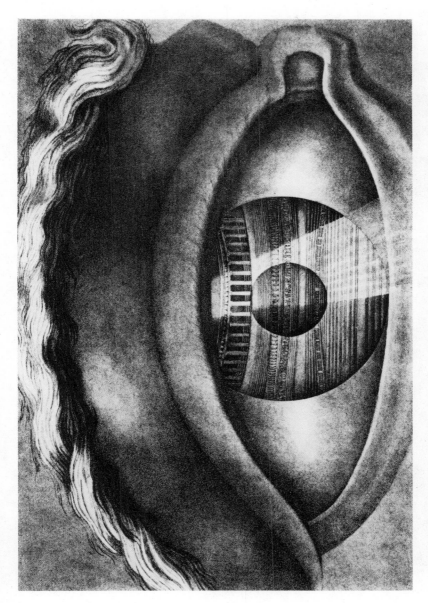

10. "Vue du Théâtre de Besançon." By Claude-Nicolas Ledoux. From Ledoux' *L'Architecture Considérée...*, 1804.

11. "Gilles." By Antoine Watteau, 1721.

12. "Polichinelle (1820)." By Maurice Sand. From Sand's *Masques et Buffons*, 1860.

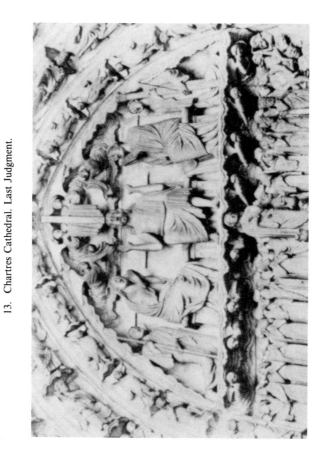

13. Chartres Cathedral. Last Judgment.

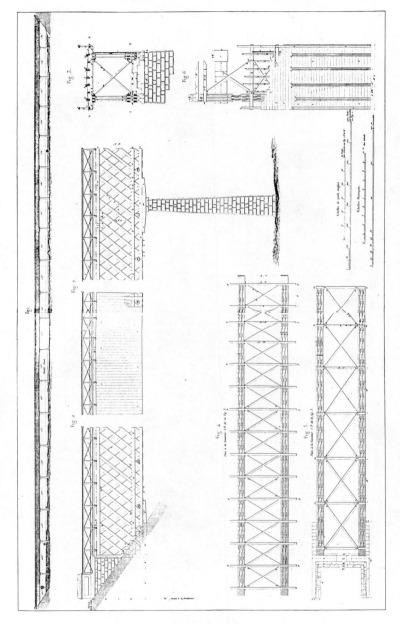

14. Bridge in Richmond, Virginia. Bridge uses truss system devised by Ithiel Town. From César Daly's *Revue Générale* I (1840).

15. Scene from a model *Crèche.* System devised by Jules Delbruck. From César Daly's *Revue Générale* VIII (1849).

16. Palais Royal. From César Daly's *Motifs Historiques*. Vol. II, 1863. Detail.

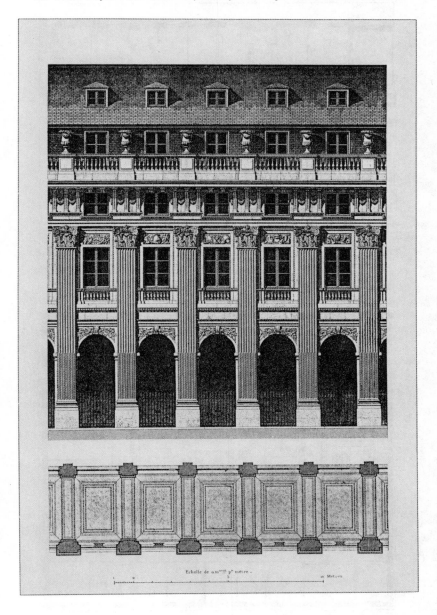

17. Reform Club. By Sir Charles Barry. From César Daly's Revue
    Générale XV (1857). Basement and second floor plan.

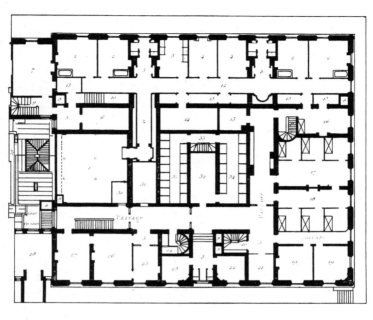

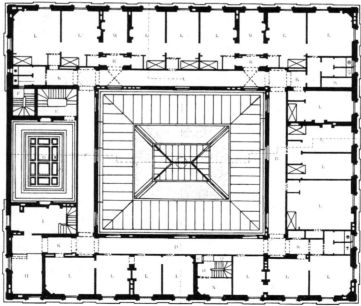

18. Travellers' Club. By Sir Charles Barry, 1830-32. From César
Daly's *Revue Générale* I (1840). Plans and elevations.

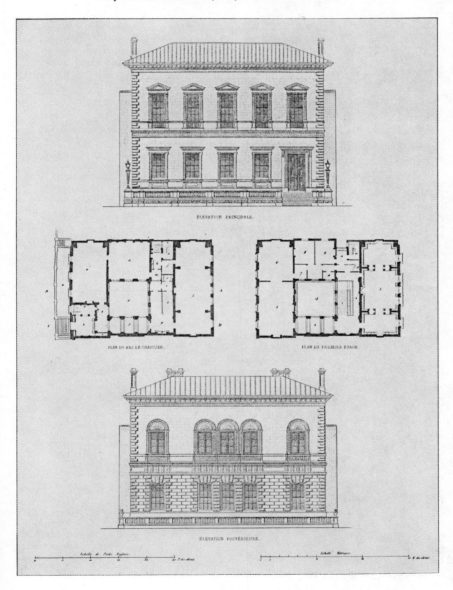

19. Plate Depicting Skulls on a Comparative Basis. From the *Encyclopédie Méthodique*, 1792.

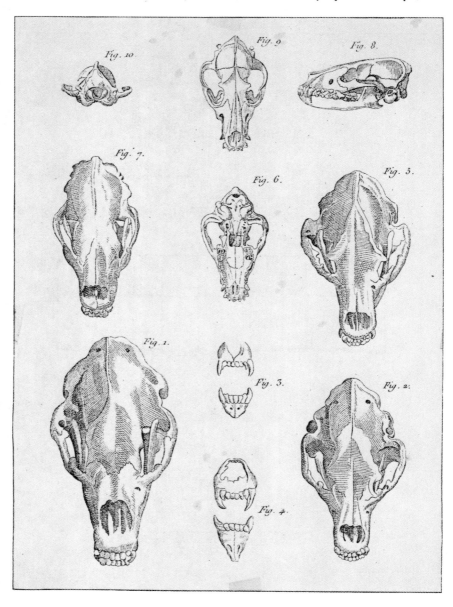

20. Musculature of the Body. By Georges Cuvier. From the *Encyclopédie Méthodique*.

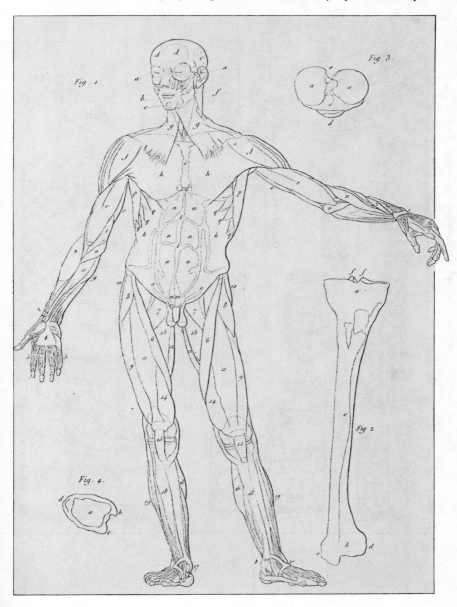

21. Fragments of Romanesque Architecture. By Arcisse de Caumont. From the *Cours d'Archéologie*, published in the *Bulletin Monumental* II (1837).

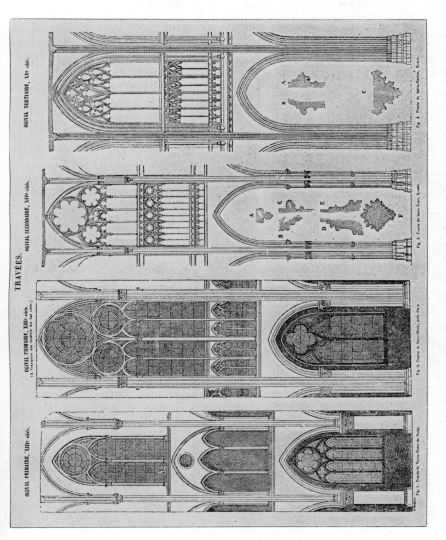

22. Travées. By Louis Batissier. From his *Histoire de l'Art Monumental,* reprinted in César Daly's *Revue Générale* VI (1845-46).

23. Synoptic Tables of Different Architectonic Elements of the Middle Ages. By Louis Batissier. From his *Histoire de l'Art Monumental,* reprinted in César Daly's *Revue Générale* VI (1845-46).

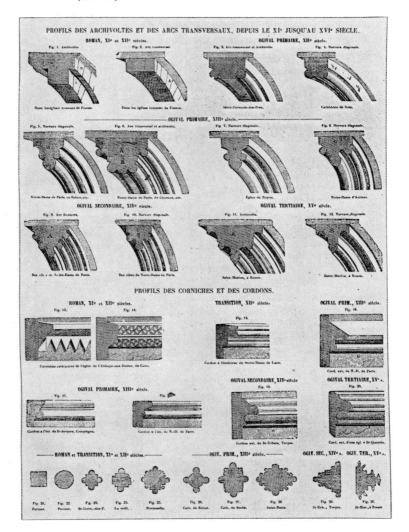

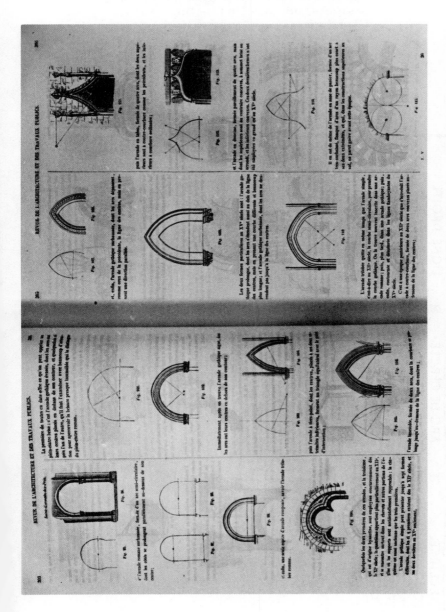

24. "Deuxième Instruction du Comité Historique: Monuments Fixes—Civilisations Chrétiennes." By Prosper Merimée, Albert Lenoir, Charles Lenormant. From César Daly's *Revue Générale* V (1844). Sample pages.

25. "Table of the Geometrical and Successive Generation of the
Style-Types of Architecture." By César Daly. From his
"L'Architecture de l'Avenir," preface to *Motifs Historiques,*
second edition (1869).

TABLEAU
DE LA GÉNÉRATION GÉOMÉTRIQUE ET SUCCESSIVE
DES STYLES-TYPES D'ARCHITECTURE [1].

	STYLES.	MOUVEMENT Géométrique des Styles.	SYSTEME DES IDÉES SOCIALES				
			Religion.	Politique.	Droit.	Etc.	Etc.
STYLES PRIMITIFS. — LIGNE DROITE. Base géométrique, comprenant — La ligne droite & ses combinaisons. structive & esthétique. (Surfaces planes [3]. Elévations [2]:	1° L'ÉGYPTIEN.	Évolution rectiligne de premier degré.	Polythéisme [4].	Unité puissante, Liberté nulle. Etc., &c., &c.	"	"	"
	2° LE GREC.	Évolution rectiligne de deuxième degré.		Liberté puissante, Unité nulle. Etc., &c., &c.	"	"	
MIXTE.	LE ROMAIN.	Transition des styles rectilignes aux styles curvilignes.		Mixte.	"		
STYLES SECONDAIRES. — ARC DE CERCLE. Base géométrique, comprenant — L'Arc de cercle & ses composés. structive & esthétique. (Surfaces planes, cylindriques ; Dômes. Elévations :	1° { LE BYZANTIN (en Orient). LE ROMAN (en Occident).	Évolutions curvilignes simples, du premier degré.	Monothéisme.	L'Ordre par l'Autorité compressive.			
	2° { L'OGIVAL (en Orient). L'OGIVAL (en Occident).	Évolutions curvilignes simples, du deuxième degré.					
MIXTE.	LE MODERNE (depuis la Renaissance jusqu'à nos jours).	Transition des styles curvilignes simples aux styles curvilignes supérieurs.		Mixte.			
STYLES TERTIAIRES. — ELLIPSE. Base géométrique, comprenant — Les Arcs elliptiques & leurs composés. structive & esthétique (Surfaces planes, cylindriques ; Dômes, &c. &. Elévations:	1° L'ELLIPTIQUE (?)	Évolution curviligne supérieure, du premier degré.		L'Ordre par la Liberté.			
	2° (?)	. . . . . .					

(Voir les notes à la page suivante.)

26. Tomb of Admiral Dumont d'Urville. By Claude-Simon
Constant-Dufeux. From César Daly's *Revue Générale* VIII
(1849). Elevation.

27. "Table of Railway Lines in the United States." From the *Railway Magazine*, reprinted in César Daly's *Revue Générale* II (1841).

Numéros d'ordre	ÉTATS dans lesquels LES CHEMINS sont situés	DÉSIGNATION DES CHEMINS.	INDICATION des années dans lesquelles les chemins ont été Concédés.	Ouverts.	LONGUEURS Totales.	Exploitées.	Pente maximum.	Rayons minimum.	POIDS et dimensions des RAILS.	MOTEUR et nombre de locomotives employées.	FRAIS D'ÉTABLISSEMENT pour la ligne entière.	par kilomètre.	Observations.
					kilom.	kilom.	millim	mètres.	mill. mill.		fr.	fr.	
1	New-York	Mohawk and Hudson	1826	1832	28.97	28.97	6.27	213.5	64 × 29	4 locomot.	5 933 058	204 702	De Albany à Schenectady, 2 Pl. incl.
2		Saratoga and Schenectady	1831	1833	34.60	34.60	5.04	132.5	64 × 43	2 id. ...	4 783 413	91 566	
3		Troy and Ballston	1833	1833	40.23	40.23	6.27	396.3	38 × 16	2 id....	2 524 536	62 710	
4		Saratoga and Whitehall	1834	»	48.22	»	7.41	»	»	»	3 444 446	48 296	Commencé et suspendu.
5		Utica and Schenectady	1833	1836	425.42	425.42	3.99	213.5	64 × 49	8 locomot.	9 255 986	73 758	
6		Syracuse and Utica	1836	1839	84.76	84.76	5.70	579.5	58 × 49	4 id...	3 006 812	39 052	
7		Auburn and Syracuse	1835	1839	44.84	44.84	5.70	305.0	64 × 49	3 id....	3 266 076	78 054	
8		Skaneateles	1836	»	8.45	»	30.40	483.0	»	Chevaux..	155 559	18 404	Rails en bois.
9		Syracuse and Onondaga	1836	1837	7.24	7.24	93.00	64.05	58 × 16	Id....	221 407	30 396	Conduisant à des carrières.
10		Auburn and Rochester	1836	»	125.52	»	5.70	244.0	20 kil.	»	7 777 778	64 927	
11		Tonawanda	1832	1837	51.50	51.50	6.52	437.5	64 × 16	3 locomot.	2 377 451	50 444	Rochester à Batavia.
12		Rochester	1832	1833	4.83	4.83	»	»	51 × 13	Chevaux..	455 559	32 208	Rochester à Carthage.
13		Scotisville and Caledonia	1836	1838	12.87	12.87	6.84	566.0	»	Id....	163 946	12 880	Sans fer.
14		Medina and Darien	1834	1836	32.49	32.49	49 95	»	»	Id....	400 800	3 450	Id. de Médina à Pembroke.
15		Buffalo aux chutes du Niagara	1834	1837	35.72	35.72	13.20	422.0	51 × 13	3 locomot.	1 041 099	23 943	
16		Buffalo and Blackrock	1833	1834	4.92	4.92	»	»	54 × 13	Chevaux..	400 800	20 439	
17		Lockpool aux chutes du Niagara	1834	1837	38.63	38.83	9.88	76.3	58 × 16	2 locomot.	831 100	26 026	
18		Lewiston branch	1835	1837	4.56	4.36	28.50	»	64 × 16	Chevaux..	434 200	28 978	De L. et N. Railway à Lewiston.
19		Zithaca and Owego	1828	1834	46.27	46.27	5.70	742.4	58 × 16	4 loc. et ch.	2 985 879	64 447	3 Plans inclinés.
20		New-York and Harlem	1834	1839	42.47	42.47	7.60	48.30	64 × 16	4 loc. et ch.	6 066 073	497 701	Chemin de fer le plus coûteux des E.-U.
21		New-York and Albany	1832	»	226.48	226.48	5.70	457.5	»	»	14 596 544	63 400	Commencé seulement.
22		New-York and Erie	1832	»	730.64	»	44.40	505.0	»	»	31 444 088	42 568	En exécution.
23		Brooklyn and Jamaica	1832	1836	47.70	47.70	45.20	4 220.0	49 kil.	»	2 477 784	124 346	
24		Long-Island	1834	1837	433.57	24.87	5.04	4 747.7	27.75 kil.	5 locomot.	8 945 905	64 475	Jamaïque à Greenport.
25		Hampstead branch	»	1830	5.62	3.62	»	»	58 × 16	Chevaux..	67 440	48 608	
26		Hudson and Berkshire	1832	1838	55.92	55.92	43.20	244.0	64 × 16	3 locomot.	2 799 997	50 053	Hudson à Westorkbridge.
27		Catskill and Canaphare	»	1839	445.87	24.44	45.20	422.0	38 × 16	4 id....	5 040 000	45 476	
28	New-England	Quincy	»	1827	6.44	6.44	3.43	»	64 × 13	Chevaux..	302 400	46 950	Le plus ancien chemin des E.-U.
29		Boston and Lowell	1830	1835	44.44	44.44	1.90	864.5	29 kil.	7 locomot.	9 346 400	225 407	
30		Charlestown branch	»	1839	2.45	2.43	2.66	467.8	24 id.	»	546 545	244 544	Du B. et L. Railway à Charlestown.
31		Nashua and Lowell	1835	1856	22.95	22.93	2.66	274.5	24.50 id.	3 locomot.	4 804 573	79 925	
32		Boston and Portland	1835	1839	54.79	54.79	»	»	29 id.	3 id....	2 735 870	86 634	B. et L. Railway à la ligne de N. Hampshire.
33		Boston and Maine	1858	1839	24.44	44.48	»	»	29 id.	»	4 247 400	54 645	New-Hampshire à Exeter.
34		Eastern (Massachusetts)	1836	1838	64.45	40.24	6.63	805.2	22.50 kil.	8 locomot.	7 459 040	442 680	Boston à Newbury Port et à la ligne de New-Hampshire.
35		Marblehead branch	»	1839	4.83	4.83	»	»	»	Chevaux..			
36		Eastern (New-Hampshire)	1836	»	24.95	»	6.63	4 640.4	22.50 kil.	»	4 562 400	62 600	
37		Boston and Providence	1831	1835	67.59	67.59	6.93	4 850.0	27.50 id.	11 locom.	10 095 624	448 493	
38		Dedham branch	»	»	5.22	5.22	6.27	349.5	54 × 16	Chevaux..			
39		Taunton branch	»	1836	47.70	47.70	5.34	»	27.50 kil.	2 locomot.	4 548 074	76 406	Mansfield à Taunton.
40		New-Bebford and Taunton	»	1839	52.49	»	»	»	27.50 id.	»	2 046 000	63 600	
41		New-York Providence and Boston	1832	1857	76.44	76.44	5.70	945.0	29 id.	5 locomot.	42 965 540	469 489	Providence à Stonington.
42		Boston and Worcester	1831	1833	70.84	70.84	5.70	294.0	49.25 id.	40 id....	9 582 199	426 036	
43		Milbury branch	»	»	5.23	5.23	»	»	»	Chevaux..			
44		Western	1833	1839	488.26	67.74	45.20	347.84	27.73 kil.	8 locomot.	22 295 455	448 240	Worcester à Westockbridge.
45		Norwich and Worcester	1832	1840	94.95	94.95	5.80	505.0	28.00 id.	6 id....	7 648 009	80 504	
46		New-Haven and Hartford	1835	1839	59.55	59.55	»	»	4 id....		3 888 864	63 270	
		À reporter			2 908.49	4 606.74	....	......	....	443 locom.	244 976 959		

28. July Monument. By Louis Duc, 1840. From César Daly's
Revue Générale 1 (1840). Elevation.

29. Colonne Vendôme. By Jacques Gondoin, 1805. View.

30. Project for the Elephant of the Bastille. By J.-A. Alavoine, circa 1810. View.

31. "Villas Italiennes par Palladio." By Jean-Nicolas-Louis Durand.
From his *Recueil et Parallèle des Edifices de Tout Genre*, 1799.

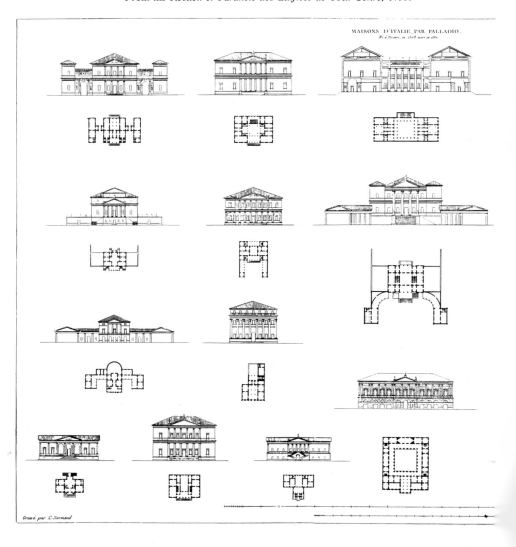

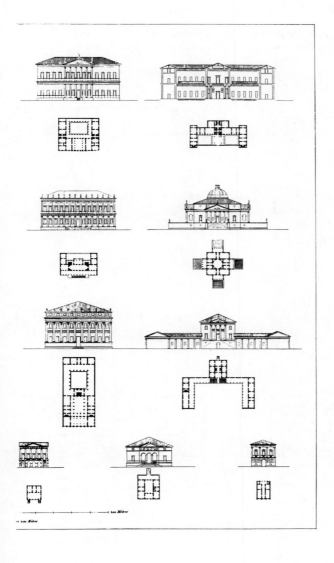

32. Plate illustrating suburban villa plans of the second class. By César Daly.
   From his *L'Architecture Privée au XIXe Siècle sous Napoléon III*, vol. II (1863).

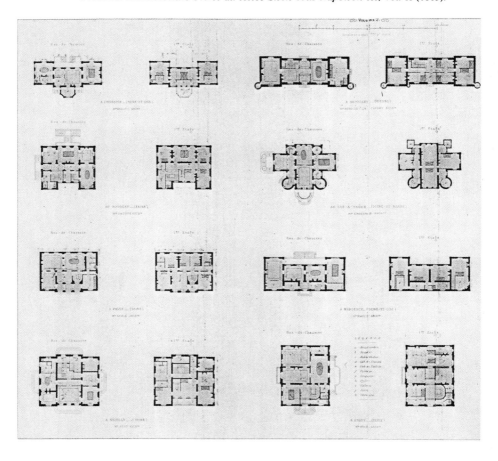

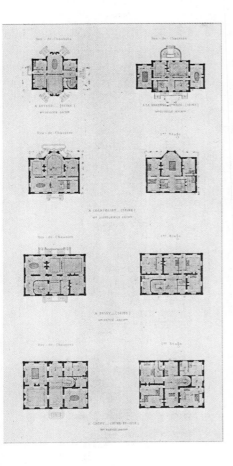

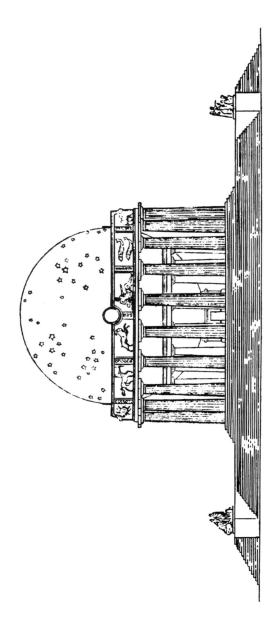

33. House of a Cosmopolite. By Charles Vaudoyer, 1802. From Charles Landon's *Le Symbolisme dans l'Art*. Reprinted in César Daly's *La Semaine des Constructeurs* VII (1882-83).

34. Laiterie. By Joseph Nicolle. From César Daly's *Revue Générale* XVII (1859).

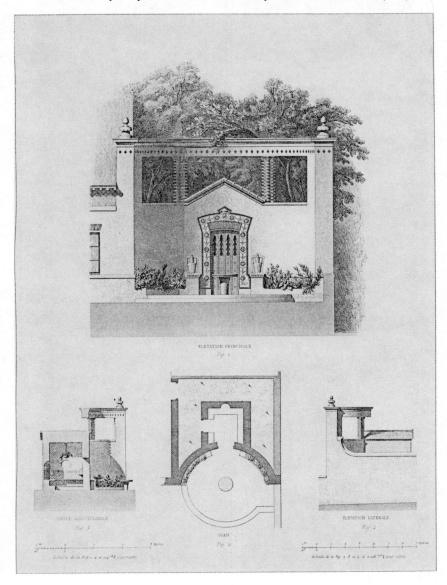

35. "North façade of Chartres Cathedral." By César Daly, 1837. From César Daly's *Revue Générale* IV (1843).

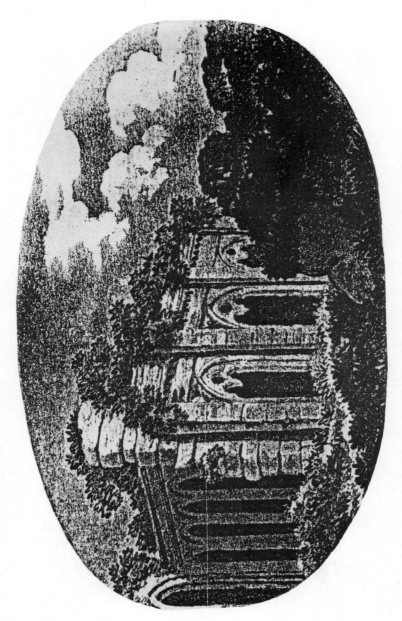

36. "Landscape with a Ruin." By William Gilpin. From Gilpin's *Observations Relative Chiefly to Picturesque Beauty ... Cumberland and Westmoreland*, 1788.

37. North facade of Chartres Cathedral. By Alexandre de Laborde. From de Laborde's *Les Monuments de la France*, 1836.

38. Chartres Cathedral. Plan.

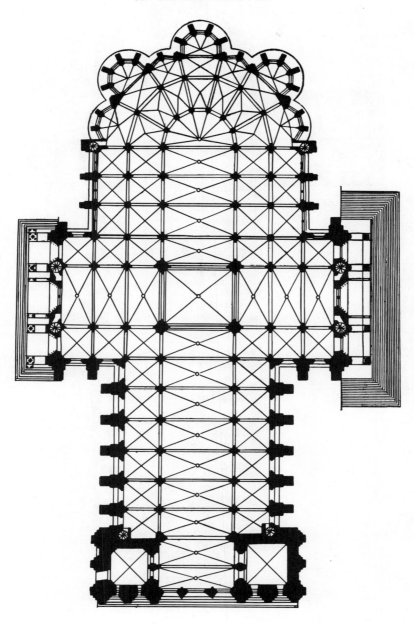

39. Albi Cathedral. Plan.

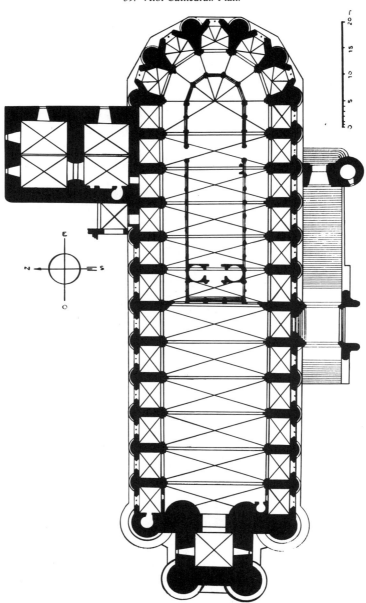

40. Albi Cathedral. Baldaquin. State in 1860.

41. Albi Cathedral. West facade. Rendering by César Daly, 1846.

42. Albi Cathedral. Section. Rendering by César Daly, 1846.

43. Albi Cathedral. Schemes for the Cathedral's completion. Designed and rendered by César Daly, 1849.

44. Albi Cathedral. Tower. Completed circa 1490.

45. Albi Cathedral. Towers on the chevet. Designed by César Daly.
Photograph taken circa 1870.

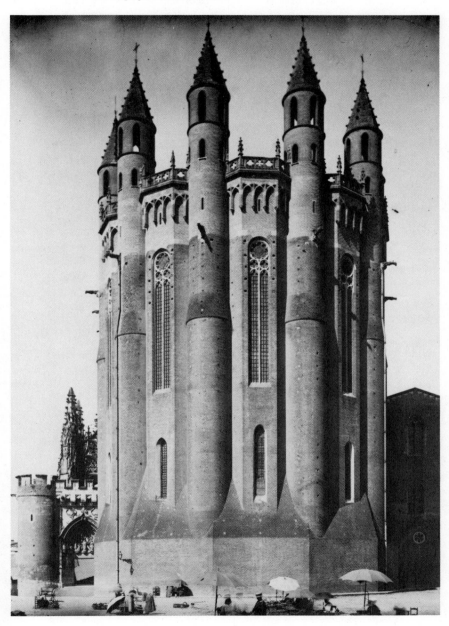

46. Albi Cathedral. Sketch detail of the Baldaquin. By César Daly, 1860.

47. Albi Cathedral. Baldaquin with nineteenth century vault.
By César Daly. Vaulting dating from 1863.

48. Albi Cathedral. View of Baldaquin. From Viollet-le-Duc's *Dictionnaire Raisonnée*, 1860.

49. Albi Cathedral. Interior with *jubé and choir*.

50. Basilica of San Francesco, Assisi. Plan, lower church.

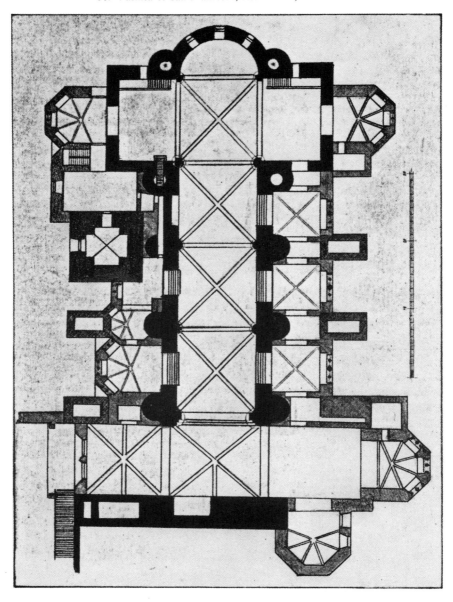

51. Church of Saint-Jacques, Toulouse. Plan.

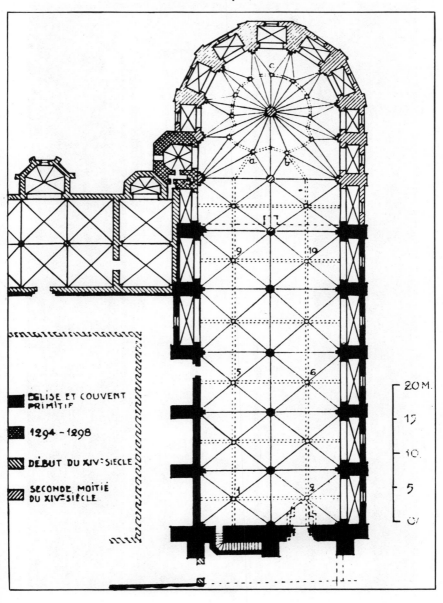

ÉGLISE ET COUVENT PRIMITIF

1294 - 1298

DÉBUT DU XIV=SIÈCLE

SECONDE MOITIÉ DU XIV=SIÈCLE

20 M.

15

10

5

0

52. Bibliotheque Sainte-Geneviève. By Henri Labrouste, designed circa 1840. Plan.

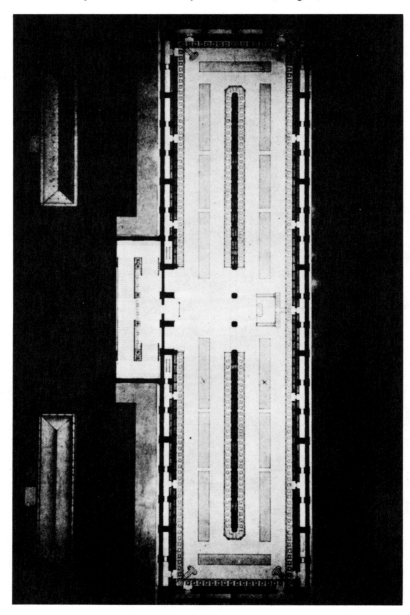

53. Square Sainte-Cécile, Albi. By César Daly, circa 1863. Scheme I. (Drawing: author)

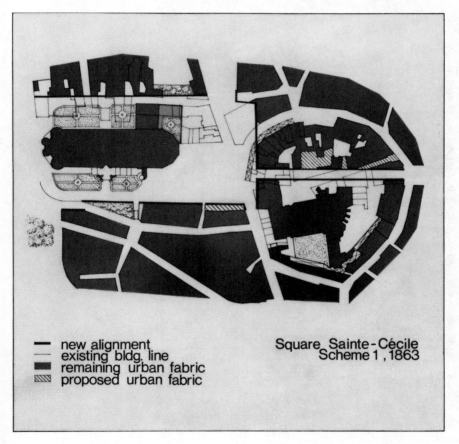

— new alignment
— existing bldg. line
■ remaining urban fabric
▨ proposed urban fabric

Square Sainte-Cécile
Scheme 1 , 1863

54. Panorama des Champs-Elysées, Paris. By Jacques-Ignaz Hittorff, 1842.
Section. Published in César Daly's *Revue Générale* II (1841).

55. Belvedere, Morfontaine. From Alexandre de Laborde's *Nouveaux Jardins de la France*, 1808.

56. "Vue Aérienne." From César Daly's *Revue Générale* III (1842).

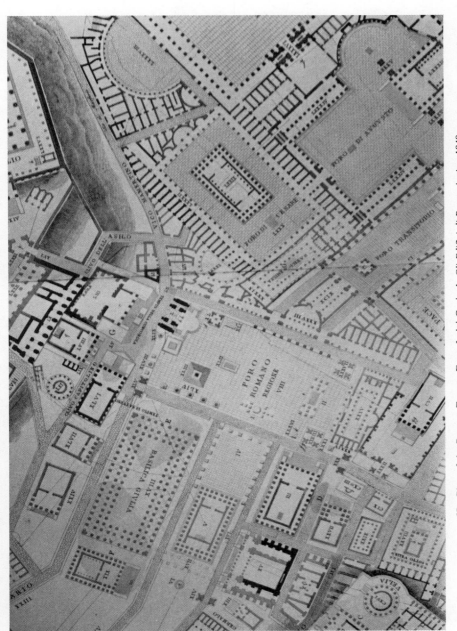

57. Plan of the Roman Forum. From Luigi Canina's *Gli Edifici di Roma Antica*, 1848.

58. "Archeological Plan of Paris." From Ferdinand de Guilhermy's *Itinéraire Archéologique de Paris.*

59. Plan of the Faubourg Saint-Antoine. From Turgot's *Plan de Louis de Bretez*, 1739.

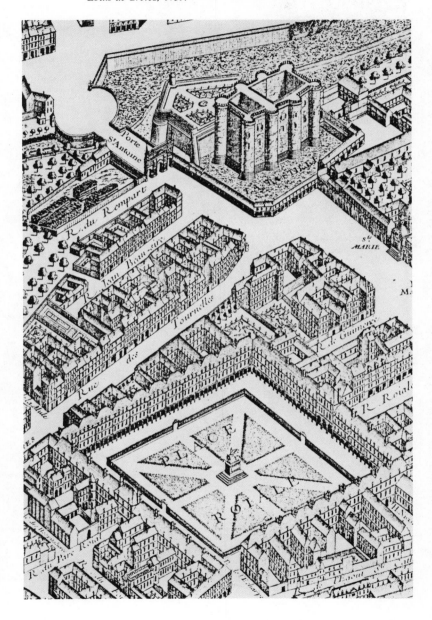

60. "Projected Embellishments for the City of Paris." From Pierre Patte's *Monuments Erigés à la Gloire de Louis XV*, 1765.

61. Project for the Palace of the King of Rome and the Planning of
Paris. By Charles Percier and Pierre Fontaine. From Percier and
Fontaine's *Résidences des Souverains*. 1833.

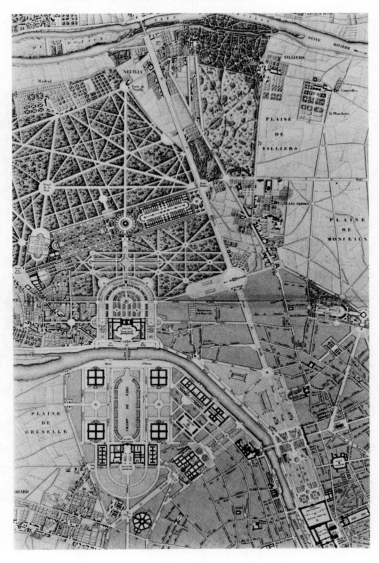

62. The Comic Scene. By Sebastino Serlio. From *Il Trattato dell'Architettura,* Book II.

63. The Tragic Scene. By Sebastino Serlio. From *Il Trattato dell'Architettura,* Book II.

64. The Satiric Scene. By Sebastiano Serlio. From *Il Trattato dell'Architettura,* Book II.

65. Versailles. By Louis Levau and Andre Le Nôtre, circa 1675. Plan.

66. Parc Monceau. By Louis-Carrogis Carmontelle, 1783. Plan.

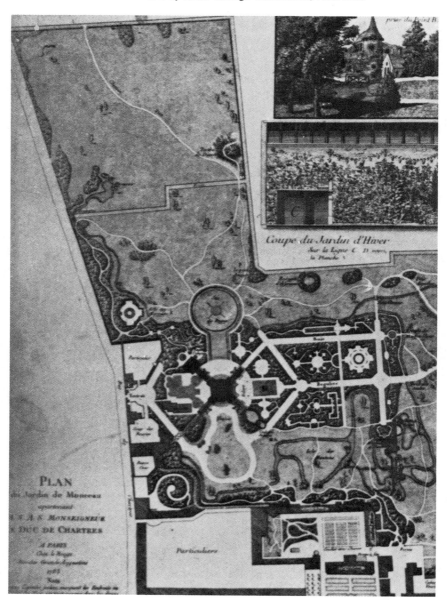

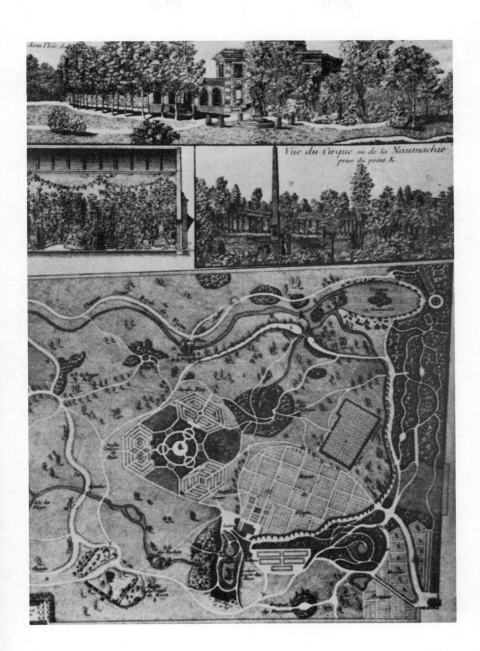

Vue du Cirque ou de la Naumachie
prise du point K.

67. Plan of the City of Paris with Modifications Proposed by M.
Perreymond. From César Daly's *Revue Générale* IV (1843).

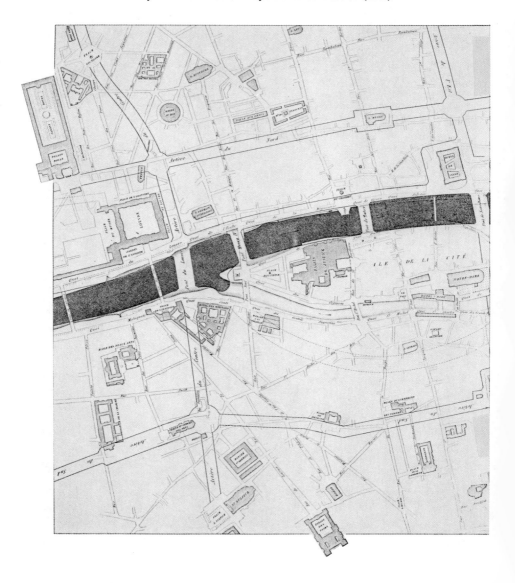

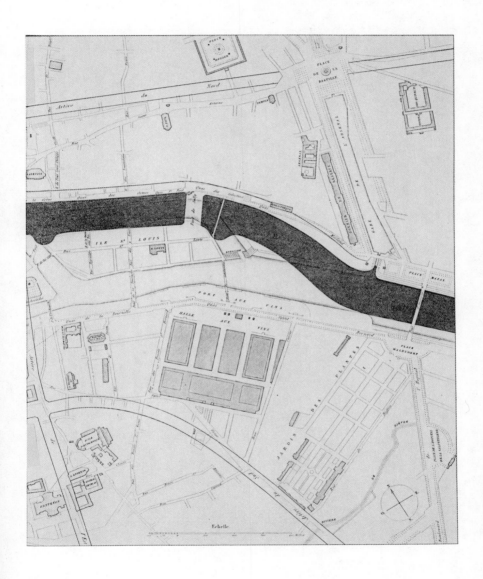

Echelle

68. Frontispiece to *L'Architecture Privée au Dix-Neuvième Siècle.* By César Daly, 1863.

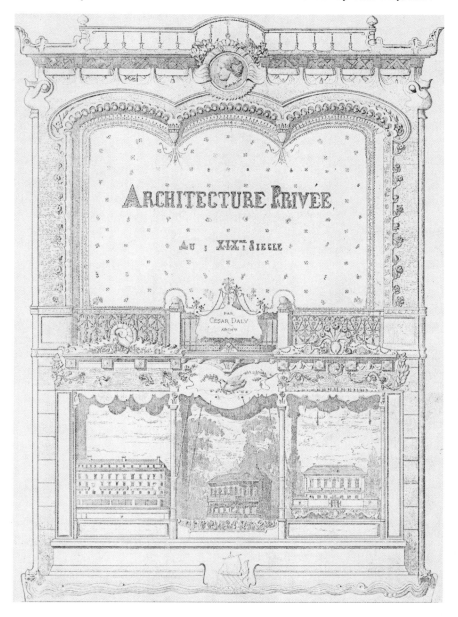

69. "*Hotel Privé* de la Deuxieme Classe." By Ruprich Robert.
Facade and detail. From César Daly's *L'Architecture Privée*.

70. "Maison à Loyer." By M. Lecomte. From César Daly's *L'Architecture Privée.*

71. Teatro Olimpico. By Andrea Palladio, circa 1580. View of interior.

72. Villa Daly, Wissous. By César Daly. Plan. Improvements made between years 1860-90. Plan includes major frontal and reciprocal readings. Diagram made from present-day condition of property. (Drawing: author)

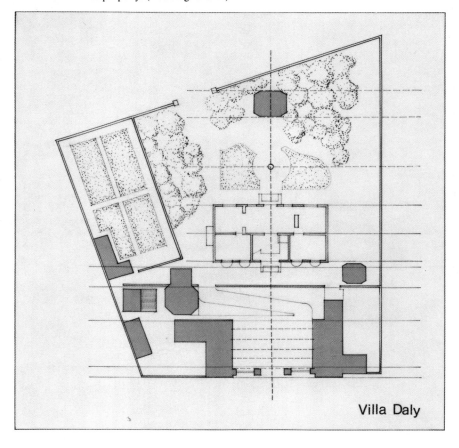

Villa Daly

73. Villa Daly. Entrance lodges.

74. Villa Daly. Front façade.

75. Villa Daly. Enfilade of reception rooms.

76. Palais de Justice, Paris. By Louis Duc, completed 1869. View of Harlay façade.

77. Bibliothèque Sainte-Geneviève, Paris. By Henri Labrouste, completed 1850. View.

78. Bibliothèque Sainte-Geneviève. Corner detail.

79. Bourse, Paris. By Antoine Brongniart, 1808. View. Note: side wings added in the twentieth century.

80. Hotel des Postes, Paris. By Julien Guadet, 1882. Detail of facade.

Notes

Introduction

1. Friedrich Nietzsche, *The Use and Abuse of History* (Indianapolis: The Library of Liberal Arts, 1977), pp. 4-6.

2. Hayden White, *Metahistory: The Historical Imagination in Nineteenth Century Europe.* (Baltimore: Johns Hopkins Press, 1973), pp. 1-2.

3. Herder speaks of the progress of mankind, or *Humanität,* as terminating in the revelation of God's kindgom on earth. Especially important in this regard is Book VII, "The Spread of Christianity," of the *Reflections on the Philosophy of the History of Mankind* (Chicago: University of Chicago Press, 1968), particularly pp. 269-70. Arthur Lovejoy's essay, "Herder and the Enlightenment Philosophy of History," focuses on the evolutionary aspect of Herder's progressive view, and although failing to address the issue of Biblical sources, recognizes in Herder's philosophy a vitalistic component akin to spiritualism. *Essays in the History of Ideas* (New York: G.P. Putnam's Sons, 1960), pp. 167-68.

4. C.J. Friederich, in his introduction to Hegel's *Philosophy of History* (New York: Dover Publications, 1956), p. 3, speaks of the centrality of the Biblical precedent to Hegel's philosophy. Indicative of this is the emphasis that Hegel places on Christ as a "world-historical" figure.

5. Nietzsche, p. 52.

6. Ibid., p. 20.

7. Roland Stromberg, *European Intellectual History Since 1789* (Englewood Cliffs, NJ: Prentice-Hall, Inc., 1975), p. 18.

8. René Wellek's *History of Criticism* (New Haven: CT: Yale Univ. Press, 1955) cites numerous examples of the use of biography to counter the generalizing, holistic tendencies of contemporary philosophy and culture. See particularly vol. 2 (1955), p. 55 (on the Schlegels) and p. 138 (on Wordsworth), and vol. 3 (1965), pp. 34-35 (on Saint-Beuve) and p. 105 (on Carlyle).

9. David Watkin, *Morality and Architecture: The Development of a Theme in Architectural History and Theory from the Gothic Revival to the Modern Movement* (Oxford: Clarendon Press, 1977); *Thomas Hope (1769-1831) and the Neoclassical Idea* (London: John Murray, 1968).

    The connection between Watkin's use of biography and critical history, countering Pevsnerian functionalism, was noted by Gavin Stamp in his review of *Morality and Architecture* in *Architectural Design,* 48: 5-6, (May-June 1978), 296, who states, "In the place of the ice-hard, anaesthetic moralism that he [Watkin] so roundly condemns, the reader is offered one alternative: the sublime genius of individual talents (like Thomas Hope or Edwin Lutyens)..."

10. The idealism of mnemosyne and rhetoric is discussed by Francis Yates in *The Art of Memory* (London: Routledge and Kegan, 1966), pp. 36-37. M.H. Abrams also treats expressive and mimetic systems and their relationship to Platonic and Horatian rhetorical structures, in *The Mirror and the Lamp* (New York: Oxford Univ. Press, 1953), pp. 21-26.

11. The problematical relationship between the progressive critic, loosely associated with the notion of the avant-gardist, and the decadence of a 'transitional period' is discussed by Renato Poggioli, in *The Theory of the Avant-Garde* (New York: Harper and Row, 1971), p. 77.

12. Northrop Frye's dependence upon biological and anatomical analogies with regard to literary analysis is fundamental to his "Polemical Introduction" to *The Anatomy of Criticism.* Frye states, "It occurs to me that literary criticism is now in such a state of naive induction as we find in a primitive science.... Criticism seems to be badly in need of a coordinating principle, a central hypothesis which, like the theory of evolution is biology, will see the phenomena it deals with as parts of a whole." (Princeton, NJ: Princeton Univ. Press, 1957), pp. 15-16.

13. Roland Barthes, *The Pleasure of the Text,* trans. Richard Miller (New York: Hill and Wang, 1975), pp. 7-10.

14. René Wellek and Austin Warren, *The Theory of Literature* (New York: Harvest Books, 1970), p. 43.

Chapter 1

1. Information on John Daley (Daly) is kept at the Service Historique de l'Armée, Château de Vincennes, carton no. 1806. In London, Daley's name is included on the "Liste Nominative de Guerre Anglaise..." ADM 103 467, item 14, at the Public Records Office, Kew.

2. For a discussion of life in Verdun, see Edward Fraser's *Napoleon the Gaoler* (London: Methuen and Co., 1914), Michael Lewis' *Napoleon and His British Captives* (London: George Allen and Unwin, 1962), and Gaston Varenne's "Les Anglais à Verdun sous le Consulat et l'Empire" *Le Pays Lorrain* XXIII:12 (December 1925) pp. 529-544. Fraser discusses the social life of the English captives, describing one English Verdun casino as Hogarthian. Varenne turns to the women describing the mistresses who follow the soldiers to Fountainebleau in 1814 as "Les Epouses de Fontainebleau."

3. César Daly's birth certificate is in the City Archives of Verdun, and in the Archives Departmentales, Bar-le-Duc.

4. Marriage certificate M-250, dated 16 December 1812, Archives de la Seine, Fonds Ancien, Rue du Temple.

5. For a catalogue of Denis Daly's library, see James Vallance, *A Catalogue of the Late Right Honorable Denis Daly* (Dublin: John Archer, 1792).

6. Letter to Mr. William White, 18 September 1888, Archives of the Royal Institute of British Architects, uncatalogued.

7. A catalogue of the art collection of Charles-Alexander de Calonne is included under Appendix II, in Robert Lacour-Gayet's *Calonne: Financier, Réformateur, Contre-*

Revolutionnaire (Paris: Librairie Hachette, 1963), p. 484. At the London sale of 1795, the collection numbered "10 Titian, 3 Veronese, 6 Tintoretto, 3 Giorgione, 1 Raphael, 1 Leonardo da Vinci, 1 Corregio, 4 Murillo, 10 Poussin, 5 Claude Lorrain, 14 Rubens, 8 Van Dyck, 7 Rembrandt, 7 Teniers, etc.".

8. "Mr. Daly and the War," *The Architect* V (4 Feb. 1871), 63.

9. John Daly's name does not appear in the naval registry of warranted officers dated 1824, Public Records Office, Kew.

10. For listings of faculty at the Collège Royale de Douai, see *Dossiers des Anciens Fonctionnaires des Enregistrements Primaire, Secondaire, et Supérieure, XIX* S., Archives Nationales, Série F[17] cartons 20 062 (Avignon), 21 231 (Mallet).

11. Daly is not included in listings of students at the Ecole. For student listings in the Ecole des Beaux-Arts, see Archives Nationales, Série AJ[52] cartons 237, 239, 244.

12. Jean Canu, *Barbey d' Aurevilly* (Paris: Robert Laffont, 1965), pp. 51-52. According to Canu, Daly remained in Caen in the circle of Barbey until 1832.

13. Letter to Mr. William White, 18 Sept. 1888.

14. David Pinckney, *The French Revolution of 1830* (Princeton, NJ: Princeton Univ. Press, 1972), p. 53.

15. In this regard, I refer to Edmund Burke's *Reflections of the Revolution in France* (1790) whose conservative political posture, i.e., pro-monarchy, was based on an argument stressing the continuity of national values. Burke and Charles-Alexander de Calonne were friends. De Calonne's *Considerations on the Past and Future State of France* was published in 1791 the year after Burke's work. De Calonne's is the more practical of the two, more economic and less philosophical.

16. H. Prentout, "Caen in 1830", *Revue d'Histoire Moderne* 6 (1931), pp. 101-103.

17. Nikolaus Pevsner, "English Antiquarians", in *Some Architectural Writers of the Nineteenth Century* (Oxford: Clarendon Press, 1972), p. 22.

18. Louis Hautecoeur, *Histoire de l'Architecture Classique en France*, VI (Paris: Editions A. et J. Picard et Cie, 1955), p. 293.

19. Jules L. Puech, *La Vie et l'Oeuvre de Flora Tristan* (Paris: Librairie des Sciences Sociales et Politiques, 1925), p. 330.

20. Claude Bellander, Jacques Godechot, Pierre Guiral, et Fernand Terrou, *L'Histoire Générale de la Presse Française* (Paris: Presses Universitaires de France, 1969), II, 130-32.

21. The election of the Comité Permanent des Architectes on 15 April 1848 to select a candidate to run for election to the Constituent Lists the following results: Labrouste, 237 votes, Duban, 215, Gilbert Aîné, 212, Vaudoyer, 180, Blouet, 173, Constant-Dufeux, 160, Daly, 158, Nicolle, 147, Huvé, 138, Grillon, 124, Lebas, 111, Viollet-le-Duc, 103. *Le Moniteur des Architectes* I :24 (15 April 1848), pp. 189-91. Daly was far from the victor in the elections, but after the first six candidates declined to run, Daly became candidate. He is listed as a socialist candidate in *La Démocratie Pacifique*, Ire S. X:106 (23 April 1848). Daly was not, however elected to the Constituent. See also Hélène Lipstadt, "César Daly et l'Habitation", *Architecture, Mouvement, et Continuité* 42 (March 1977), 39 n. 8.

23. Archives Nationales, Séries F[19] carton 7220; Archives Départementales du Tarn 1 V 418.

24. Jean Laran, *La Cathédrale d'Albi* (Paris: Henri Laurens, 1931), p. 46.

25. Letter to the Prefect of the Tarn, 14 July 1851, Archives Départementales du Tarn, carton I V 439.

26. Letter to the Prefect of the Tarn, 16 February 1855, Archives Départementales du Tarn, carton 1 V 418.

27. "The Late M. César Daly", *The Builder* LXVI: 2659 (20 Jan. 1894), 46.

28. César Daly, "De la Liberté dans l'Art: Lettre à M. Ludovic Vitet," *La Démocratie Pacifique* X:30 (4 Feb. 1848), cols. 10-12; X:31 (5 Feb. 1848), cols. 8-11 and *Revue Générale de l'Architecture* (hereafter abbreviated as RGA)VII (1847), 392-408.

29. Daly's progress was published in the Fourierist *Bulletin de la Société de Colonisation Européo-Americaine au Texas* (Brussels: J.-H. Briand, 1855-57). This sequence of events does not replicate Daly's own as published the *Revue Générale.* The *Bulletin* records that he left New York in the company of Considérant on 14 April, arriving in New Orleans on 28 April, reaching Houston on 30 May, and La Réunion about 18 June. Daly in the *Revue* states that he travelled down the Ohio and Mississippi Rivers to New Orleans, where he met Considérant and others. The *Bulletin* also mentions the "chefs d'ordre" at the communal meeting of 22 June 1855, as Considérant, Cantagrel, Savardan, Daly, Cousin, Roger. However, Daly does not appear in the "Conseil d'Administration" by the October meeting. César Daly, "Introduction" RGA XIV (1856), 10.

30. For histories of the colony at La Réunion, see George Henry Santerre, *White Cliffs of Dallas: The Story of La Réunion* (Dallas: Book Craft, 1955), and Margaret F. and William J. Hammond, *La Réunion: A French Settlement in Texas* (Dallas: Royal Publishing Co., 1958).

31. César Daly, "Introduction," RGA XIV (1856), 10.

32. César Daly, "A Propos de M. Viollet-le-Duc et des Réformes à l'Ecole des Beaux-Arts", RGA XXII (1864), 129-36.

33. "M. César Daly and the War", *The Architect* V (4 Feb. 1871), 63.

34. César Daly, "Introduction", RGA XXIX (1872), 3.

35. Archives Nationales, Séries F^{19} carton 7230.

36. The nominations made to the Committee of Council for the R.I.B.A. Gold Medal included George Frederick Bodley, Thomas Colleutt, Honoré Daumet, Ernest George, Richard Morris Hunt, Philip Webb, César Daly, Auguste Choisy, Fernand de Durbein, Dr. William Dorpfeld, Edward A. Freeman, and Baron Henry Geymüller. Contrary, to French learned societies, this English one recognized in Daly "an architect (who) was engaged for many years on the restoration of Albi Cathedral; but he is best known (for) his *Revue Générale de l'Architecture*...(and for his)...*Semaine de Constructeurs,* a weekly journal..." He was selected as recipient on 1 February 1892. Minutes, Royal Gold Medal Committee of Council, Archives of the R.I.B.A.

37. Peter Collins, *Changing Ideas in Modern Architecture* (Montreal: McGill University Press, 1976), p. 156. Sigfried Giedion, *Space Time, and Architecture,* 5th ed. (Cambridge, MA: Harvard Univ. Press, 1967), p. 214. Donald Drew Egbert. *Social Radicalism and the Arts* (New York: Knopf Press, 1970), pp. 140-43.

38. Giedion, p. 214.

39. Collins, p. 185.

40. Pierre Le Muet, *Manière de Bien Bastir* (Paris, 1664), introd. Anthony Blunt (Paris, 1664; rpt. Farnborough, England: Gregg International Publishing, 1972). Blunt in his introduction,

p. 1, views the first part of the treatise as a "strictly practical guide to an architect or patron to build a house," J. Cordemoy, *Nouveau Traité de Toute l'Architecture* (Paris: 1714; rpt. Farnborough, England: Gregg International Publishing, 1966). Robin Middleton emphasizes understanding Cordemoy within the structural rationalist tradition, extending out of Philibert de l'Orme. See Middleton "The Abbé de Cordemoy and the Graeco-Gothic Ideal," *Journal of the Warburg and the Courtauld Institutes* XXV: 3-4 (July-December 1962), pp. 290-93. Jean Rondelet, *Traité Théorique et Pratique de l'Art de Batir,* 7th ed. (Paris: Firmin Didot, 1864).

41.   Collins, p. 203.

42.   Jean le Rond d'Alembert and Denis Diderot, eds. *Encyclopédie ou Dictionnaire Raisonnée des Sciences, des Arts, et des Métiers,* I (Paris: Chez Briasson, David, Le Breton, (Durand, 1751), prospectus.

43.   Renato Poggioli stresses that the basic artistic impulsion which he describes as "the will to style," was based in the artist's experimental desire to expand his craft via technique. *The Theory of the Avant-Garde* (New York: Harper and Row, 1971), p. 134.

44.   It is in exactly such terms that Thomas Hastings describes the magnanimity of architecture's liberal institution *par excellence,* the Ecole des Beaux-Arts: "It is a most interesting and challenging feat that in the last few years more than half the entire number of the students in the Beaux-Arts, who were not Frenchmen, were Americans. The generous and noble way which we have been received by French authorities and students alike, without any favoritism to their own kinsmen, should always be gratefully remembered by all interested in the growth and development of American architecture." Thomas Hastings, "The Influence of the Ecole des Beaux-Arts upon American Architecture" in *Architectural Record: The Beaux-Arts Number* (January 1901), p. 66.

45.   Friedrich A. Hayek, *The Counterrevolution of Science* (Glencoe, IL.: The Free Press, 1955), pp. 104, 126, 163. Hayek notes the importance of the Ecole Polytechnique on the shaping of positivistic position in Saint-Simon, Comte, and Considérant. Egbert, p. 141, incorrectly points to Daly's ostensible enrollment in Douai's Ecole Polytechnique (no such school ever existed) in shaping Daly's interest in the social sciences.

46.   The bardic tradition was especially important in Aenghus O'Daly's discussion of the Daly family. He cites the poet Spenser who mentions the inflammatory nature of the bards who "fired the minds of the young with rebellion." John O'Donovan, ed., *The Tribes of Ireland: a Satire* (Dublin: John O'Daly, 1882), p. 19.

47.   Letter to Bodin-Légendre, from Cyprian Magne, 21 March 1871, Archives Départementales du Tarn, carton 1 V 418.

48.   Letter from the Minister of Instruction to the Légion d'Honneur, July 1859, Archives *Nationales, Séries F*^{19} carton 7230.

49.   Jules Barbey d'Aurevilly, *Oeuvres Romanesques Complètes,* (Paris: Editions Gallimard, 1966) II, p. 1429.

50.   Barbey d'Aurevilly, pp. 690-92.

51.   *The Painter of Modern Life* was first published in 1859. My references are to a volume of Baudelaire's prose selected and edited by Peter Quennell, *The Essence of Laughter* (New York: Meridian Press, 1956), pp. 46-50.

52.   Ellen Moers, *The Dandy: Brummell to Beerbohm* (New York: The Viking Press, 1960), p. 263.

53. Ibid., p. 262.

54. Martin Green in *The Children of the Sun* (London: Constable and Co., 1977), pp. 37-40, speaks of the way in which the fashion-conscious dandy introduced a new fashion, "cultic lives", hence restyled bourgeois social norms. See especially his discussion of dandy ritualization in action in England particularly in the late Victorian and particularly Edwardian periods.

55. Michel Foucault discusses the development of early modern historical method from the point of view of taxonomy. See especially *The Order of Things: An Archeology of the Human Sciences* (New York: Vintage Books, 1973), pp. 125-65.

56. Moers, pp. 14, 254.

Chapter 2

1. "De la Liberté dans l'Art" appears in the *Revue Générale* VII (1847), 392-408, and in the Fourierist periodical *La Démocratie Pacifique* X:30 (4 Feb 1848), 10-12, X:31 (5 Feb 1848), 8-11, and in the *légitimiste* journal *Revue du Monde Catholique* I (1848), 163-65.

2. Daly avoids the subject of criticism in the early numbers of the *Revue Générale*. In 1841, he advances that he prefers a purely practical to a critical journalistic stand. Daly states, "Beaucoup de mes lecteurs se sont étonnés de rencontrer dans *Le Revue* si peu de travaux de critique, et nous avons souvent reçu des observations à ce sujet... Ensuite on aurait pu se méprendre sur notre but, et confondre *La Revue* avec les publications qui n'ont pas pour object principal la diffusion des connaissances utiles." RGA II (1841), 4.

3. Vitet's discourse, apart from its publication in the *Revue Générale,* also appeared in the *Revue des Deux Mondes* XIX (1847 3e partie, 762-68. I use this pagination.

4. Ibid., 767.

5. Ibid.

6. Daly, "De la Liberté," 396.

7. Ibid., 398.

8. In this regard, I think of Daly's assertion concerning the futility of man's denial of history which he likens to suicide. Daly states, "Négliger l'histoire, le souvenir, ce qui est dû aux ancêtres, c'est donc se nier soi-même, c'est commencer le suicide." *Vue Intérieure d'un Tombeau Etrusque à Corneto* (Paris: Extrait de la Revue Générale de l'Architecture et des Travaux Publics, Imprimerie de J. Claye, 1862), p. 8. Moreover, an important parallel exists between Daly's position and Emile Durkheim's conception of "fatalistic" suicide, conceptualized as man's alienation from society's collective unconscious, of which history and tradition are important components. See especially Dominick La Capra, "Society and Suicide," *Emile Durkheim: Sociologist and Philosopher* (Ithaca, NY: Cornell Univ. Press, 1972), esp. pp. 175-77.

9. Mikhail Bakhtin introduced the important concept of *mésalliance* to criticism. He describes the fundamental characteristics of literary carnivalization as new modes of interaction between characters, *mésalliances,* profanation, and the breakdown of traditional genres. The dwarf is a symbol of this process. Mikhail Bakhtin, *Problems of Dostoevsky's Poetics,* trans. R.W. Rotsel (Ann Arbor, MI: Ardis Publishers, 1973), pp. 100-103.

10. Karl Marx, "The Eighteenth Brumaire of Louis Bonaparte", in *The Marx-Engels Reader,* ed. Robert Tucker, (New York: W.W. Norton and Co., 1972), p. 444. "Order and Liberty" was a

conservative slogan calling for social unity and political stability during the 1848 revolution. See also Roger Price, ed., *1848 in France* (Ithaca, NY: Cornell Univ. Press, 1975), pp. 92, 120, 141.

11.   Louis-Antoine Garnier-Pages, *Histoire de la Révolution de 1848,* Vol. I (Paris: Bibliothèque Libérale Dégorce-Cadot, 1861-72), p. 275.

12.   Jean le Rond d'Alembert, *Preliminary Discourse to the Encyclopedia of Diderot,* trans. Richard N. Schwab. (Indianapolis: Bobbs-Merrill Co., 1963), p. 49.

13.   Ibid., p. 49.

14.   Schwab implies an important connection between d'Alembert and such natural scientists as Buffon, especially with regard to the *Encyclopédie's* interest in classification. Moreover, he notes the simultaneous importance of the notion of filiation, as described by Lovejoy in *The Great Chain of Being,* explicitly articulated only with the arrival of Cuvier on the editorial board of the *Encyclopedia.* d'Alembert, p. 49. n. 59.

15.   Michel Foucault, *The Origin of Things: An Archaeology of the Human Sciences,* (New York: Pantheon Books, 1970), pp. 263-68.

16.   d'Alembert, p. 50.

17.   Ibid., p. 48.

18.   Helen Rosenau, *Social Purpose in Architecture* (London: Studio Vista, 1970), frontispiece, p. 13.

19.   In this regard, I refer the reader to Michael H. Abrams, *The Mirror and the Lamp* (New York: Oxford University Press, 1976), especially the section entitled "German Theories of Vegetable Genius," pp. 201-13.

20.   Gertrude Bussey, Appendix, *Man a Machine,* by Julien Offray de la Mettrie (LaSalle, IL: Open Court Press, 1977), p. 166-67.

21.   Denis Diderot, *Le Neveu de Rameau et Autres Dialogues Philosophiques,* introd. Jean Varloot (Paris: Editions Gallimard, 1972), p. 16.

22.   Jean-Jacques Rousseau, *Du Contrat Social,* introd. Pierre Buguelin, (Paris: Garnier Flammarion, 1966), p. 101.

23.   Rousseau, *Du Contrat Social,* p. 23.

24.   Ibid., p. 24.

25.   Frank Manuel, *The Prophets of Paris* (Cambridge, MA: Harvard Univ. Press, 1962), p. 30 n. 23.

26.   Jonathan Culler provides an illuminating discussion of the synchronic/diachronic distinction, informed largely by researches into Derridean *différance.* Jonathan Culler, *Ferdinand de Saussure* (Harmondsworth, England: Penguin Books, 1977) pp. 35-36.

27.   Karl Uitti describes a polarizing process at work in his analysis of literature, involving literary criticism and linguistics. He perceives the Cartesian language, as formalized by the Port Royal Grammar, as breaking into two distinct strains by the mid-eighteenth century, the personal prose of Diderot and Rousseau and the philosophical language of Condillac. Karl Uitti, *Linguistics and Literary Theory* (New York: W.W. Norton and Co., 1969), pp. 66-92.

28.   Manuel, *Prophets,* pp. 64-67.

29. This schematization of Saint-Simon's cosmology is indebted to Friederich Hayek's *The Counterrevolution of Science* (Glencoe, IL: The Free Press, 1955), pp. 121-24.

30. Manuel, p. 26.

31. Ibid., p. 27.

32. F.R. Leavis, introd., *Mill on Bentham and Coleridge* (London: Chatto and Windus, 1959), p. 3.

33. Kurt R. Eissler, *Talent and Genius* (New York: Grove Press, 1971), p. 249. Eissler supports his analysis by frequent reference to Thomas Kuhn's concept of "paradigm," first articulated in Kuhn's *The Copernican Revolution* (Cambridge, MA: Harvard Univ. Press, 1957) pp. 122-32, 270-271, as "perspectivism" and fully articulated in *The Structure of Scientific Revolutions* (Chicago: Univ. of Chicago Press, 1962), pp. 10-11.

34. Frank Manuel emphasizes that Saint-Simon considers his own to be the final period in the dialectical historical process. Frank Manuel, *The New World of Henri de Saint-Simon* (Cambridge, MA: Harvard Univ. Press, 1956), pp. 234-35.

35. Nicholas Riasanovsky provides an excellent discussion of Fourier's cosmology in the section entitled "Fourier's Teaching" of his *The Teaching of Charles Fourier* (Berkeley, CA: Univ. of California Press, 1969), esp. pp. 86-89. Riasanovsky does not refer, however, to the apocalyptic character of the cosmology. For this interpretation, especially interesting is Paul Chanson's *Trois Socialistes Français: Quatre Etudes* (Paris: Les Editions de la Nouvelle France, 1945), p. 93.

36. Fourier attacks philosophy as source of the social fragmentation and repression of the day. He states, "It is easy to repress passions by violence; philosophy suppresses them with the stroke of the pen..." Riasanovsky, p. 215.

37. Riasanovsky discusses literary analogy as important to Fourier's philosophical scheme of scale shift and increasing generalization. For a more complete treatment of the literary forms and techniques prevalent in nineteenth-century historical writing, it is useful to refer to Hayden White's theory of tropes. Hayden White, *Metahistory: The Historical Imagination in Nineteenth Century Europe* (Baltimore: Johns Hopkins Press, 1973), pp. 31-38.

38. Riasanovsky, *Fourier*, p. 184; Manuel, *Prophets*, p. 211. Mark Poster, ed. and introd. *Harmonian Man: Selected Writings of Charles Fourier* (New York: Anchor Books, 1971), p. 20.

39. John Veitch, "Victor Cousin", *The Encyclopedia Britannica*, 11th ed. (1910), p. 332.

40. In 1828 Cousin was named an underminister of Public Education, and as such, nationalized his philosophy and theory of education. His importance as educator is the object of Walter Brewer's *Victor Cousin as a Comparative Educator* (New York: Teacher's College Press, 1971).

41. Cited in Emile Bréhier, *The Nineteenth Century: Period of Systems*, trans. Wade Baskin, (Chicago: Univ. of Chicago Press, 1968), pp. 83-84.

42. Ibid., p. 84.

43. Ibid.

44. In their articles, "Architecture", composed for the *Encyclopédie* and *Encyclopédie Méthodique,* Jacques-François Blondel and Quatremère de Quincy emphasize the triadic nature of architecture, relating to both classical and enlightenment epistemologies. Both distinguish three types of architecture—naval, military, civil—but reflect primarily upon civil

architecture as "l'art de bâtir." They discuss it as a mediate discipline between liberal and fine arts, or between "vrai" and "beau" stressing it as "l'utile." Hence, *L'Utile* takes the place of *Le Bien* in the Platonic theory of knowledge. For Blondel and Quatremère, architecture reverberates the epistemological triad: construction (vrai), disposition (utile), and decoration (beau). Jacques-François Blondel, *Cours d'Architecture, ou Traité de La Décoration, Distribution et Construction des Bâtiments* (Paris: Desaint, 1771-77), V. 1., 123-29 and 388-92. Antoine-Chrysostome Quatremère de Quincy, "Architecture", *Encyclopédie Méthodique*, XVII, (1788), 109.

45. Victor Cousin, *Lectures on the True, Beautiful and Good*, trans. O.W. Wright (New York: D. Appleton and Co., 1893), p. 34.

46. Ibid., p. 368.

47. Ibid., p. 226.

48. Cousin discusses genius and "je ne sais quoi" in Lecture VIII, p. 155.

49. Louis Hautecoeur describes the alternative schools which spring out of a single aesthetic. He ties schools of realism, idealism, and *l'art pour l'art* simultaneously to the idealistic school of philosophy, centering upon both Cousin and Quatremère. See Louis Hautecoeur, *Littérrature et Peinture en France du XVIIIᵉ Siècle*, 2nd ed. (Paris: Libraire Armand Colin, 1963), pp. 88-110.

50. Neil Levine's elaborate exegesis of the Bibliothèque Ste. Geneviève gives an excellent idea of the interpretive issues and formal techniques at play in this classic work of the rationalist school. "The Romantic Idea of Architectural Legibility: Henry Labrouste and the Néo-Grec" in *The Architecture of the Ecole des Beaux-Arts*, ed. Arthur Drexler (Cambridge, MA: MIT Press, 1976), pp. 325-57.

51. Cousin was frequently compared with Abelard in terms of the enormous popularity of his rhetorical prose and speaking style. Veitch, pp. 330-31.

52. Claude-Nicolas Ledoux, *L'Architecture Considérée sous les Rapports de l'Art, des Moeurs et de la Législation*, (Paris: Chez l'Architecte, 1804), I, 104.

53. Plato, *The Republic*, trans. Francis Cornford (London: Oxford Univ. Press, 1941), pp. 254-55.

54. Hayden White, *Metahistory: the Historical Imagination in Nineteenth Century Europe*, p. 9.

55. Maurice Sand, *Masques et Buffons (Comédie Italienne)* (Paris: Michel Lévy Frères, 1860), I, 129.

56. Ibid., 123.

57. Ibid., 123-24.

58. David Lodge, "The Language of Modernist Fiction: Metaphor and Metonymy", in *Modernism 1890-1930*, eds. Malcolm Bradbury and James McFarlane (Harmondsworth, England: Penguin Books, 1976), p. 483.

59. Hayden White makes a distinction between synechdoche and metonymy which neither Jakobson nor Barthes specify. For the sake of his argument, White uses metonymy to signify mechanistic progress, synechdoche organic. Both are part of a generally optimistic historical scheme. White, p. 36.

60. These are Colin Rowe's distinctions between literal and phenomenal spatial readings as discussed in his "Transparency: Literal and Phenomenal", reprinted in *The Mathematics of the Ideal Villa and Other Essays* (Cambridge, MA: MIT Press, 1977), 160-61.

61. Roland Barthes, *Writing Degree Zero/Elements of Semiology*, introd. Susan Sontag, trans. Annette Lavers and Colin Smith (Boston: Beacon Press, 1968), pp. 60-61.

62. Ibid., p. 13.

63. Richard Jackson, "The Romantic Metaphysics of Time," *Studies in Romanticism* 19:1 (Spring 1980), 19-20.

64. George-Wilhelm-Friedrich Hegel, *The Phenomenology of Mind*, trans. J.B. Baillie (rpt. New York City: Harper Torchbooks, 1967), esp. pp. 222-27.

65. Sand, 124.

66. Bakhtin, pp. 101-103. Bakhtin discusses a similar notion, "dégradation," in *Rebelais and His World*, trans. Helen Iswolsky (Cambridge, MA: MIT Press, 1968), pp. 19-20.

67. Jurij Tynjanov, "On Literary Evolution", in *Readings in Russian Poetics: Formalist and Structuralist Vision*, eds. Ladislav Majetka and Krystyna Pomorska (Ann Arbor, MI: Univ. of Michigan Press, 1978), p. 70.

68. Karl Marx, "The Eighteenth Brumaire of Louis Bonaparte" in *The Marx-Engels Reader*, Robert C. Tucker, ed. (New York: W.W. Norton, 1972), p. 436.

69. Friedrich Nietzsche, *Ecce Homo*, trans. R.J. Hollingsworth. (Harmondsworth, England: Penguin Books, 1979). See especially the section "Why I am a Destiny", pp. 126-34.

70. Emile Mâle, *The Gothic Image* (New York: Harper Torchbooks, 1958), p. vii.

71. Sand, 124.

72. Walter Benjamin makes a similar assertion when he speaks of the world as a "puppet show" operated by the invisible hands of a "little hunchback." He associates the dwarf with theology. See "Theses on the Philosophy of History" in his *Illuminations*, ed. and introd. Hannah Arendt, trans. Harry Zohn. (New York: Schocken, 1969), p. 255.

73. George Sand and Charles Nodier contributed essays on Punchinello to Maurice Sand's *Masques et Buffons*.

74. Victor Considérant coined the phrase "En Avant" in the 1840s and used it in his chronicle of La Réunion, *Au Texas*. The term, however, was quickly absorbed into Fourierist aesthetics as Gabriel-Desiré Laverdant's neologism "avant-garde" of 1845 would tend to indicate. See Renato Poggioli, *The Theory of the Avant-Garde* (New York: Harper and Row, 1971), p. 9. Daly reflects the idea in his essay "De L'Architecture de l'Avenir" by ending his discussion with the imperative "marche devant". He also uses Considérant's expression "En avant" for explicitly critical reasons, notably, in support of the student protest against the pedagogy of Viollet-le-Duc in 1864. See "Ecole Impériale des Beaux-Arts: Ouverture des Cours d'Histoire et d'Esthétique", RGA XXII (1864), 69.

75. White, pp. 37-38.

Chapter 3

1. Frank Manuel, *The Prophets of Paris* (Cambridge, MA: Harvard Univ. Press, 1962), p. 5.

2. César Daly, "Exposition de la Théorie Sociétaire à Chartres, par M. Considérant", *La Phalange* 2ᵉS.: I (1836-37), 617.

3. Mary Warnock, Introd., *Utilitarianism and Other Writings* by John Stuart Mill (New York: New American Library, 1962), pp. 13-14.

4. Daly, "Exposition," 795.

5. Ibid., 797.

6. César Daly, "Système Sociale de M. Owen," *La Phalange* 2ᵉS, II: 4 (15 Feb 1838), 49.

7. César Daly, "Peinture du Bâtiment," RGA III (1842), 323.

8. Ibid., 323.

9. César Daly, "Architecture Rurale: Introduction," RGA III (1842), 68.

10. César Daly, "Nouvelle Architecture à l'Usage des Prolétaires Anglais," *La Démocratie Pacifique* VI:25 (25 Jan. 1846), 11.

11. Charles Pellarin, *The Life of Charles Fourier*, trans. George Shaw, (New York: Wm. H. Graham, 1848), p. 122.

12. César Daly, "De l'Architecture Domestique Monumentale," RGA I (1840), 202.

13. César Daly, "Reform Club (Londres)", RGA XV (1857), 343.

14. Ibid., 344.

15. César Daly, "Architecture Privée Monumentale: Club des Voyageurs," RGA I (1840), 333.

16. Ibid., 333.

17. César Daly, *Introduction Traitant du Symbolisme dans l'Architecture* (Paris: Aux Bureaux de la Revue Générale de l'Architecture et Travaux Publics, 1847), p. 6.

18. Georg G. Iggers, introd. and trans, *The Doctrine of Saint-Simon: An Exposition* (New York: Shocken Books, 1972), p. xiii.

19. W.D. Robson-Scott, *The Literary Background of the Gothic Revival in Germany* (Oxford: Clarendon Press, 1965), pp. 304-305.

20. César Daly, *Du Projet d'Achèvement de la Cathédrale de Cologne* (Paris: Aux Bureaux de la Revue de l'Architecture et des Travaux Publics, 1842), pp. 13-15.

21. Ibid., p. 12.

22. Ibid., pp. 11-12.

23. Ibid., p. 21.

24. Daly, *Du Symbolisme*, p. 7.

25. Ibid.

26. César Daly, "Des Rapports Qui Existent entre l'Archéologie Monumentale et l'Architecture Contemporaine," *Congrès des Architectes Français: Premier Session.* (Paris: Librairie Générale de l'Architecture et des Travaux Publics, 1873), p. 124.

27. César Daly, "Hygiène Publique en Angleterre" RGA XXIX (1872), 37.

28. Gertrude Lenzer, ed. and introd., *Auguste Comte and Positivism: The Essential Writings* (New York: Harper Torchbooks, 1975), p. 72.

29. Cited in D.G. Charlton, *Positivist Thought in France during the Second Empire, 1852-1870* (Oxford: Clarendon Press, 1959), p. 7.

30. I cannot hope to do justice to either Friedrich Hayek's or Karl Popper's critiques of vulgar positivist method. Hence, I refer the reader to the former's *The Counterrevolution of Science*

(Glencoe, Ill: The Free Press, 1952), pp. 42-43, and the latter's *The Poverty of Historicism* (New York: Harper Torchbooks, 1964), pp. 35-37 and 43-44, especially with regard to the issue of prediction in the social sciences.

31. Charlton, pp. 36-38.

32. César Daly, "Les Collection d'Objets d'Art et d'Industrie Anciens," RGA VIII (1849-50), 303.

33. Eugène Viollet-le-Duc, "Essai sur l'Origine et les Développements de l'Art de Bâtir en France" RGA X (1852), 348.

34. César Daly, "L'Architecture de l'Avenir", preface to *Motifs Historiques,* 2nd ed. (Paris: A. Morel, 1869), I, 38.

35. César Daly, "Bibliographie: De l'Entretien des Routes d'Empressement à l'Etat Normal, au Système du Balayage," RGA III (1842), 532-33.

36. César Daly, "Du Comité Historique des Arts et Monuments", RGA V (1844), 50.

37. César Daly, "La Science et l'Industrie: Sont-Elles les Ennemies de l'Art?" RGA VI, 54.

38. Daly, "L'Architecture de l'Avenir," I, 24.

39. Ibid.

40. Ibid., p. 26.

41. Ibid., p. 24.

42. César Daly, "Introduction," RGA VI (1846), 6.

43. Daly, "La Science et l'Industrie," 54.

44. Daly first alludes to the "moi/non-moi" distinction in *Du Symbolisme,* p. 17, stating "... il faut recommencer pour avoir une âme au dedans de soi-même, une forme vivante, qui suite et comprende ce que c'est qu'une foi qui en sache trouver les accents."

45. César Daly, "Introduction" RGA XXXIX (1882), 12-13.

46. Daly, "La Science et l'Industrie," 53-54.

47. César Daly, "L'Alhambra" RGA VI (1846), 7-8.

48. Daly, "La Science et l'Industrie," 54.

49. Ibid.

50. On the distinction between the natural imitation of Aristotle and "la belle nature" of Poussin, see Rensselaer Lee, *Ut Pictura Poesis* (New York: Norton, 1967), especially pp. 9-17.

51. César Daly, "Introduction", RGA XII (1854), 1-4.

52. César Daly, "Mausolée de Dumont d'Urville," RGA VIII (1849-50), 438.

53. Daly, "L'Architecture de l'Avenir", I, 38.

54. César Daly, "L'Art et la Critique," RGA XXV (1867), 154.

55. F. Cantagrel, "Bibliographie—'Revue de l'Architecture et des Travaux Publics, par César Daly'," *La Démocratie Pacifique* V:91 (29 Sept. 1845), 11.

56. My treatment of the biological analogy in architecture has been shaped especially by Michel Foucault's discussions of "Classifying" and "Labor, Life, Language" in *The Order of Things* (New York: Vintage Books, 1971), pp. 125-56 and 250-302.

57. César Daly, "Tables Synoptiques de Divers Elements de l'Architecture du Moyen Age," RGA VI (1845), 97.

58. Ibid., 98.

59. Jean-Baptiste de Lamarck, *Histoire Naturelle des Animaux sans Vertèbres,* vol. I (Paris: Verdière, 1815), préface.

60. Daly, "Reform Club (Londres)," 347.

61. Prosper Merimée, "Deuxième Instruction du Comité Historique des Arts de Monuments," RGA V (1844), 314.

62. Eugène Viollet-le-Duc, "Entretien et Restauration: Des Cathédrales de France," RGA IX (1850-51), 113.

63. Ibid., 114.

64. César Daly, "Introduction," RGA XXVII (1869), 3.

65. César Daly, "Exposition des Projets de Tombeau pour Napoléon," RGA II (1841), 524.

66. Simon-Claude Constant-Dufeux, "Discours de M. Constant-Dufeux," RGA VIII (1849-50), 443.

67. Included in Auguste Comte, *Catéchisme Positiviste ou Sommaire Exposition de la Religion Universelle* (Paris: Chez l'Auteur, 1852), p. 338, appendix.

68. César Daly, "L'Archéologie aux Prises avec l'Architecture," RGA VI (1846), 275.

69. César Daly, "L'Esthétique, La Science, l'Art, et l'Histoire: Leurs Apports," RGA XLII (1885), 74.

70. César Daly, "Introduction," RGA VIII (1848-49), 5-6.

71. César Daly, *Conférences de M. César Daly à la Session de 1873 du Congrès des Architectes Français* (Paris: Libraire Générale de l'Architecture et des Travaux Publics, 1875), p. 11.

72. My view of "scientific" documentary historical style derives from Peter Gay's discussion of Leopold von Ranke in *Style in History* (New York: McGraw-Hill, 1974), pp. 67-76.

73. Daly advocates Spencer's synthetic philosophy in a letter of 6 September 1888 addressed to William H. White, but he criticizes Spencer's application of his own theory to architectural history, in the Englishmen's "Origin and Development of the Styles of Architecture." Moreover, he criticizes eclecticism calling it a process rather than an ideology, "... l'Eclectisme est une pratique et non une doctrine," thus deviating from Cousin's notion of an eclectic philosophy. Archives, Royal Institute of British Architects.

74. César Daly, "Introduction," RGA II (1841), 4.

75. César Daly, "Monument de Juillet: Elevé sur la Place de la Bastille," RGA I (1840), 751 n. 1.

76. César Daly, *Première Causerie d'Histoire et d'Esthètique: Ce Qui Peut Raconter une Grille de Fer* (Paris: Bureaux de "La Revue d' Architecture," 1864), p. 16.

77. Ibid., p. 17.

78. Ibid., p. 18.

79. Ibid., p. 24.

80. Ibid.

81. Ibid., pp. 30-32.

82. César Daly, "Mausolée de Dumont d'Urville," RGA VIII (1849-50), 438.

83. Ibid., 439.

84. César Daly, "Ce Que C'est *la Semaine des Constructeurs*", LSC I (1876-77), 2.

85. César Daly, "Le Monument de Juillet," RGA I (1840), 750.

86. Antoine-Chrysostome Quatremère de Quincy, "Allegory" *Loudon's Architectural Magazine* IV:35 (Jan 1837), 2-3.

87. Ibid., 3.

88. Daly, "Monument de Juillet," 751, n. 1.

89. Ibid.

90. Ibid., 750.

91. Ibid., 758.

92. César Daly, "Varia no. 3" *LSC* XVII :41 (8 April 1893), 481.

93. César Daly, "L'Alhambra," RGA VI (1846), 47.

94. César Daly, L'Architecture de l'Avenir", I, 38.

95. César Daly, Paul Planat, "Chronique: Le Symbolisme dans l'Art," LSC VII:47 (19 May 1883), 555.

96. Ibid., 553-54.

97. The RGA makes a comparison between Léonce Reynaud's *Traité d'Architecture* and itself, "Traité d'Architecture," RGA XVI (1858), 236-37. See also Léonce Reynaud, "Colonne", *Encyclopedie Nouvelle* (1836-39), vol. III.

98. Henry Van Brunt, "Greek Lines," *Atlantic Monthly* VIII:45 (July 1861), 87.

99. Ruprich Robert, César Daly, "Salon de 1852", RGA X, 156. Ruprich Robert engraved the plate 'L'Architecture Contemporaine,' which accompanied Daly's text of the same title, in 1849. Robert also succeeded Daly as *architecte-diocésain* of the Tarn in 1877.

100. César Daly, "Lettres sur l'Esthétique Architecturale, Première Lettre," LSC XV (1890-91), 194.

101. César Daly, "Concours pour le Grand Opera de Paris: 2ᵉ Partie," RGA (1861) XIX, 80.

102. César Daly, "Une Laiterie à Marly-le-Roi," RGA XVII (1859), 70.

103. Daly, "Des Rapports...", p. 122.

104. Ibid., p. 123.

105. Ibid.

106. Mary Warnock, *Imagination* (Berkeley: Univ. of California, 1978). See especially pp. 13-21.

107. Jackson, "The Romantic Metaphysics of Time," pp. 19-20.

108. Cited by Anna Balakian in *The Literary Origins of Surrealism* (New York: New York Univ. Press, 1947), p. 147.

Chapter 4

1. Victor Hugo, *Notre-Dame de Paris* (New York: D. Appleton and Co., 1902), pp. 176-77.

2. Ibid., p. 176.

3. Ibid., pp. 175, 177.

4. Karl Marx, "The Economic and Philosophical Manuscripts of 1844," in *The Marx-Engels Reader,* ed. Robert Tucker (New York: W.W. Norton & Co., 1972), p. 98.

5. Anthony Vidler, "Type: Quatremère de Quincy," *Oppositions* VIII (Cambridge, MA: MIT Press, 1976), 148.

6. Ibid., 148-89.

7. Ibid., 148.

8. Antoine-Chrysostome Quatremère de Quincy, *Essai sur l'Imitation dans Beaux-Arts* (Paris: Treuttel et Wurtz, 1823), p. 298.

9. Ibid., pp. 307, 310.

10. Ibid., p. 275.

11. *Le Glâneur: Journal d'Eure et Loire* makes this connection, stating, "M. Daly s'est définitivement adressé à des artistes anglais, à des hommes spéciaux, habitués à graver l'architecture. C'est la première fois peut-être qu' un morceau d'architecture d'une si grande dimension se trouve executé dans le style des vignettes anglaises." "Cathédrale de Chartres: Première Gravure de César Daly," *Le Glâneur* IX:9 (7 June 1838), 279.

12. Paul Frankl notes that the taste for romantic architectural rendering followed the example of English work, whose provenance extends from Gilpin. Of this *genre,* most important in France was Nodier's, Taylor's, and de Cailleux' *Voyages Pittoresques.* Paul Frankl, *The Gothic: Literary Sources and Interpretations through Eight Centuries* (Princeton, NJ: Princeton Univ. Press, 1960), p. 510.

13. William Gilpin, *An Essay on Prints* (London: R. Blamire, 1792), p. 14.

14. William Gilpin, *Three Essays, on Picturesque Beauty, on Picturesque Travel, and on Sketching Landscape* (London: R. Blamire, 1792), p. 7.

15. Gilpin discusses the differences between engraving, etching, and etching heightened by engraving in his *Essay on Prints,* pp. 14-20. His own work, however, is done in mezzotint, which he prefers for its softness. It is interesting to note a difference in taste between the English and French publics. R. Blamire reprinted Gilpin's *Observations... of Cumberland and Westmoreland,* probably the most popular of the various picturesque voyages. The second edition was printed in English in 1788, in French in 1789. The English version uses Gilpin's mezzotint process. The French uses a high contrast etching technique. It seems that French audiences preferred the more movemented *chiaroscuro* of the etching process to other techniques allowing for great control and subtlety. Lithography continued these preferences. Nodier's and Taylor's *Voyages Pittoresques* maintain an interest in strong shadow and highlights, although using this more advanced printing technique.

16. Roland Barthes maintains a similar point of view in his interpretation of the plates in the *Encyclopédie.* He notes the scale differences, as well as rarified descriptive techniques implicit in the visual documentation of this work tend to de-naturalize, and mystify the object

represented. He further notes that the various implements depicted are paired with a *genre* scene which treats the object as a catalyst of happiness. The machine works instrumentally upon the lives of the people who use it. The implement takes on a benevolent personality, bestowing upon society the promise of a better tomorrow. Such benign fatalism comprises what Barthes calls the "epic function" of the *Encyclopédie's* imagery. This phenomenon is not unlike that implicit in Daly's representation of Chartres. Roland Barthes, "The Plates of the *Encyclopedia*" in his *New Critical Essays,* trans. Richard Howard (New York: Hill and Wang, 1980), pp. 32-33.

17.   For a discussion of the conflict between the Young Romantics and Quatremère, see R. Schneider, *Quatremère de Quincy et Son Intervention dans les Arts (1788-1830)* (Paris: Librairie Hachette et Cᵉ, 1910), pp. 300-311.

18.   César Daly, "Les Envois de Rome et Considérations Générales sur l'Architecture" *Le Glâneur* VII:38 (22 Sept. 1836), 467.

19.   An application of the Roman forum to modern urbanistic situations is not unheralded in France. For example, Héré de Corny's Place Stanislaus must be compared to the Forum of Trajan to understand the full extent of the reference. The new emphasis of mid-eighteenth-century urbanistic projects which stress simultaneous and transparent spatial readings has been cited by Dora Wiebenson in her discussion of Pierre Patte's *Monuments Erigés à la Gloire de Louis XV* of 1748. She cites Boffrand's market project as seminal for Héré's Nancy scheme. She does not, however, mention the importance of Roman spatial prototypes, now all too apparent to the French at mid-century after the publication of the Nolli plan of Rome. Dora Wiebenson, *The Picturesque Garden in France* (Princeton, NJ: Princeton Univ. Press, 1978), p. 108.

20.   Daly, "Les Envois," 467.

21.   Robert Branner advanced, "To the modern tourist and historian alike, the Cathedral of Chartres is the monument most representative of the Gothic style.... Chartres was not only a culmination of the early Gothic experiments of the twelfth century, but was also the pace-setter for the century that was to follow." Robert Branner, ed. and introd., *Chartres Cathedral* (New York: Norton, 1969), p. 69.

22.   Antoine-Pierre-Marie Gilbert, *Description Historique de l'Eglise Cathédrale de Chartres* (Chartres: Gernier Allabre, 1824), p. 4.

23.   Henri Jouin, "La Cathédrale d'Albi," *Gazette des Beaux-Arts,* XXVI:2ᵉ Série (1882), 406.

24.   Prosper Merimée, *Notes d'Un Voyage dans le Midi de la France* (Paris: Librairie de Fournier, 1835), p. 468.

25.   Letter from Viollet-le-Duc to the Ministère des Travaux Publics, dated 28 July 1841, *Archives de la Ministère des Affaires Culturelles,* carton Tarn 1474 bis, Albi Cathedral, Sainte-Cécile, 1ᵉʳ dossier.

26.   Arcisse de Caumont, "Histoire Sommaire de l'Architecture au Moyen Age," *Bulletin Monumental* II (1836), 7-8.

27.   Louis Grodecki's very useful introduction to his *Gothic Architecture* divides the historiography of the subject into a number of approaches: the Componental, Structural, Spatial, Historical, Iconographic, and Social. For my purposes, I have grouped the componental and structural, for both approaches imply construction based upon a number of distinct structural elements, hence, the designation "structuralist." Louis Grodecki, *Gothic Architecture* (New York: Harry Abrams, 1977), especially pp. 9-13.

28. *Congrès Archéologique de la France: XXXe Session* (Paris: Rue Montmartre, 1864), p. 325.

29. Alphonse de Cailleux, Charles Nodier, Isidor-Justin Taylor, *Voyages Pittoresques dans l'Ancienne France: Languedoc I* (Paris: Firmin Didot, 1833), p. 124.

30. Alphonse de Cailleux, Charles Nodier, Isidor-Justin Taylor, *Voyages Pittoresque et Romantiques dans l'Ancienne France,* vol. II (Paris: Firmin Didot frères, 1840), p. 94.

31. Grodecki, p. 58.

32. Robert Branner, *St. Louis and the Court Style* (London: A Zwemmer Ltd., 1965), p. 109.

33. Victor Hugo, *Notre-Dame de Paris,* pp. 180-81.

34. Ibid., p. 181.

35. *Congrès Archéologiques de France: Séances Générales Tenues à Sens, Tours, Angoulême, Limoges en 1847* (Paris: Devaches, 1848), p. 291.

36. César Daly, "L'Archéologie aux Prises avec l'Architecture: Réponse à Une Critique des *Annales Archéologiques*", *RGA* VI (1846), 71.

37. Ibid., 27.

38. Ibid., 71.

39. Ibid., 73.

40. Jules Michelet, *L'Histoire de la France,* 2nd ed. (Paris: Librairie Classique de l'Hachette, 1835), II, 665.

41. *Congrès Archéologique... 1847,* p. 297.

42. Michael Abrams notes that distinctions between the mechanical and the organic in his discussion of "German Theories of Vegetable Genius." He notes that the parts of the mechanism can be organized and analyzed with regard to the "cause" determining each component. Organic forms develop in accord with ends that are immanent in the organism itself. He further discusses the organic work as "unconsciously teleological," implying the presence of a soul as self-organizing power. M.H. Abrams, *The Mirror and the Lamp* (New York and London: Oxford Univ. Press, 1971), p. 208.

43. *Congrès Archéologique...* 1847, p. 297.

44. David Watkin has traced functionalism as an architectural ethic from Pugin to Pevsner in his *Morality and Architecture.* Structural logic is the explicit stand of functionalism. Implicit, however, is a moral and social order, an ideological posture based on an ideology using logic and instrumental discourse. David Watkin, *Morality and Architecture* (Oxford: Clarendon Press, 1977), esp. pp. 22-29.

45. César Daly, "Salon de 1846," *RGA* VI (1846), 325.

46. Michelet, 686.

47. Ibid., 668.

48. Ibid., 668.

49. César Daly, "Tableau de l'Evolution des Styles d'Architecture en Regard des Civilisations Correspondantes," *LSC* XIV:3 (13 July 1889), 39.

50. Michelet, 666.

51. Ibid., 696.

52. Louis Baltard, *Paris et Ses Monuments, Mésurés, Dessinés, et Gravés* (Paris: Chez l'Auteur, 1803-05), p. 9.

53. Alexandre de Laborde, *Les Monuments de la France, Classés Chronologiquement et Considerées sous le Rapport des Faits Historiques et de l'Etude des Arts*, vol. II (Paris: Imprimerie Jules Didot l'Ainé, 1836), Avant-propos.

54. Ibid.

55. Ibid., vol. I, p. ii.

56. César Daly, "L'Architecture de l'Avenir', I, 31.

57. Eugène Viollet-le-Duc, "Préface", *Dictionnaire Raisonnée*, vol. I (Paris: B. Bance, 1858), ii-v.

58. César Daly, "Exposition de 1840," RGA I (1840), 296.

59. Ibid.

60. César Daly, "Salon de 1846," RGA VI, 325.

61. The movement of the chevet walls reported to Daly by the architecte inspecteur Dobrosielsky in 1853: "Je m'empresse de vous signaler, Monsieur l'Architecte, le mouvement bien positif et fort dangereux des vieux murs extérieurs du chevet de Ste. Cécile. Ces murs sont déjà en plomb. Leur mouvement consecutif sera probablement plus rapide, compromettra la solidité de l'édifice et ménacera la sécurité publique, si aucun moyen efficace n'est promptement employé pour en arrester la progression." There was a similar letter addressed to the Prefect of the Tarn from Archbishop Eugène, dated 20 May 1853. *Archives Départementales du Tarn*, carton Tarn 1 V, 440.

62. Work on the church was halted in 1851, resumed in 1853, halted in 1854, resumed under a new entrepreneur in 1856, halted again in 1857, and resumed again in 1859. Work continued uninterrupted until the 1870 Revolution.

63. Léon Vaudoyer reveals his ambivalence about the towers. He nonetheless recommends that the final three towers be built on the chevet in order to observe the total effect. "... il reste encore à élever les tourelles en nombre égal à celui des contreforts qui flanquent les murs de l'abside et de la nef, et forment au sommet de cette Cathédrale un couronnenent d'un genre particulier et dont on ne saurait content le grand effet ... l'exécution des autres soît continués sans interruption." "Rapport pour le Comité des Inspecteurs des Travaux Diocésains," 28 March 1863, p. 1, *Archives Nationales*, F[11] 4551.

64. "Motion no. 298" *Le Moniteur Universel*, 122 (2 May 1866), p. 525.

65. Daly's successors, both Ruprich Robert and Hardy, did nothing with regard to the towers. However, Hardy's successor, M. Poitevin, proposed a number of schemes for their alteration in the 1890s. He returned to fourteenth-century fortified prototypes, with crenelation and shorter, more pyramidal roofs rather than the more elegant, flamboyant proportion of Daly's scheme.

66. Daly's stand in 1847 alternated between the *Beau*, which he feels is based in "lois géométriques," and the *Pittoresque*, subject to "conditions imprévus". This second, imaginative consideration Daly contrasts with Didron's scientific iconography. *Congrès Archéologiques le France* (1847), p. 293.

67. Krautheimer describes the hall churches as, "Vier Wände und eine flache Decke: das ist alles..." Richard Krautheimer, *Die Kirchen der Bettelörden in Deutschland* (Cologne: F.J. Marcan, 1925), p. 13.

68. John Kenneth Conant, in *Carolingian and Romanesque Architecture, 800-1200* (Harmondsworth, England: Penguin Books, 1959), p. 132, notes that the hall church, i.e., a nave type with broad side aisles, has a very similar spatial quality to a nave church, i.e., a clear interior space with a sense of openness. Paul Frankl makes a similar assertion. Paul Frankl, *Gothic Architecture* (Harmondsworth, England: Penguin Books, 1962), p. 141.

69. Grodecki in *Gothic Architecture,* pp. 11-12, stresses that it was the distinction between structure and membrane, especially in vaulting, that was especially important to those exponents of the "structural" approach in the mid-nineteenth century.

70. César Daly, "Salon de 1846," RGA VI (1846), 327.

71. Emile Mâle, *La Cathédrale d'Albi* (Paris: Paul Hartmann, ed., 1950), p. 48 ff.

72. Jean Laran, *La Cathédrale d'Albi* (Paris: Henry Laurens, ed., 1931), p. 23, n. 1. César Daly advanced, in 1863, that the chevet went from a five to a six-sided figure, so that northernmost and southernmost buttresses of the chevet could directly resolve their outward forces. This was a continuation of Daly's functionalist interpretation of Albi's structure, following the example of the Northern Gothic flying buttress systems. *Congrès Archéologique...* XXXe Session, p. 404.

73. Paul Frankl in *Gothic Architecture,* p. 141, recognizes important mendicant symbolism in plan type, and similarly compares San Francesco, Assissi with Sainte-Cécile.

74. F. Lambert, "L'Eglise et le Couvent des Jacobins de Toulouse," *Bulletin Monumental* (1946), 168-69. Also Louis Gillet, *Histoire Artistique des Ordres Mendiants* (Paris: Librairie Renouard, 1912), p. 57.

75. Arcisse de Caumont, *Abécédiare ou Rudiment d'Architecture* (Caen: F.le Blanc Hardel, 1876), p. 593.

76. César Daly, "La Cathédrale de Sainte-Cécile à Albi," *RGA* XV (1857), pp. 252-60. Moreover, archeology at mid-century did recognize Dominican iconography as an important formalizing factor in thirteenth century religious architecture. Representative of this awareness was Le Comte de Montalembert's "Les Artistes Dominicains," *Annales Archéologiques* II (1845), 238-41.

77. See especially J.L. Talmon, *The Rise of Totalitarian Democracy* (Boston: The Beacon Press, 1952), pp. 132-35. Also Charles Coulston Gillespie, "The *Encyclopédie* and the Jacobin Philosophy of Science: A Study in Ideas and Consequences," *Critical Problems in the History of Science,* ed. Marshall Clagett (Madison, WI: Univ. of Wisconsin Press, 1962), pp. 255-89.

78. Levine, "The Romantic Idea of Architectural Legibility: Henri Labrouste and the Néo-Grec," pp. 352-57.

79. César Daly, "Introduction," RGA XXIX (1872), 3.

80. *Congrès Archéologique...* XXXe Session, p. 403.

81. Ibid., p. 400.

82. Ibid., p. 403.

83. Daly's displeasure with De Caumont and his circle grew as the *Bulletin Monumental* published an unfavorable review of Daly's and Duban's restoration of Chartres Cathedral. See especially M. LeBaron de Contencin "Rapport sur La Situation des Edifices Religieux" *Bulletin Monumental* XVII (1851), pp. 342-43.

84. "Instruction pour la Conservation, L'Entretien et la Restauration des Edifices Diocésains et Particulièrement des Cathédrales," dated 7 Feb. 1849, p. 2. *Archives Nationales,* carton F^{19} 4545. Also letter from Hippolyte Crozès to the Ministère de l'Instruction Publique, dated 1 Feb. 1869, stressing the honorific and physical necessities of isolating local monuments in public squares: "L'honneur et la renommée des villes ne se fonde pas par la création de places plus ou moins regulière, de rues larges et artistement alignées. Ces améliorations sont sans doute infiniment appréciables. Elles procurent aux habitants plus de confort de l'agrément pour leur existence, la facilité pour le commerce, de sécurité, dans la circulation des voies publiques, le jour, la lumière, le charme des beaux aspects, enfin des conditions hygiéniques essentiellement favorables au bien-être à la santé publique. Mais la repartition des cités s'établit par les monuments qu'elles possèdent dans leur sein, c'est là, en dehors des affaires, l'attrait qui attire les visitateurs et les étrangers..." *Archives Départementales du Tarn,* carton Tarn 1-V 447.

Chapter 5

1. Victor Considérant, *Description du Phalanstère et Conditions Sociales sur l'Architectonique* (Paris: Librairie Sociétaire, 1848), p. 57.

2. Hugo, *Notre Dame of Paris,* p. 134.

3. In this regard, I am indebted to Brand Blanshard's analysis of perception, treated in the first book of his *The Nature of Thought* (London: Allen and Unwin, 1939). Especially pertinent are sections 2 and 3, addressing the problem of defining perception, distinguishing between sensory reaction, or "sensation" and rational inquiry, I, 51-54.

4. Choay's interpretation of Haussmann's project focuses upon such issues as economic growth, circulatory and ventilation systems, and program. Although an organic allusion is implicit, it is an interpretation different from Hugo's, due primarily to her anatomizing and classification of city functions. Françoise Choay, *The Modern City: Planning in the Nineteenth Century* (New York: George Braziller, 1969), pp. 15-19.

5. The traditionalism of Napoleonic Paris and its pre-urbanistic existence is tied to retardataire political and economic theory, so Choay advances: "This schema of regularization emerges during the last third of the nineteenth century as the fundamental verity of the capitalist-industrialist order" (p. 19). There is more than a hint of Choay's fundamental Marxian stance in this statement.

6. Baron Georges-Eugène Haussmann, *Mémoires du Baron Haussmann* (Paris: Victor-Havard, 1870), II, 382.

7. Louis-Napoléon Bonaparte, *Oeuvres de Napoléon III* (Paris: Henri Plon, 1856), III, 112.

8. Haussmann, I, xxi.

9. David H. Pinckney, *Napoleon III and the Rebuilding of Paris* (Princeton, NJ: Princeton Univ. Press, 1958), pp. 214-215.

10. Jeanne Gaillard, in her *Paris, La Ville 1852-1870* (Paris: Editions Honoré Champion, 1977), pp. 37-54, argues persuasively for an interpretation of Paris as an artistic and social phenomenon only secondarily concerned with production, consciously limiting the growth of industry within the city. She notes that Louis-Napoleon wanted to ensure the public order and stability of the capital, hence removing the working classes, in Louis Chevalier's terms "Les Classes Laborieuses et Dangereuses", from the city proper.

11. César Daly, "Panorama du Mouvement Architectural du Monde," RGA XX (1862), 112.

12. Ernst Gombrich addresses the problem of the linkage of ideational concepts to didactic structure in his essay "Icones Symbolicae" included in his *Symbolic Images* (London: Phaidon Press, 1972), especially in the section "Society of Concepts", pp. 130-32. See also Frances Yates, *The Art of Memory*, pp.3-4.

13. Choay, pp. 7, 104.

14. Walter Benjamin cites the panorama as having given rise to a new urban consciousness, most apparent in "littérature panoramique," a literary genre extending the romantic picturesque voyage into the urban sphere. Walter Benjamin, "Paris Capitale du XIXe Siècle," in his *L'Homme, Le Language, et La Culture*, ed. and trans. Maurice Gandillac, (Paris: Denoel/Gonthier, 1971), pp. 121-23.

15. The history of the belvedere as building type extends from the renaissance. Two examples from its genealogy are especially noteworthy. The first is Bramante's Vatican Belvedere, which Julius II built on the site of an earlier fifteenth century construction. Its elevated site provided a location from which to view both the Roman skyline and the *campagna*. For the eighteenth century, Lucas von Hildebrandt's Vienna Belvedere functioned in much the same way, its central pavilion providing a panorama of Vienna. Saloman Kleiner depicted this feature in his views of the belvedere. See Bruno Grimschitz, *Johann Lucas von Hildebrandt* (Vienna: Verlag Herold, 1959), plate 126.

16. Alexandre de Laborde, *Description des Nouveaux Jardins de la France et de Ses Anciens Châteaux* (Paris: L. Imprimerie de Delance, 1808), plates 23, 52, 59.

17. Louis Carrogis Carmontelle, *Jardins de Monceau prés de Paris, Appartenant à Son Altesse Serenissime Monseigneur le Duc de Chartres* (Paris: Chez Delafosse, Née, et Masquelier, 1779), pp. 8-9.

18. Charles Percier and Pierre Fontaine, *Résidences des Souverains: Parallèle entre Plusieurs Résidences des Souverains de France, d'Allemagne, de Suède, de Russie, d'Espagne, et d'Italie* (Paris: Chez les Auteurs, 1833), p. 13.

19. Ibid., p. 342.

20. Ibid.

21. César Daly, "De la Locomotion Aérienne", *RGA* IV (1843), 17.

22. I am especially indebted to Antoine Grumbach's article "The Promenades of Paris," *Oppositions* VIII (Spring 1977), 52, which discusses the contributions of Haussman's landscaper, Alphonse Alphand. Grumbach makes an important connection between eighteenth century "promenade" literature and the mid-nineteenth-century urbanistic promenade.

23. Charles Nodier, *Paris Historique: Promenade dans les Rues de Paris* (Paris: F.G. Levrault, 1838), p. 4.

24. Ibid., p. 7.

25. Edmond Texier, *Tableau de Paris* (Paris: Paulin et LeChevalier, 1850), p. iii.

26. Ibid.

27. César Daly, "Chronique: une Question Intéressante—Réponse à un Lecteur," *LSG* XII:34 (18 February 1888), 397.

28. Sigmund Freud, *Civilization and Its Discontents*, trans. James Strachey (New York: Norton, 1961), p. 17.

29.   Ibid.

30.   Nicholas Riasanovsky makes this allegation in *The Teaching of Charles Fourier* (Berkeley, CA: Univ. of California Press, 1969), p. 238. Roland Barthes in his *Sade, Fourier, Loyola,* trans. Richard Miller (New York: Hill and Wang, 1976), p. 100, posits a similar theory. The positivism of Freud's treatment of *libido* as cause was an object of Jung's disaffection, leading to the latter's development of analysis in terms of "free association" and an ambivalent, mythic structure underlying man's motivations. Carl Jung, *Man and His Symbols* (Garden City, NY: Doubleday and Co., 1964), pp. 26-31.

31.   Luigi Canina, *Gli Edifici di Roma Antica* (Roma: Stresso Canina, 1848), II, pls. I-XV.

32.   André Rossel, "Le Plan de Louis Bretez." *Le Plan de Louis Bretez dit de Turgot* (Paris: Editions les Yeux Ouverts, 1966), introduction.

33.   Patte discusses the need for comprehensive public works suitable for the grandeur of Paris as spiritual center of France in his *Monuments Erigés en France à la Gloire de Louis XV* (Paris: Librairies Desaint et Saillant, 1765). His concerns are in part practical, but more importantly, he stresses the necessary formal and artistic components suitable to such a city, "Les villes sont supposés immortelles; et il seroit digne de nous de laisser à la posterité une grande idée de notre siècle, des vues qu'on avoit pour le bien public, et du haut degré de perfection où les arts ont été portés de nos jours . . .", p. 221.

34.   Percier and Fontaine, pp. 12-13.

35.   Conversation of 1808, reported by Goethe in German. J. Christopher, Herold, ed., *The Mind of Napoleon* (New York: Columbia Univ. Press, 1955), p. 149.

36.   It was Laugier who first spoke of architecture in terms of a transference of natural imagery, particularly trees. Moreover, it was he who proposed a reordering of the city of Paris based upon the forms of the baroque garden. Wolfgang Herrmann, *Laugier and Eighteenth Century French Theory* (London: A. Zwemmer Ltd., 1962), esp. pp. 140-147.

37.   Le Comte de Las Cases, *Le Mémorial de Sainte Helena* (Paris: Bibliothèque de la Pléiade, 1956), I, 970.

38.   Arthur Clough in his introduction to Dryden's standard edition of Plutarch's *Lives* (New York: Modern Library, 1932) distinguishes between the Roman biographer as historian and moralist. See especially pp. xvii-xviii. Napoleon drew upon the example of Plutarch's *Lives,* and surely upon the virtuous example of Plutarch. Like Plutarch, Napoleon sought a truth beyond historical circumstances. Regarding Napoleon's debt to Plutarch, see André Maurois "Avant-propos: Napolèon d'après le Mémorial," included in De Las Cases, I, ix.

39.   Rensselaer Lee, *Ut Pictura Poesis,* pp. 5, 9.

40.   Concerning the process of moralization and inspiration viz. the ideational realm of *historia,* Ian Scott-Kilvert in his introduction to Plutarch's *Lives* notes "that knowledge is virtue and that cause and effect are really operative within the sphere of Ideas." *The Rise and Fall of Athens* (Harmondsworth, England: Penguin Books, 1960), p. 11.

41.   Plato, *The Republic,* trans. Francis Cornford. (Oxford: Oxford Univ. Press, 1945), Book III, p. 85.

42.   Plutarch, trans. Dryden, pp. 182-83.

43.   Leon Battista Alberti, *On Painting,* introd. and trans. John Spencer, (New Haven, CT: Yale Univ. Press, 1956), esp. pp. 17-18.

44.   Elizabeth Gilmore Holt, ed., "The Painting of the Sabines." *From the Classicists to the Impressionists* (Garden City, NY: Doubleday Press, 1966), p. 4.

45.   Jean-Jacques Rousseau, "An Epistle from J.J. Rousseau, Citizen of Geneva, to Mr. d'Alembert," *The Miscellaneous Works of Mr. J.J. Rousseau* (London: T. Becket and P.A. De Hondt, 1767), III, 181.

46.   Ibid., 183.

47.   Ibid., 181-182.

48.   Hautecoeur discusses the *fêtes republicaines* in his *L'Histoire de l'Architecture Classique en France,* V (Paris: A. and J. Picard, 1953), 118-26.

49.   Françoise Choay treats the Artist's Plan as pre-positivist and, hence, *retardataire.* She fails to acknowledge the idealistic component at play. Choay, *The Modern City,* pp. 16-17.

50.   Napoleon's hostility to museums was encouraged by the aesthetician of the First Empire, Quatremère de Quincy. In this regard, see R. Schneider, *Quatremère de Quincy et Son Intervention dans les Arts* (Paris: Librairie Hachette et Cie., 1910), p. 256.

51.   De Las Cases, II, 385.

52.   Ibid., I, 293.

53.   Ibid., I, 966. See also Schneider, p. 54.

54.   Ibid., II, 359-60.

55.   Cited in A. Perreymond, "Troisième Etude sur la Ville de Paris," RGA IV (1843), 37.

56.   De Las Cases, I, ix.

57.   Plutarch, trans. Dryden, 191-92.

58.   Ibid., pp. 192-93.

59.   De Las Cases, I, 260.

60.   Especially instructive à propos public works is Louis-Napoleon's *History of Julius Caesar* (New York: Harper and Brothers, 1866), II, 477-78. Napoleon III expresses admiration for Caesar's campaign of Roman embellishments, particularly in the Roman Forum and the Campus Martius.

61.   Louis-Napoléon Bonaparte, *Oeuvres de Napoléon III* (Paris: Henri Plon, ed., 1856), III, 273.

62.   Ibid., III, 221.

63.   Hermann, *Laugier,* p. 137; Dora Wiebenson, *The Picturesque Garden in France,* pp. 108-9; Nicolas Le Camus de Mezières, *Le Génie de l'Architecture ou l'Analogie de Cet Art avec Nos Sensations* (Paris: Chez l'Auteur, 1780), pp. 73-82.

64.   A. Barlett Giamatti, *The Earthly Paradise and the Renaissance Epic* (Princeton, NJ: Princeton Univ. Press, 1966), pp. 16-17.

65.   Indicative of this iconographic approach is the work of Claudia Lazzaro-Bruno, especially her "The Villa Lante at Bagnaia: An Allegory of Art and Nature" in *The Art Bulletin* LIX:4 (Dec. 1977), 553-60, where she discusses the architectonic structure of landscape in terms of the periods of classical history.

66.   Carmontelle, p. 4.

67. Ibid., 5.

68. Béatrice de Andia, ed. *De Bagatelle à Monceau: Les Folies du XVIIIe Siècle à Paris* (Paris: Musée Carnavalet, 1978), p. 30.

69. Lazzaro-Bruno, p. 553.

70. Robert Nesbit discusses this aspect of millenialism in his *History of the Idea of Progress* (New York: Basic Books, 1980), pp. 66-68.

71. This reference has a specifically Augustinian provenance. In *The City of God* St. Augustine speaks of the Vine of Judea as it pertains to the geneology of the Jewish people (Book XVI, chapter 2). He further speaks of their descent ending with Christ, specifically in the Passion (Book XVIII, chapter 31). Here, the vine can be seen as establishing a connection with the crown of thorns. Ultimately, the Vine of Judea has a dual significance, one historical and the other biographical. Christ's life can be seen as taking on a generalized meaning as summarized historical narrative. This reference is important to both pictorial and architectural iconography during the sixteenth century, especially in the understanding of Michelangelo's Sistine Ceiling and Alessi's Sacra Monte in Varallo. See Esther Dotson, "The Augustinian Interpretation of Michelangelo's Sistine Ceiling: Part I," *The Art Bulletin* LXI:2 (June 1979), especially p. 240 n. 91, and Galeazzo Alessi, *Libro dei Misteri: Progetto di Pianificazione Urbanista Architectonica e Figurativa del Sacra Monte di Varallo in Valsesia (1565-1569),* preface Anna Maria Brizio (Bologna; Arnaldo Forni, 1974).

72. Carmontelle, p. 4.

73. For example, Pierre Lavedan's interpretation of Perreymond is essentially materialistic. See his *La Nouvelle Histoire de Paris* (Paris: Diffusion Hachette, 1975), p. 410.

74. A. Perreymond, "Première Etude sur la Ville de Paris," RGA III (1842), p. 542.

75. A. Perreymond, "Deuxième Etude sur la Ville de Paris," RGA III (1842), pp. 570-71.

76. Ibid., 571.

77. Albert Lenoir, "La Théorie des Villes: Comment les Villes Se Sont Formées," RGA XII (1854), 296.

78. Perreymond, "Première Etude," 554.

79. Lavedan, pp. 401-3.

80. César Daly, "Fortifications de Paris," *La Phalange* 3e S., I:27 (1 Nov 1840), 467. Daly provides a definition of positive production, as opposed to neutral or negative production, stating, "On peut dire de la *Production,* qu'elle est ou *positive,* ou *neutre,* ou *négative.* La production positive existe dès qu'il y a un bénéfice réel, *une augmentation,* de capitale. Le produit est neutre lorsqu'il n'y a ni bénéfice ni perte, mais seulement *conservation.* Le produit est négatif quand il y a perte. On peut dire qu'un capital est improductif quand il ne rapporte pas un produit positif."

81. Ibid.

82. In this regard, see especially A. Perreymond, "Quatrième Etude sur la Ville de Paris," where the architect discusses the three categories of new building for Paris and the proposed circulation system, RGA IV (1843), 73-79.

83. The "Grande Croisée" was an urbanistic feature of great formal and historical importance for both Louis-Napoleon and Haussmann. See Haussmann, III, 47.

84. Joerg Garms discusses Delamaire's influence on Patte's plan for Paris. His interest, however, focuses more upon projects for the Place Dauphine than upon schemes for the consolidation of the Iles de la Cité and St. Louis. "Projects for the Pont Neuf and the Place Dauphine in the First Half of the Eighteenth Century," *Journal of the Society of Architectural Historians* XXVI: 2 (May 1967), 102-13.

85. A Perreymond, "Sixième Etude sur la Ville de Paris," RGA IV (1843), 415-22.

86. Perreymond, "Deuxième Etude," 579.

87. Perreymond, "Cinquième Etude," 87-88.

88. Perreymond, "Sixième Etude," 416.

89. César Daly, *L'Architecture Privée au Dix-Neuvième Siècle* (Paris: A. Morel et Cie., 1863), I, 5.

90. César Daly, "Monument de Juillet Elevé sur la Place de la Bastille," *La Phalange* 3ᵉ S. II:15 (31 December 1840-3 January 1841), 238.

91. Ibid., 239.

92. Ibid., 238.

93. César Daly, "Monument de Juillet Elevé sur la Place de la Bastille," *La Phalange* 3ᵉ S. II: 16 (4,5 February 1841), 267.

94. Ibid.

95. Ibid., 268.

96. César Daly, "Concours pour le Grand-Opéra de Paris: Deuxième Partie," RGA XIX (1861), 77.

97. Ibid., 79-80.

98. César Daly, "Cours de Composition d'Ornement: Grand Concours Annuel de l'Ecole Impériale de Dessin á Paris," RGA XX (1862), 158.

99. César Daly, "Panorama du Mouvement Architectural du Monde," RGA XX (1862), 175.

100. Ibid., 30.

101. Daly, *L'Architecture Privée*, I, 6.

102. César Daly, "Maisons d'Habitation de Londres," RGA XIII (1855), 146.

103. César Daly, "De l'Architecture Domestique Monumentale," RGA I (1840), 202.

104. Daly, "Panorama," p. 175.

105. César Daly, "Observations du Directeur de la Revue," RGA XI (1853), 335.

106. Ibid.

107. César Daly, "Peintures Murales des XIIᵉ et XIIIᵉ Siècles," RGA XI (1853), 434.

108. Charles Percier and Pierre Fontaine, *Choix des Plus Célèbres Maisons de Plaisance de Rome et des Environs*, 2d. ed. (Paris: Didot Aîné, 1824), pp. 4-5.

109. *The Building News* (London) notes the parallel between Letarouilly's and Daly's handbooks. The English statement was recorded in the *Revue Générale* XIX (1861), 233.

110. Charles Letarouilly, *Edifices de Rome Moderne ou Recueil des Palais, Maisons, Eglises, Couvents et Autres Monuments Publics et Particuliers les Plus Remarquables,* pirated edition (Liège: D. Avanzo et Cie., 1849), p. 54.

111. Letarouilly quotes from book 5 of Plato's *Republic,* a dialogue concerning, the artwork, ontology, and inspiration, p. 57.

112. Ibid., p. 54.

113. Charles-Pierre Legrand and Jacques-Guillaume Landon, *Monuments de Paris* (Paris: Chez Landon, 1806), book II was prepared by Quatremère de Quincy, vol. I, pt. ii, 4.

114. Ibid., p. 90.

115. Daly, *L'Architecture Privée,* I, 11.

116. César Daly, "Maisons de Paris," RGA XV (1857), 278.

117. Daly, *L'Architecture Privée,* I, 11.

118. Ibid., I, 11-12.

119. Ibid., I, 12.

120. Daly, "Maisons de Paris," 396.

121. Cited by Marcel Cornu, *La Conquête de Paris* (Paris: Mercure de France, 1972), p. 53.

122. Daly, *L'Architecture Privée,* I, 21.

123. César Daly, "Maisons d'Habitation de Londres," RGA XIII (1855), 58.

124. The notion of art as the presence of human will in the orchestration of nature is present in Letarouilly's *Edifices de Rome,* p. 57, who describes the villa in terms similar to Daly: "C'est qu'elles ne sont pas seulement l'élan spontané d'une inspiration isolée, mais l'accomplissement d'une volonté générale; et cette association d'une peuple à l'oeuvre de l'architecte, loin d'en diminuer le mérite, l'augmente au contraire ou toute la grandeur du programme."

125. César Daly, "Une Villa," RGA XXV (1867), 157.

126. *The Builder* provides us with a description of the town of Wissous and the Villa Daly at the time of the 1889 Paris Exposition,"... Wissous was a little too inaccessible for journalizing the exhibition from... A slow, stopping train brought one at length to the small characteristically French country town of Antony, with its white-shuttered houses and broad paved streets with not a soul to be seen in them, and a drive in a country omnibus through the bare-looking unfenced country to the little hamlet of Wissous, with its odd little Gothic church. Adjoining the village our friend had found a French country house, which he had altered and added to, putting a grille flanked by exactly symmetrical lodges towards the little street. Inside this a courtyard gave access to the double ramp of external stone steps leading to the house door, and on the other side of the house was a large garden, laid out when what was then called "English gardens" were the fashion in France, with winding walks, shrubberies, a "wilderness", clumps of trees, and a little artificial "mount" near the extremity, whence Paris, on clear days, just asserted itself in the shape of the outline of the Eiffel Tower in the distance. On the first floor, our host had his suite of rooms, forming a library, packed as close as they could with every sort of book on architecture. No place could be more quiet, no seclusion more complete..." "The Late M. César Daly," *The Builder* LXXVI: 2659 (20 Jan 1894), 47.

127. Dora Wiebenson notes the utilitarian involvements of the *ferme ornée* and *hameau,* party to the productive interests of the physiocrats and agronomes, in the eighteenth-century French

picturesque garden. The forms of these concerns surely continued into the nineteenth century. *The Picturesque Garden in France* (Princeton, NJ: Princeton Univ. Press, 1978), pp. 98-104.

128. Daly, "Panorama du Mouvement Architectural," RGA XX (1862), 30-31.

129. César Daly, "Promenades et Plantations," RGA XXI (1863), 247.

130. Ibid., pp. 176-77.

131. A Bartlett Giamatti, *The Earthly Paradise and the Renaissance Epic* (Princeton, NJ: Princeton Univ. Press, 1966), p. 71.

132. Neil Levine, "The Romantic Idea of Architectural Legibility: Henri Labrouste and the Néo-Grec," p. 350.

133. Ibid., p. 352.

134. Ibid.

135. Daly, "Panorama," 177.

136. Ibid., 178.

137. César Daly, *Les Théâtres de la Place du Châtelet* (Paris: Ducher et Cie., 1874), p. 8.

138. Daly, "Panorama," 271.

139. César Daly, "Cérémonie de la Translation des Cendres de l'Empéreur Napoléon," RGA II (1841), 46.

140. Albert Lenoir, "Théorie des Villes," RGA XII (1854), 295.

141. César Daly, "Conférence sur les Hautes-Etudes d'Architecture," LSC XIV:3 (13 July 1889), 26.

142. Ibid.

143. Especially important in this regard is the conception of "Geist" (alternately translated as "mind" or "spirit") in Hegel, or Baudelaire's use of "esprit," the opposite of "sens" or sensation in his poem "Correspondences." This dichotomy between sense experience and mind or spirit is mediated in *synesthésie*. Charles Baudelaire, *Les Fleurs du Mal,* introd. Claude Pichois (Paris: Editions Gallimard, 1972), p. 38.

144. Charles Baudelaire, "Rêve Parisien," in *The Flowers of Evil and Other Poems of Charles Baudelaire,* trans. Francis Duke (Charlottesville, VA: Univ. of Virginia Press, 1961), pp. 178-79.

145. César Daly, "Introduction," RGA XVIII (1860), 3-6.

146. Gustave Flaubert, *Madame Bovary,* trans. Paul de Man (New York: W.W. Norton and Co., 1965), p. 87.

147. Baudelaire, "Paysage," trans. Duke *The Flowers of Evil,* pp. 144-45.

148. Baudelaire, "Le Soleil," trans. Duke *The Flowers of Evil,* pp. 146-47.

149. Baudelaire, "Rêve Parisien," trans. Duke *The Flowers of Evil,* p. 178-179.

150. Daly, *L'Architecture Privée,* I, 7.

151. Walter Benjamin, "On Some Motifs in Baudelaire," in *Illuminations* (New York: Harcourt Brace, 1968), pp. 157-58.

152. Yates, *The Art of Memory,* pp. 4-10.

153.   A. Craig Baird, *Rhetoric: a Philosophical Inquiry* (New York: The Ronald Press, Co., 1965), p. 51.

154.   I.A. Richards notes the importance of metaphor in portraying ambiguity and alogical continuities in rhetorical form in *The Philosophy of Rhetoric*. (London, Oxford, 1936; rpt. Oxford: Oxford Univ. Press, 1976), pp. 123-25.

Conclusion

1.   Arthur Drexler, ed., *The Architecture of the Ecole de Beaux-Arts* p. 428.

2.   David Van Zanten called attention to this detail of the Bibliotheque Ste. Geneviève in his lecture on Labrouste, fall 1976, Cornell University.

3.   Julien Guadet, *Eléments et Théorie de l'Architecture* (Paris: Librairie de la Construction Moderne, 1902), p. 9.

4.   Ibid., p. 10.

5.   Ibid., pp. 9-10/

6.   It is interesting to compare the projects of two of Laloux students, Paul Bigot's Institut de l'Histoire de l'Art et l'Archéologie of 1928 and Auguste Perret's Musée des Travaux-Publics of 1929-30, to illustrate the nature of the growing dichotomy.

7.   My consideration of Nietzsche's *Ecce Homo* is indebted to Jacques Derrida's interpretation of the work, discussed in a lecture entitled, "Nietzsche's Ear," Cornell University, fall 1979.

8.   César Daly, *Vue Intérieure d'un Tombeau Etrusque à Corneto* (Paris: J. Claye, 1862), p. 8.

Works Consulted

Major Writing of César-Denis Daly

Daly, César-Denis, directeur. *Revue Générale de l'Architecture et des Travaux Publics; Journal des Architectes, des Ingénieurs, des Archéologues*... Paris, 1839-90.

——. *Concours pour le Grand-Prix d'Architecture de 1842*. Paris: Lacampe, 1842.

——. *Du Projet d'Achèvement de la Cathédrale de Cologne,* Paris: Bureaux de la "Revue Générale d'Architecture," 1842.

——. "Introduction Traitant du Symbolisme dans l'Architecture." Excerpt from *Mémoire sur Trente-Deux Statues Symboliques Observées dans la Partie Haute des Tourelles de Sainte Denys* by Mme. Félicie Marie Emilie d'Ayzac. Paris: Bureaux de la "Revue Générale de l'Architecture et Travaux Publics, 1847.

Congrès Archéologique de France. Séances Générales Tenues à Sens, Tours, Angoulême, Limoges en 1847 par la Société Française pour la Conservation des Monuments Historiques. Paris: Deraches, Rue de Boulov, 1848. Especially pp. 288-98.

Daly, César-Denis. *Profession du Foi du Citoyen César Daly*. Paris: Martinet, 1848.

——. *Adresse du Bureau de 1852 aux Membres de la Société Centrale des Architectes*. Paris: E. Thénot, 1852.

——. *Des Concours pour les Monuments Publics dans le Passé, le Présent, et l'Avenir*. Paris: Bureaux de la "Revue Générale de l'Architecture," 1861.

——. *Des Concours pour les Monuments Publics dans le Passé, le Présent, et l'Avenir*. Paris: Bureaux de la "Revue Générale de l'Architecture," 1861.

——. *Blanchissage du Linge, Etude Comparative des Divers Systèmes*. Paris: J. Claye, 1861.

——. *Chemin de Fer Bourbonnais, Gare de Vichy.* Paris: J. Claye, 1862.

——. *Vue Intérieure d'un Tombeau Etrusque à Corneto*. Paris: J. Claye, 1862.

——. *L'Architecture Privée au XIXe Siècle sous Napoléon III*. Première Série. 3 vols. Paris: A. Morel, 1863.

——. *Motifs Historiques d'Architecture et de Sculpture d'Ornement pour la Composition et la Decoration Extérieure des Edifices Publics et Privés. Choix de Fragments, Empruntés à des Monuments Français du Commencement de la Renaissance à la Fin de Louis XVI*. 2 vols. Paris: A. Morel, 1863.

Congrès Archéologiques de France: XXXe Session. Séances Générales Tenues à Rodez, à Albi, et au Mans en 1863, par la Société Française d'Archéologie pour la Conservation des Monuments Historiques. Paris: 48, Rue Montmartre, 1864. Especially pp. 324-407.

Daly, César-Denis. *Nos Doctrines: Réponse à Deux Objections Addressés à la Direction de la Revue de l'Architecture*. Paris: J. Claye, 1863.

——. *Le Premier des Décorateurs, C'est l'Architecte*. Paris: Extrait de la Revue Générale de l'Architecture et des Travaux Publics, 1863.

———. *Première Causerie d'Histoire et d'Esthétique: Ce Que Peut Raconter une Grille de Fer. De l'Influence des Femmes sur l'Architecture au XVIII° Siècle.* Paris: Bureau de "la Revue d'Architecture," 1864.

———. *Deuxième Causerie d'Histoire et d'Esthétique: à Propos d'un Vase d'Amortissement du Palais de l'Institut, à Paris.* Paris: Bureau de "la Revue d'Architecture," 1867.

———. *L'Architecture Privée au XIX° Siecle. Deuxième Série. Nouvelles Maisons et des Environs.* Paris: Ducher et Cᵉ, 1868-72.

———. *Motifs Historiques d'Architecture et de Sculpture d'Ornement pour la Composition et la Décoration Extérieure des Edifices Publics et Privés, Choix de Fragments, Empruntés à des Monuments Français du Commencement de la Renaissance à la Fin de Louis XVI.* 2d ed. 2 vols. Paris: A. Morel, 1869.

———. *Architecture Funéraire Contemporaine. Specimens de Tombeaux, Chapelles Funeraires, Mausolées, Sarcophages, Stèles, Pierres Tombales, Croix, etc., Choisis Principalement dans les Cimetières de Paris et Exprimant les Trois Idées Radicales de l'Architecture Funéraire.* Paris: Ducher, 1871.

———. *Funérailles de Félix Duban, Architecte du Gouvernement... Redigé sur l'Invitation de la Commission Générale des Funérailles et du Monument de Félix Duban.* Paris: Ducher, 1871.

———. *De la Société et de l'Architecture, à Propos de Notre Architecture Funéraire.* Paris: Ducher at Cᵉ, 1872.

———. *Architecture Contemporaine: Les Théâtres de la Place du Châtelet; Théâtre du Châtelet, Théâtre Lyrique; Construits d'après les Dessins et sous la Direction de M. Gabriel Davioud, Architecte, Publiée sous le Patronage et avec le Concours de la Ville de Paris.* Paris: Ducher et Cᵉ, 1874.

Société Centrale des Architectes: Annales Iᵉʳ Volume—Année 1874. Congrès des Architectes Français: Première Session (1873). Paris: Librairie Générale de l'Architecture et Travaux Publics—Ducher et Cᵉ, 1875. Especially pp. 99-130.

Daly, César-Denis. *Conférences de M. César Daly... à la Session de 1873 du Congrès des Architectes Français.* Paris: Ducher, 1875.

———. "Des Rapports Qui Existent entre l'Archéologie Monumentale et l'Architecture Contemporaine, Ainsi Que Des Ressources Toutes Spéciales et Peu Connues Qui Fournit à l'Histoire Générale des Civilisations l'Etude Historique et Philosophique de Notre Art," *Société Centrale des Architectes: Annales des Congrès des Architectes Français. Comptes Rendus et Mémoires.* Paris: Société Centrale des Architectes, 1874-75. Vols. I-II. especially pp. 99-130.

———. *L'Architecture Privée au XIX° Siecle, Troisième Série. Décorations Intérieures Peintes.* 2 vols. Paris: Ducher et Cᵉ, 1877.

———, ed. *La Semaine des Constructeurs, Journal Hebdomadaire Illustré des Travaux Publics et Privés.* Paris, 1877-95.

———. *Ingénieurs et Architectes (un Toast et Son Commentaire).* Paris: Ducher, 1877.

———. *Motifs Historiques d'Architecture et de Sculpture d'Ornement (Deuxieme Série). Décorations Intérieures, Empruntées à des Edifices du Commencement de la Renaissance à la Fin de Louis XVI.* 2 vols. Paris: Ducher, 1880.

———. *Motifs Divers de Serrurerie; Extrait de la Revue Générale de l'Architecture et des Travaux Publics et Divers Autres Ouvrages de César Daly.* Paris: Librairie Générale de l'Architecture et des Travaux Publics, 1881-82.

———. *Des Hautes-Etudes d'Architecture et de l'Académie des Beaux-Arts à Propos du Prix Duc.* Paris: Ducher et Cᵉ, 1884.

———. *Des Hautes-Etudes d'Architecture; un Appel à Nos Corps Constituée et aux Architectes Indépendants.* Paris: André, Daly Fils, et Cᵉ, 1888.

———. "L'Architecture et l'Ethnographie." *Bibliothèque Internationale de l'Alliance Scientifique Universelle* I (1891), 41-48.

_____. "De l'Evolution Historique de l'Architecture et de la Place Qui Y Occupe l'Architecture Américaine." *Archives de la Société Americaine de France*, N.S. VIII (1892), 29-34.
_____. "Presentation of the Royal Gold Medal." *The Builder* LXIII: 2578 (2 July 1892), 5-8.

Articles by César Daly

Abbreviations of Periodicals

> *Le Glâneur: Journal d'Eure et Loire*   (LG)
> *La Phalange*   (LP)
> *La Démocratie Pacifique*   (LDP)
> *La Revue Générale de l'Architecture et des Travaux Publics*   (RGA)
> *La Semaine des Constructeurs*   (LSC)

"Le Glâneur"

"Des Envois de l'Ecole Française à Rome, et Considérations Générales sur l'Architecture", VII:36 (8 September 1836), 444-45.
"Des Envois... Deuxième Partie", VII:38 (22 September 1836), 467.
"Nouvelle Organisation Sociale", VII (29 December 1836), 641.
"De l'Ecole Sociétaire et du Système de Charles Fourier", VIII:1 (5 January 1837), 5-6.
"De l'Ecole Sociétaire... Deuxième Partie", VIII (16 February 1837), 76-77.
"De l'Ecole Sociétaire... Troisième Partie", VIII:8 (23 February 1837), 86-87.
"Fourier et Son Système", IX:41 (11 October 1838), 509.
"Exposition des Tableaux au Musée de Paris", X:12 (21 March 1839), 142-43.

"La Phalange"

"Exposition de la Théorie Sociétaire à Chartres", 2ᵉ Série, I (January 1836-December 1837), 615-17.
"Exposition... Deuxième Partie", 2ᵉ Série, I (January 1836-December 1837), 793-99.
"Système Sociale de M. Owen", 2ᵉ Série, II:2 (15 January 1838) 17-20.
"Système Sociale... Deuxième Partie", 2ᵉ Série, II:4 (15 February 1838), 49-53.
"Système Sociale... Troisième Partie", 2ᵉ Série, II:6 (15 March 1838), 81-84.
"Fortifications de Paris", 3ᵉ Série, I:27 (1 November 1840), 465-69.
"Morning Star", 3ᵉ Série, I:50 (25 December 1840), 854-56.
"Monument de Juillet Elevé sur la Place de la Bastille: du Monument de Juillet Considérée comme Oeuvre d'Art", 3ᵉ Série, II:15 (31 January 1841), 238-40.
"Monument de Juillet... Deuxième Partie", 3ᵉ Série, II:16 (5 February 1841), 267-72.

"La Démocratie Pacifique"

"Concours: Halle aux Blés de Blois", V:5 (5 July 1845), 8-9.
"Nouvelle Architecture à l'Usage des Prolétaires Anglais", VI:25 (25 January 1846), 12-14.
"La Pologne et la Presse Anglais", VI:76 (17 March 1846), 7.
"Une Découverte de la Féodalité Financière", VII:61 (11 September 1846), 7.
"Concours pour les Grands Prix de Rome", VII:63 (14, 15 September 1846) 11-12.
"Concours... Deuxième Partie", VII:64 (16 September 1846), 9-12.
"Fête au Profit de l'Association des Peintres", VIII:46 (22, 23 February 1847), 6.

"De l'Architecture Industrielle et des Gares de Chemin de Fer", VIII:44 (20 February 1847), 10-12.
"Vandalisme et Désordre", VIII:107 (3 May 1847), 5-6.
"Du Symbolisme dans l'Architecture", VIII:108 (6 May 1847), 1-6.
"Du Symbolisme... Deuxième Partie", VIII:109 (7 May 1847), 1-6.
"Du Symbolisme... Troisième Partie", VIII:101 bis (8 May 1847), 1-6.
"Solidarité entre l'Industrie et l'Art: Distribution de Prix de l'Ecole de Dessin", IX:90 (14 October 1847), 8-11.
"Le Panorama d'Egypte et de Nubie", IX:104 (30 October 1847), 10-11.
"De la Liberté dans l'Art", X:30 (4 February 1848), 10-12.
"De la Solidarité Politique", XI:114 (9 August 1848), 3-4.
"Le Rapport de la Commission d'Enquête", XI:114 (9 August 1848), 3.

"Revue Générale de l'Architecture et des Travaux Publics: Journal des Architectes, des Ingénieurs, des Archéologues, des Industriels, et des Propriétaires sous la Direction de M. César Daly, Architecte"

RGA I (1840)

"Introduction", 1-7.
"De l'Examen, de la Défense, et du Produit des Voies de Communication", 100.
"Resumé d'un Architecte en Angleterre", 157-61.
"De l'Architecte Domestique de Paris", 165-69.
"Nouvelles et Faits Divers", 191.
"De l'Architecture Domestique Monumentale", 197-205.
"Architecture Domestique: Des Habitations des Emigrés et des Maisons Mobiles", 276-85.
"Architecture Privée Monumentale", 285-86.
"Exposition de 1840", 295-302.
"Architecture Privée Monumentale", 327-33.
"Nouveau Robinet à Clapet", 396-99.
"Monument de Juillet: Elevé sur la Place de la Bastille", 406-19.
"Architecture Domestique: Des Bains dans les Maisons Particulières", 590-95.
"Des Fortifications de Paris", 601-5.
"Etudes sur l'Architecture Moderne Anglaise par M. W.H. Leeds", 616-18.
"Monument de Juillet Elevé sur la Place de la Bastille", 665-92.
"Monument de la Bastille Considéré comme Oeuvre d'Art", 746-59.

RGA II (1841)

"Introduction", 1-8.
"Projet de Conservation des Pavillons de l'Institut", 19-23.
"Les Fortifications de Paris", 26-29.
"Cérémonie de la Translation des Cendres de l'Empéreur Napoléon", 46-48.
"Notes à Propos d'un Article sur l'Emploi de Bitume", 96-98, 102.
"Aperçu Historique de l'Emploi du Bronze dans les Ouvrages d'Art", 113-29.
"Salon de 1841", 143-44, 185, 190.
"Rabelais et l'Architecture de la Renaissance. Restitution de l'Abbaye de Thélème, 196-208.
"Architecture Domestique par M.A. de Chateauneuf", 208-9.
"Salon de 1841", 319-31.
"Excursion dans les Environs de Birmingham (Angleterre): Note Historique sur les Châteaux de Warwick et de Kenilworth", 353.

"Fragments de Serrurerie du Moyen-Age", 362-63.
"Nouveau Cimetière de Glasgow", 374-77.
"Candelabras du Pont de la Concorde", 377-79.
"Mâts du Pont-Neuf (Fêtes de Juillet)", 380-81.
"Chemins de Fer des Etats-Unis de l'Amérique du Nord", 397-400.
"Maison Suédois en Bois (XVᵉ Siècle)", 401-10.
"Le Concours pour le Grand Prix d'Architecture et Envois de Rome en 1841", 466-71.
"Exposition des Projets de Tombeau pour Napoléon", 521-28.
"Paris", 544.
"Exposition des Projets de Tombeau de Napoléon", 571-81, 593-629.
"Le Tombeau de Napoléon à la Madeleine", 639-40.

RGA III (1842)

"Introduction", 1-5.
"Eléphant de la Bastille", 40-42.
"Nouvelles et Faits Divers", 42-47.
"Architecture Rurale: Introduction", 66-74.
"Note sur M. Donaldson", 80.
"De l'Achèvement de la Cathédrale de Cologne", 82-87.
"Du Concours pour la Bourse de Marseille", 122.
"Railway Atmosphérique", 207-13.
"Concours pour le Grand Prix d'Architecture", 261-74.
"Dialogues sur la Concurrence sans Limites dans la Peinture du Bâtiment", 323-30. [Review by Daly of book by M. Leclair.]
"La Manutention des Vivres de la Guerre", 355-63.
"Bibliographie: De l'Entretien des Routes d'Empierrement à l'Etat Normal, ou du Système du Balayage par L. Dumas", 532-36.
"Des Rez-de-Chaussée et des Boutiques à Paris", 561-66.
"Railway Atmosphérique", 566-70.

RGA IV (1843)

"Introduction", 1-2.
"Mémoire de M. Willis sur la Construction des Voûtes au Moyen-Age", 3-14. Translated by Daly.
"De la Locomotion Aérienne", 15-25.
"De l'Enseignement de l'Architecture en Angleterre", 121-24.
"L'Exposition Annuelle d'Architecture au Louvre", 124-37.
"Restauration Projetée de Notre-Dame de Paris", 137-41.
"L'Exposition Annuelle d'Architecture au Louvre", 160-66.
"Correspondance: Première Lettre d'Angleterre", 281-84.
"Correspondance: Deuxième Lettre d'Angleterre", 329-32.
"Machine à Balayer de M. Whitworth", 359-63.
"Rapport Adressé à M. Le Ministre de l'Intérieur par la Commission Chargée d'Examiner l'Appareil de M. Rouillet", 374-84.
"A. M. A.Villy, Mettreur, Vérificateur en Serrurerie", 413.
"Aux Constructeurs: Un Conseil Vieux de Trois Siècles", 431-32.
"Ancien Hotel de Ville de Paris", 543-44.
"Portail Septentrional et Pourtour du Choeur de la Cathédrale de Chartres", 544.

RGA V (1844)

"Introduction", 1-2.
"Du Comité Historique des Arts et Monuments", 49-57.
"Sa Nomination de Membre Honoraire et Correspondant de l'Institut Royal des Architectes Brittaniques", 96.
"L'Alhambra", 97-105.
"Grandes Portes d'Atelier", 117.
"Du Chauffage et de la Ventilation: Introduction à un Mémoire du M. René Duvoir", 118.
"Salon de 1844: Pourquoi la Presse Parle si Peu de l'Exposition des Projets d'Architecture", 178-84.
"Salon de 1844", 214-25.
"Le Restauration de Notre-Dame de Paris Confiée à MM. Lassus et Viollet-le-Duc", 237-38.
"Des Ecuries au Premiér Etage", 337-45.
"Etude sur les Théâtres: Noe Précédant un Article de M. Janniard sur Rouen", 453.
"L'Alhambra", 529-38.
"Concours pour un Projet de Halle aux Grains pour la Ville de Blois", 558-60.

RGA VI (1845-46)

"Introduction", 1-6.
"L'Alhambra", 7-14.
"Concours de Blois", 36-38.
"L'Alhambra", 49-52.
"La Science et l'Industrie: Sont-Elles les Ennemies de l'Art?" 53-55.
"L'Archéologie aux Prises avec l'Architecture: Réponse à une Critique des Annales Archéologiques", 70-76.
"Tables Synoptiques de l'Architecture du Moyen-Age", 97-98.
"Nouvelle Architecture à l'Usage des Prolétaires Anglais," 150-55.
"Communication de la Mer Mediterranée et de la Mer Rouge", 155-57.
"Ecole des Beaux-Arts de Paris: Ouverture des Cours de M. Constant-Dufeux et de M. Lebas", 177-79.
"La Grande Tour de Saint-Denis. S'Ecoulera-t-Il?" 180-82.
"Nouvelle Architecture à l'Usage des Ouvrières", 210-22.
"L'Archéologie aux Prises avec l'Architecture", 273-85.
"Opinion de l'Académie Royale des Beaux-Arts sur l'Architecture Gothique", 313-16.
"Le Salon de 1840", 322-25, 374-83.
"Concours pour les Grands Prix de Rome", 413-21.
"Les Habitations des Ouvrières", 449-56.
"De la Profession de l'Architecte", 456-65.
"L'Eglise Futur de Vaugirard", 473-78.
"Des Gares de Chemin de Fer", 509-18.
"Les Habitations des Ouvrières", 449-56.
"De la Profession de l'Architecte", 456-65.
"L'Eglise Futur de Vaugirard", 473-78.
"Des Gares de Chemin de Fer", 509-18.
"Ecole Royale des Beaux-Arts de Paris: Ouverture des Cours", 518-22.
"Gare du Chemin de Fer du Nord", 529-46.
"Notes Nécrologiques", 547-52.
"Nouvelles: De Paris, des Départements, de l'Etranger", 545-48.

RGA VII (1847)

"Introduction", 1-2.
"Une Révolution dans l'Art de Bâtir", 34-36.
"Concours pour de Projet d'une Nouvelle Salle d'Opéra", 47-48.
"Du Symbolisme dans l'Architecture", 49-64.
"Gare de Chemin de Fer du Nord (Paris)", 81-86.
"Decoration du Pont du Carrousel", 96.
"Tombeau Elevé au Cimetière Mont-Parnasse, à Paris, sur les Dessins de M.H. Labrouste", 197-202.
"Grilles et Charpentes de la Gare du Nord (Paris)", 202-5.
"De l'Architecture Religieuse au XIXe Siècle", 205-8.
"Projets d'Eglises Paroissales", 228-29.
"Solidarité entre l'Industrie et l'Art: Distribution des Prix de l'Ecole Royale Spéciale de Dessin", 290-96.
"Tombeau de Napoléon", 300-301.
"Bibliothèque Royale", 306.
"De la Liberté dans l'Art. A Monsieur Ludovic Vitet", 392-408.
"Ecole des Beaux-Arts (Paris)", 408-10.
"Jardins d'Hiver de Paris et de Lyons", 410-12.
"Médaille Royale de l'Institut des Architectes Britanniques", 412-13.
"Panorama d'Egypte et de Nubie", 412-13.
"Enseignement de la Théorie de l'Architecture", 431-36.
"Des Cours d'Histoire et de Construction à l'Ecole des Beaux-Arts de Paris", 436-441.
"Adresse à Nos Lecteurs", 449-54.
"Panorama d'Egypte et de Nubie", 454-69.
"Voyage de Deux Artistes. Discussions d'Art—Histoire Générale du Pavage", 486-541 (with H. Sirodot).

RGA VIII (1849)

"Introduction", 1-6.
"Une Grange du XIIIe Siècle", 7-8.
"Antiquités d'Athènes", 9-16.
"Architecture de l'Avenir", 26-27.
"Eglise Saint-Clothilde", 44.
"Essai sur l'Architecture Religieuse au XIXe Siècle", 64-68.
"Comble Circulaire de la Remise des Locomotives à Birmingham, Chemin de Fer de Londres à Birmingham", 80-83.
"Bibliographie: Visite à la Crèche Modèle, par M. Jules Delbrouck", 102-6.
"L'Art Contemporaine", 104-6.
"Salon de 1849", 166.
"Bibliographie: Villa Medicis (Académie de France à Rome)", 170-71.
"Guide du Voyageur dans la France Monumentale", 171-72.
"Mémoires de la Société Archéologique", 173-74.
"Maisons du Moyen Age et de la Renaissance", 184-88.
"Salon de 1849 (Revue Retrospective)", 206-20.
"Edifices pour l'Instruction Publique: Ecoles Primaires Communales", 258-61.
"Nouvelles et Faits Divers: Guerre entre Sainte-Chapelle et Le Palais de Justice de Paris", 276-88.
"Les Collections d'Objets d'Art et d'Industrie Anciens", 302-12.

"Nouveau Système de Persiennes", 327-29.
"Concours Publics", 344-46.
"Des Collections d'Objets d'Art", 368-82.
"Des Bibliothèques Publics", 415-37.
"Mausolée de Dumont d'Urville", 437-40.

RGA IX (1851)

"Introduction", 1-2.
"Restauration de Notre-Dame de Paris", 43-45.
"Industries de Bâtiment (Suite de l'Exposition de 1849)", 66-80.
"Envois de Rome et d'Athènes", 283-85.
"Nouvelles et Faits Divers: Politique et l'Architecture", 412-13, 460-70.

RGA X (1852)

"Introduction", 3-4.
"Ferronerie du Moyen-Age", 33-34.
"Ecole des Beaux-Arts de Paris", 42-43.
"Ferronerie du Moyen Age: Grille de Clôture (XIIᵉ et XIIIᵉ Siècle)", 129-30.
"Armoire Peinte du XIIIᵉ Siècle (Construite dans la Salle du Trésor de la Cathédrale de Bayeux)", 130-34.
"Ferronerie du Moyen Age: Poignées et Heurtoirs de Portes (XVᵉ et XVIᵉ Siècles)", 193-94.
"Bibliothèque Sainte-Geneviève", 379-81.
"Maison de Santé de Charenton", 384-95.
"Maisons de Paris", 396-403.
"Maisons Ouvrières d'Angleterre", 403-5.

RGA XI (1853)

"Introduction", 1-2.
"Eglise de Saint-Genou (Indre—XIᵉ Siècle)", 161-64.
"Ecole des Beaux-Arts de Paris: Du Successeur de M. Blouet à la Chaire de Théorie d'Architecture—De l'Avenir de l'Ecole", 208-10.
"Salon de 1853", 210-13.
"Observations du Directeur de la Revue", 335-36.
"Porte du XIIIᵉ Siècle: Sacristie de la Cathédrale de Rouen", 385-86.
"Peintures Murales des XIIᵉ et XIIIᵉ Siècles", 433-34.
"Croix Porte-Cierge (XVIᵉ Siècle)—à l'Eglise du Grand Saint Martin", 434-35.
"La Mairie du IIIᵉ Arrondissement de Paris", 441-48.

RGA XII (1854)

"Introduction", 1-4.
"Peinture à Fresque au XIVᵉ Siècle", 5.
"Halles Centrales de Paris", 5-34.
"M. Achille Leclère—Tombeau de Cherubini", 51-52.
"Martyrologie des Constructeurs de 1853", 52-57.
"Une Maison de Tréport", 83-86.

"La Question des Planchers de Fer (Discutée en Angleterre)", 86-96.

"Nomination de M. Duban à l'Institut", 99.

"Porte de l'Eglise de l'Abbaye de Saint-Jean-des-Chou (Bas-Rhin)", 114.

"Fenêtre du Palais de la Guadagna (Palermo)", 115.

"Eglise de Saint-Genou", 115.

"Martyrologie des Constructeurs de 1853", 139-44.

"Quelques Mots sur la Rédaction de la Revue, sur Nos Projets Futurs, et sur Nos Tendances", 192-94.

"Couvertures en Tuiles Emaillées", 289-92.

"Constructions en Briques", 370-71.

"Portes en Bois", 371.

"Bibliographie: Album de Broderie Religieuse par Rev. Père Martin", 374-76.

RGA XIII (1855)

"Introduction", 104.

"Décoration d'un Magasin de Parfumerie", 19-22.

"De la Floriculture Associée à l'Architecture", 22-24.

"Maisons d'Habitation de Londres", 57-63, 145-49.

RGA XIV (1856)

"Introduction", 1-10.

RGA XV (1857)

"Introduction", 1-2.

"La Cathédrale de Sainte-Cécile, à Albi (Département du Tarn)", 247-52.

"Mairie, Justice de Paix et Halles aux Grains, à Thoissey (Ain)", 273-74.

"Maisons de Paris", 272-78.

"Une Terre Cuite Antique Tiré du Musée de Pérouse-Italie", 297-98.

"De l'Architecture Polychrome Naturelle: Exemples de Décorations en Lave de Monuments Siciliens", 333-36.

"Reform Club (Londres)", 342-48.

RGA XVI (1858)

"Introduction", 1-6.

"La Fontaine du Palmier, de Paris. Sa Transition Tout d'une Pièce", 42-44.

"Fontaine Monumentale—Le Projet Couronnée au Concours de Bordeaux", 44-45.

"Maison d'un Peintre", 45-46.

"L'Abbaye-aux-Dames à Caen", 46-47.

"Le Télégraphe Transatlantique", 47-48.

"Tableau à l'Usage des Constructeurs-Practiciens", 78-79.

"Traité d'Architecture par M. Léonce Reynaud", 189.

"Hôtel Privé à Paris: Rue de la Victoire, no. 98", 220-26.

"Bibliographie: Rapport de l'Académie des Beaux-Arts sur le Traité d'Architecture de M. Léonce Reynaud", 236-37.

"Petites Habitations d'Eté des Environs de Paris", 264-66.

"Exemples de Serrurerie, Grilles, Portes, Fenêtres, Treilles", 267-68.

RGA XVII (1859)

"Introduction", 1-4.
"Antéfixe Etrusque Colorée", 3-4.
"Etablissements d'Instruction Primaire", 19-27.
"L'Architecture des Chemins de Fer: Gare de Paris, de la Ligne de Paris à Lyon", 27-33.
"Hôtel d'un Architecte (Cité Malesherbes—Paris)", 33-34.
"Grille d'Entrée de la Villa Montmorency", 35.
"La Russie et les Artistes Français", 36.
"Etablissements d'Instruction Primaire: Salles d'Asile", 56-62.
"L'Architecture des Chemins de Fer... Deuxième Partie", 62-65.
"L'Hôtel d'un Architecte (Cité Malesherbes—Paris)", 66-68.
"Une Laiterie à Marly-le-Roi", 68-70.
"Etablissements d'Instruction Primaire", 125-27.
"Le Grand Séminaire de Kouba près d'Alger", 127-28.
"Mur de Soutènement à la Terrasse de Meudon", 243-44.
"Maisons d'Eté des Environs de Paris", 269-70.

RGA XVIII (1860)

"Introduction", 1-8.
"Maisons d'Eté des Environs de Paris", 24-25.
"Bibliographie: L'Architecture Privée au XIXᵉ Siècle", 33-37.
"Fragments Antiques Tiré du Musée de Naples", 62.
"Appel de la Société Anglaise de Photographie Architecturale aux Photographes Français", 75.
"Les Decorés du 15 Août", 92-93.
"L'Architecture des Chemins de Fer: Gare de Perrache (Lyon), de la Ligne de Paris à Lyons", 130-32.
"Travaux à Paris", introduction by Daly, 132-42.
"Etablissements d'Instruction Primaire. Salles d'Asile—Le Mobilier", 164.
"L'Architecture des Chemins de Fer", 210-18.
"Une Maison de Paris", 222-24.
"Constructions en Bois à Strasbourg", 224-26.
"Programme d'une Salle d'Asile", 262-66.

RGA XIX (1861)

"Introduction", 1-10.
"Concours pour le Grand Opéra de Paris: Note Introductive", 14-18.
"Des Concours pour les Monuments Publics, dans le Passé, le Présent, et l'Avenir", 19-52.
"Fragments de Cheneaux Antiques de Pompeii", 65-66.
"Concours pour le Grand Opéra de Paris: Deuxième Partie", 76-107.
"Troisième Partie: Du Concours Définitif pour l'Opéra entre les Cinq Lauréats du Concours Générale", 107-33.
"Un Critique d'Art Critique", 191-92.
"Le Nouvel Hospice de Gisors", 208-15.
"L'Architecture des Chemins de Fer (Stations Intermédiaires)", 215-22.

RGA XX (1862)

"Introduction", 1-4.
"Vue Intérieure d'un Tombeau Etrusque", 3-8.
"De la Propriété Artistique et Littéraire", 29.
"Panorama du Mouvement Architecturale du Monde", 30-33.
"Une Porte Chinoise à Deux Auvents", 49-51.
"Cours de Composition d'Ornement: Grand Concours de l'Ecole Impériale de Dessin, à Paris", 158-62.
"Panorama du Mouvement Architectural du Monde Accompli dans Ces Dernières Années", 164-200.
"Les Décorés du 15 Août", 200-1.
"Concours Publics", 201-4.
"Grands Prix de Rome", 205.
"Nécrologie", 205-6.
"Panorama du Mouvement Architectural du Monde... Deuxième Partie", 271-86.

RGA XXI (1863)

"Introduction", 1-21.
"Un Puits de la Renaissance à Toulouse", 13-19.
"Hotel des Ventes Mobilières à Paris", 19-22.
"Concours Publics: Concours de Montpellier", 27-34.
"A.-N. Caristie: Notice Nécrologique", 34-41.
"Une Leçon de Decoration: Donnée par un Membre de l'Académie Française", 41-43.
"L'Architecture des Chemins de Fer", 61-62.
"Bureau d'Octroi, à Lyon", 63.
"Une Salle de Billiard", 63-66.
"L'Architecture des Chemins de Fer", 109-13.
"Modèle de Blanchisserie: Système Bouillon, Mulle et Cie", 118-22.
"Le Nouveau Théâtre de Covent-Garden", 122-28.
"Promenades et Plantations. Parcs. Jardins Publics. Squares et Boulevards de Paris", 128-32.
"Concours Publics: le Concours de Montpellier et le *Builder*", 134.
"Nécrologie: Lebrun et Benoist-Victor Lenoir", 139-42.
"Architecture des Chemins de Fer", 160-61.
"Ma Nouvelle Publication: Motifs Historiques d'Architecture et de Sculpture d'Ornement", 162-67.
"Promenades et Plantations... Deuxième Partie", 173-76.
"Concours Publics: Concours International Ouvert par l'Art-Union de Londres", 176-79.
"Modèle de Blanchisserie: Système Bouillon... Deuxième Partie", 221-29.
"Une Château près d'Odessa", 229-31.
"Le Projet-d'Hôtel de Ville: Couronne au Concours de Tourcoing (Nord)", 234-37.
"Promenades et Plantations... Troisième Partie", 245-49.
"Grand Prix de Rome", 254.
"Des Grilles de Saint-Germain-l'Auxerrois", 257.
"Fontaine de la Villa Montmorency", 278-79.
"Un Hôtel Rue du Cherche-Midi", 279-82.
"Le Nouvel Associé Etranger de Notre Académie des Beaux-Arts: T.-L. Donaldson", 284-85.

RGA XXII (1864)

"Introduction", 1-4.

"Détails du Château Grand-Ducal de Bâde", 3-4.

"Lycée Saint-Louis à Paris", 5-6.

"L'Architecture des Chemins de Fer: Maison de Gardien de Passage à Niveau", 6-7.

"Un Congé Accordé à Regret", 19-20.

"De la Réorganisation de l'Ecole des Beaux-Arts", 21-29.

"Causerie d'Histoire et d'Esthétique: Ce Qui Peut Raconter une Grille de Fer: L'Influence des Femmes sur l'Architecture au XVIIIe Siècle", 81-103.

"A Propos de M. Viollet-le-Duc et des Réformes à l'Ecole des Beaux-Arts", 129-36.

"Phidias par Beule", 159.

"Etude de la Construction des Etablissements Hospitaliers", 180.

"Architecture Historique de l'Allemagne: Divers Détails de Château de Bâde", 225-28.

"Les Petites Portes du Panthéon de Paris (Eglise Sainte-Geneviève)", 228-29.

"La Nouvelle Morgue de Paris", 229-30.

"Reposoir de la Paroisse Saint-François à Lyon", 230-31.

"Cylindrage des Chaussées à la Vapeur", 252-54.

"Une Société Internationale de Photographie d'Architecture: Appel aux Architectes Français", 254-56.

"Concours Publics", 256-57.

"Gare de Vichy: Chemin de Fer du Bourbonnais", 274-77.

"Château du Duc de Trevise à Sceaux", 277-78.

"Cours d'Esthétique et d'Histoire d'Art", 279-82.

"Des Etablissements de Librairie Architecturale de France et d'Angleterre", 282-90.

RGA XXIII (1865)

"Introduction", 1-6.

"A Nos Confrères des Départements", 22-25.

"Prospectus de la Publication: Les Théâtres de la Place de Châtelet", 31-34.

"Du Style Louis XVI: A Propos la Porte Principale du Lycée Impériale Louis-le-Grand, à Paris", 50-55.

"Du Style Louis XIII", 97-100.

"L'Eglise Saint-Paul, à Paris", 145-46.

"L'Architecture Commerciale à Paris: Maison Rue du Conservatoire, N° 11", 159-61.

"Magasins Généraux de Melun", 161-66.

"Ecole Impériale des Beaux-Arts (Section d'Architecture): Grands Prix—Envois de Rome", 166-68.

"Prêtre et Artiste", 171-72.

"Société Académique d'Architecture de Lyon: Compte-Rendu des Travaux des Années 1863-1864", 181-84.

"Du Style XIII: A Propos des Portes de l'Eglise Saint-Laurent à Paris", 193-94.

"Porte Cochère: Rue des Francs-Bourgeois, à Paris", 194.

"Croix des Cimetières", 195-96.

"Tribunal de Commerce de Paris", 248-54.

"De la Condition des Artistes dans l'Antiquité Grecque par M. H. Bazin," 254-55.

RGA XXIV (1866)

"Introduction", 1-10.
"Porte Quai Voltaire", 18.
"La Chapelle de l'Asile des Aliénés de Braqueville (Haute-Garonne)", 18-19.
"Boutique du XVIIIᵉ Siècle: Rue des Prouvaires, à Paris", 49-50.
"Porte, Rue Saint-Nicolas-du-Chardonnet, à Paris", 50-51.
"Tribunal de Commerce (Paris)", 51-52.
"Portes de Maisons (Paris)", 51-52.
"Palais de Justice, à Paris", 98-99.
"Etude sur l'Arc de Triomphe de Louis XIV (Porte de Paris), à Lille par M.J.-B. Godey", 140-41.
"D'un Confessional dans l'Eglise Saint-Germain-l'Auxerrois, à Paris", 158-60.
"Les Ecuries de l'Empereur (Paris) par M. Tetaz, Architecte", 216-21.
"Nécrologie: Ingres et Cousin", 232-33.
"Une Petition en Faveur des Concours Publics", 256-58.

RGA XXV (1867)

"Introduction", 1-9.
"Fontaine Medicis dans le Jardin du Luxembourg, à Paris", 7-9.
"Le Palais de Justice, à Paris", 9-10.
"Du Casernement des Troupes en France et en Algérie", 10-13.
"Causerie sur l'Esthétique: a Propos d'un Vase d'Amortissement du Palais de l'Institut", 50-56.
"Le Marché Saint-Maur-Saint-Germain", 76-79.
"Le Banquet de l'Union Centrale des Beaux-Arts Appliqués à l'Industrie", 90-91.
"Concours Publics", 120.
"Atelier de Preparation aux Ecoles d'Architecture", 126-27.
"Le Nouvel Opéra de Paris", 141-42.
"Hôtel de Biseul, XVIIᵉ Siècle", 152-54.
"L'Art et la Critique", 154.
"Une Villa", 155-58.
"Que Faut-il Entendre par Ces Mots: "Architecture de la Renaissance: Specimens des XVIᵉ et XVIIᵉ Siècles", 207-16.

RGA XXVI (1868)

"Introduction", 1-5.
"Exposition Universelle de 1867: Pavillon Impériale", 16-25.
"Château de Fournil (Dourdogne)", 27-29.
"Le Beau dans l'Utile", 34-37.
"Hôtel d'Aumont (XVIIᵉ Siècle)", 103-9.
"Habitations d'Artistes: Hôtel d'un Peintre", 113-16.
"Habitations d'Artistes: Hôtel d'un Sculpteur", 157-58.

RGA XXVII (1869)

"Introduction", 1-7.
"L'Architecture Funéraire: Spécimens de Tombeaux, Mausolées, Chapelles Funéraires, Sarcophages, Stèles, Pierres Tombales, etc.", 5-7.

Works Consulted

"De l'Architecture de l'Avenir: A Propos la Renaissance Française", 10-71.
"Le Prix de Cent Mille Francs", 177-84.
"Notice Historique sur la Vie et les Ouvrages de M. Lebas", 244-51.
"Nécrologie: M.A. Morel", 234.
"Monastère de l'Assomption (Bordeaux)", 277-78.

RGA XXVIII (1870)

"Introduction", 1-12.
"Des Honoraires de l'Architecte Appel aux Sociétés d'Architecture de France", 31-33.
"Introduction: Reprise du XXVIIIe Volume", 97-102.
"Traité de l'Art de la Charpenterie: Eléments de la Charpenterie Métallique", 142-44. Review by Daly.
"Nécrologie: Constant-Dufeux", 187-90.
"Funérailles de Félix Duban", 199-222.
"Maison de Boston", 236-37.
"Grand Prix de Rome", 246-49.
"Congrès Achille Leclère: Pour un Monument Funéraire de la Défense de Paris", 249-55.

RGA XXIX (1871)

"Introduction", 1-10.
"Panneau de Bois Sculpté: Fin du XVe Siècle", 9-11.
"Console du XVIIIe Siècle", 12.
"Porte-Grille de l'Hôtel Demidoff, à Paris", 18-20.
"De l'Institut Américain des Architectes", 29-33.
"Les Haute-Etudes en Architecture: le Prix Duc", 33-36.
"Hygiène Publique en Angleterre", 36-37.
"Exposition de la Société des Amis des Arts, à Pau", 37-38.
"Société Nationale des Architectes Français", 38-40.
"Vase de Plomb du Bassin de Neptune, à Versailles", 49-50.
"Une Figure Antique à Gaine", 50-51.
"Constant-Dufeux", 81.
"De la Société et de l'Architecture: à Propos de Notre Architecture Funéraire", 97-107.
"Société Nationale des Architectes de France", 137.
"Ministère de l'Agriculture du Commerce et des Travaux Publics, à Paris", 203-5.
"Figures à Gaine (XVIe et XVIIe Siècles)", 242.

RGA XXX (1873)

"Introduction", 1-4.
"Vase en Plomb", 5.
"Tourelle de l'Hôtel Lamoignon, à Paris", 5-6.
"Hôtel Privé Rue Francois Ier, à Paris", 6-8.
"Concours de l'Hôtel de Ville de Paris", 24-37, 107-18.
"Conférences Nationales de la Société Centrale des Architectes: Conférences de M. Daly", 122-24.
"Nouvelle Méthode d'Encourager les Arts", 236-37.
"A Propos du Concours de Lunéville", 268.
"Concours Publics—Concours à Maçon pour l'Erection d'une Statue de Lamartine", 269-73.
"Livres-Reçus", 273-74. Review by Daly.

RGA XXXI (1874)

"Introduction", 1-4.
"Monument Funéraire Elevé en l'Honneur de Constant-Dufeux: Discours de M. César Daly", 19-23.
"Nouvelle Méthode d'Encourager les Arts", 36-42.
"Miroir avec Cadre en Bois Sculpté (XVIe Siècle)", 97.
"La Société d'Encouragement pour la Propagation des Livres d'Art", 128-129.
"Théâtre d'Angers", 145-48.
"Souscription pour les Fouilles à Exécuter à l'Acropole d'Athènes", 175.

RGA XXXII (1875)

"Introduction", 1-4.
"Nécrologie", 76-78.
"Cartouche (XVIe Siècle) au Siècle de Bournazel (Aveyron)", 97-98.
"Les Travaux Publics depuis l'Antiquité jusqu'aux Temps Modernes par Sir John Hawksmoor", 176. Review by Daly.
"Une Réclamation", 182.
"Une Tourelle (XVe Siècle), Rue Vieille-du-Temple, à Paris", 193.
"Escalier (XVIIe Siècle) d'un Hôtel Privé, Rue Séguier, à Paris", 193-94.
"Tombeaux des Généraux Thomas et Lecomte au Cimetière de l'Est, à Paris", 242-54.
"Villa à Croissy (Seine et Oise) par M. Duc", 269-74.

RGA XXXIII (1876)

"Introduction", 1-6.
"Concours Publics: Concours pour le Prix Duc", 38-40.
"Concours à Billy (Belgique): De Quelques Devises des Concurrents", 40-41.
"Groupe Scolaire, Rue d'Alésia, à Paris par M.E. Vaudremer", 98.
"Le Nouveau Journal, La Semaine des Constructeurs", 162-68.
"Monument d'Ingres à l'Ecole des Beaux-Arts à Paris", 207-9.
"A Propos de la Reconstitution des Tuileries", 211-13.

RGA XXXIV (1877)

"Introduction", 1-4.
"Nécrologie: Baltzar Cronstad", 33-34.
"Tombeau de Deux Enfants Jumeaux", 56-57.
"Henri Labrouste: Architecte, Membre de l'Institut", 60-65.
"La Question des Concours Publics au Concours National des Architectes", 114-19.
"Chronique: Mort de Sir Digby Wyatt et de M.E. Sharpe", 138.
"Ingénieurs et Architectes", 160-65.
"Congrès National des Architectes (5e Session—1877): Discours de M. César Daly", 185-86.

RGA XXXV (1878)

"Introduction", 1-4.
"De l'Hygiène Publique et Privée", 13-14.
"Stalles de l'Eglise Saint-Sernin (XVIIe Siècle)", 49.

"Balcons en Fer Forge: Hôtel Privé, Rue Magnan, à Paris", 50-51.
"Les Deux Plans de l'Exposition Considérée dans Leurs Rapports avec l'Art", 178-200.

RGA XXXVI (1879)

"Introduction", 1-4.
"Les Deux Plans de l'Exposition Considérée dans Leurs Rapports avec l'Art", 194-224.
"De l'Etablissement des Arches du Pont Réalisant le Maximum de Stabilité", 242.

RGA XXXVII (1880)

"Introduction", 1-6.

RGA XXXVIII (1881)

"Chronique: la Médaille d'Or de l'Institut Royale des Architectes Brittaniques", 136-39.
"Le Panthéon et Ses Peintures Murales", 230-31.

RGA XXXIX (1882)

"Introduction", 1-16.
"La Maçonnerie Egyptienne", 49-54.
"La Gargouille la Plus Ancienne du Monde", 97-106.
"Une Porte de la Première Moitié du XVIIe Siècle", 103-6.
"Une Nouvelle Recrue en Architecture", 135.
"La Voûte Egyptienne: Son Origine Préhistorique", 145-60.
"Fontaine de Gaillon", 161-62.
"Le Jubé de Saint-Etienne, à Toulouse", 198.
"La Peinture Décorative de la Chapelle de la Vierge, à la Cathédrale de la Rochelle", 199-203.
"Le Monument du Générale de Division Saget à Grand Villiers", 242-44.
"Tombeau de F.B. Lambert par M. Huguelin", 247-48.

RGA XL (1883)

"Le Nouveau Musée Zoologique du Jardin des Plantes". Extended note to article by F. Monmory,
   19n. 2.
"L'Amérique à la Recherche d'un Procédé de Délassement", 81-83.
"Une Question à Traiter à l'Ecole des Beaux-Arts", 83-84.
"Le Mont Saint-Michel", 138-39.
"Mosquée de Medine", 198-99.

RGA XLI (1884)

"Introduction", 1-9.
"Concours Trimestriels d'Architecture à l'Ecole Nationale Décoratif (Nîmes)", 25-27.
"Discours de M. César Daly sur le Diplôme d'Architecture", 27-35 (with M. Daly).
"Toast de M. César Daly", 35.
"Bas Relief à l'Hôtel de Strasbourg (Imprimerie Nationale)", 49-51.
"Un Meuble-Vestiaire par M. Edmond Guillaume", 63-66.
"Les Deux Congrès de Nice: Congrès International", 77-79.
"Un Meuble Vestiaire par M. Edmond Guillaume. Deuxième Partie", 100-12.

"Première Excursion en Algérie", 193.
"Des Hautes-Etudes d'Architecture et l'Académie des Beaux-Arts", 223-32.

RGA XLII (1885)

"Ce Qui Peut Raconter les Pierres d'un Tombeau et du Symbolisme Funéraire Considérée dans Ses Phases Successives à Propos du Tombeau d'un Sceptique Romain à Akbou (Kabylie)", 49-61.
"L'Esthétique, la Science, l'Art et l'Histoire, Leurs Apports", 64-75.
"Villa B...à Chatou (Seine et Oise) par M. Bardon", 80.
"Funérailles de Victor Hugo", 81-83.
"Congrès Annuel des Architectes", 91-93.
"Le Livre de M. White: de l'Architecture et des Edifices Publics dans Leurs Rapports avec l'Ecole, l'Acadèmie et l'Etat, Tant à Paris, Qu'on à Londres", review by Daly, 94-95.
"A Nos Abonnés", 97.
"L'Architecte et Ses Critiques", 118-22.
"Congrès Annuel des Architectes (à Paris)", 135-43.
"Ce Qui Peuvent Raconter les Pierres d'un Tombeau", 145-46.
"Grille au Château de Wideville", 149-51.
"Restitution du Temple de Jerusalem d'après Ezéchiel", 151-67.
"Congrès Annuel des Architectes (à Paris)", 179-87.
"Trois Livres Anglais Qui Devraient Etre Français", 189-92.
"Porte du Collège des Infantes (Tolède)", 238-40.
"Palais del Consiglio à Verone (Italie)", 242-43.

RGA XLIII (1886)

"Incrustations de Marbre et Faience (XV^c S.) à Damas", 5.
"Maisons Américaines", 23-25.
"Renaissance Hollandaise", 49.
"Les Temples Japonais", 50-51.
"Salon de 1886", 88-94.
"La Medaille d'Or de la Reine Victoria et M. Ch. Garnier, de l'Institut", 94.
"Les Temples Bouddhistes du Japon", 97.
"Fenêtre de la Salle à Manger", 184-85.
"Boudoir et Cabinet de Travail", 185-86.
"Hôtel de Ville d'Angers (Renaissance Flamande)", 210-11.
"Décorations Polychromes sur Surfaces Plates au Japon", 211-12.
"Peintures Décoratives Françaises du XVII^c Siècle", 213-14.
"Tombeau de Victor Masse par M. Ch. Garnier", 258.

RGA XLIV (1887)

"Introduction", 1-4.
"Les Temples Bouddhistas du Japon", 7-8.
"Deuxième Note: Procédés de Construction pour Régistrer aux Effets des Tremblements de Terre", 15-18.
"Un Temple Rustique au Japon", 23-25.
"Une Laterne Qui Parle", 57-61.
"Une Porte d'Angle de la Renaissance à Périgueux", 61-62.
"Monument de l'Affranchissement de l'Escaut à Anvers (Belgique)", 64-72.

"Tombeaux Lyciens et Phrygiens Tailles dans le Roc", 104-9.
"Un Arc de Triomphe (XVII S.)", 110.
"Marbre Incrusté: Architecture Orientale", 151.
"L'Hôtel de Burges à Londres", 163-71.
"L'Architecture Funéraire au Japon", 201-5.
"Hôtel de Burges à London. Deuxième Partie", 206-18.

RGA XLA (1888-1890)

"Introduction: des Hautes-Etudes d'Architecture—Un Appel à Nos Corps Continués et aux Architectes Indépendants", 1-24.
"La Maison aux Masques ou de l'Animalité dans l'Architecture", 24-28.
"Porte du Palais Brignole, à Gênes", 32.
"Les Hautes-Etudes d'Architecture", 57-62.
"Congrès International des Architectes à Paris (1889)—Compte-Rendu du Discours de César Daly", 146-48.

"La Semaine des Constructeurs: Journal Hebdomadaire Illustré des Travaux Publics et Privés

LSC I (1876-77)

"Ce Que C'est Que la Semaine des Constructeurs," I:15 (22 July 1876), 1-3.
"Correspondance: Une Réclamation." I:6 (19 August 1876), 69.

LSC II (1877-78)

"Chronique: Ingénieurs et Architectes—Un Toast et Son Commentaire." II:28 (12 January 1878), 325-26.
"Une Conférence de Notre Directeur Général." II:33 (16 February 1878), 389-90.
"Congrès Scientifique de France." II:36 (9 March 1878), 421-22.
"Les Arts à Nice." II:37 (16 March 1878), 435.
"Denfert Rochereau." II:46 (18 May 1878), 459.
"Chronique: en Avant les Architectes." II:48 (1 June 1878), 565-66.
"Chronique: un Bon Conseil aux Administrateurs Communales." II:49 (8 June 1878), 577.
"Chronique: un Mot d'Avis." II:50 (15 June 1878), 589.

LSC III (1878-79)

"A Propos du Congrès des Architectes." III (20 July 1878), 25.
"Un Premier Mot sur les Conférences Architecturales du Trocadéro." III:5 (3 August 1878), 49-50.
"A Propos de la Conférence de M. Hermant." III:7 (17 August 1878), 73-74.
"Le Nouveau Théâtre de Monte Carlo de Ch. Garnier." III:31 (1 February 1879), 361-62.

LSC IV (1879-80)

"La Prochaine Exposition des Beaux-Arts de Nice." IV:17 (25 October 1879), 193.
"La Revue Générale de l'Architecture et des Travaux Publics." IV:45 (8 May 1880), 529-30.

LSC V (1880-81)

"Courrier de Nice: Banquet Annuel de la Société des Beaux-Arts." V:29 (15 January 1881), 337-38.

LSC VI (1881-82)

"Les Etudes Historiques en Architecture." VI:41 (8 April 1882), 481-83.

LSC VII (1882-83)

"Chronique: Le Symbolisme dans l'Art." VII:47 (19 May 1883), 553-56. With Paul Planat.

LSC IX (1884-85)

"Ce Que C'est Que l'Esthétique." IX:38 (21 March 1885), 445.
"Lettre à P. Planat." IX:39 (28 March 1885), 457.

LSC X (1885-86)

"Bibliographie: Anvers à Travers les Ages." X:28 (9 January 1886), 334.

LSC XI (1886-87)

"L'Origine de l'Astragale." XI:7 (14 August 1886), 76-77.
"Chronique: des Musées Commerciaux et Pourquoi *La Semaine* S'y Interesse." XI:16 (16 October 1886), 181-82.
"Chronique: les Trois Questions Parisiennes et le Métropolitain." XI:19 (6 November 1886), 217-18.
"Extrait du Discours sur le Diplôme des Architectes Prononcé au Congrès de Nice en 1885." *LSC* XI:28 (8 January 1887), 327.
"Nécrologie: R. Robert." XI:46 (14 May 1887), 551.
"Du Rationalisme en Architecture." XI:47 (21 May 1887), 553-55.
"Vieux Souvenirs: une Causerie avec Henri Labrouste à Propos de L'Ecole de "la Verité dans l'Art." XI:52 (25 June 1887), 613-14.

LSC XII (1887-88)

"Chronique: Une Question Intéressante—Réponse à un Lecteur." XII:34 (18 February 1888), 397.
"La Liberté dans l'Art." XII:52 (23 June 1888), 613-15.

LSC XIII (1888-89)

"Le Paysan Architecte et Décorateur." XIII:1 (1 July 1888), 1-5.
"Pour le Progrès—Par le Travail." XIII:3 (14 July 1888), 25.
"L'Ecole du 'Cela Fait Bien'." XIII:21 (17 November 1888), 241.
"Opéra Comique et les Concours Publics." XIII:22 (24 November 1888), 265-66.
"Varia: Reflections, Extraits, Anecdotes, Pensées, etc." XIII:24 (8 December 1888), 277-78.

"La Germination de l'Architecture de l'Avenir." XIII:27 (29 December 1888), 313-15.
"La Révolution Architecturale en Voie d'Accomplissement." XIII:31 (26 January 1889), 361-63.

LSC XIV (1889-90)

"Conférence sur les Hautes Etudes d'Architecture Faite par M. César Daly." XIV:3 (13 July 1889), 25-28.
"Conférence sur les Hautes Etudes... Deuxième Partie." XIV:4 (20 July 1889), 37-41.
"Clôture de l'Exposition du Centenaire." XIV:29 (9 November 1889), 229.
"De l'Origine du Plus Ancien Style d'Architecture." XIV:34 (15 February 1890), 397-98.
"Comment On Peut Comprendre la Grandeur de l'Architecture." XIV:36 (1 March 1890), 421.
"L'Union Générale des Architectes." XIV:44 (26 April 1890), 517-20.
"Appendice." XIV:44 (26 April 1890), 520-21.
"Evolution dans l'Architecture Considérée dans Ses Rapports avec l'Ethnographie." XIV:50 (7 June 1890), 598-99.
"De l'Enseignement de l'Architecture: Une Grave Cause d'Erreurs." XIV:52 (21 June 1890), 613.

LSC XV (1890-91)

"Le Progrès en Architecture." XV:6 (2 August 1890), 61-62.
"Lettres sur l'Esthétique Architecturale (Première lettre)." XV:17 (18 October 1890), 193-96.
"Le Croyant et l'Artiste." XV:29 (10 January 1891), 339.
"Un Vrai Concours Public et Inofficiel." XV:51 (15 June 1891), 601.

LSC XVI (1891-92)

"L'Union Centrale des Arts Décoratifs." XVI:1 (27 June 1891), 1-2.
"Voix de Dehors." XVI:5 (25 July 1891), 49-50.
"Souvenirs Anciens et Récents." VI:11 (5 September 1891), 120-21.

LSC XVII (1892-93)

"Varia (No. 2)." XVII:40 (1 April 1893), 469.
"Varia (No. 3)." XVII:41 (8 April 1893), 481.

LSC XVIII (1893-94)

"A Propos des Concours Publics." XVIII:8 (19 August 1893), 85-86.

Archival Sources

A. Archives Nationales. Paris.

Carton Number	Description
AJ^{52} 190	Catalogue des Projets Ayant Obtenu les Grands Prix ou des Médailles de Composition d'Architecture et de Construction dans les Concours de l'Institut et de l'Ecole de 1723 à 1867.

AJ⁵² 237	Régistres Matriculés des Elèves de la Section d'Architecture. 1801-Jan. 1836. Nos. 1 à 1000.

AJ^{52} 237 — Régistres Matriculés des Elèves de la Section d'Architecture. 1801-Jan. 1836. Nos. 1 à 1000.

AJ^{52} 239 — Régistres Matriculés des Elèves de la Section d'Architecture. 1800-76. Nos. 1 à 3032.

AJ^{52} 244 — Régistre Chronologique des Elèves Architectes Donnant Leur Date d'Entrée en 1ere Classe et à Partir de 1869, Leur Date d'Admission en 2e Classe. 1819-98.

AJ^{52} 245 — Listes des Elèves—Architectes de 1ere Classe (2) 1819-93. Classement Alphabétique et Chronologique.

AJ^{52} 361 — Dossiers Individuels des Elèves. (Beginning with Second Empire). Surnames Couvrecher—Deglane.

AJ^{52} 448 — Collection du Musée des Etudes et de la Bibliothèque: Dons et Legs. XIXe—XXe S. Dossiers Alphabétiques des Donateurs Composés de Correspondance et d'Inventaires des Donateurs—Daly fils.

AJ^{52} 454 — Inventaire sur Fiches des Moulages, des Copies et des Dessins Provenant de Collections et de Concours. d'Elèves, Conservés à l'Ecole des Beaux-Arts.

F^{17} 1404 — Academie de Douai. Correspondance Générale. College Royal de Douai. Collèges Communales.

F^{17} 20 062 (AVA-AVR) — Dossiers des Anciens Fonctionnaires de Enregistrements Primaire, Secondaire, et Supérieure. XIXe S.

F^{17} 21 231 (MALL—MALLET) — Dossiers des Anciens Fonctionnaires des Enregistrements Primaire, Secondaire, et Supérieure. XIXe S.

F^{17}* 317^2 — Elèves de gouvernement dans les Lycées et Collèges Royaux par Académies: Douai 1811-1831.

F^{17}* 322 — Elèves du Gouvernement dans les Lycées et Collèges Royaux par les Académies: Douai 1811-31.

F^{17}* 340 — Répertoire d'Elèves du Gouvernement dans les Collèges Royaux. 1822-46. Douai.

F^{18} 413 — Répertoire Alphabétique des Directeurs, Gérants et Propriétaires de Journaux Parisiens, 1820-94. Revue Générale de l'Architecture, 1874.

F^{19} 4536 — Edifices Diocésains: Organisation du Service Centrale et des Inspections. 1814-1900.

F^{19} 4544	Commission de Repartition des Fonds pour les Edifices Religieux. Commission des Arts et Edifices Religieux; Rapports, Procès-Verbaux et Correspondance. Système de Construction d'Eglises Boileau.
F^{19} 4545	Conservation des Edifices Religieux: Rapports et Correspondance (dans l'Ordre des Conservations) 1849-50.
F^{19} 4546	Comité des Inspecteurs Diocésains: Procès-Verbaux et Pièces Jointes. 1853-54.
F^{19} 4547	Comité des Inspecteurs Diocésains... 1854-55.
F^{19} 4548	Comité des Inspecteurs Diocésains... 1855-57.
F^{19} 4549	Comité des Inspecteurs Diocésains... 1858-59.
F^{19} 4550	Comité des Inspecteurs Diocésains... 1859-61.
F^{19} 4551	Comité des Inspecteurs Diocésains... 1861-64.
F^{19} 4552	Comité des Inspecteurs Diocésains... 1864-67.
F^{19} 4553	Comité des Inspecteurs Diocésains... 1868-70.
F^{19} 4554	Comité des Inspecteurs Diocésains... 1871-74.
F^{19} 4555	Comité des Inspecteurs Diocésains... 1874-77.
F^{19} 4556	Comité des Inspecteurs Diocésains... 1878-79.
F^{19} 4561	Comité des Inspecteurs Diocésains: Fournitures; Copies de Plans, Dessins; Etats des Architectes Diocésains 1828-75.
F^{19} 4595	Edifices Diocésains: Liquidation des Dépenses (dans l'Ordre des Diocèses): Albi.
F^{19} 7218	Contrôle des Edifices Diocésains: Organisation (1840-1907); Personnel (1854-1906); Honoraires (1895-1907).
F^{19} 7219	Contrôle des Travaux Diocésains: Organisation (1840-1907). Personnel (1854-1906).
F^{19} 7220	Comité des Inspecteurs Généraux des Edifices Diocésains et Paroissales: Personnel (1840-1907); Organisation des Services Diocésains (1848-1904); Frais de Voyages des Inspecteurs Généraux (1855-1906); Nominations (1853-1883); Arreté des 18 Février 1882. Divisions de la France en 3 Circonscriptions. 1862-1906.
F^{19} 7224	Cours d'Architecture (1886-1901); Relevés et Copies de Places; Publication Intitulée: Les Cathédrales de France (1879-1909).

F^{19} 7230	Dossier Personnel des Architectes et des Inspecteurs Diocésains: CALS à DUSSIERE.
F^{19} 8043	Personnel, Generalités.
F^{19} 8044	Dossiers Personnels, Architectes Diocésains, Surveillants, Contrôleurs et Travaux Diocésains; 1858-1907; AIGUE-SPARSSE—LITZ.
F^{19} 8045	Dossiers Personnels, Architectes Diocésains, Surveillants, Contrôleurs de Travaux Diocésains; 1858-1907; MAGNE-WOTLING.
F^{19}* 1439	Commission des Arts et Edifices Religieux: Mouvement des Dossiers (Enregistrement Numérique). 1849-70.
F^{19}* 1440	Commision des Arts et Edifices Religieux: Mouvement des Dossiers (Enregistrement Numérique). 1849-70.
F^{19}* 1443	Nominations aux Bourses (Bourses Entières et Demi-Bourses). Par Diocèses. AGEN-GRENOBLE, LANGRES-VIVIERS (1862-77).
F^{21} 1905	Eglise Metropolitaine (ALBI)—4 Articles. Plans, Coupes, Elévations à l'Encre sur Calque. October 1842.

B. Archives Départmentales du Tarn. Albi, Tarn.

Dossier Number	Description
1 V 418	Edifices Diocésains. Architectes. 1849-94.
1 V 438	Cathédrale d'Albi. Travaux de Restauration et Entretien, Rapports, Devis, Approbation, Adjudication, Mémoires, Reglement. 1848-50.
1 V 439	Cathédrale d'Albi. 1851.
1 V 440	Cathédrale d'Albi. 1852-53.
1 V 441	Cathédrale d'Albi. 1854.
1 V 442	Cathédrale d'Albi. 1855.
1 V 443	Cathédrale d'Albi. 1856-57.
1 V 444	Cathédrale d'Albi. 1858-59.
1 V 445	Cathédrale d'Albi. 1860-61.
1 V 446	Cathédrale d'Albi. 1862-65.

1 V 447	Cathédrale d'Albi. 1866-70.
1 V 448	Cathédrale d'Albi. 1871-74.
1 V 449	Cathédrale d'Albi. 1875-79.
1 V 461	Cathédrale d'Albi. Correspondance Générale. 1839-98.

C. Archives des Services Historiques de l'Armée, Château de Vincennes. Paris.

Dossier of John Daley. Including Letters written by Daley dated 30 Jan 1810, 19 Dec 1811, 24 Dec 1811, 9 Jan 1812, 29 Jan 1812, 13 Feb 1812, 19 Feb 1812, 4 Mar 1812, 10 Mar 1812, 26 Mar 1812, 3 Apr 1812. 2 Letters of good conduct written by M. Le Sage at Sarrelouis, dated 30 Jan 1810, and Duc de Feltre at Sarrelouis, dated 24 Jan 1811.

D. Archives de la Ministère des Affaires Culturelles. Paris

Carton (Département 81). Albi-Cathédrale. Tarn. Includes drawings by Daly, and sucessors to his post as architects-diocésain Ruprich Robert and Hardy.

Dossier Tarn 1474 bis. Albi-Cathédrale Ste Cecile. Premier dossier. Includes letter from Viollet-le-Duc to the Ministre des Travaux Publics.

E. Public Record Office. Kew, Surrey, England.

Carton Number	**Description**
ADM 103 467	Dossiers—Prisoners of War. Napoleonic Wars.
ADM 103 468	Records of English Prisoners of War in France. Napoleonic Wars.

F. Archives of the Royal Institute of British Architects, London.

Minutes: Royal Gold Medal Committee of Council. Especially dates 22 Jan 1892, 1 Feb 1892.

Dossier of César-Denis Daly. Correspondant. Includes obituary, with complete list of his academic and professional honors. Letters to William H. White dated 6 Sept 1888, 18 Sept 1888, 25 Sept 1888, 1 Oct 1888, 22 Aug 1891, 31 Mar 1892, 1 Sept 1892, 3 Sept 1892, 8 Nov 1893, 29 Nov. 1893, 12 Dec 1893.

Biographical Sources

Auvray, Louis and Bellier de la Chavignerie, Emile. "César Daly." *Dictionnaire Générale des Artistes de l'Ecole Française Depuis l'Origine des Arts du Dessin Jusqu'à Nos Jours.* Paris: Librairie Renouard, 1882, 331-32.
Barbey d'Aurevilly, Jules. "César Daly." *Critiques Diverses,* Paris: Alphonse Lemerre, 1909.
Becherer, Richard. "Caution: Irony at Play in César Daly's 'L'Architecture Contemporaine'." *Modulus* XV (1982), 56-72.

"Biographies d'Amis des Monuments et des Arts: César Daly." *L'Ami des Monuments et des Arts (Organe du Comité des Monuments Français) VIII* (1894), 81-85.

Bulletin de la Société de Colonisation Européo-Américaine au Texas. Brussels: J.H. Briand, 1855-57.

Delaire, Roux, and David de Penandrun. *Les Architectes Elèves de l'Ecole des Beaux-Arts (1793-1907).* Paris: Librairie de la Construction Moderne, 1907.

"César Daly." *American Architect and Building News* 43 (1894), 37, 151.

"César Daly." *Inland Architect and News Record* XXIII (February 1894), 2.

"César Daly." *La Rénovation* VII:40 (31 August 1894), 1.

"César Daly." *Thieme-Becker Künstler Lexicon.* Leipzig: E.A. Seemann, 1913, VIII, 310.

"Daly, César-Denis." *Dictionnaire de Biographie Française,* Paris: Librairie Letouzey et Ane, 1965, X, 18.

Daly, Marcel. "Chronique: Une Question Brûlante:—Les Architectes et les Elections! Un Vieux Souvenir de 1848." *LSC* X:11 (12 September 1885), 121-22.

_____. "Architecture au Jour le Jour." *LSC* XV:24 (6 December 1890), 277-78.

_____. "César Daly." *LSC* XVIII:30 (20 January 1894), 349-51.

_____. "La Médaille d'Or de la Reine d'Angleterre." *LSC* XVI:47 (14 May 1892), 549-50.

Favardin, Patrick. "La Villa, ou l'Avènement d'un Nouveau Monde d'Habitation." *Monuments Historiques de la France* 102: 2 (April 1979), 57-60.

Hautecoeur, Louis. *L'Histoire de l'Architecture Classique en France.* Vols. VI, VII. Paris: Picard Press, 1955, 1957.

"Hero of the Ateliers." *Northwest Architect* VII (June 1943), 6.

"The Late M. César Daly." *The Builder,* LXVI:2659 (20 January 1894), 46-47.

"The Late César Daly." *RIBA Journal* 3ᵉS. I(1894), 232-34, 433-34.

Lipstadt, Hélène. "César Daly et l'Habitation." *Architecture, Mouvement, Continuité* 42 (March 1977), 37-39.

_____. "César Daly: Revolutionary Architect?" *Architectural Design* 48:11-12 (Nov-Dec. 1978), 18-28.

_____. "Housing the Bourgeoisie: César Daly and the Ideal Home." *Oppositions* VIII (Spring 1977), 34-47.

_____. "Pour une Histoire Sociale de la Presse Architecturale *La Revue Générale de l'Architecture* et César Daly (1840-1888)." Thèse de Troisième Cycle, Ecole des Hautes Etudes en Sciences Sociales, Paris, 1979.

_____. "Toast aux Ingénieurs: César Daly 1811-1894." *Cahiers de Recherche Architecturale* 2 (1978), 28-30.

_____and Mendelsohn, Harvey. *Architecte et Ingénieur dans la Presse: Polémique, Débat, Conflit.* Paris: CORDA-IERAU, 1980.

Merimée, Prosper. Ed. Maurice Paturier. *Correspondence Générale.* Toulouse: Edouard Privat, 1964.

"M. César Daly and the War." *The Architect* V (4 February 1871), 63.

"Nécrologie: M. César Daly." *La Construction Moderne* IX:16 (20 January 1894), 191.

"Presentation of the Royal Gold Medal." *The Builder* LXIII:2578 (2 July 1892), 5-8.

Sturgis, Russell. *A Dictionary of Architecture and Building.* New York: The Macmillan Company, 1904.

Van Zanten, Ann Lorenz. "César Daly and the *Revue Générale de l'Architecture.*" Diss. Harvard 1980.

_____. "Form and Society: César Daly and the *Revue Générale de l'Architecture.*" *Oppositions* VII (Spring 1977), 137-45.

Family History

Burke, Sir Bernard. *History of the Landed of Ireland.* 10th ed. London: Harrison and Sons, 1904.

Dictionary of National Biography. London: Smith, Elder, and Co., 1888.

D'Amat, Roman and M. Prévost. *Dictionnaire de Biographie Française.* Paris: Librairie Letouzey et Ané, 1956. Tome VII.

De Calonne, Alexandre. *Considerations on the Past, Present, and Future State of France.* London: J. Evans, 1791.

Fraser, Edward. *Napoleon the Gaoler.* London: Methuen and Co., 1914.

Lacour-Gayet, Robert. *Calonne: Financier, Réformateur, Contre-Révolutionnaire.* Paris: Librairie Hachette, 1963.

Lewis, Michael. *Napoleon and His British Captives.* London: George Allen and Unwin, 1962.

MacLysaght, Edward. *Irish Families, Their Names, Arms, and Origins.* Dublin: Hodges, Figgis, and Co., 1957.

O'Byrne, William. *Naval Biographical Dictionary.* London: John Murray, 1849.

O'Daly, Aenghus. ed. John O'Donovan. *The Tribes of Ireland: a Satire.* Dublin: John O'Daly, 1852.

Vallance, James. *A Catalogue of the Library of the Late Honorable Denis Daly.* Dublin: John Archer, 1793.

Varenne, Gaston. "Les Anglais sous le Consulat et l'Empire." *Le Pays Lorrain* XXIII:12 (December 1926), 529-544.

Other Articles—Nineteenth Century

Constant-Dufeux, Simon-Claude. "Discours de M. Constant-Defeux," RGA VIII (1849), 440-48.

de Caumont, Arcisse. "Histoire Sommaire de l'Architecture au Moyen Age." *Bulletin Monumental* II (1836).

de Contencin, Le Baron. "Rapport sur la Situation des Edifices Réligieux" *Bulletin Monumental* XVII (1881), 337-58.

de Montalembert, Le Comte. "Les Artistes Dominicains." *Annales Archéologiques* II (1845), 238-41.

Jouin, Henri, "La Cathédrale d'Albi." *Gazette des Beaux-Arts* XXVI: 2ᵉ Série (1882), 404-19.

Lenoir, Albert. "La Théories des Villes: Comment les Villes Se Sont Formées." RGA XII (1854), 292-98.

Lenoir, Albert, Charles Lenormant, Prosper Merimée. "Deuxième Instruction du Comité Historique des Arts et Monuments." RGA VI (1845), 241-55, 289-314.

Perreymond, A. "Première Etude sur la Ville de Paris." RGA III (1842), 540-54.

———. "Quatrième Etude sur la Ville de Paris." RGA IV (1843), 72-88.

———. "Sixième Etude sur la Ville de Paris." RGA IV (1843), 413-29.

Ruprich, Robert. "Salon de 1852." RGA X(1852), 155-57, 253-63.

Van Brunt, Henry. "Greek Lines." *Atlantic Monthly* VII:44 (June 1861), 654-667.

———. "Greek Lines." *Atlantic Monthly* VIII:45 (July 1861), 76-88.

Viollet-le-Duc, Eugène. "Entretiens et Restauration: Des Cathédrales de France, Notre-Dame de Paris." RGA IX (1851), 113-20, 209-17.

———. "Essai sur l'Origine et les Développements de l'Art de Bâtir en France." RGA X (1852), 35-42, 74-81, 134-46, 242-53, 343-52.

Vitet, Ludovic. "Des Etudes Archéologiques en France." *Revue des Deux Mondes* XIX: 3ᵉ Partie (1847), 762-68.

Secondary Sources

Architectural and Artistic Context

Alberti, Leon Battista. *On Painting.* Trans. John Spencer. New Haven, CT: Yale Univ. Press, 1956.

Alphand, Alphonse. *Les Promenades de Paris: Histoire, Description des Embellishments, Dépenses de Création et d'Entretien.* Paris: J. Rothschild, 1867-73.

Alphand, Alphonse, and Ernouf Le Baron. *L'Art des Jardins.* Paris: J. Rothschild, 1887.

Appell, J.W. *The Dream of Poliphilus.* London: W. Griggs, 1889.

Baltard, Louis-Pierre. *Paris et Ses Monuments, Mesurés, Dessinés, Gravés.* Paris: L'Auteur, 1803-05.

Becamel, Marcel. *A la Decouverte de la Cathédrale d'Alby: Les Trente Chapelles, les Peintures de la Voûte, le Jugement Dernier.* Albi, 1976.

Bosc, Ernest. *Dictionnaire Raisonnée d'Architecture et des Arts Qui S'y Rattachent.* Paris: Librairie de Firmin-Didot et Cie, 1877.

Braham, Allan. *The Architecture of the French Enlightenment.* Berkeley, CA: Univ. of California Press, 1980.

Branner, Robert. *Chartres Cathedral.* New York: W.W. Norton, 1969.

———. *St. Louis and The Court Style.* London: A. Zwemmer Ltd., 1965.

Bulletin Monumental: Publié sous les Auspices de la Société Française pour le Conservation (et la Descrption) des Monuments Historiques.

Canina, Luigi. *Gli Edifici di Roma Antica.* Rome: Stesso Canina, 1848.

Carmontelle, Louis Carrogis. *Jardins de Monceau, près de Paris, Appartenant à Son Altesse Serenissime Monseigneur le Duc de Chartres.* Paris: Chez Delafosse, Nee, et Masquelier, 1779.

Charageat, Marguerite. *L'Art des Jardins.* Paris: Presses Universitaires de France, 1962.

Choay, Françoise. *The Modern City: Planning in the Nineteenth Century.* New York: George Braziller, 1969.

Collins, Peter. *Changing Ideals in Modern Architecture.* Montreal: McGill Univ. Press, 1976.

Columna, Franciscus. *Le Songe de Poliphile.* Trans. Charles Nodier. Introd. Mario Roques. Paris: Les Bibliôâtres de France, 1949.

Conant, John Kenneth. *Carolingian and Romanesque Architecture 800 to 1200.* Harmondsworth, England: Penguin Books, 1959.

Cordemoy, J. *Nouveau Traité de Toute l'Architecture: ou l'Art de Bastir, Utile aux Entrepreneurs et aux Ouvriers.* Paris, 1714. Rpt. Farnborough, England: Gregg Press, 1966.

Crozès, Hippolyte. *Le Diocèse d'Albi: Ses Evêques et Archêveques.* Toulouse: A. Chauvin et Fils, 1878.

———. *Monographe de la Cathédrale de Sainte-Cécile d'Albi.* Paris: Victor Didron; Toulouse: Delboy Librairie, 1873.

de Andia, Béatrice. *De Bagatelle à Monceau: les Folies du XVIIIe Siècle à Paris.* Paris: Musée Carnavalet, 1978.

de Cailleux, Alphonse, Charles Nodier, and Isidore-Justin-Séverin Taylor. *Voyages Pittoresques dans l'Ancienne France: Languedoc I.* Paris: L'Imprimerie Firmin Didot, 1833.

———. *Voyages Pittoresques et Romantiques dans l'Ancienne France,* Vol. II. Paris: Firmin Didot Frères, 1840.

de Caumont, Arcisse. *Abécédaire ou Rudiments d'Archéologie.* Caen: Le Blanc-Hardel, 1876.

———. "Histoire Sommaire de l'Architecture au Moyen-Age." *Bulletin Monumental* II (1836), 5-425.

———. *Statistique Monumentale de Calvados.* Paris: Derache, 1846.

de Laborde, Comte Alexandre. *Les Monuments de la France, Classés Chronologiquement et Considérées sous le Rapport des Faits Historiques et l'Etude des Arts,* Vol. 2. Paris: Imprimerie Jules Didot l'Ainé, 1836.

Didron l'Ainé. *Annales Archéologiques.* Paris, 1844-81.

Durand, Jacques-Nicolas-Louis. *Recueil et Parallèle des Edifices de Tout Genre, Anciens et Modernes, Remarquables par Leur Beauté, par Leur Grandeur et par Leur Singularité, et Dessinés sur une Même Echelle.* Paris: Ecole Polytechnique, 1800.

Egbert, Donald Drew, and David Van Zanten. *The Beaux-Arts Tradition in French Architecture.* Princeton, N.J.: Princeton Univ. Press, 1981.

Exposition Universelle de Londres de 1862. *Documents Officiels Complétant les Rapports du Jury International sur l'Ensemble et l'Exposition.* Paris: Imprimerie et Librairie Centrale des Chemins de Fer, 1864.

Fontaine, Pierre, and Charles Percier. *Choix des Plus Célèbres Maisons de Plaisance de Rome et des Environs.* Paris: Didot Aîné, 1824.

Fouquier, Marcel. *De l'Art des Jardins du XVe au XXe Siècle.* Paris: Emile Paul, 1911.

Frankl, Paul. *Gothic Architecture.* Harmondsworth, England: Penguin Books, 1962.

———. *The Gothic: Literary Source and Interpretations through Eight Centuries.* Princeton, NJ: Princeton Univ. Press, 1960.

Gaillard, Jeanne. *Paris, la Ville 1852-1870.* Paris: Editions Honoré Champion, 1977.

Garms, Joerg. "Projects for the Pont-Neuf and the Place Dauphine in the First Half of the Eighteenth Century." *Journal of the Society of Architectural Historians,* XXVI:2 (May 1967), 102-13.

Giedion, Sigfried. *Space, Time, and Architecture.* Cambridge, MA: Harvard Univ. Press, 1967.

Gilbert, Antoine-Pierre-Marie. *Description Historique de l'Eglise Cathédrale de Chartres.* Chartres: Gernier Allabre, 1824.

Gilpin, William. *An Essay on Prints.* 4th ed. London: R. Blamire, 1792.

———. *Observations Relative Chiefly to Picturesque Beauty, Made in the Year 1772, on Several Parts of England; Particularly the Mountains and Lakes of Cumberland and Westmoreland.* Second edition. London: R. Blamire, 1788.

———. *Three Essays: On Picturesque Beauty, on Picturesque Travel, on Sketching Landscape, to Which Is Added a Poem, on Landscape Painting.* London: R. Blamire, 1772.

———. *Voyage en Différents Parties de l'Angleterre, et Particulièrement dans les Montagnes, et sur les Lacs du Cumberland et du Westmoreland, Contenant des Observations Rélatives aux Beautés Pittoresques.* Paris: Chez Defer de Maisonneuve, London: Chez Blamire, 1789.

Gillet, Louis. *Histoire Artistique des Ordres Mendiants: Etude sur l'Art Réligieux en Europe du XIIIe Siècle.* Paris: Librairie Renouard, 1912.

Gloag, John. *Mr. Loudon's England: The Life and Work of John Claudius Loudon, and His Influence on Architecture.* Newcastle-upon-Tyne, England: Oriel Press, Ltd., 1970.

Grodecki, Louis. *Gothic Architecture.* New York: Abrams, 1977.

Grumbach, Antoine. "Les Promenades de Paris." *Oppositions* VIII (Spring 1977), 50-67.

Hastings, Thomas. "The Influence of the Ecole des Beaux-Arts upon American Architecture." *The Architectural Record: the Beaux-Arts Number* (January 1901), 66-90.

Hautecoeur, Louis. *L'Histoire de l'Architecture Classique en France,* Vols. VI, VII. Paris: A. and J. Picard et Cie, 1955, 1957.

———. *Littérature et Peinture en France du XVIIe au XXe Siècle.* 2d ed. Paris: Librairie Armand Colin, 1963.

Hénard, Robert. *Les Jardins et les Squares.* Paris: Librairie Renouard, 1911.

Hermann, Wolfgang. *Laugier and Eighteenth Century French Theory.* London: A. Zwemmer Ltd., 1962.

Holt, Elizabeth Gilmore. *From the Classicists to the Impressionists.* Garden City, NY: Doubleday Press, 1966.

Hugo, Victor. *Notre-Dame de Paris.* New York: D. Appleton and Co., 1902.

Jacobs, Stephen W. *"Architectural Preservation's American Development and Antecedents Abroad."* Diss. Princeton 1972.

Jouin, Henri. "La Cathédrale d'Albi." *La Gazette des Beaux-Arts* 2ᵉ S., XXVI (1882), 403-19.

Krautheimer, Richard. *Die Kirchen der Beitelörden in Deutschland.* Cologne: F.J. Marcan, 1925.

Lambert, E. "L'Eglise et le Couvent des Jacobins de Toulouse et l'Architecture Dominicaine en France." *Bulletin Monumental* 104 (1946), 141-86.

Landon, Charles-Pierre and Jacques-Guillaume Legrand. *Description de Paris et de Ses Edifices.* Paris: Chez C. Landon, 1806.

Laran, Jean. *La Cathédrale d'Albi.* Paris: Henri Laurens, 1931.

_____. Adhémar, Jean, and Prinet, Jean. *L'Estampe.* Paris: Presses Universitaires de France, 1959.

Lavedan, Pierre. *La Nouvelle Histoire de Paris.* Paris: Diffusion Hachette, 1975.

Lazzaro-Bruno, Claudia. "The Villa Lante at Bagnaia: an Allegory of Art and Nature." *The Art Bulletin* LIX:4 (December 1977), 553-60.

Lee, Rensselaer. *Ut Pictura Poesis: the Humanistic Theory of Painting in the Renaissance.* New York: W.W. Norton, 1967.

Le Camus de Mezières, Nicolas. *Le Génie de l'Architecture ou l'Analogie de Cet Art avec Nos Sensations.* Paris: Chez l'Auteur, 1780.

Ledoux, Claude-Nicolas. *L'Architecture Considérée sous les Rapports de l'Art, des Moeurs, et de la Législation.* Paris, 1804; rept. Paris: F. de Noble, 1961.

Le Muet, Pierre. *Manière de Bien Bastir.* Introd. Anthony Blunt. Paris, 1664; rpt. Farnborough, England: Gregg International Publishers, 1972.

Letarouilly, Charles. *Edifices de Rome Moderne ou Recueil des Palais, Maisons, Eglises, Couvents, et Autres Monuments Publics Particulières les Plus Remarquables.* Pirated edition. Liège: D. Avanzo et Cⁱᵉ, 1849.

Levine, Neil. "The Romantic Idea of Architectural Legibility: Henry Labrouste and the Néo-Grec." *The Architecture of the Ecole des Beaux-Arts.* Ed. Arthur Drexler. Cambridge, MA: MIT Press, 1977.

_____. "*Architectural Reasoning in the Age of Positivism.*" Diss. Yale 1975.

Lipstadt, Hélène. "De la Montonie Chez Fourier." *Werk/Archithèse* 64:1 (1977), 34-36.

Mâle, Emile. *L'Art Religieux du XIIIᵉ Siècle en France: Etude sur l'Iconographie du Moyen Age et sur les Sources d'Inspiration.* Paris: Librairie Armand Colin, 1902.

_____. *La Cathédrale d'Albi.* Paris: Paul Hartmann, 1950.

_____. *The Gothic Image.* New York: Harper Torchbook, 1958.

Mariette, Jean. *L'Architecture Françoise ou Recueil des Plans, Elévations, Coupes, et Profiles des Eglises, Palais, Hotels, et Maisons Particulières de Paris, et des Chasteaux et Maisons de Campagne ou de Plaisance des Environs et des Plusieurs Autres Endroits.* Paris: Chez Jean Mariette, 1727-29.

Markus, Thomas. "Pattern of Law." *Architectural Review* 116:694 (October 1954), 251-56.

Merimée, Prosper. *Notes d'Un Voyage dans le Midi de la France.* Paris: Librairie de Fournier, 1835.

Middleton, Robin. "The Abbé de Cordemoy and the Graeco-Gothic Idea." *Journal of the Warburg and Courtauld Institutes* XXV:3-4 (July-December, 1962), 278-320; XXVI:1-2 (January-June, 1963), 90-123.

_____, ed. *The Beaux-Arts and Nineteenth Century French Architecture.* Cambridge, MA: MIT Press, 1982.

_____ and Watkin, David. *Neoclassical and Nineteenth Century Architecture.* New York: Abrams, 1979.

Moniteur des Architectes: Indicateur Général et Spécial à l'Usage des Architectes, des Vérificateurs et des Entrepreneurs. Paris, 1847-1900.

Nodier, Charles. *Francesco Colonna: A Fanciful Tale of the Writing of The Hypnerotomachia.* Introd. Theodore Koch. Chicago: Lakeside Press, 1929.

_____. *Paris Historique: Promenade dans les Rues de Paris.* Paris: F.G. Levrault, 1838.

Patte, Pierre. *Monumens Erigés en France à la Gloire de Louis XV.* Paris: Librairies Desaint et Saillant, 1765.

Pevsner, Nikolaus. *Some Architectural Writers of the Nineteenth Century.* Oxford: Clarendon 1972.

Pinckney, David H. *Napoleon III and the Rebuilding of Paris.* Princeton, NJ: Princeton Univ. Press, 1958.

Philip, Lotte Rand. *The Ghent Altarpiece.* Princeton: NJ: Princeton Univ. Press, 1971.

Planat, Paul, ed. *Encyclopédie de l'Architecture et de la Construction.* Paris: Aulanier et Cⁱᵉ, eds., 1888-92.

Quatremère de Quincy, Antoine-Chrysostome. *Essais sur l'Imitation dans les Beaux-Arts.* Paris: Treuttel et Wurtz, 1823.

_____. *Dictionnaire Historique de l'Architecture, Comprenant dans Son Plan les Notions Historique Descriptives, Archéologiques... de Cet Art.* Paris: Adrien, 1832.

Rickman, Thomas. *An Attempt to Discriminate the Styles of Architecture in England from the Conquest to the Reformation, with a Sketch of the Grecian and Roman Orders.* 6th ed. Oxford and London: John Henry and James Parker, 1862.

Roger-Marx, Claude. *La Gravure Originale au XIXᵉ Siècle.* Paris: Editions Aunery Somogy, 1962.

Rondelet, Jean. *Traité Théorique et Pratique de l'Art de Bâtir.* 7th ed. Paris: F. Didot, 1864.

Rosenau, Helen. *Social Purpose in Architecture.* London: Studio Vista, 1972.

Rossel, André. "Le Plan de Louis Bretez." *Le Plan de Louis Bretez Dit de Turgot.* Paris: Editions les Yeux Ouverts, 1966.

Rowe, Colin, and Fred Koetter. *Collage City.* Cambridge, MA: MIT Press, 1979.

Rowe, Colin. *The Mathematics of the Ideal Villa and Other Essays.* Cambridge, MA: MIT Press, 1976.

Safaret, P.-F. *Almanach et Annuaire des Bâtiments,* Paris: Au Bureau de l'Annuaire des Batiments, 1841 onward.

Sand, Maurice, *Masques et Buffons (Comédie Italienne).* Paris: Michel Lévy Frères, 1860.

Schneider, R. *Quatremère de Quincy et Son Intervention dans les Arts, 1788-1830.* Paris: Librairie Hachette et Cⁱᵉ, 1910.

Société Centrale des Architectes. *Annales des Congrès des Architectes Français; Comptes Rendus et Mémoires.* Vols. I-II. Paris, 1874-75.

Société Centrale des Architectes. *Bulletin Mensuel de la Société Centrale.* Paris, 1843-93.

Texier, Edmond. *Tableau de Paris.* Paris: Paulin et LeChevalier, 1850.

Van Zanten, David. *The Architectural Polychromy of the 1830's.* New York: Garland, 1977.

Vidler, Anthony. "Type: Quatremère de Quincy." *Oppositions* VIII (Spring 1977), 95-113.

Viollet-le-Duc, Eugène. *Dictionnaire de l'Architecture ou Dictionnaire Raisonné de l'Architecture Française du XI au XVIᵉ Siècle,* Paris: B. Bance, ed., 1863.

Vitet, Ludovic. "Des Etudes Archéologiques en France." *Revue des Deux Mondes* XIX, 3ᵉ partie (1847), 762-68.

Watkin, David. *Morality and Architecture: the Development of a Theme in Architectural History and Theory from the Gothic Revival to the Modern Movement.* Oxford: Clarendon, 1977.

_____. *Thomas Hope 1769-1831 and the Neoclassical Idea.* London: John Murray, 1968.

Wiebenson, Dora. *The Picturesque Garden in France.* Princeton, NJ: Princeton Univ. Press, 1978.

Intellectual History and Philosophy

Barthes, Roland. "Image, Raison, Déraison." *L'Univers de l'Encyclopédie.* Paris: Les Libraires Associés, 1964.

_____. *New Critical Essays.* Trans. Richard Howard. New York: Hill and Wang, 1980.

Becker, Carl L. *The Heavenly City of the Eighteenth Century Philosophers.* New Haven, CT: Yale Univ. Press, 1932.

Benjamin, Walter. *Illuminations.* Trans. Harry Zohn. New York: Harcourt, Brace and World, 1968.

Blanshard, Brand. *The Nature of Thought.* London: Allen and Unwin, 1939.

_____. *Reason and Analysis.* LaSalle, IL: Open Court Press, 1964.

Bréhier, Emile. *The Nineteenth Century: Periods of Systems 1800-1850.* Chicago and London: Univ. of Chicago Press, 1968.

Brewer, Walter. *Victor Cousin as a Comparative Educator.* New York: Teacher's College Press, 1971.

Chanson, Paul. *Trois Socialistes Français: Quatre Etudes.* Paris: Les Editions de la Nouvelle France, 1945.

Charlton, D.C. *Positivist Thought in France During the Second Empire.* Oxford: Clarendon, 1959.

Comte, Auguste. *Catéchisme Positiviste ou Sommaire Exposition de la Religion Universelle.* Paris: Chez l'Auteur, 1852.

_____. *Cours de Philosophie Positive, Augmenté par une Préface de E. Littré.* 2d ed. France, 1864.

Cousin, Victor. *Lectures on the True, the Beautiful, and the Good.* Trans. O.W. Wright, New York: D. Appleton and Co., 1893.

d'Alembert, Jean le Rond, and Denis Diderot eds. *Encyclopédie ou Dictionnaire Raisonnée des Sciences, des Arts, et des Métiers.* Paris: Chez Briasson, David, Le Breton, Durand, 1751-80.

de Lamarck, Jean-Baptiste. *Histoire Naturelle des Animaux sans Vertebres.* 7 vols. Paris: Verdière, 1815-22.

de la Mettrie, Julian Offray. *Man a Machine.* Appendix Gertrude Bussey. La Salle, IL, 1912; rpt. La Salle, IL: Open Court, 1977.

Eissler, Kurt R. *Talent and Genius.* New York: Grove Press, 1971.

Foucault, Michel. *The Order of Things: an Archaeology of the Human Sciences.* New York: Vintage Books, 1970.

Freud, Sigmund. *Civilisation and Its Discontents.* Trans. James Strachey. New York: W.W. Norton and Co., 1961.

Gombrich, Sr. Ernst. "Icones Symbolicae." *Symbolic Images.* London: Phaidon Press, 1972.

Hegel, George-Wilhelm-Friederich. *The Phenomenology of Mind.* Trans. J.B. Baillie. New York: Harper Colophon Book, 1967.

_____. *The Philosophy of History.* Intro. C.J. Friederich. New York: Dover, 1956.

Herder, Johann Gottfried von. *Reflections in the Philosophy of the History of Mankind.* Introd. Frank E. Manuel, Chicago: Univ. of Chicago Press, 1968.

Iggers, Georg, introd. and trans. *The Doctrine of Saint-Simon: an Exposition.* New York: Schocken Books, 1972.

Jung, Carl. *Man and His Symbols.* Garden City, NY: Doubleday, 1964.

Kuhn, Thomas. *The Copernican Revolution.* Cambridge, MA: Harvard Paperback, 1971.

_____. *The Structure of Scientific Revolutions.* Chicago: Univ. of Chicago Press, 1962.

La Capra, Dominick. *Emile Durkheim: Sociologist and Philosopher,* Ithaca, NY: Cornell Univ. Press, 1972.

Lasteyrie, Robert de, and Alexandre Vidier. *Bibliothèque Générale des Travaux Historiques Publiés par les Sociétés Savantes de la France.* Paris: Imprimerie Nationale, 1902.

Leavis, F.R., ed. and introd. *Mill on Bentham and Coleridge.* London: Chatto and Windus, 1959.

Lovejoy, Arthur. *The Great Chain of Being.* Cambridge, MA: Harvard Univ. Press, 1936.

Manuel, Frank. *The New World of Henri de Saint-Simon.* Cambridge, MA: Harvard Univ. Press, 1962.

Nesbit, Charles. *History of the Idea of Progress.* New York: Basic Books, 1980.

Nietzsche, Friedrich. *The Use and Abuse of History.* Indianapolis: Bobbs Merrill, 1949.

_____. *Ecce Homo.* Trans. R.J. Hollingsworth. Harmondsworth, England: Penguin Books, 1979.

Plato. *The Phaedrus.* Trans. Walter Hamilton. Harmondsworth, England: Penguin Books, 1973.

―――. *The Republic.* Trans. Francis Cornford. New York: Oxford Univ. Press, 1945.

Poster, Mark, ed. and introd. *Harmonian Man: Selected Writings of Charles Fourier.* New York: Anchor, 1971.

Plutarch. *The Lives of the Ancient Greeks and Romans.* Trans. John Dryden. Introd. Arthur Clough. New York: Modern Library, 1932.

―――. *The Rise and Fall of Athens.* Trans. Ian Scott-Kilvert. Harmondsworth, England: Penguin Books, 1960.

Poggioli, Renato. *The Theory of the Avant-Garde.* New York: Harper and Row (Icon Editions), 1971.

Popper, Karl R. *The Poverty of Historicism.* New York: Harper Torchbooks, 1964.

Riasanovsky, Nicholas. *The Teaching of Charles Fourier.* Berkeley, CA: Univ. of California Press, 1969.

Ripley, George, ed. *Philosophical Miscellanies Translated from the French of Cousin, Jouffroy, and B. Constant.* Boston: Hilliar, Gray, and Co., 1938.

Robson-Scott, W.D. *The Literary Background of the Gothic Revival in Germany.* Oxford: Clarendon Press, 1965.

Rousseau, Jean-Jacques. "A Discourse on a Subject Proposed by the Academy of Dijon: What is the Origin of Inequality among Men, and Is It Authorized by Natural Law." In *The Miscellaneous Works of Mr. J.J. Rousseau.* London: T. Becket and P.D. De Hondt, 1767.

Stromberg, Roland. *European Intellectual History Since 1789.* Englewood Cliffs, NJ: Prentice Hall, 1975.

Taine, Hippolyte: *Essais de Critique et d'Histoire.* Paris: Librairie Hachette et Ce, 1908.

Veitch, John. "Victor Cousin." *The Encyclopedia Britannica.* 11th ed., Vol. VII, pp. 330-35.

White, Hayden. *Metahistory: The Historical Imagination in Nineteenth Century Europe.* Baltimore, MD: Johns Hopkins Press, 1975.

Yates, Frances. *The Art of Memory.* London: Routledge and Kegan, 1966.

Literary Theory

Abrams, M.H. *The Mirror and the Lamp.* New York: Oxford Univ. Press, 1953.

Bakhtin, Mikail. *Problems of Dostoevsky's Poetics.* Trans. R.W. Rotsch: Ann Arbor, MI: Ardis Publishers, 1973.

―――. *Rabelais and His World.* Trans. Helene Iswolsky. Cambridge, MA: MIT Press, 1968.

Balakian, Anna. *The Literary Origins of Surrealism.* New York: New York Univ. Press, 1947.

Barbey D'Aurevilly, Jules. *Oeuvres Romanesques Complètes.* Ed. Jacques Petit. Paris: Bibliothèque de la Pléiade, 1966.

Barthes, Roland. *The Pleasure of the Text.* New York: Hill and Wang, 1975.

―――. *Writing Degree Zero/Elements of Semiology.* Introd. Susan Sontag. Boston: Beacon Press, 1968.

Baudelaire, Charles. *Les Fleurs du Mal.* Paris: Editions Gallimard. 1972.

―――. *The Flowers of Evil and Other Poems of Charles Baudelaire.* Trans. Francis Duke. Charlottesville, VA: Univ. of Virginia Press, 1961.

Bellanger, Claude, Jacques Godechot, Pierre Guiral, and Fernand Terrou. *Histoire Générale de la Presse Française.* Paris: Presses Universitaires de France, 1969.

Bradbury, Malcolm, and James McFarlane, eds. *Modernism 1890-1930.* Harmondsworth, England: Penguin Books, 1976.

Canu, Jean. *Barbey d'Aurevilly.* Paris: Robert Laffont, 1965.

Chartier, Armand D. *Barbey d'Aurevilly.* Boston: Twayne Publishers, 1977.

Culler, Jonathon. *Ferdinand de Saussure.* Harmondsworth, England: Penguin Books, 1977.

Dale, R.C. *The Poetics of Prosper Merimée.* The Hague and Paris: Mouton and Co., 1966.

Dembo, L.S. *Criticism.* Madison, WI: Univ. of Wisconsin Press, 1968.

Dempsey, Madeleine. *A Contribution to the Study of the Sources of the Génie du Christianisme.* Paris: Librairie Honoré Champion, 1938.

Derrida, Jacques. *Speech and Phenomena: and Other Essays on Husserl's Theory of Signs.* Trans. David B. Allison. Pref. Newton Garver. Evanston, IL: Northwestern Univ. Press, 1973.

Diderot, Denis. *Le Neveu de Rameau et Autres Dialogues Philosophiques.* Introd. Jean Varloot, Paris: Gallimard, 1972.

Flaubert, Charles. *Madame Bovary.* Trans. Paul de Man. New York: W.W. Norton and Co., 1965.

Frye, Northrop. *The Anatomy of Criticism.* Princeton, NJ: Princeton Univ. Press, 1957.

Gay, Peter. *Style in History.* New York: McGraw-Hill, 1974.

Giamatti, A. Bartlett. *The Earthly Paradise and the Renaissance Epic.* Princeton, NJ: Princeton Univ. Press, 1966.

Hugo, Victor. *Notre-Dame of Paris.* New York: D. Appleton and Co., 1902.

Majetka, Ladislav, and Krystina Pomorska, eds. *Readings in Russian Poetics: Formalist and Structuralist Views,* Ann Arbor, MI: Univ. of Michigan Press, 1978.

Quennell, Peter, ed. *The Essence of Laughter.* New York: Meridian Press, 1956.

Richards, I.A. *The Philosophy of Rhetoric.* London and New York: Oxford Univ. Press, 1976.

Rousseau, Jean Jacques. *Du Contrat Social.* Introd. Pierre Burgelin. Paris: Garnier Flammarion, 1966.

Uitti, Karl. *Linguistics and Literary Theory.* New York: W.W. Norton and Co., 1969.

Warnock, Mary. *Imagination.* Berkeley, CA: University of California Press, 1978.

Warren, Austin, and René Wellek. *The Theory of Literature.* 3d ed. New York: Harcourt Brace, 1977.

Wellek, René. *A History of Criticism.* Vol. 2. New Haven, CT: Yale Univ. Press, 1955.

Social and Political History

Bonaparte, Louis-Napoléon. *History of Julius Caesar.* New York: Harper and Brothers, 1866.

———. *Oeuvres de Napoléon III.* Paris: Editions Henri Plon, 1856.

Bulletin de la Société de Colonisation Européo-Américaine au Texas. Brussels: J.H. Briand, 1855-1857. Ten numbers.

Burke, Edmund. *Reflections on the Revolution in France.* New York: Dolphin Books, 1961.

Christie, Thomas. *Letters on the Revolution of France, and on the New Constitution Established by the National Assembly, Occasioned by the Publications of the Right Honorable Edmund Burke, M.P. and Alexandre de Calonne.* London: J. Johnson, 1791.

Clagett, Marshall, ed. *Critical Problems in the History of Science.* Madison, WI: Univ. of Wisconsin Press, 1962.

Cornu, Marcel. *La Conquête de Paris.* Paris: Mercure de France, 1972.

de Calonne, Alexandre. *Considerations on the Past and Future State of France.* London: J. Evans, 1791.

de la Cases, Le Comte. *Le Mémorial de Sainte-Hélène.* Paris: Bibliothèque de la Pléiade, Editions Gallimard, 1956.

Durkheim, Emile. *Socialism and Saint-Simon.* Pref. Marcel Mauss. Trans. Charlotte Staller. Yellow Springs, OH: Antioch Press, 1958.

Egbert, Donald Drew. *Social Radicalism and the Arts.* New York: A. Knopf Press, 1970.

Fourier, Charles. *Design for Utopia.* Introd. Charles Gide. Trans. Julia Franklin. New York: Schocken Books, 1971.

Garnier-Pagès, Louis-Antoine. *Histoire de la Révolution de 1848.* Paris: Bibliothèque Libérale Dégorce-Cadot, 1861-1872.

Greene, Martin. *Children of the Sun.* London: Constable and Co., Ltd., 1977.

Hammond, Margaret F. and William J. *La Réunion: A French Settlement in Texas.* Dallas: Royal Publishing Co., 1958.

Haussmann, Baron Georges-Eugène. *Mémoires du Baron Haussmann.* Paris: Victor-Havard Editions, 1840.

Herold, J. Christopher, ed. *The Mind of Napoleon.* New York: Columbia Univ. Press, 1955.

Iggers, Georg G., introd. and trans. *The Doctrine of Saint-Simon.* New York: Schocken Books, 1972.

Jolly, Pierre. *Calonne 1732-1802.* Paris: Librairie Plon, 1949.

La Capra, Dominick. *Emile Durkheim: Sociologist and Philosopher.* Ithaca, NY: Cornell Univ. Press, 1972.

Lenzer, Gertrude, ed. and introd. *Auguste Comte and Positivism: The Essential Writings.* New York: Harper Torchbooks, 1975.

Manuel, Frank. *The New World of Henry Saint-Simon.* Cambridge, MA: Harvard Univ. Press, 1956.

_____. *The Prophets of Paris.* Cambridge, MA: Harvard Univ. Press, 1962.

Marcus, Thomas A. "Pattern of the Law." *The Architectural Review* 116: 694 (October 1954), 251-56.

Marx, Karl. "The Economic and Philosophical Manuscripts of 1844." *The Marx-Engels Reader.* Ed. Robert Tucker. New York: W.W. Norton and Co., 1972.

_____. "The Eighteenth Brumaire of Louis-Napoléon." *The Marx-Engels Reader.* New York: W.W. Norton and Co., 1972.

Michelet, Jules. *Histoire de France.* 2d ed. Paris: Librairie Classique de l'Hachette, 1835.

_____. *History of the French Revolution.* Intro. Gordon Wright. Trans. Charles Locke. Chicago: The Univ. of Chicago Press, 1967.

Mill, John Stuart. *On Liberty.* Ed. Alburey Castell. New York: Appleton-Century-Crofts, 1947.

_____. *Utilitarianism and Other Writings.* Introd. Mary Warnock. New York: Meridian Books (New American Library), 1962.

Moers, Ellen. *The Dandy: Brummell to Beerbohm.* New York: Viking Press, 1960.

Le Moniteur Universel: Journal Officiel de la République Française. Especially numbers 120 (29 Avril 1848), 127 (5 Mai 1848), 128 (7 Mai 1848).

Pellarin, Charles. *The Life of Charles Fourier.* New York: Wm. H. Graham, 1848.

Pinckney, David. *The French Revolution of 1830.* Princeton, NJ: Princeton Univ. Press, 1972.

Prentout, H. "Caen en 1830." *Revue d'Histoire Moderne* 6:32 (May-April 1939), 101-14.

Price, Roger. *1848 in France.* Ithaca, NY: Cornell Univ. Press, 1975.

Puech, Jules. *La Vie et l'Oeuvre de Flora Tristan.* Paris: Librairie des Sciences Sociales et Politiques, 1925.

Riasanovsky, Nicholas. *The Teaching of Charles Fourier.* Berkeley and Los Angeles: Univ. of California Press, 1969.

Santerre, George H. *White Cliffs of Dallas: The Story of La Réunion, the Old French Colony.* Dallas: The Books Craft, 1955.

Talman, J.L. *The Rise of Totalitarian Democracy.* Boston: The Beacon Press, 1952.

Taylor, Keith, introd. and trans. *Henri Saint-Simon.* New York: Holmes and Meier, Inc., 1975.

Williams, Raymond. *Culture and Society: 1780-1950.* New York: Harper and Row, 1858.

Index

Commune and communism, 74, 124, 171
composition: and style, 24, 109, 132-33;
architectural, 92-101, 103, 132, 218, 232-34;
as essential basis of form, 129, 144, 152,
167, 220, 226, 247; at the Villa Daly, 228-29,
plates 72-75
Comte, Auguste: 80-83, 100-101, 121;
Calendrier Positiviste, 232; *Cours de
Philosophie Positive,* 82. *See also*
positivism
Condillac, Etienne, 42, 114
Les Concours pour les Grands Prix (Daly). *See*
Daly: Writings
"Les Concours des Hautes-Etudes"(Daly). *See*
Daly: Writings
Condé-sur-Vesgre, 5-6, 10
*Congrès Scientifiques et Archéologiques de
France,* 5, 13, 25, 140-41, 166-67
consciousness: and Encyclopedist
epistemology, 36-41; and ideality, 27, 57,
110, 119, 149, 242; and the city, 169-70, 235-
36; and theory of vision, 31; collective, 39,
54; critical, 48, 67; Daly's sense of, 58, 103;
self-, xxviii, 24, 51-52, 173, 180, 193, 237;
un-, 237. *See also* criticism, vision
Conseil des Batiments Civils, 6, 149
Considérant, Victor, 6, 7, 9, 14, 179;
Description du Phalanstère, 169-70
Constant-Dufeux, Simon-Claude, 99, 107-10,
plate 26
La Construction Moderne (Planat), 249
Cordemoy, J., 16, 248, 340-41 n.40
cosmology, 46, 121, 344 n.29
cottage orné, 227-28
Cours d'Antiquités Monumentales
(Caumont), 93, 136, 163
*Cours d'Archéologie. See Cours d'Antiquités
Monumetales*
Cours de Philosophie Positive (Comte), 82
Cousin, Victor: and eclecticism, 49-55, 77, 81,
86, 102; faculties of mind, 51, 120;
Fragments Philosophiques, 49-50, 63;
Neoplatonism, 51, 248; *Le Vrai, le Beau, le
Bien,* 52. *See also* eclecticism;
Neoplatonism
"Crèche"(Daly), 72, plate 15
Critique of Judgement (Kant), 49
Critique of Pure Reason (Kant), 49
criticism: and genius, 45, 92; and separate
consciousness
cult. *See* ritual
Cuvier, Georges, 35, 46, 84, 93, 94, 237, plates 7,
20. *See also* catastrophe; synoptic tables

d'Alembert, Jean le Rond: 16; "Discours
Préliminaire", 35-37; *Encyclopédie,* 38

Daley, John (father of César Daly), 1-2
Daly, César-Denis:
and epistemology, 34-35, 81-92, 120, 143-44,
166-67
and history, xxx, 1-3, 140-41, 143-44, 146
as romantic figure, 22, 88-89, 142, 151
family, 1-3, 9-10, 18, plate 1
health, 8-9, 228
honors, 13-14
life, 1-14, 17, 228
on the city, 177-83, 209-36
on society, 72-81, 131, 140-41, 145-46, 163,
167
personality of, xxxi, 71-72, 88-89, 146
politics of, 7-10, 72-81, 165; during of
Revolution of 1848, 25-29, 32, 63; during
Second Empire
restoration, Albi Cathedral,
interpretation of cathedral, 131-33, 156,
165-66, 166-67
drawings: *Schemes for Albi Cathedral's
Reconstruction,* 151-55, plate 43;
Sketch of Baldaquin, 157, 158, plate
46; *Transverse Section,* 151, 156, 157,
plate 42; *West Front,* 150, plate 41
restoration, Chartres Cathedral,
interpretation of cathedral, 127-30
drawing: North Portal, 78, plate 35
Square Sainte-Cécile, 167-68, plate 53
Writings
*L'Architecture Privée du Dix-neuvième
Siècle,* 10, 115, 201, 209, 217-19, 222-
30, plate 68
*Concours pour le Grand Prix
d'Architecture,* 115
Des Hautes Etudes d'Architecture, 13-14
*Du Projet d'Achèvement de la Cathédrale
de Cologne,* 78-79
Le Glâneur d'Eure et Loire, 6, 129
*Introduction Traitant du Symbolisme
dans l'Architecture,* 78
Motifs Historiques d'Architecture: theory
of, 13, 76, 97, 149, 218; "L'Architecture
de l'Avenir," 87, 98, 149; "Tableau de
la Génération Géométrique et
Successive des Styles-Types," 97, plate
25
*Première Causerie d'Histoire et
d'Esthétique: Ce Qui Peut Raconter
une Grille de Fer,* 104-7, 117
*Revue Générale de l'Architecture et des
Travaux Publics:* conception and
major themes, xxxii, 7, 72; "Crèche,"
72, plate 15; "De la Liberté dans l'Art,"
25-28, 69; "Des Etudes Archéologiques
en France" (Vitet), 26; "Etudes sur la
Ville de Paris" (Perreymond), 202-9;

philosophy, 48-49, 78, 86, 103, 349 n.73. *See also* eclecticism, Platonism, reason, sensationalism

picturesque, the, 126, 140, 155-58, 199, 206, 230. *See also* promenade

Pinckney, David, 172

Plans, Coupes, Elévations des Plus Belles Maisons de Paris (Krafft and Ransonette), 218

"Plan du Centre de Paris" (Perreymond), 201-9, plate 67

"Plan of the Faubourg Saint-Antoine" (Turgot map), 183, plate 59

Planat, Paul, 117, 121, 249

Plato, and Platonism, xxx, xxxiii, 26-27, 114, 189-90, 216, 219, 241

Plotinus, 53

Plutarch, 189-91, 195-96

poetry, 106-11, 212, 240-41

"Pont à Richmond, Virginia" (Daly), 72, plate 14

Port-Royal grammar, 114, 343 n.27. *See also* Cartesianism

positivism: aesthetics, 104, 110, 111; and Daly's intellectual background, xxxiii, 71, 83; and Saint-Simon, 45, 75; and scientific method, 14-15, 81, 90, 120-21; development of, 164, 341 n.45. *See also* epistemology; Comte

prediction, 100

prevision *(prévoyance),* xxx, 146, 147, 149, 238

profanation, 65-68

progress: and history, xxvii-xxix, 101, 187; and social order, 74, 183; as scientific law, 80, 83-84, 97, 146, 200; cyclical, 56, 200; in architecture, 65, 140, 143, 233; metaphor-mechanism, xxxi-xxxii, 28, 34, 138, 237-38; metaphor-organism, 41-42, 43, 65-66. *See also* organicism; mechanism

"Project for the Palace of the King of Rome" (Percier and Fontaine), 185, plate 61

"Projected Embellishments for the City of Paris" (Patte), 182-84, plate 60

promenade, 200, 205, 214, 230, 233, 235, 239-41. *See also* picturesque, the

Les Promenades de Paris (Alphand), 177

"Promenades et Plantations" (Daly). See Daly: Writings, *Revue Générale*

propaganda, 15

psychological method: in Cousin, 49, 87; in Daly, 87, 110. *See also* consciousness; ontology

psychology, and esthetics, 213-15

Pugin, A.W.N., 7

Punchinello, 58-70, plate 12. *See also Commedia dell'Arte*

quarter, urban, 184-86, 206-8

Quatremère de Quincy, A.C.: and Encyclopedism, 17; and Neoplatonism, 53, 248; and typology, 90, 125-26, 219; and urban embellishment, 116, 192, 219; on artistic language, 112-15, 125, 129; on imitation, 219-21. *See also* imitation; language; monumentality; type

Raumgestaltung, 174

realism, 103, 107, 129

reason: and aesthetics, 120, 250-52; and Daly's *L'Architecture Contemporaine,* 31; and eclecticism, 51-55; and epistemology, xxix, 37, 182; and instrumental language, 115, 118; apotheosis of, xxxiv, 48; as philosophical faculty, 34, 40-41

Recueil et Parallèle des Edifices (Durand), 115, 124, 136

reflection, 88

Reflections on the Philosophy of History (Herder), xxvii

Reflections on the Revolution in France (Burke), xxxi

Reflexions sur les Langues (Turgot), 41

"Le Réforme Club" (Barry), 76, plate 17

religion, 32-33, 79, 86, 118-22, 128. *See also* ritual; dogma

The Republic (Plato), 189

Résidences des Souverains (Percier and Fontaine), 175-76

restoration, of historic structures, 139-42, 149-66, 207

Rêveries du Promeneur Solitaire (Rousseau), 177, 230

Revue Générale de l'Architecture et des Travaux Publics. See Daly: Writings

Reynaud, Léonce, 117

rhetoric: and ideology, 18, 173, 338 n.10; and synthetic activity of mind, 92, 103, 118-22, 253; in Cousin, 49, 54; structure of, 243, 357 n.12. *See also* language

Richelieu, 197

Rickman, T., 154

ritual, 118-22. *See also* dogma, religion

Robert, Ruprich, 28, 118, 223, plates 2, 69

Robespierre, M., 164

romanticism and architectural language, 125, 247; and French philosophy, 49; and ideology, 106, 124; criticism of (in Daly), 23, 54, 129, 217-18; and historical consciousness, 70; in painting, 150, 156-57; in writing style, 105. *See also* consciousness; Daly: as romantic figure, language